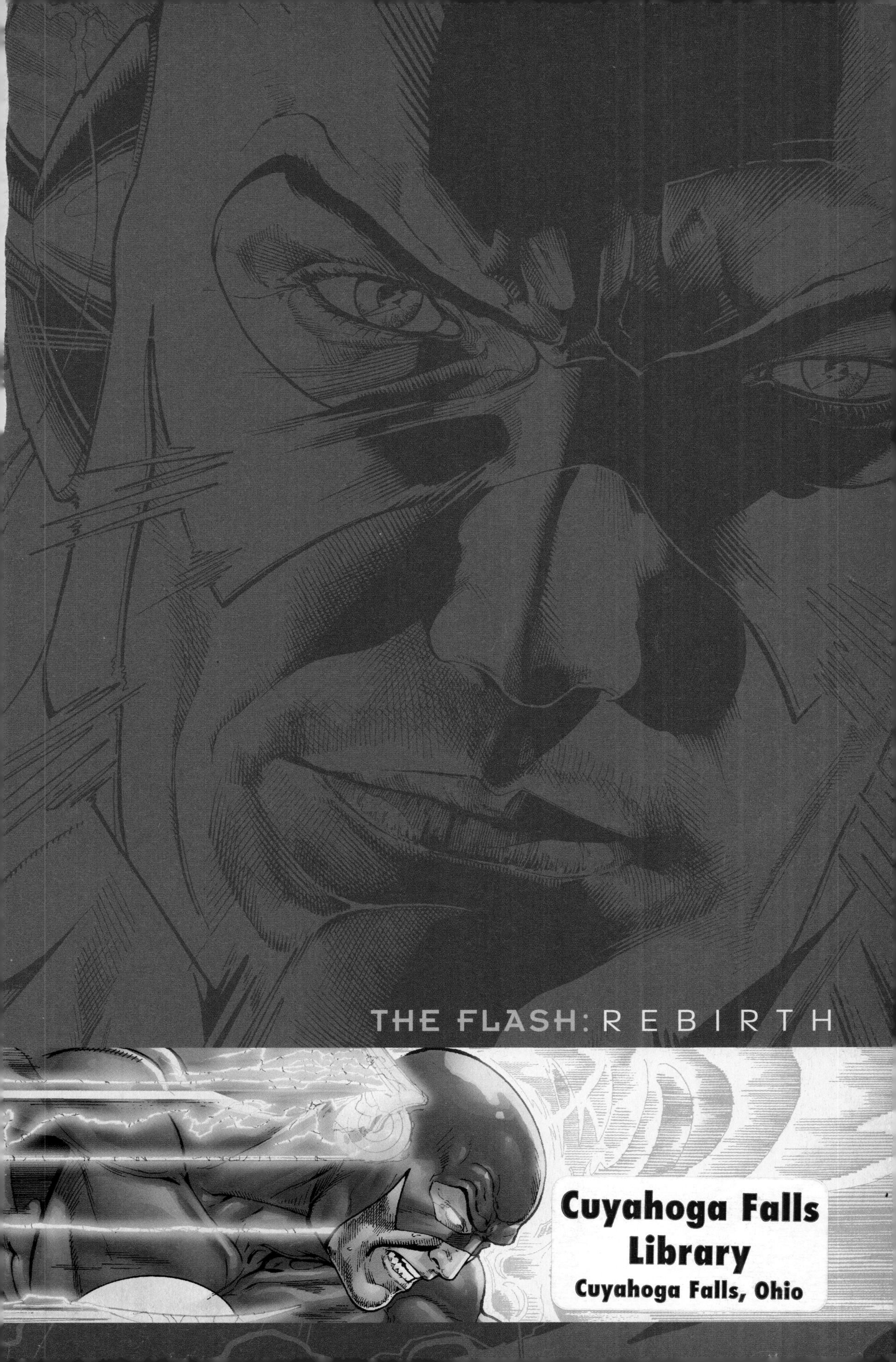
THE FLASH: REBIRTH

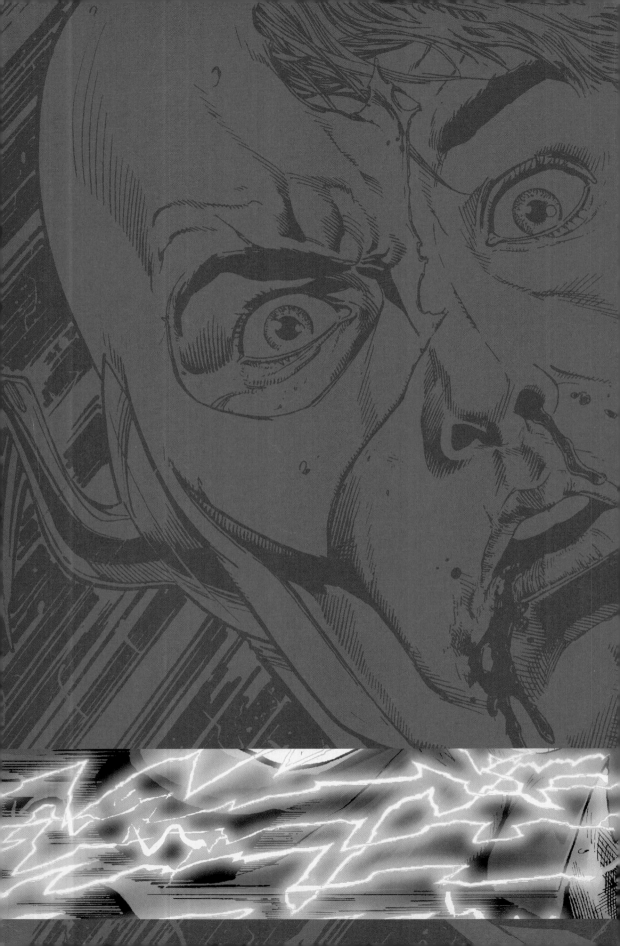

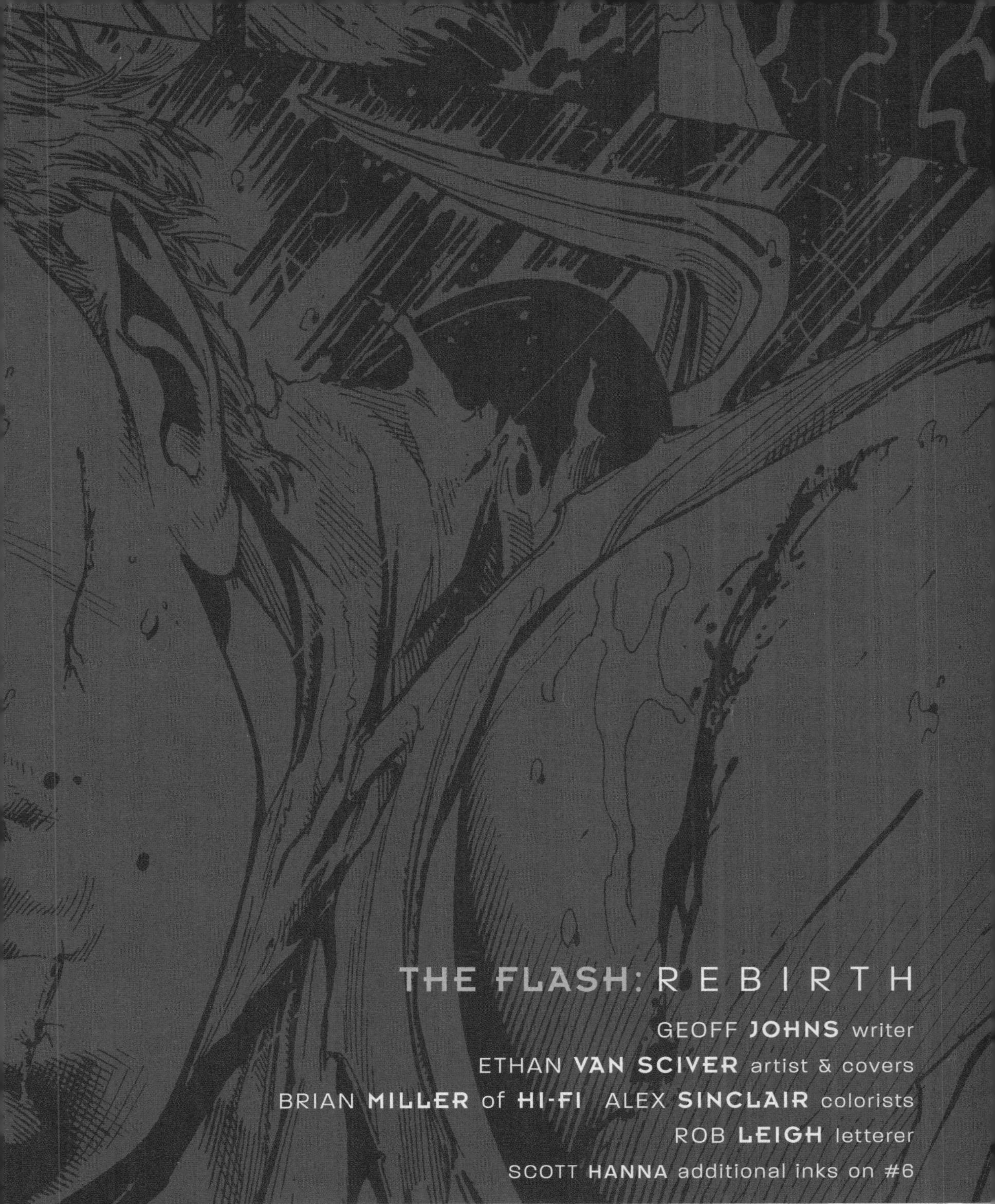

THE FLASH: REBIRTH

GEOFF **JOHNS** writer

ETHAN **VAN SCIVER** artist & covers

BRIAN **MILLER** of **HI-FI** ALEX **SINCLAIR** colorists

ROB **LEIGH** letterer

SCOTT **HANNA** additional inks on #6

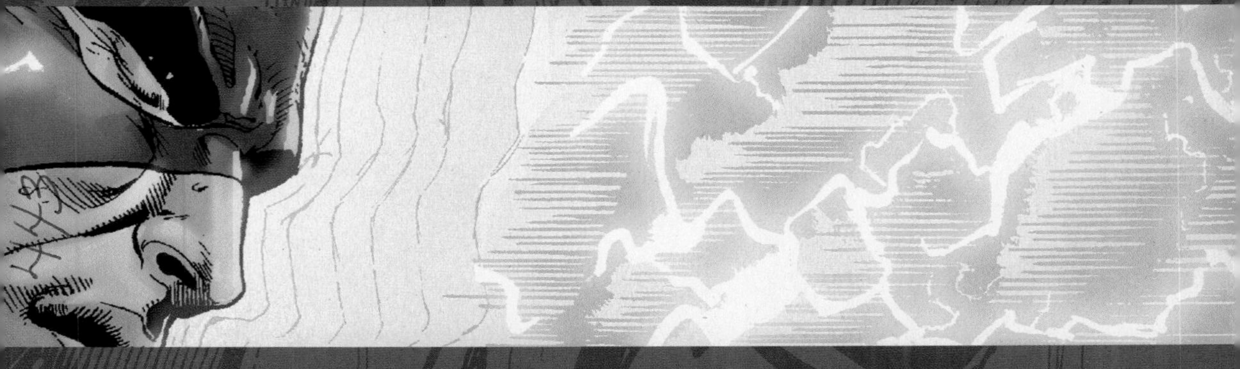

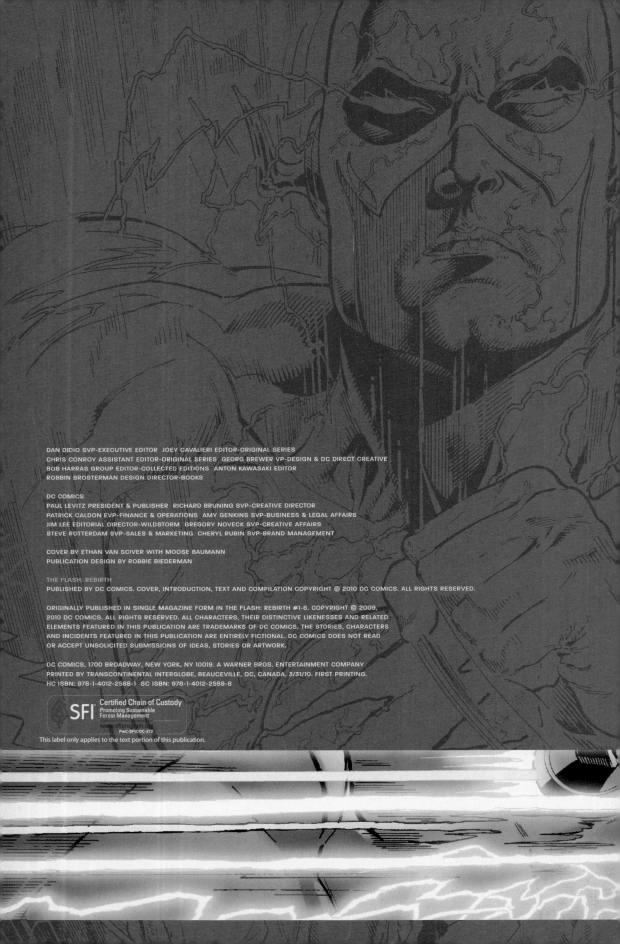

DAN DIDIO SVP-EXECUTIVE EDITOR JOEY CAVALIERI EDITOR-ORIGINAL SERIES
CHRIS CONROY ASSISTANT EDITOR-ORIGINAL SERIES GEORG BREWER VP-DESIGN & DC DIRECT CREATIVE
BOB HARRAS GROUP EDITOR-COLLECTED EDITIONS ANTON KAWASAKI EDITOR
ROBBIN BROSTERMAN DESIGN DIRECTOR-BOOKS

DC COMICS
PAUL LEVITZ PRESIDENT & PUBLISHER RICHARD BRUNING SVP-CREATIVE DIRECTOR
PATRICK CALDON EVP-FINANCE & OPERATIONS AMY GENKINS SVP-BUSINESS & LEGAL AFFAIRS
JIM LEE EDITORIAL DIRECTOR-WILDSTORM GREGORY NOVECK SVP-CREATIVE AFFAIRS
STEVE ROTTERDAM SVP-SALES & MARKETING CHERYL RUBIN SVP-BRAND MANAGEMENT

COVER BY ETHAN VAN SCIVER WITH MOOSE BAUMANN
PUBLICATION DESIGN BY ROBBIE BIEDERMAN

THE FLASH: REBIRTH
PUBLISHED BY DC COMICS. COVER, INTRODUCTION, TEXT AND COMPILATION COPYRIGHT © 2010 DC COMICS. ALL RIGHTS RESERVED.

ORIGINALLY PUBLISHED IN SINGLE MAGAZINE FORM IN THE FLASH: REBIRTH #1-6. COPYRIGHT © 2009,
2010 DC COMICS. ALL RIGHTS RESERVED. ALL CHARACTERS, THEIR DISTINCTIVE LIKENESSES AND RELATED
ELEMENTS FEATURED IN THIS PUBLICATION ARE TRADEMARKS OF DC COMICS. THE STORIES, CHARACTERS
AND INCIDENTS FEATURED IN THIS PUBLICATION ARE ENTIRELY FICTIONAL. DC COMICS DOES NOT READ
OR ACCEPT UNSOLICITED SUBMISSIONS OF IDEAS, STORIES OR ARTWORK.

DC COMICS, 1700 BROADWAY, NEW YORK, NY 10019. A WARNER BROS. ENTERTAINMENT COMPANY
PRINTED BY TRANSCONTINENTAL INTERGLOBE, BEAUCEVILLE, QC, CANADA. 3/31/10. FIRST PRINTING.
HC ISBN: 978-1-4012-2568-1 SC ISBN: 978-1-4012-2569-8

A FLASH FORWARD BY MATT CHERNISS

It's a funny thing about superheroes; keeping them dead is often harder than actually killing them in the first place. We want our fantasies to be grounded in reality, our character's flaws to be real, and their sacrifices to carry weight. Sometimes that means our favorite heroes must die. Those moments, rare as they are, remind us why we love our heroes. But that is where the conflict begins. Keeping them dead means not having the joy of reading them every month. Yet, in bringing them back to life, we run the risk of minimizing their heroism, the tragedy of their death, or the power of their sacrifice. We care too much about them to do that, either.

It's also true that the longer a character remains dead, the greater the importance and scrutiny is put on his return. A character who returns from death after being absent for 6 months or a year? His return is generally accompanied by a fanboy in the new arrivals section uttering, "I knew they'd bring him back." A beloved character who is absent for years on end? That is an event. Barry Allen's absence of 23 years most certainly falls into that category.

When you think about it, it's almost unfathomable Barry was gone as long as he was. . This isn't some "B" grade superhero. This is an Icon. The character that launched the Silver Age in SHOWCASE #4, introduced us to the Multiverse in THE FLASH #123, and helped found the Justice League in THE BRAVE AND THE BOLD #28. A character with arguably one of the best two or three Rogues' Galleries in all of comics, and my favorite DC villain (more on that later). Twenty-three years! It makes Hal Jordan's 10-year absence seem like the blink of an eye.

I suppose one of the things that helped keep Barry out of the world of the living was what he died doing. Some heroes die saving a loved one, others save their beloved city, maybe even their home planet. Barry literally saved the entire Universe from being erased from existence. If a hero does that, and then just happens to show up a few months later, it would have surely minimized one of the seminal events in Comic Book History.

All that is to say this: If you are going to bring Barry Allen back, you better not screw it up. A satisfying hero's return is remembered fondly. A disastrous one becomes part of comic book lore. I don't even need to mention them by name, we all know which ones they are. We still complain about them to this day. That's a lot of responsibility for any writer to carry on their shoulders. Which leads me to my last reason Barry was gone for so long: we were waiting for the right writer to bring Barry back.

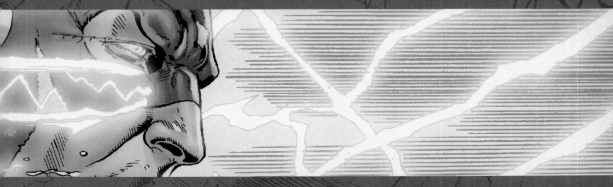

Over the past 23 years there have been many great writers, some of whom have written the Flash. Again, I don't need to name them. We all know who they are. We buy their books every month. But to take on this task, in my mind only Geoff had the ability, knowledge, and most importantly, the affinity for the character to take on the challenge and succeed. For both Geoff and myself, Barry Allen's death in CRISIS ON INFINITE EARTHS was one of those moments that came early in our introduction to comic books, and had an impact that would endear us to comics for years to come. These magical moments, more often than not, happen when you are young, and stay with you long after. In many genres, it would be sacrilege for a writer to continue someone else's story. In comic books, it is tradition. And I think it is for the best, because in many instances, that young boy whose imagination was captured by a single moment will take greater care of it than someone burdened by years of storytelling.

The fact that Geoff would approach THE FLASH: REBIRTH more as an honor than as a task also speaks to why he was the right person to tell this story. Barry's return wasn't the trickiest in terms of narrative. It was the emotional significance of Barry's return and the impact it would have on the DC universe that was most difficult. That is where Geoff's stories always stand out.

I'm also grateful that Reverse Flash found his way into the story as well. I'm not sure if it is the striking yellow costume, with the red lightning bolt/black circle insignia, or the fact that his villainy included the murder of Barry's wife, Iris, long before such things were done regularly in comics, but every time Reverse Flash graces a comic cover, I can't help but look inside.

No matter how strong, how fast, or how intelligent a super-hero is, they all share a common weakness. Every hero is susceptible to a bad story. It can bring them to their knees faster than any weapon or arch-nemesis. I have never read a bad story from Geoff, and THE FLASH: REBIRTH is no exception. Enjoy!

MATT CHERNISS
LOS ANGELES, CALIFORNIA JANUARY, 2010

Matt Cherniss is a TV Development Executive for the FOX Broadcasting Company, where he developed shows including *Glee* and *Human Target*. In his previous job at FX, he took part in the development of shows including *Nip/Tuck*, *Rescue Me*, *Sons of Anarchy*, *Damages*, and *It's Always Sunny in Philadelphia*. Outside of his day job, he is a part-time comic writer, and full-time comic fanatic.

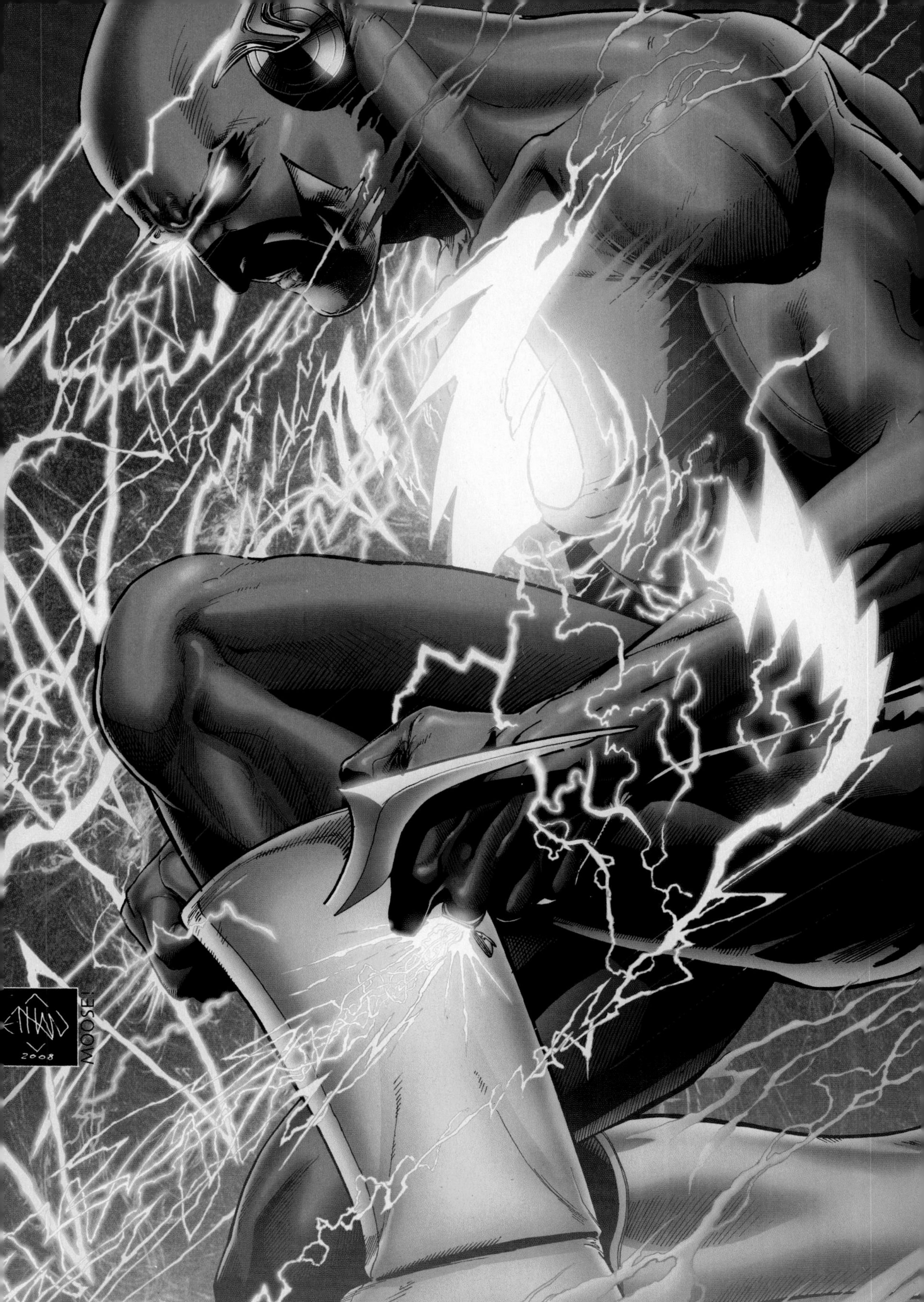
ETHAN 2008
MOOSE!

THE FLASH: REBIRTH #1 COVER BY ETHAN VAN SCIVER WITH MOOSE BAUMANN

THE FLASH: REBIRTH #1 VARIANT COVER BY **ETHAN VAN SCIVER** WITH **ALEX SINCLAIR**

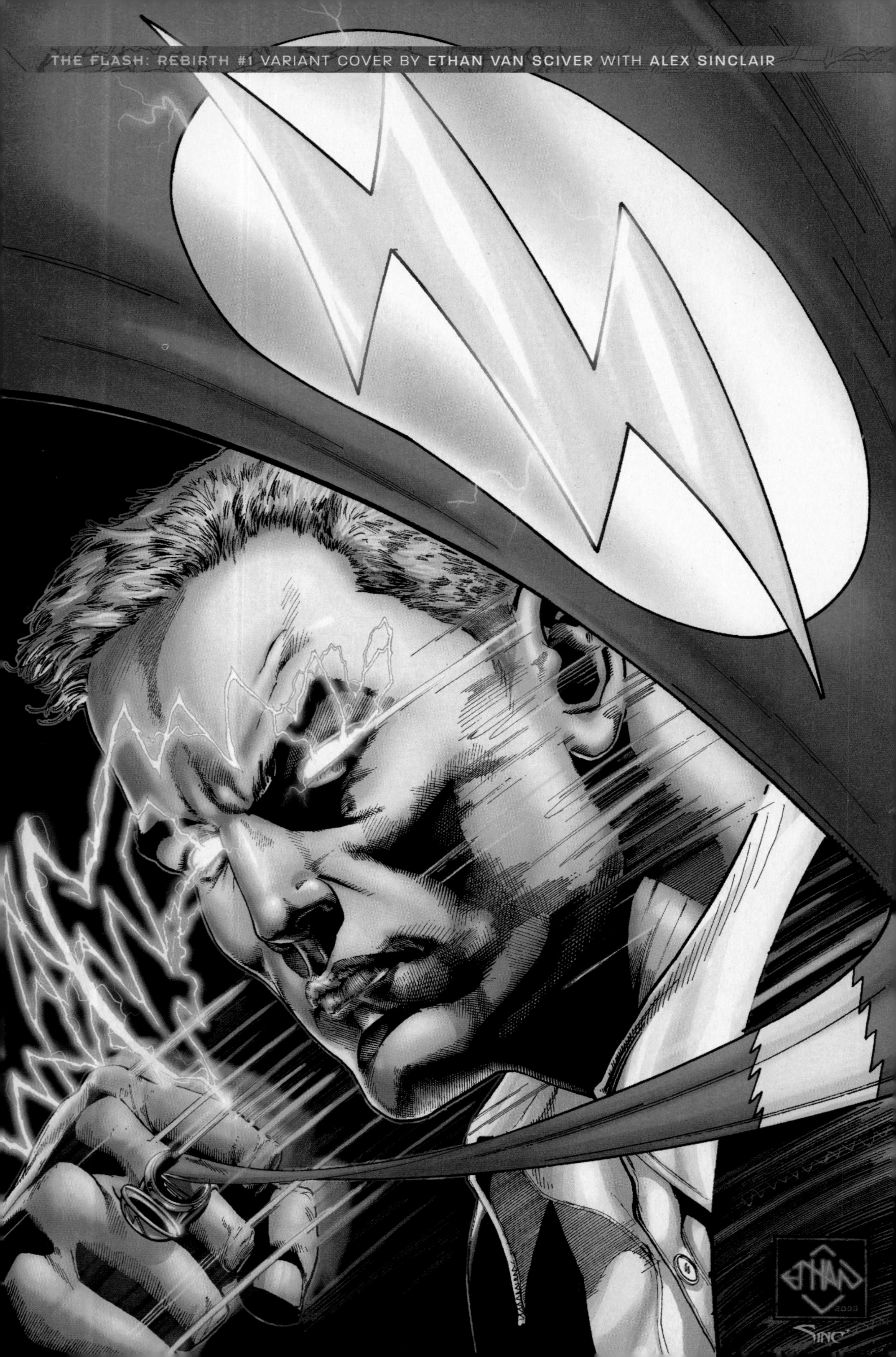

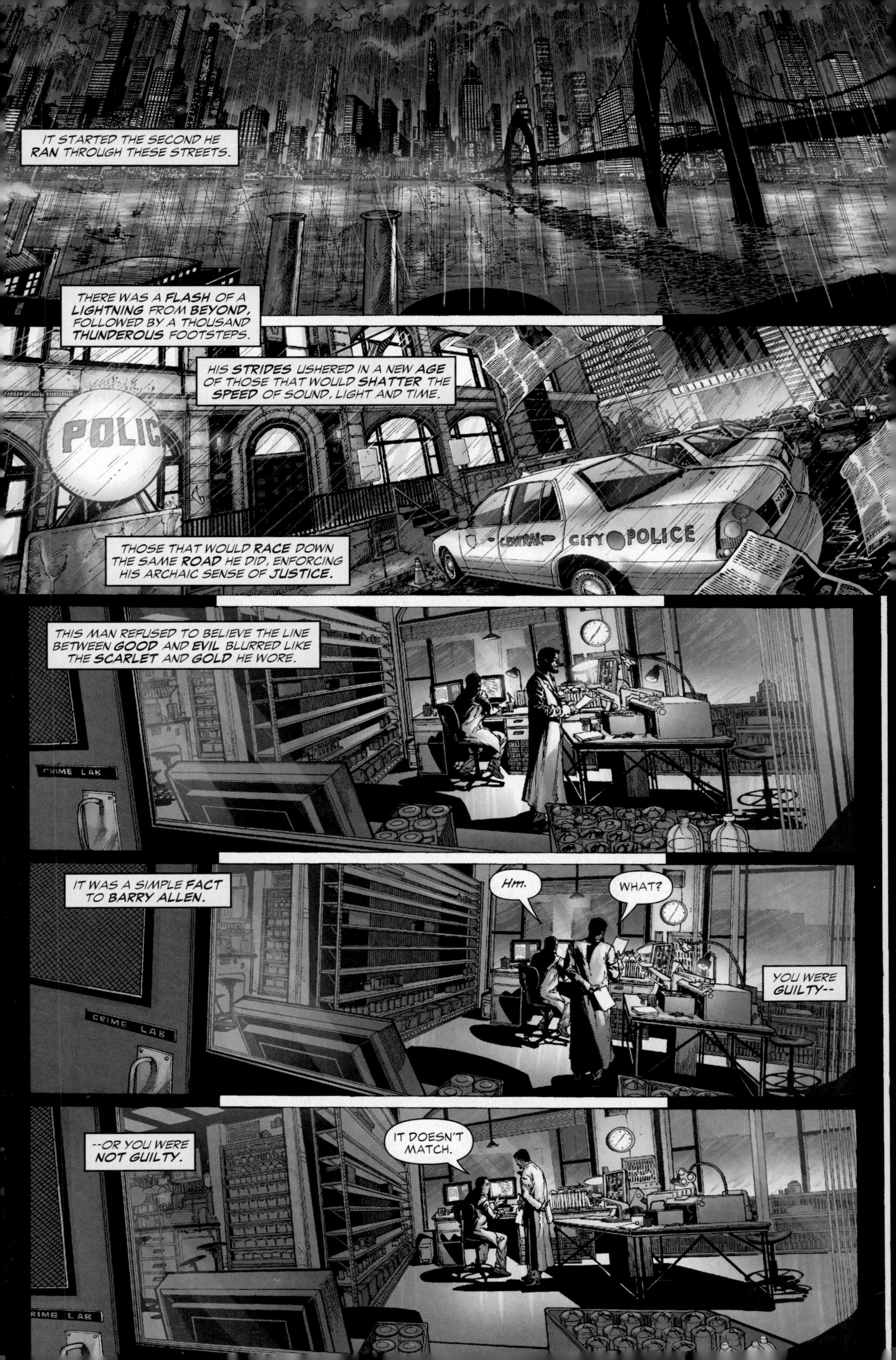
IT STARTED THE SECOND HE RAN THROUGH THESE STREETS.
THERE WAS A FLASH OF A LIGHTNING FROM BEYOND, FOLLOWED BY A THOUSAND THUNDEROUS FOOTSTEPS.
HIS STRIDES USHERED IN A NEW AGE OF THOSE THAT WOULD SHATTER THE SPEED OF SOUND, LIGHT AND TIME.
POLIC
THOSE THAT WOULD RACE DOWN THE SAME ROAD HE DID, ENFORCING HIS ARCHAIC SENSE OF JUSTICE.
CENTRAL CITY POLICE
THIS MAN REFUSED TO BELIEVE THE LINE BETWEEN GOOD AND EVIL BLURRED LIKE THE SCARLET AND GOLD HE WORE.
CRIME LAB
IT WAS A SIMPLE FACT TO BARRY ALLEN.
Hm.
WHAT?
YOU WERE GUILTY--
CRIME LAB
--OR YOU WERE NOT GUILTY.
IT DOESN'T MATCH.
CRIME LAB

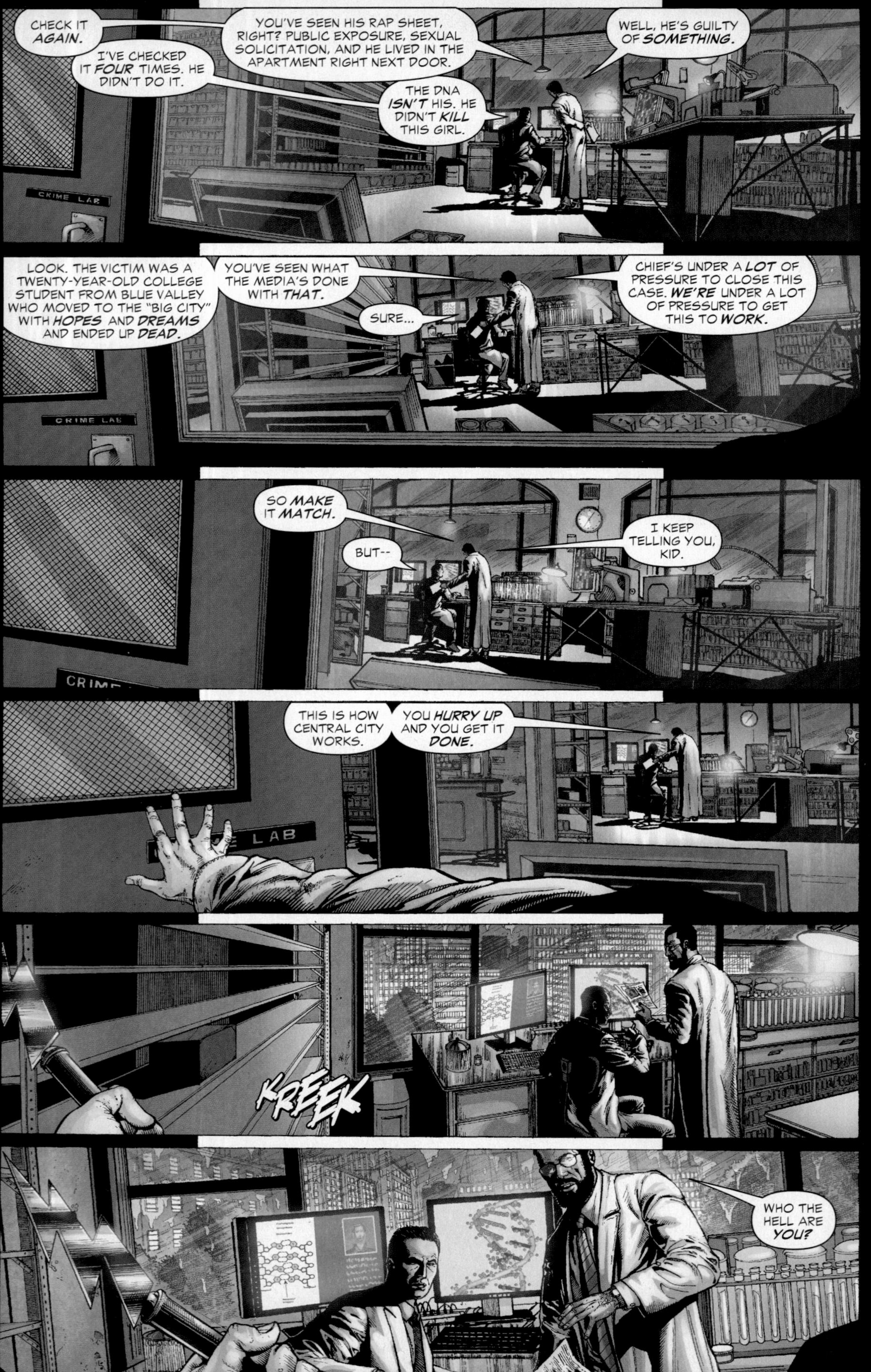
CRIME LAB
CHECK IT AGAIN.
I'VE CHECKED IT FOUR TIMES. HE DIDN'T DO IT.
YOU'VE SEEN HIS RAP SHEET, RIGHT? PUBLIC EXPOSURE, SEXUAL SOLICITATION, AND HE LIVED IN THE APARTMENT RIGHT NEXT DOOR.
THE DNA ISN'T HIS. HE DIDN'T KILL THIS GIRL.
WELL, HE'S GUILTY OF SOMETHING.
CRIME LAB
LOOK. THE VICTIM WAS A TWENTY-YEAR-OLD COLLEGE STUDENT FROM BLUE VALLEY WHO MOVED TO THE "BIG CITY" WITH HOPES AND DREAMS AND ENDED UP DEAD.
YOU'VE SEEN WHAT THE MEDIA'S DONE WITH THAT.
SURE...
CHIEF'S UNDER A LOT OF PRESSURE TO CLOSE THIS CASE. WE'RE UNDER A LOT OF PRESSURE TO GET THIS TO WORK.
SO MAKE IT MATCH.
BUT--
I KEEP TELLING YOU, KID.
THIS IS HOW CENTRAL CITY WORKS.
YOU HURRY UP AND YOU GET IT DONE.
KREEK
WHO THE HELL ARE YOU?

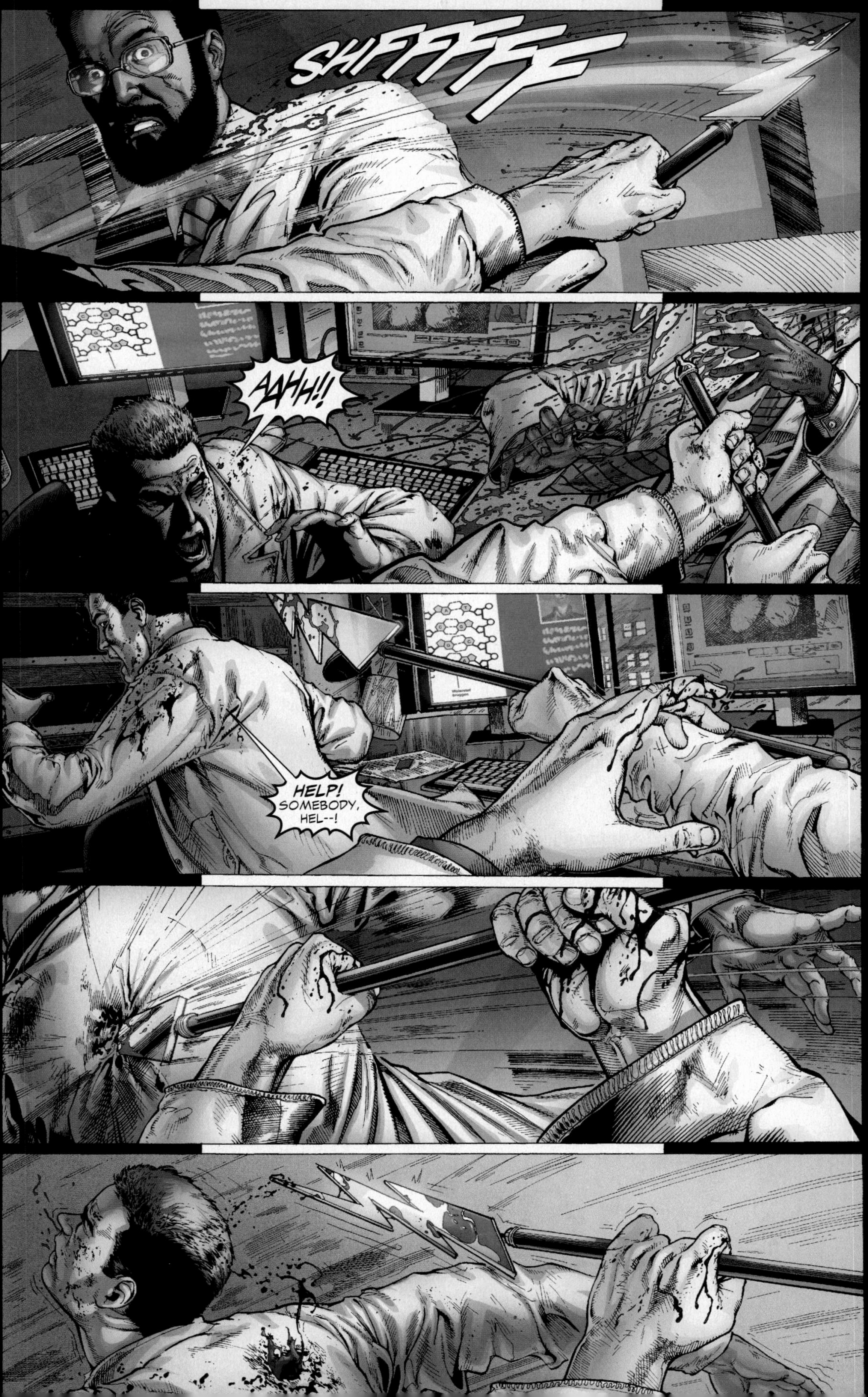
SHFFFFF
AAHH!!
HELP! SOMEBODY, HEL--!

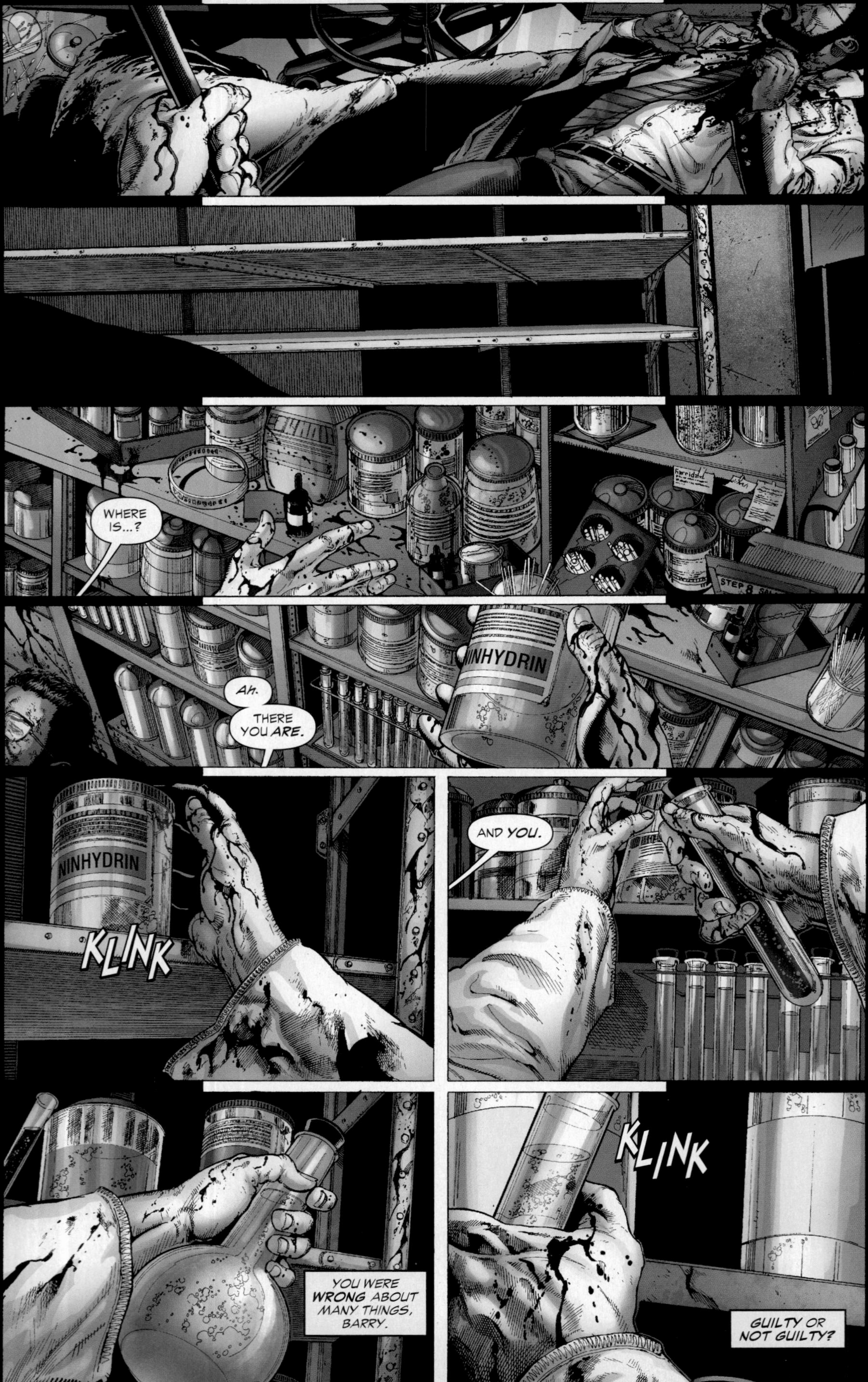
WHERE IS...?
NINHYDRIN
Ah.
THERE YOU ARE.
NINHYDRIN
KLINK
AND YOU.
YOU WERE WRONG ABOUT MANY THINGS, BARRY.
KLINK
GUILTY OR NOT GUILTY?

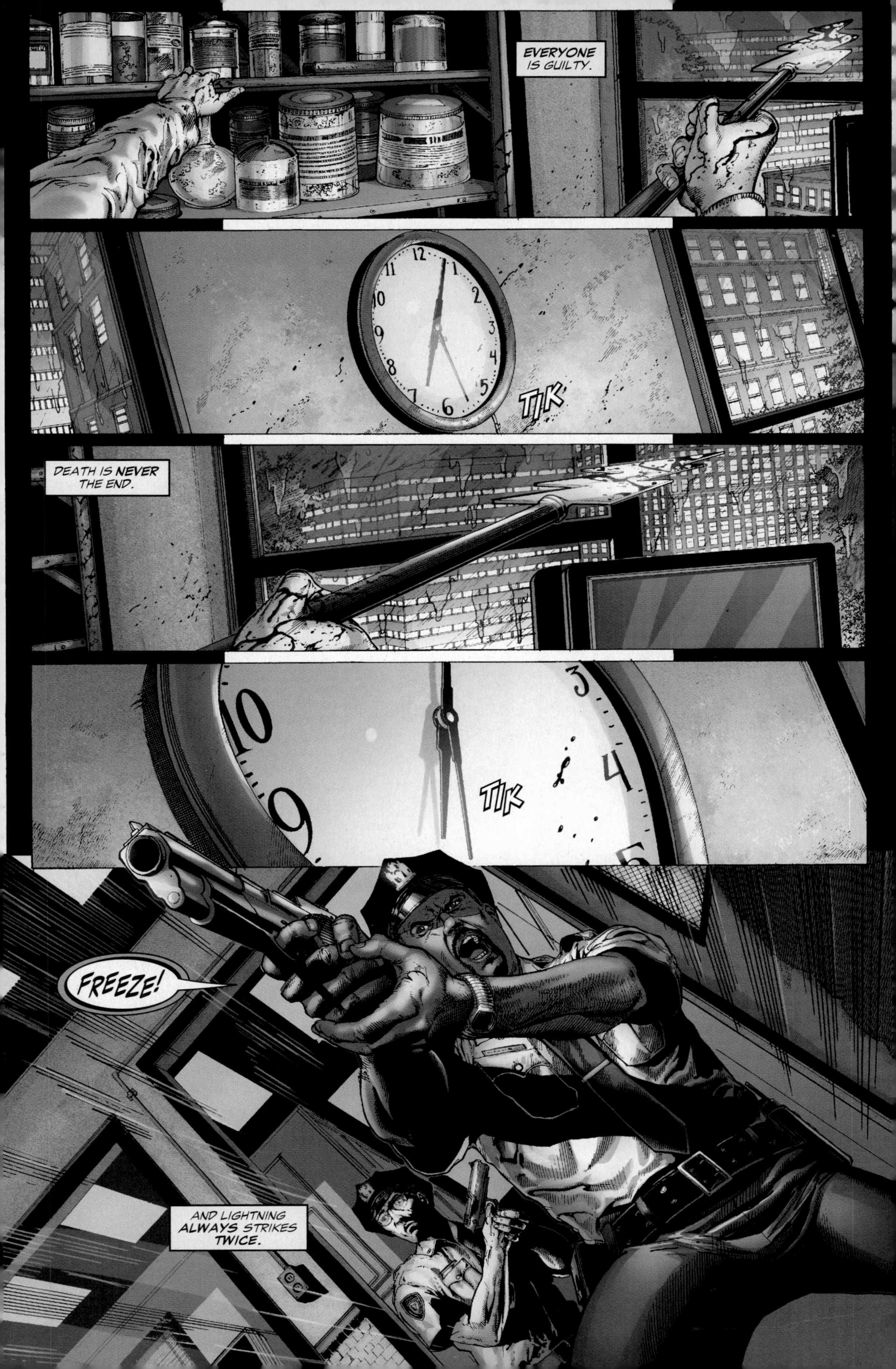
EVERYONE IS GUILTY.
TIK
DEATH IS NEVER THE END.
TIK
FREEZE!
AND LIGHTNING ALWAYS STRIKES TWICE.

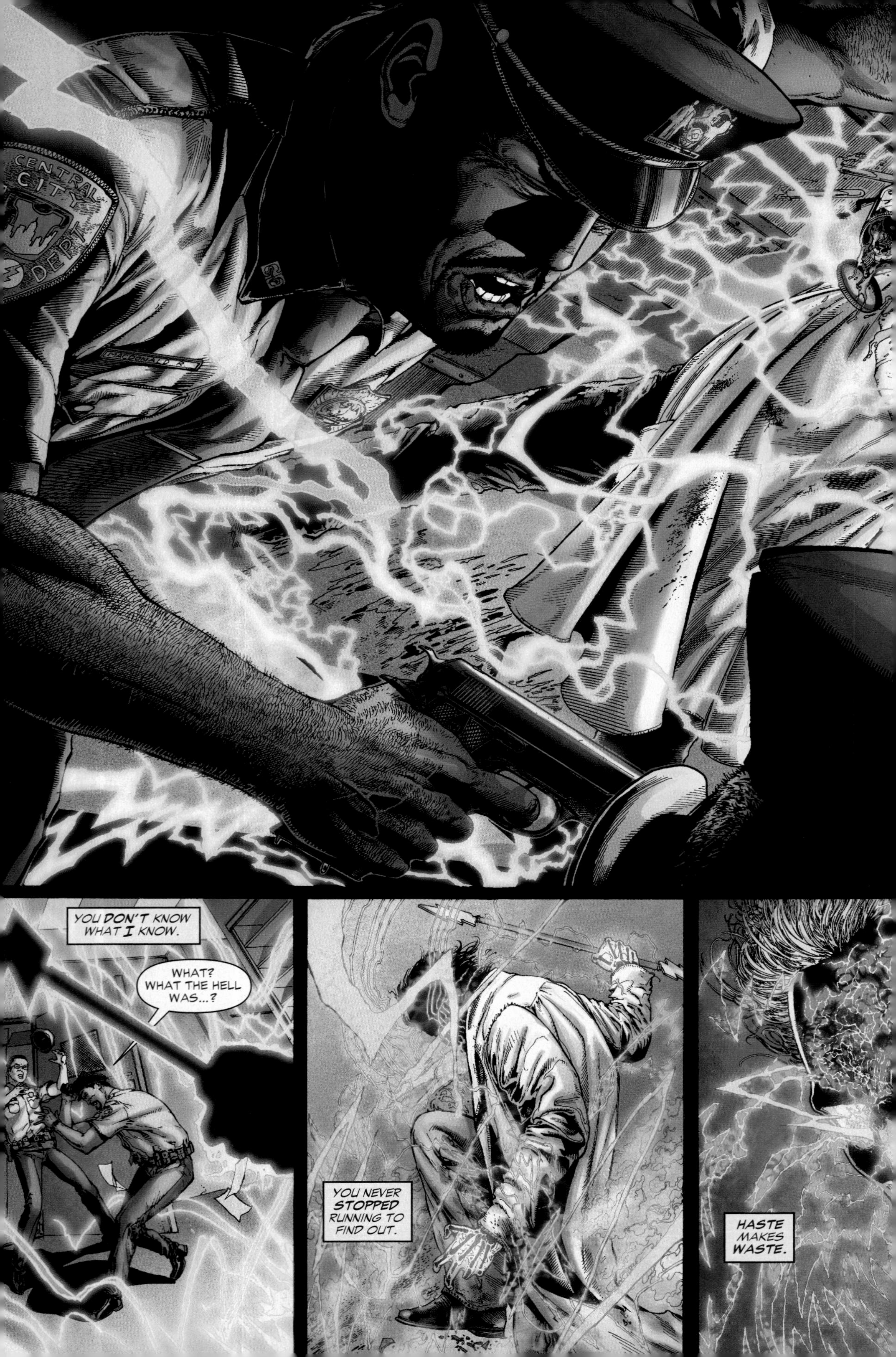

CENTRAL CITY DEPT
YOU DON'T KNOW WHAT I KNOW.
WHAT? WHAT THE HELL WAS...?
YOU NEVER STOPPED RUNNING TO FIND OUT.
HASTE MAKES WASTE.

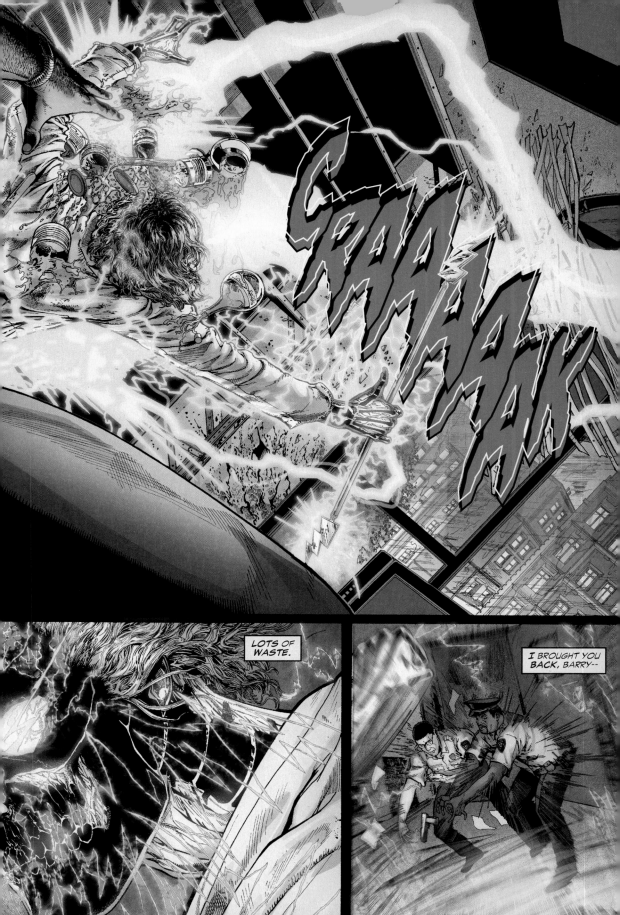

SRAAAKKK

LOTS OF WASTE.

I BROUGHT YOU BACK, BARRY--

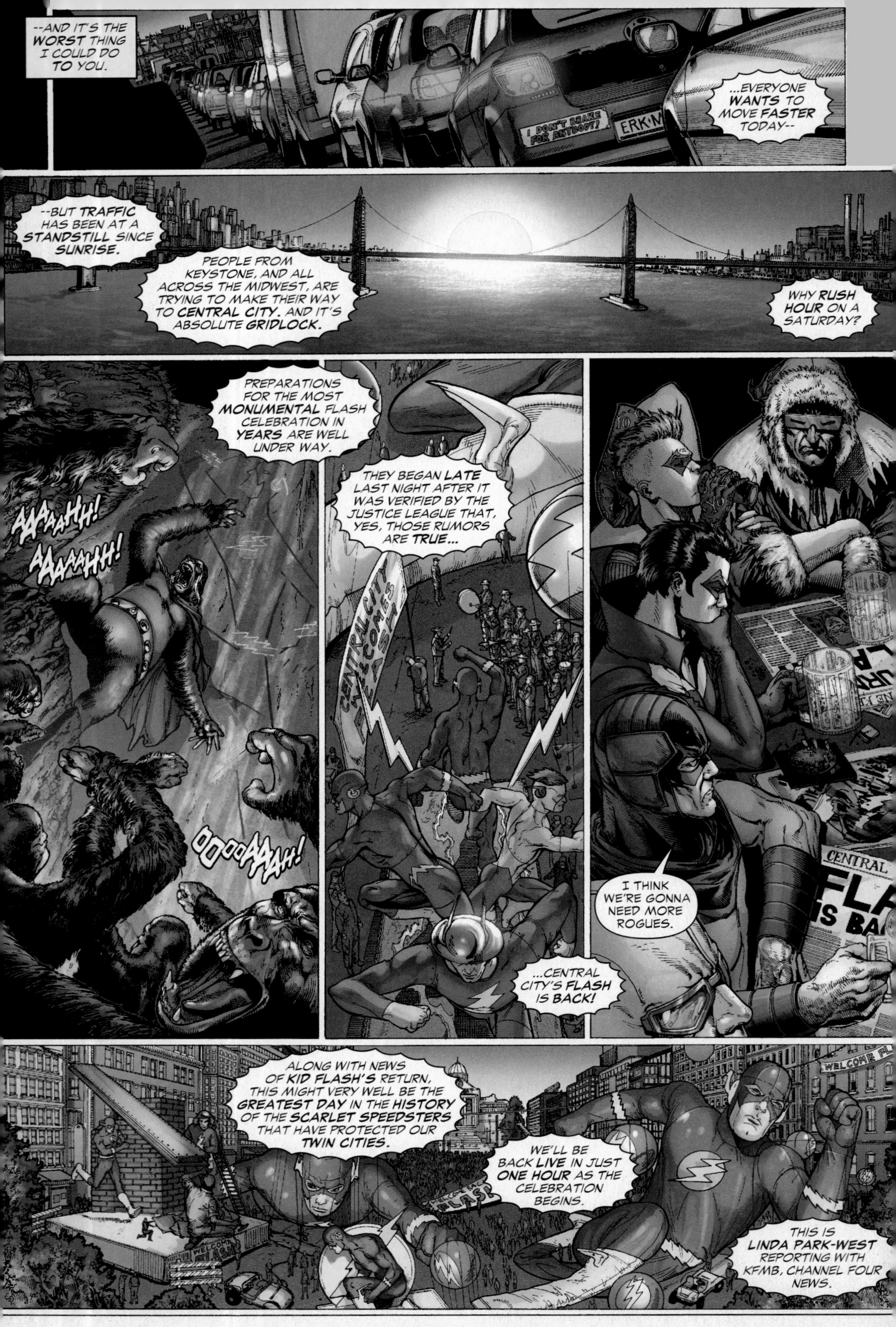
--AND IT'S THE WORST THING I COULD DO TO YOU.
I DON'T BRAKE FOR ANYBODY!
...EVERYONE WANTS TO MOVE FASTER TODAY--
--BUT TRAFFIC HAS BEEN AT A STANDSTILL SINCE SUNRISE.
PEOPLE FROM KEYSTONE, AND ALL ACROSS THE MIDWEST, ARE TRYING TO MAKE THEIR WAY TO CENTRAL CITY. AND IT'S ABSOLUTE GRIDLOCK.
WHY RUSH HOUR ON A SATURDAY?
PREPARATIONS FOR THE MOST MONUMENTAL FLASH CELEBRATION IN YEARS ARE WELL UNDER WAY.
AAAAAHH!
AAAAAHH!
OOOOAAAAH!
THEY BEGAN LATE LAST NIGHT AFTER IT WAS VERIFIED BY THE JUSTICE LEAGUE THAT, YES, THOSE RUMORS ARE TRUE...
CENTRAL CITY WELCOMES FLASH
...CENTRAL CITY'S FLASH IS BACK!
I THINK WE'RE GONNA NEED MORE ROGUES.
CENTRAL
FLA
IS BA
ALONG WITH NEWS OF KID FLASH'S RETURN, THIS MIGHT VERY WELL BE THE GREATEST DAY IN THE HISTORY OF THE SCARLET SPEEDSTERS THAT HAVE PROTECTED OUR TWIN CITIES.
WE'LL BE BACK LIVE IN JUST ONE HOUR AS THE CELEBRATION BEGINS.
THIS IS LINDA PARK-WEST REPORTING WITH KFMB, CHANNEL FOUR NEWS.

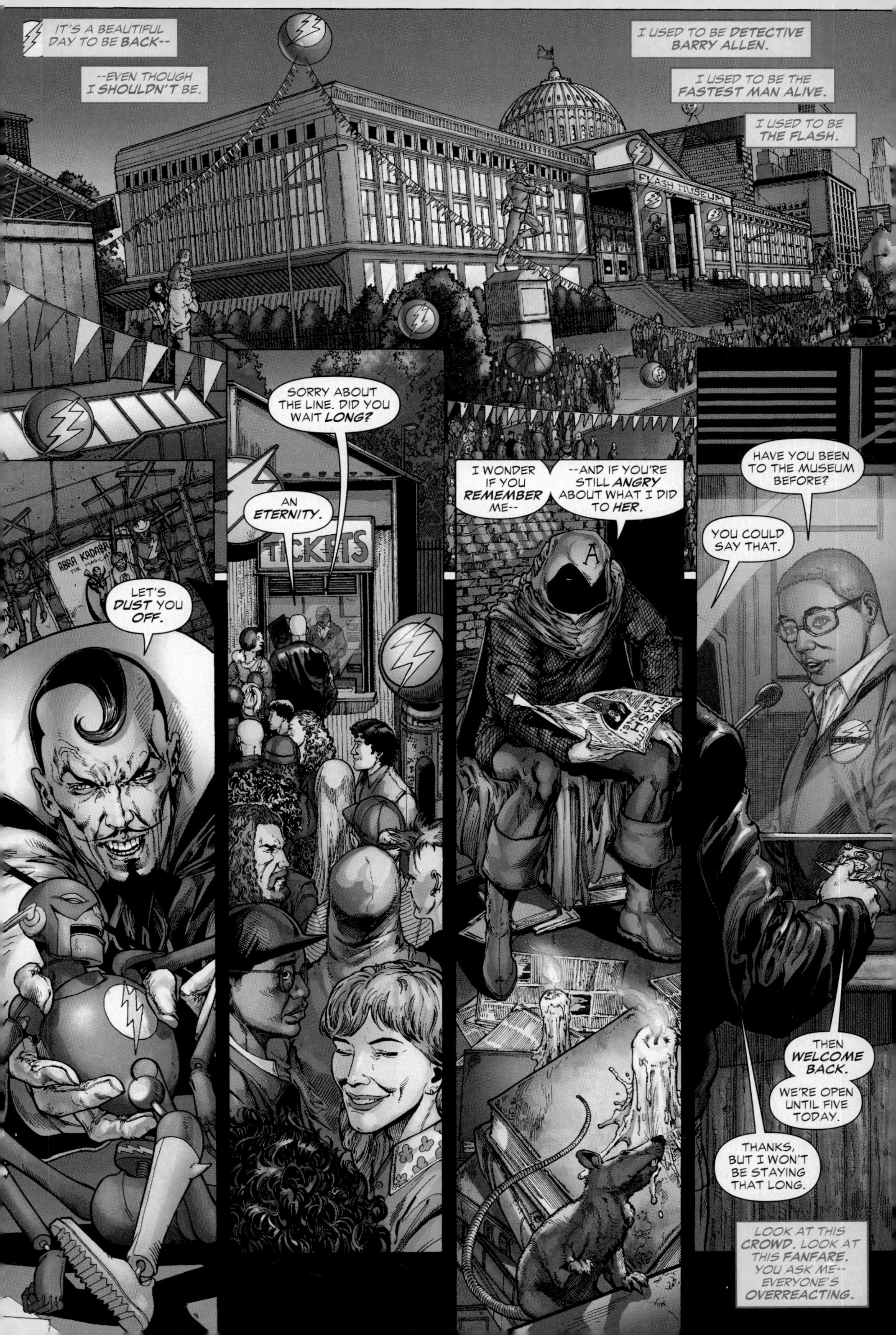
IT'S A BEAUTIFUL DAY TO BE BACK--
--EVEN THOUGH I SHOULDN'T BE.
I USED TO BE DETECTIVE BARRY ALLEN.
I USED TO BE THE FASTEST MAN ALIVE.
I USED TO BE THE FLASH.
FLASH MUSEUM
ABRA KADABRA THE MAGICIAN
LET'S DUST YOU OFF.
SORRY ABOUT THE LINE. DID YOU WAIT LONG?
AN ETERNITY.
TICKETS
I WONDER IF YOU REMEMBER ME--
--AND IF YOU'RE STILL ANGRY ABOUT WHAT I DID TO HER.
HAVE YOU BEEN TO THE MUSEUM BEFORE?
YOU COULD SAY THAT.
THEN WELCOME BACK.
WE'RE OPEN UNTIL FIVE TODAY.
THANKS, BUT I WON'T BE STAYING THAT LONG.
LOOK AT THIS CROWD. LOOK AT THIS FANFARE. YOU ASK ME-- EVERYONE'S OVERREACTING.

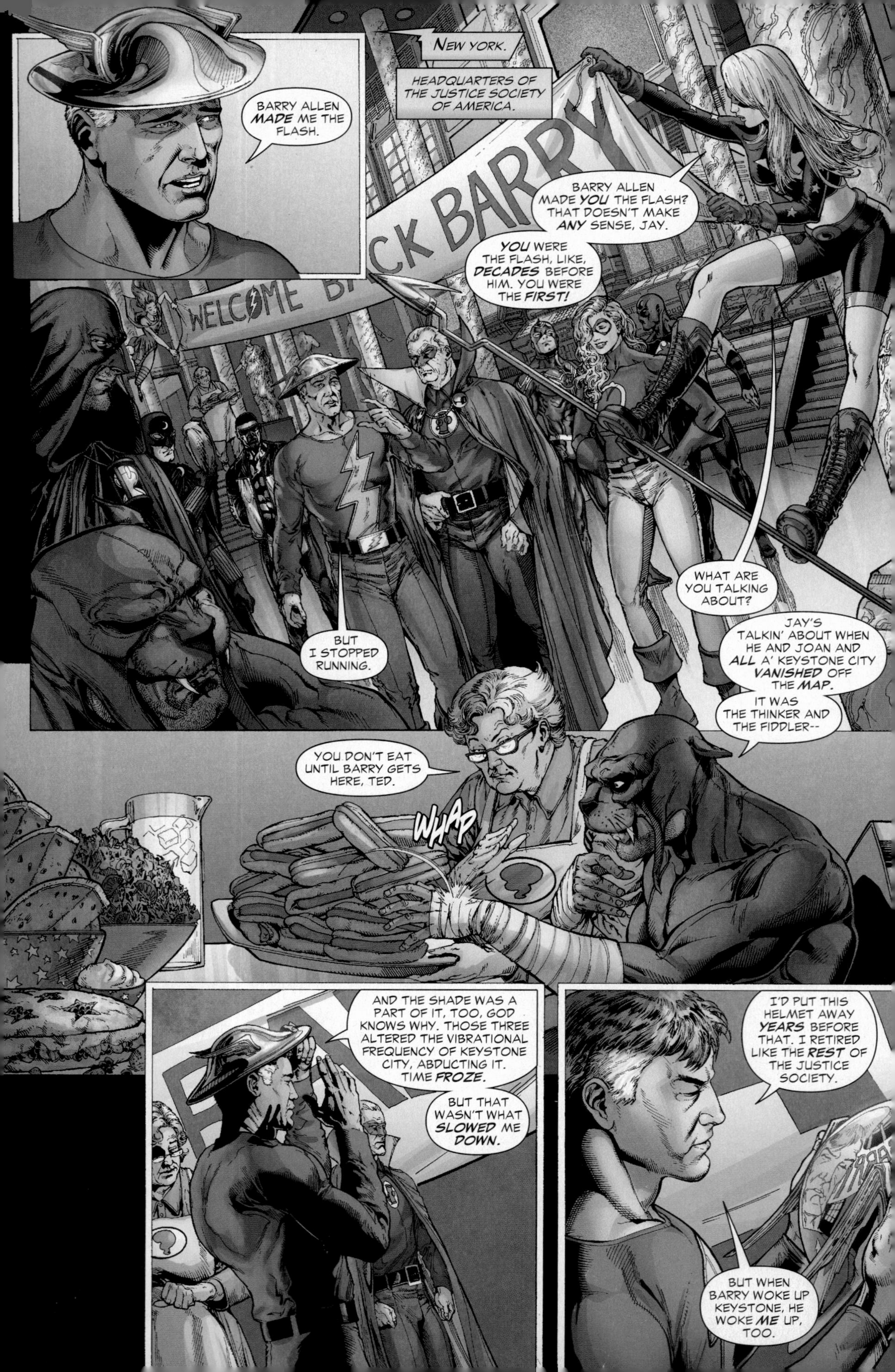
BARRY ALLEN MADE ME THE FLASH.
NEW YORK.
HEADQUARTERS OF THE JUSTICE SOCIETY OF AMERICA.
BARRY ALLEN MADE YOU THE FLASH? THAT DOESN'T MAKE ANY SENSE, JAY.
YOU WERE THE FLASH, LIKE, DECADES BEFORE HIM. YOU WERE THE FIRST!
WELCOME BACK BARRY
BUT I STOPPED RUNNING.
WHAT ARE YOU TALKING ABOUT?
JAY'S TALKIN' ABOUT WHEN HE AND JOAN AND ALL A' KEYSTONE CITY VANISHED OFF THE MAP.
IT WAS THE THINKER AND THE FIDDLER--
YOU DON'T EAT UNTIL BARRY GETS HERE, TED.
WHAP
AND THE SHADE WAS A PART OF IT, TOO, GOD KNOWS WHY. THOSE THREE ALTERED THE VIBRATIONAL FREQUENCY OF KEYSTONE CITY, ABDUCTING IT. TIME FROZE.
BUT THAT WASN'T WHAT SLOWED ME DOWN.
I'D PUT THIS HELMET AWAY YEARS BEFORE THAT. I RETIRED LIKE THE REST OF THE JUSTICE SOCIETY.
BUT WHEN BARRY WOKE UP KEYSTONE, HE WOKE ME UP, TOO.

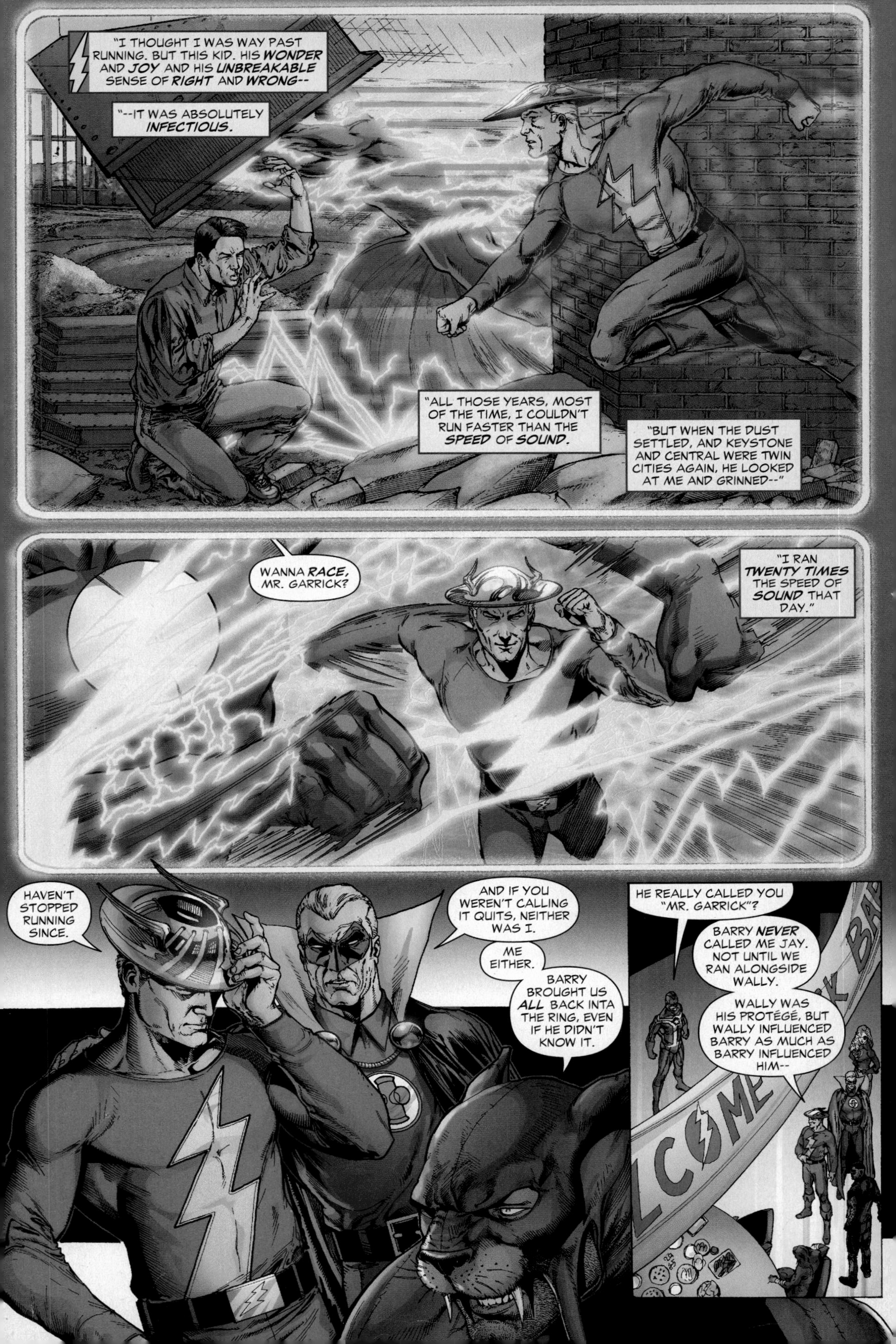
"I THOUGHT I WAS WAY PAST RUNNING. BUT THIS KID. HIS WONDER AND JOY AND HIS UNBREAKABLE SENSE OF RIGHT AND WRONG--
"--IT WAS ABSOLUTELY INFECTIOUS.
"ALL THOSE YEARS, MOST OF THE TIME, I COULDN'T RUN FASTER THAN THE SPEED OF SOUND.
"BUT WHEN THE DUST SETTLED, AND KEYSTONE AND CENTRAL WERE TWIN CITIES AGAIN, HE LOOKED AT ME AND GRINNED--"
WANNA RACE, MR. GARRICK?
"I RAN TWENTY TIMES THE SPEED OF SOUND THAT DAY."
HAVEN'T STOPPED RUNNING SINCE.
AND IF YOU WEREN'T CALLING IT QUITS, NEITHER WAS I.
ME EITHER.
BARRY BROUGHT US ALL BACK INTA THE RING, EVEN IF HE DIDN'T KNOW IT.
HE REALLY CALLED YOU "MR. GARRICK"?
BARRY NEVER CALLED ME JAY. NOT UNTIL WE RAN ALONGSIDE WALLY.
WALLY WAS HIS PROTÉGÉ, BUT WALLY INFLUENCED BARRY AS MUCH AS BARRY INFLUENCED HIM--

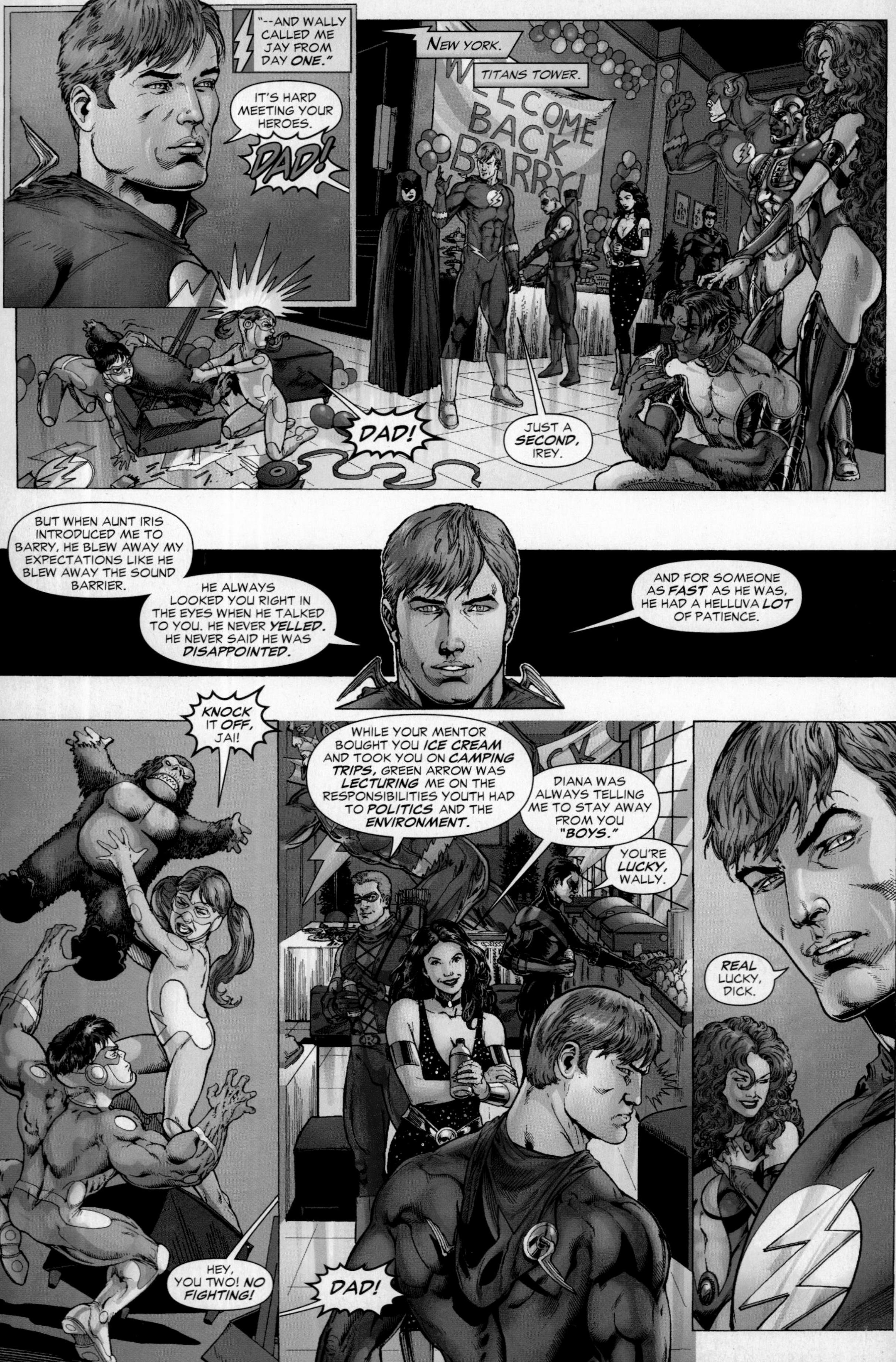
"--AND WALLY CALLED ME JAY FROM DAY ONE."
IT'S HARD MEETING YOUR HEROES.
DAD!
NEW YORK.
TITANS TOWER.
WELCOME BACK BARRY!
DAD!
JUST A SECOND, IREY.
BUT WHEN AUNT IRIS INTRODUCED ME TO BARRY, HE BLEW AWAY MY EXPECTATIONS LIKE HE BLEW AWAY THE SOUND BARRIER.
HE ALWAYS LOOKED YOU RIGHT IN THE EYES WHEN HE TALKED TO YOU. HE NEVER YELLED. HE NEVER SAID HE WAS DISAPPOINTED.
AND FOR SOMEONE AS FAST AS HE WAS, HE HAD A HELLUVA LOT OF PATIENCE.
KNOCK IT OFF, JAI!
HEY, YOU TWO! NO FIGHTING!
WHILE YOUR MENTOR BOUGHT YOU ICE CREAM AND TOOK YOU ON CAMPING TRIPS, GREEN ARROW WAS LECTURING ME ON THE RESPONSIBILITIES YOUTH HAD TO POLITICS AND THE ENVIRONMENT.
DIANA WAS ALWAYS TELLING ME TO STAY AWAY FROM YOU "BOYS."
YOU'RE LUCKY, WALLY.
DAD!
REAL LUCKY, DICK.

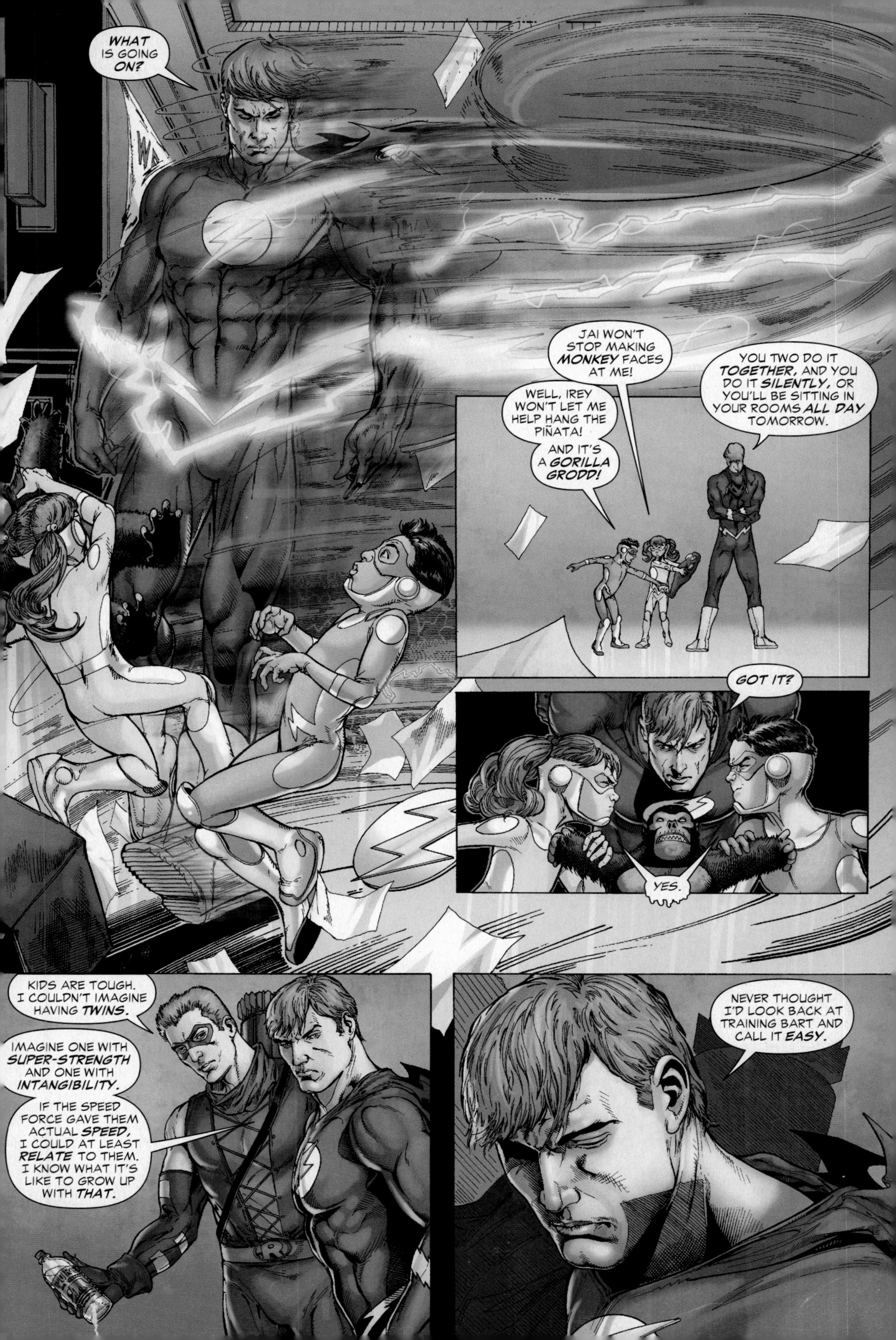
WHAT IS GOING ON?
JAI WON'T STOP MAKING MONKEY FACES AT ME!
WELL, IREY WON'T LET ME HELP HANG THE PIÑATA!
AND IT'S A GORILLA GRODD!
YOU TWO DO IT TOGETHER, AND YOU DO IT SILENTLY, OR YOU'LL BE SITTING IN YOUR ROOMS ALL DAY TOMORROW.
GOT IT?
YES.
KIDS ARE TOUGH. I COULDN'T IMAGINE HAVING TWINS.
IMAGINE ONE WITH SUPER-STRENGTH AND ONE WITH INTANGIBILITY.
IF THE SPEED FORCE GAVE THEM ACTUAL SPEED, I COULD AT LEAST RELATE TO THEM. I KNOW WHAT IT'S LIKE TO GROW UP WITH THAT.
NEVER THOUGHT I'D LOOK BACK AT TRAINING BART AND CALL IT EASY.

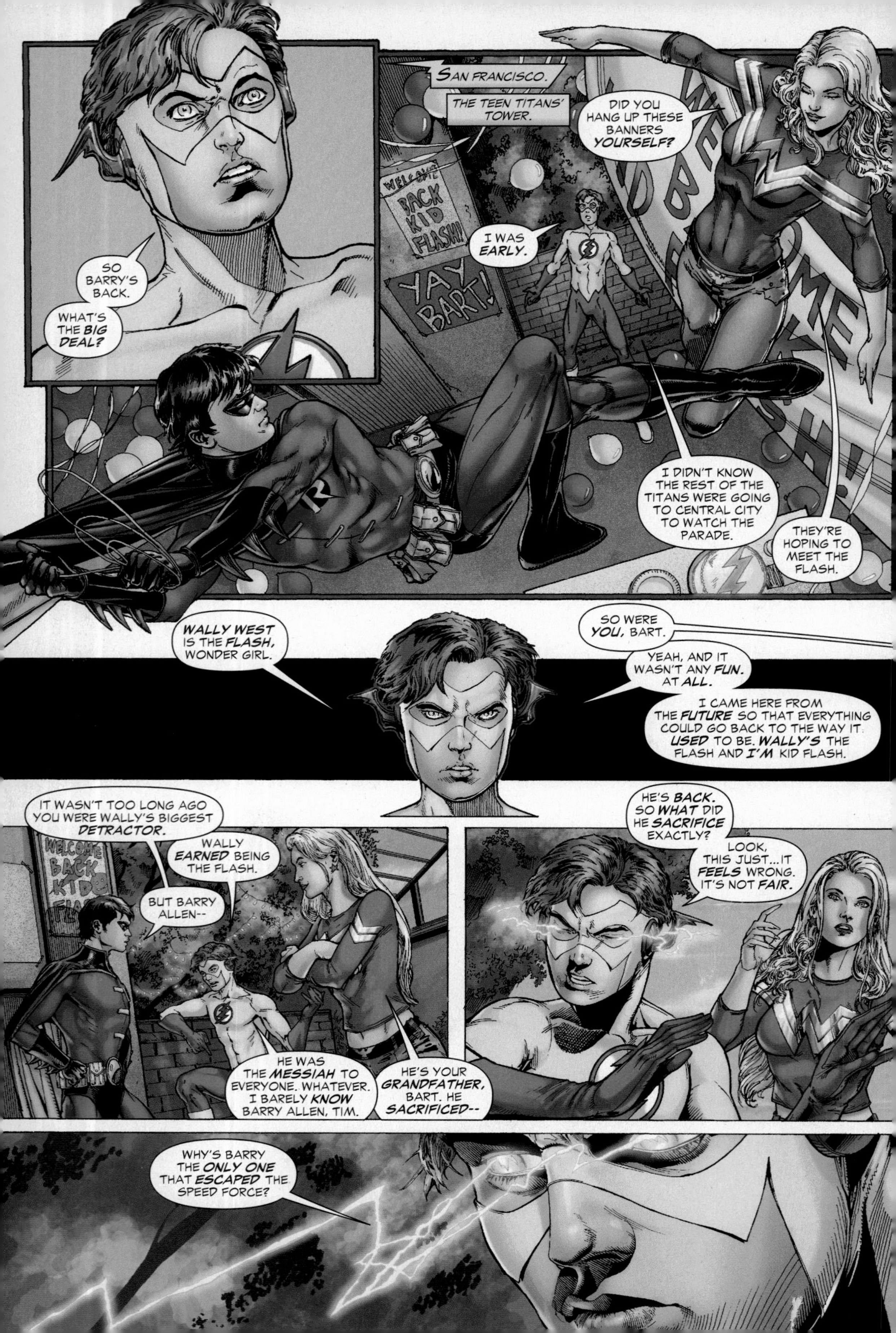
SAN FRANCISCO.
THE TEEN TITANS' TOWER.
DID YOU HANG UP THESE BANNERS YOURSELF?
I WAS EARLY.
WELCOME BACK KID FLASH!
YAY BART!
SO BARRY'S BACK.
WHAT'S THE BIG DEAL?
I DIDN'T KNOW THE REST OF THE TITANS WERE GOING TO CENTRAL CITY TO WATCH THE PARADE.
THEY'RE HOPING TO MEET THE FLASH.
WALLY WEST IS THE FLASH, WONDER GIRL.
SO WERE YOU, BART.
YEAH, AND IT WASN'T ANY FUN. AT ALL.
I CAME HERE FROM THE FUTURE SO THAT EVERYTHING COULD GO BACK TO THE WAY IT USED TO BE. WALLY'S THE FLASH AND I'M KID FLASH.
IT WASN'T TOO LONG AGO YOU WERE WALLY'S BIGGEST DETRACTOR.
WALLY EARNED BEING THE FLASH.
BUT BARRY ALLEN--
HE WAS THE MESSIAH TO EVERYONE. WHATEVER. I BARELY KNOW BARRY ALLEN, TIM.
HE'S YOUR GRANDFATHER, BART. HE SACRIFICED--
HE'S BACK. SO WHAT DID HE SACRIFICE EXACTLY?
LOOK, THIS JUST...IT FEELS WRONG. IT'S NOT FAIR.
WHY'S BARRY THE ONLY ONE THAT ESCAPED THE SPEED FORCE?

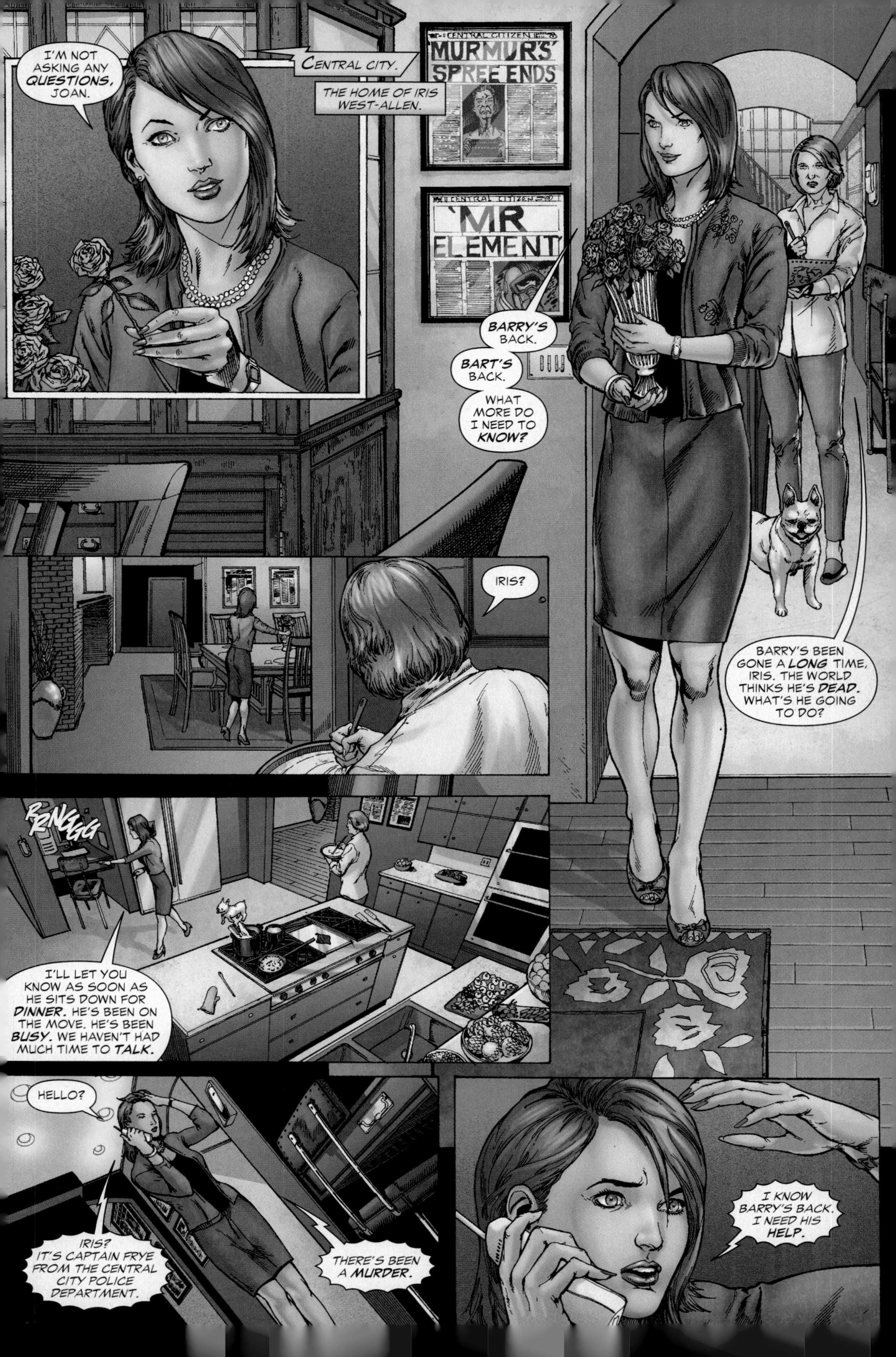

I'M NOT ASKING ANY QUESTIONS, JOAN.
CENTRAL CITY.
THE HOME OF IRIS WEST-ALLEN.
CENTRAL CITIZEN
MURMUR'S' SPREE ENDS
CENTRAL CITIZEN
'MR ELEMENT
BARRY'S BACK.
BART'S BACK.
WHAT MORE DO I NEED TO KNOW?
BARRY'S BEEN GONE A LONG TIME, IRIS. THE WORLD THINKS HE'S DEAD. WHAT'S HE GOING TO DO?
IRIS?
RRNGGG
I'LL LET YOU KNOW AS SOON AS HE SITS DOWN FOR DINNER. HE'S BEEN ON THE MOVE. HE'S BEEN BUSY. WE HAVEN'T HAD MUCH TIME TO TALK.
HELLO?
IRIS? IT'S CAPTAIN FRYE FROM THE CENTRAL CITY POLICE DEPARTMENT.
THERE'S BEEN A MURDER.
I KNOW BARRY'S BACK. I NEED HIS HELP.

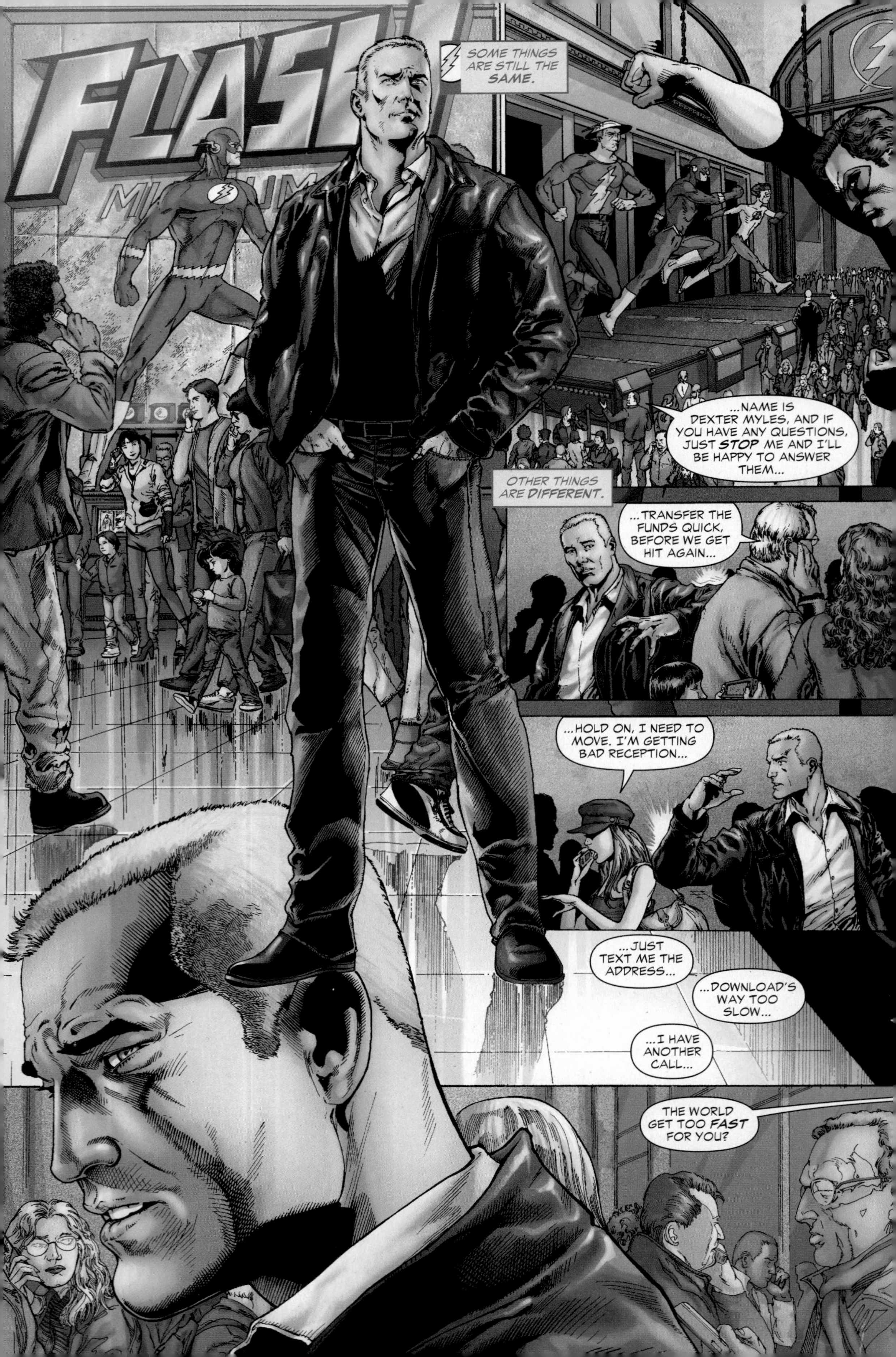
FLASH MUSEUM
SOME THINGS ARE STILL THE SAME.
...NAME IS DEXTER MYLES, AND IF YOU HAVE ANY QUESTIONS, JUST STOP ME AND I'LL BE HAPPY TO ANSWER THEM...
OTHER THINGS ARE DIFFERENT.
...TRANSFER THE FUNDS QUICK, BEFORE WE GET HIT AGAIN...
...HOLD ON, I NEED TO MOVE. I'M GETTING BAD RECEPTION...
...JUST TEXT ME THE ADDRESS...
...DOWNLOAD'S WAY TOO SLOW...
...I HAVE ANOTHER CALL...
THE WORLD GET TOO FAST FOR YOU?

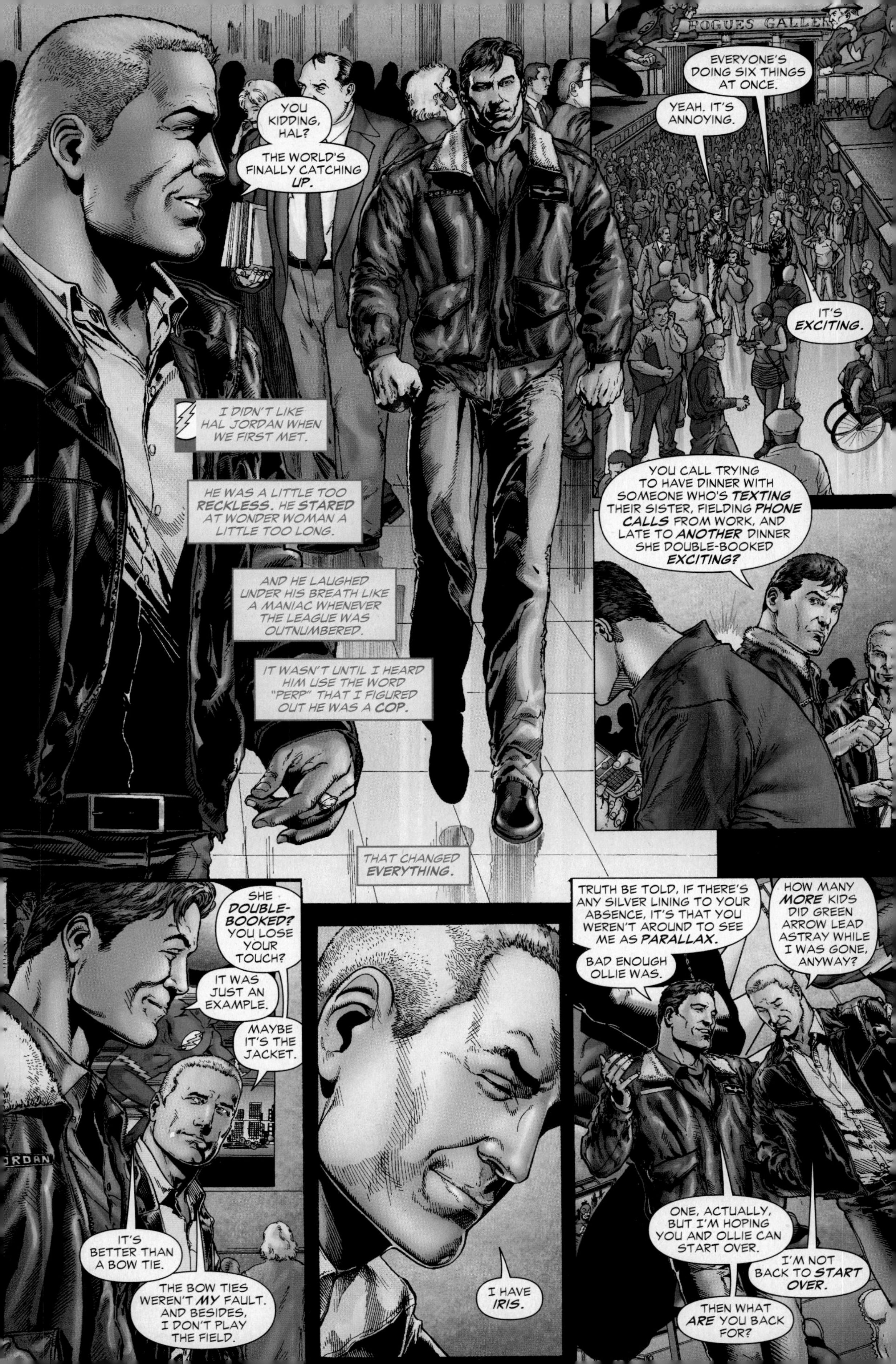

YOU KIDDING, HAL?
THE WORLD'S FINALLY CATCHING UP.
I DIDN'T LIKE HAL JORDAN WHEN WE FIRST MET.
HE WAS A LITTLE TOO RECKLESS. HE STARED AT WONDER WOMAN A LITTLE TOO LONG.
AND HE LAUGHED UNDER HIS BREATH LIKE A MANIAC WHENEVER THE LEAGUE WAS OUTNUMBERED.
IT WASN'T UNTIL I HEARD HIM USE THE WORD "PERP" THAT I FIGURED OUT HE WAS A COP.
THAT CHANGED EVERYTHING.
ROGUES GALLER
EVERYONE'S DOING SIX THINGS AT ONCE.
YEAH. IT'S ANNOYING.
IT'S EXCITING.
YOU CALL TRYING TO HAVE DINNER WITH SOMEONE WHO'S TEXTING THEIR SISTER, FIELDING PHONE CALLS FROM WORK, AND LATE TO ANOTHER DINNER SHE DOUBLE-BOOKED EXCITING?
SHE DOUBLE-BOOKED? YOU LOSE YOUR TOUCH?
IT WAS JUST AN EXAMPLE.
MAYBE IT'S THE JACKET.
IT'S BETTER THAN A BOW TIE.
THE BOW TIES WEREN'T MY FAULT. AND BESIDES, I DON'T PLAY THE FIELD.
I HAVE IRIS.
TRUTH BE TOLD, IF THERE'S ANY SILVER LINING TO YOUR ABSENCE, IT'S THAT YOU WEREN'T AROUND TO SEE ME AS PARALLAX.
BAD ENOUGH OLLIE WAS.
HOW MANY MORE KIDS DID GREEN ARROW LEAD ASTRAY WHILE I WAS GONE, ANYWAY?
ONE, ACTUALLY, BUT I'M HOPING YOU AND OLLIE CAN START OVER.
I'M NOT BACK TO START OVER.
THEN WHAT ARE YOU BACK FOR?

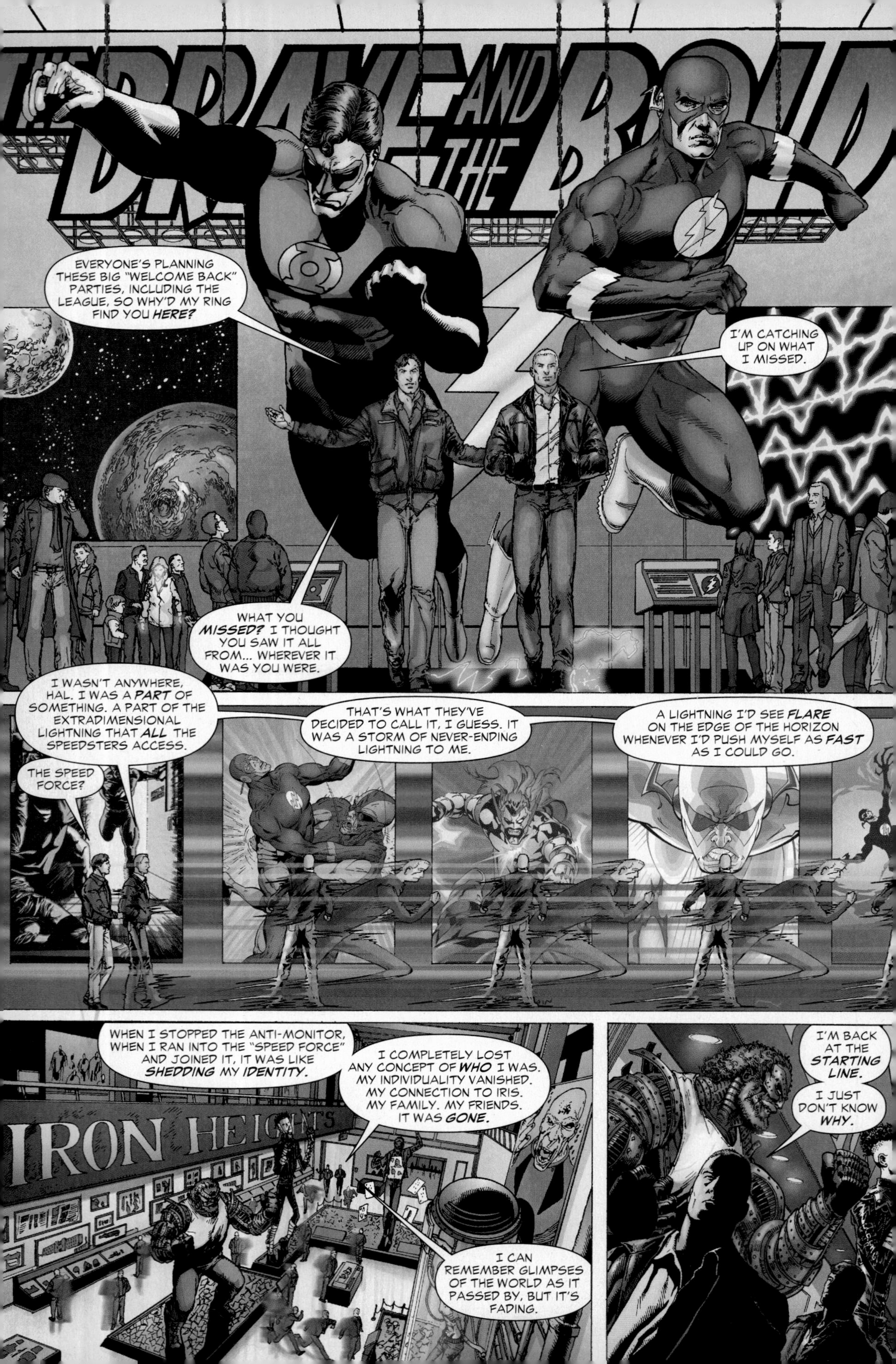
THE BRAVE AND THE BOLD
EVERYONE'S PLANNING THESE BIG "WELCOME BACK" PARTIES, INCLUDING THE LEAGUE, SO WHY'D MY RING FIND YOU HERE?
I'M CATCHING UP ON WHAT I MISSED.
WHAT YOU MISSED? I THOUGHT YOU SAW IT ALL FROM... WHEREVER IT WAS YOU WERE.
I WASN'T ANYWHERE, HAL. I WAS A PART OF SOMETHING. A PART OF THE EXTRADIMENSIONAL LIGHTNING THAT ALL THE SPEEDSTERS ACCESS.
THE SPEED FORCE?
THAT'S WHAT THEY'VE DECIDED TO CALL IT, I GUESS. IT WAS A STORM OF NEVER-ENDING LIGHTNING TO ME.
A LIGHTNING I'D SEE FLARE ON THE EDGE OF THE HORIZON WHENEVER I'D PUSH MYSELF AS FAST AS I COULD GO.
WHEN I STOPPED THE ANTI-MONITOR, WHEN I RAN INTO THE "SPEED FORCE" AND JOINED IT, IT WAS LIKE SHEDDING MY IDENTITY.
I COMPLETELY LOST ANY CONCEPT OF WHO I WAS. MY INDIVIDUALITY VANISHED. MY CONNECTION TO IRIS. MY FAMILY. MY FRIENDS. IT WAS GONE.
IRON HEIGHTS
I CAN REMEMBER GLIMPSES OF THE WORLD AS IT PASSED BY, BUT IT'S FADING.
I'M BACK AT THE STARTING LINE.
I JUST DON'T KNOW WHY.

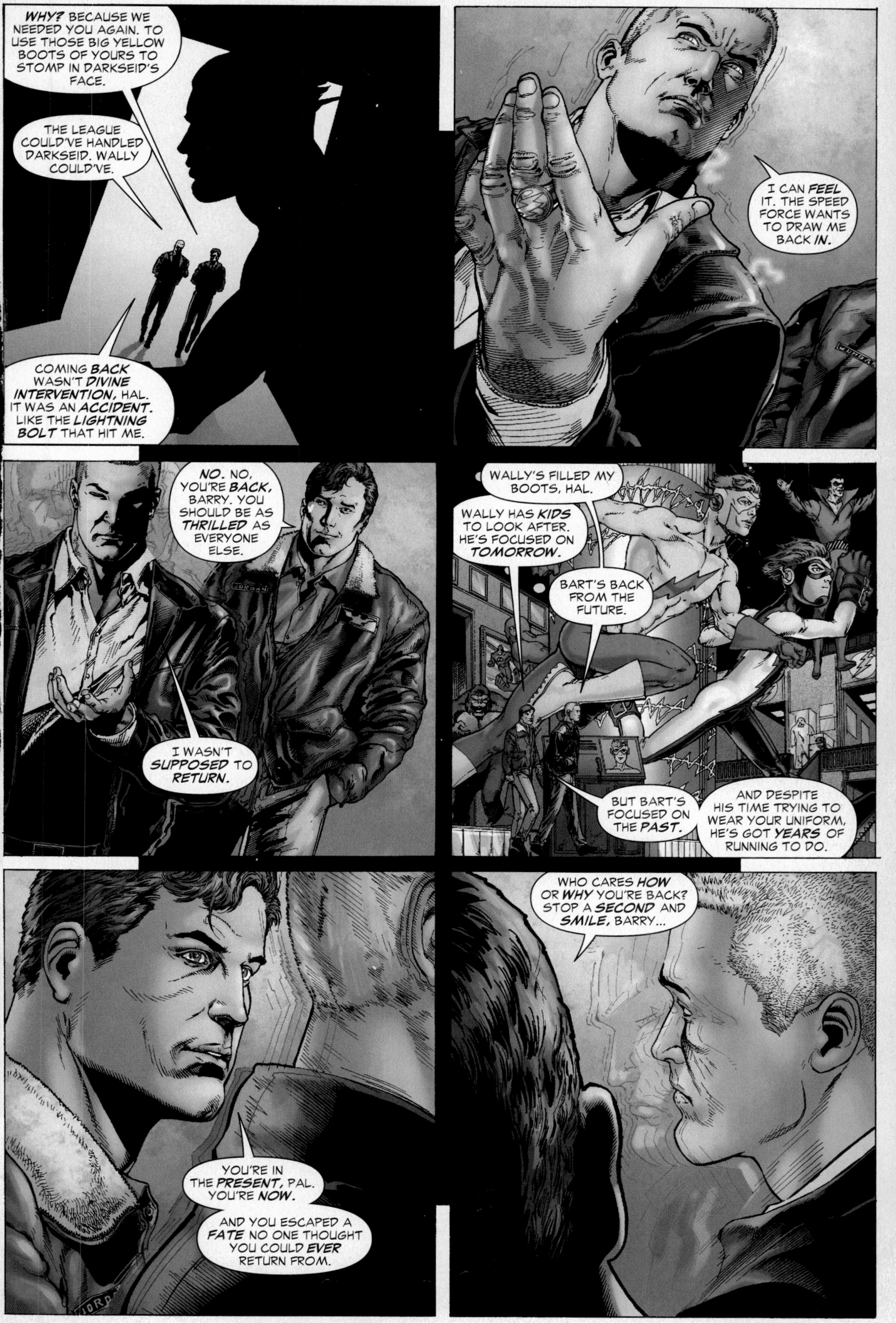
WHY? BECAUSE WE NEEDED YOU AGAIN. TO USE THOSE BIG YELLOW BOOTS OF YOURS TO STOMP IN DARKSEID'S FACE.
THE LEAGUE COULD'VE HANDLED DARKSEID. WALLY COULD'VE.
COMING BACK WASN'T DIVINE INTERVENTION, HAL. IT WAS AN ACCIDENT. LIKE THE LIGHTNING BOLT THAT HIT ME.
I CAN FEEL IT. THE SPEED FORCE WANTS TO DRAW ME BACK IN.
NO. NO, YOU'RE BACK, BARRY. YOU SHOULD BE AS THRILLED AS EVERYONE ELSE.
I WASN'T SUPPOSED TO RETURN.
WALLY'S FILLED MY BOOTS, HAL.
WALLY HAS KIDS TO LOOK AFTER. HE'S FOCUSED ON TOMORROW.
BART'S BACK FROM THE FUTURE.
BUT BART'S FOCUSED ON THE PAST.
AND DESPITE HIS TIME TRYING TO WEAR YOUR UNIFORM, HE'S GOT YEARS OF RUNNING TO DO.
YOU'RE IN THE PRESENT, PAL. YOU'RE NOW.
AND YOU ESCAPED A FATE NO ONE THOUGHT YOU COULD EVER RETURN FROM.
WHO CARES HOW OR WHY YOU'RE BACK? STOP A SECOND AND SMILE, BARRY...

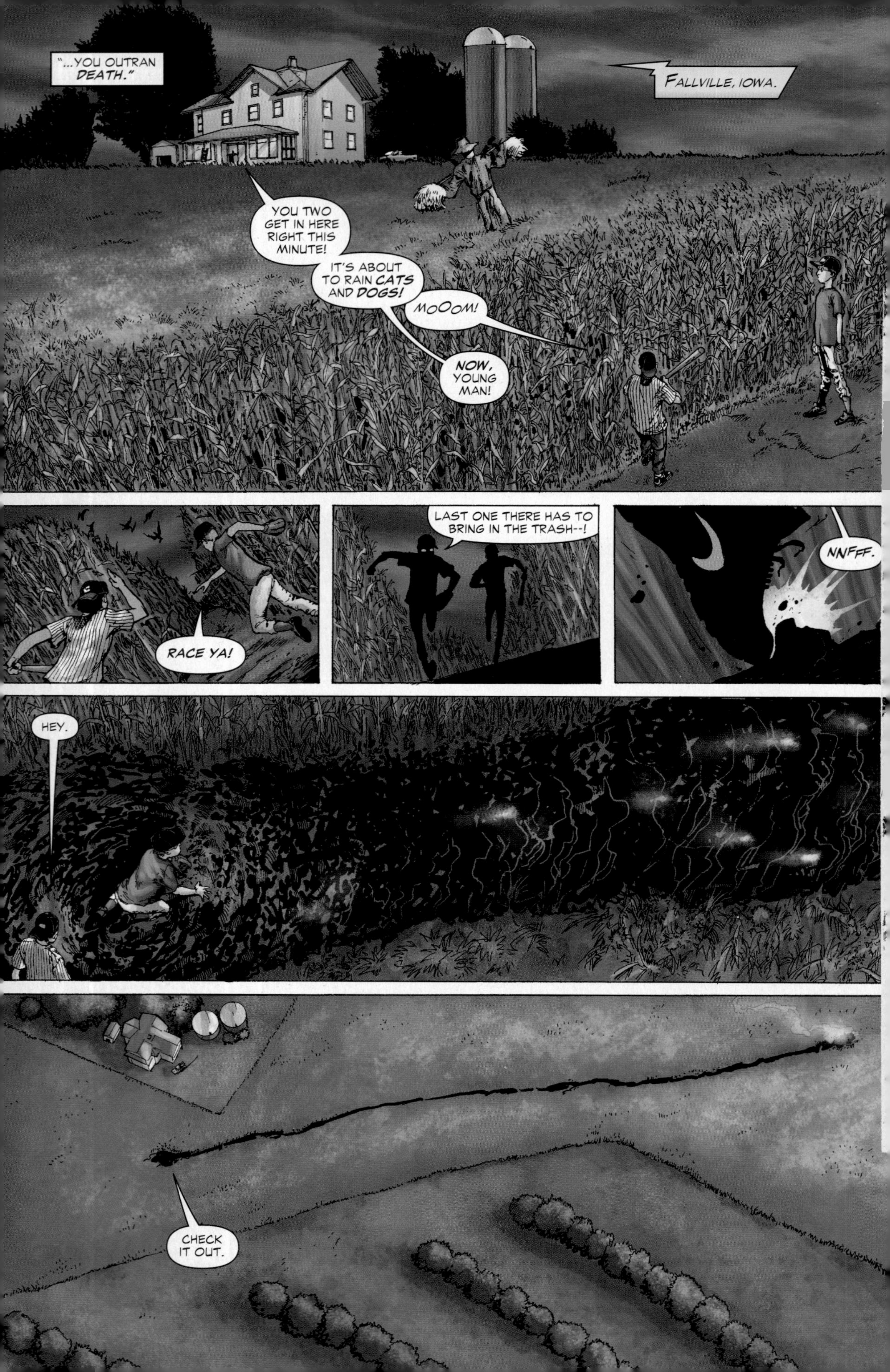
"...YOU OUTRAN DEATH."
FALLVILLE, IOWA.
YOU TWO GET IN HERE RIGHT THIS MINUTE!
IT'S ABOUT TO RAIN CATS AND DOGS!
MOOOOM!
NOW, YOUNG MAN!
RACE YA!
LAST ONE THERE HAS TO BRING IN THE TRASH--!
NNFFF.
HEY.
CHECK IT OUT.

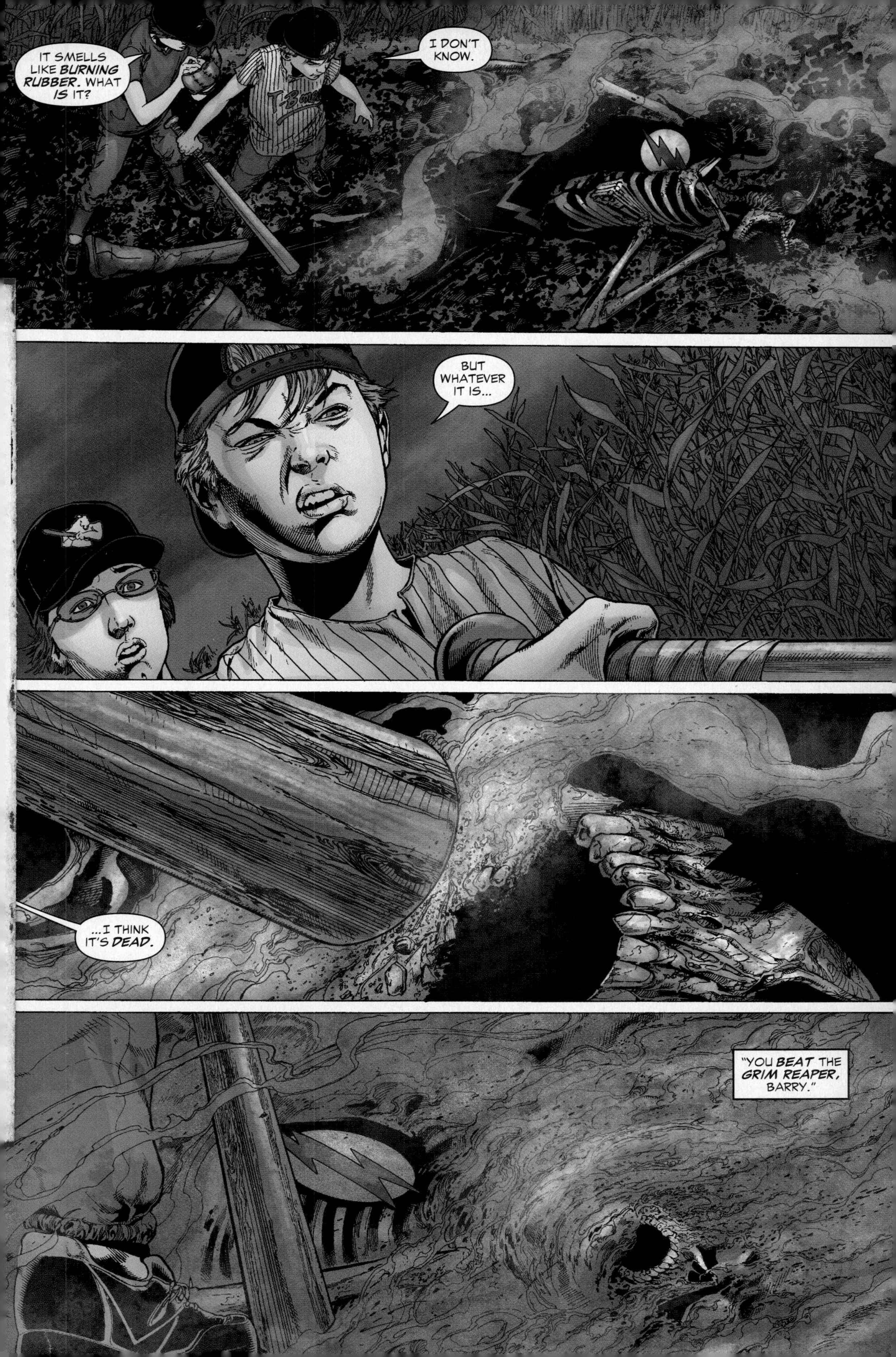
IT SMELLS LIKE BURNING RUBBER. WHAT IS IT?
I DON'T KNOW.
BUT WHATEVER IT IS...
...I THINK IT'S DEAD.
"YOU BEAT THE GRIM REAPER, BARRY."

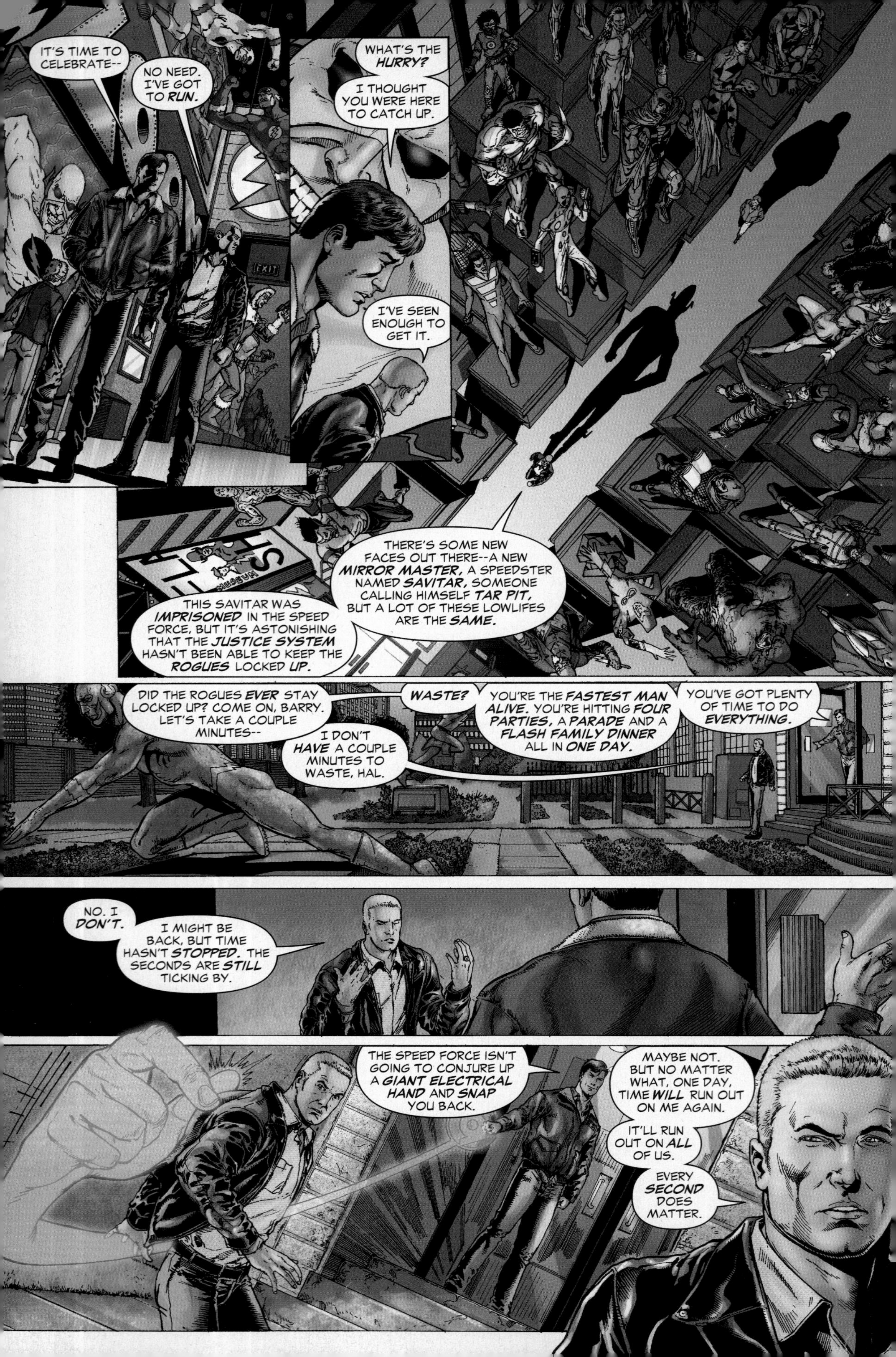
IT'S TIME TO CELEBRATE--
NO NEED. I'VE GOT TO RUN.
WHAT'S THE HURRY?
I THOUGHT YOU WERE HERE TO CATCH UP.
I'VE SEEN ENOUGH TO GET IT.
THERE'S SOME NEW FACES OUT THERE--A NEW MIRROR MASTER, A SPEEDSTER NAMED SAVITAR, SOMEONE CALLING HIMSELF TAR PIT, BUT A LOT OF THESE LOWLIFES ARE THE SAME.
THIS SAVITAR WAS IMPRISONED IN THE SPEED FORCE, BUT IT'S ASTONISHING THAT THE JUSTICE SYSTEM HASN'T BEEN ABLE TO KEEP THE ROGUES LOCKED UP.
DID THE ROGUES EVER STAY LOCKED UP? COME ON, BARRY. LET'S TAKE A COUPLE MINUTES--
I DON'T HAVE A COUPLE MINUTES TO WASTE, HAL.
WASTE?
YOU'RE THE FASTEST MAN ALIVE. YOU'RE HITTING FOUR PARTIES, A PARADE AND A FLASH FAMILY DINNER ALL IN ONE DAY.
YOU'VE GOT PLENTY OF TIME TO DO EVERYTHING.
NO. I DON'T.
I MIGHT BE BACK, BUT TIME HASN'T STOPPED. THE SECONDS ARE STILL TICKING BY.
THE SPEED FORCE ISN'T GOING TO CONJURE UP A GIANT ELECTRICAL HAND AND SNAP YOU BACK.
MAYBE NOT. BUT NO MATTER WHAT, ONE DAY, TIME WILL RUN OUT ON ME AGAIN.
IT'LL RUN OUT ON ALL OF US.
EVERY SECOND DOES MATTER.

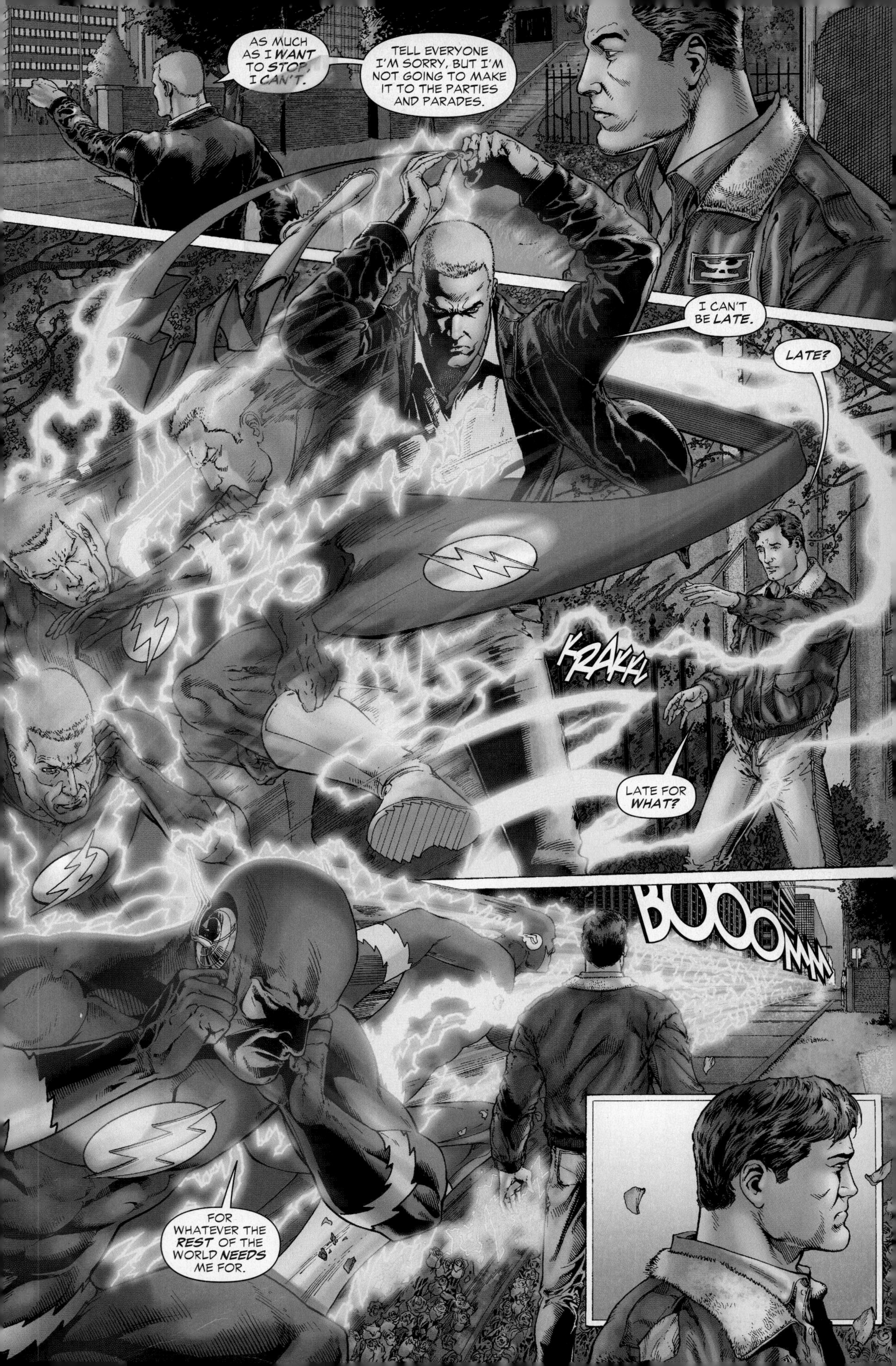
AS MUCH AS I WANT TO STOP, I CAN'T.
TELL EVERYONE I'M SORRY, BUT I'M NOT GOING TO MAKE IT TO THE PARTIES AND PARADES.
I CAN'T BE LATE.
LATE?
KRAKKL
LATE FOR WHAT?
BOOOMM
FOR WHATEVER THE REST OF THE WORLD NEEDS ME FOR.

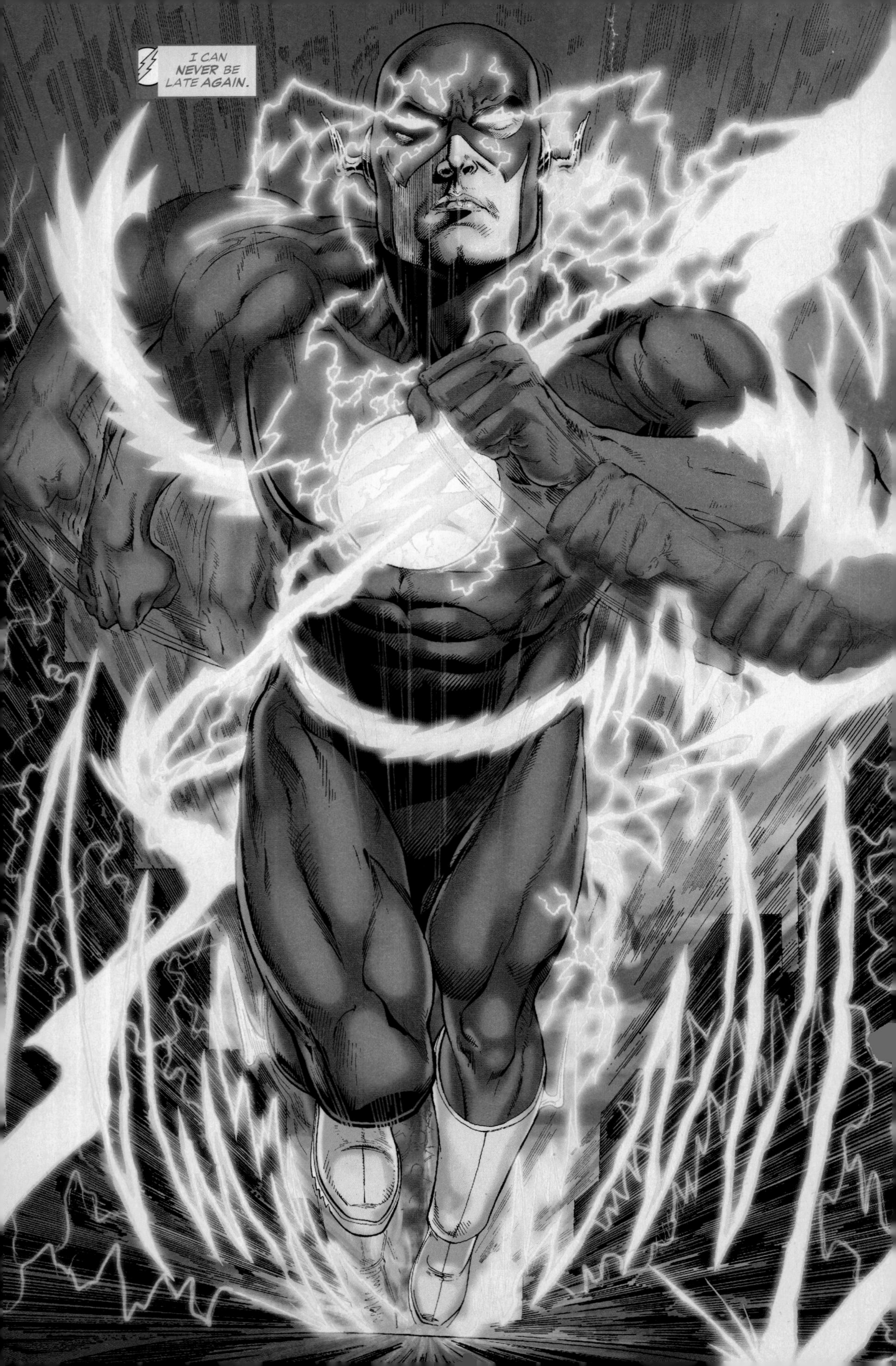
I CAN NEVER BE LATE AGAIN.

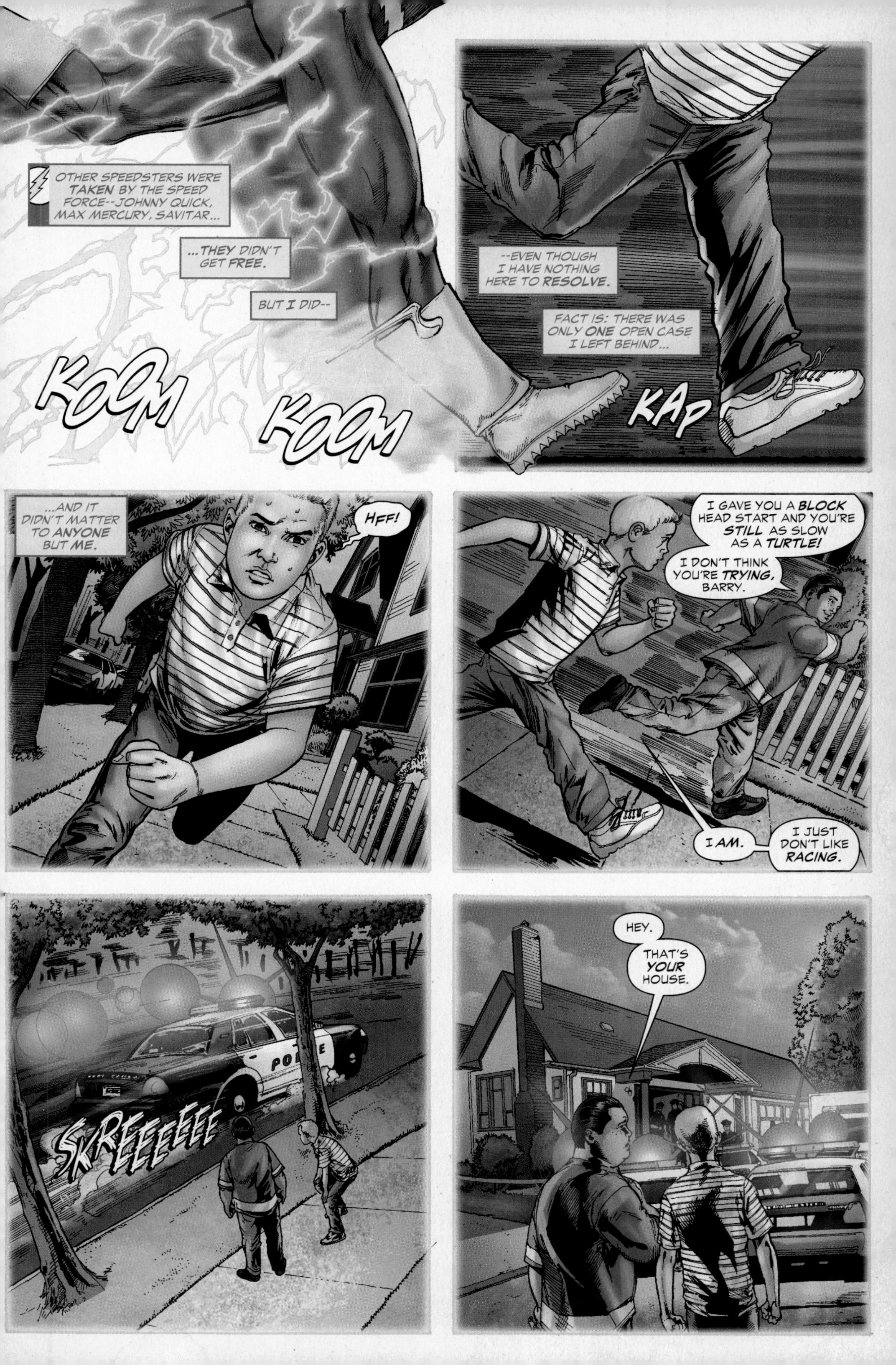
OTHER SPEEDSTERS WERE TAKEN BY THE SPEED FORCE--JOHNNY QUICK, MAX MERCURY, SAVITAR...
...THEY DIDN'T GET FREE.
BUT I DID--
KOOM
KOOM
--EVEN THOUGH I HAVE NOTHING HERE TO RESOLVE.
FACT IS: THERE WAS ONLY ONE OPEN CASE I LEFT BEHIND...
KAP
...AND IT DIDN'T MATTER TO ANYONE BUT ME.
HFF!
I GAVE YOU A BLOCK HEAD START AND YOU'RE STILL AS SLOW AS A TURTLE!
I DON'T THINK YOU'RE TRYING, BARRY.
I AM.
I JUST DON'T LIKE RACING.
SKREEEEEEE
HEY.
THAT'S YOUR HOUSE.

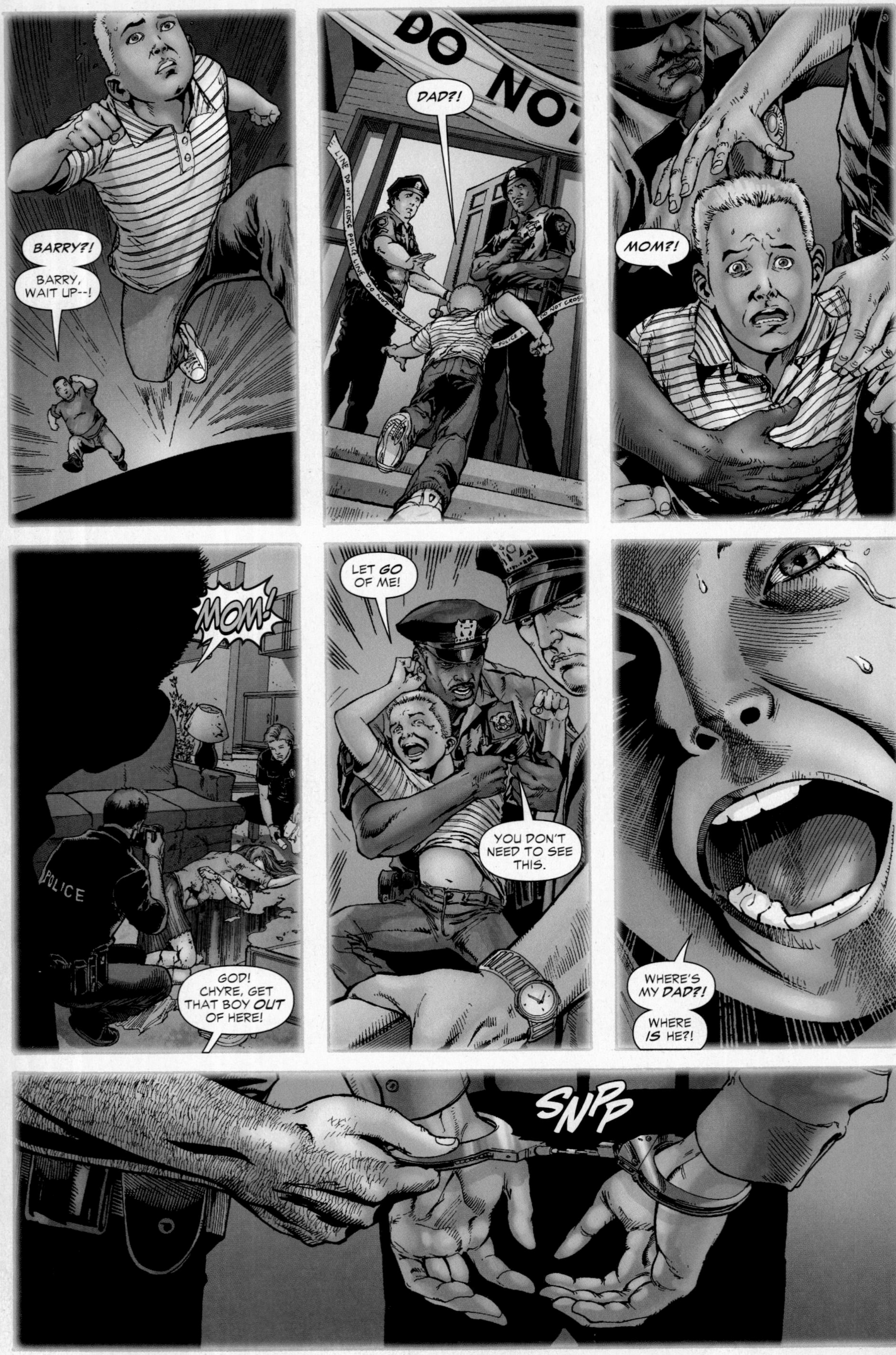
BARRY?!
BARRY, WAIT UP--!
DO NOT
DAD?!
MOM?!
MOM!
GOD! CHYRE, GET THAT BOY OUT OF HERE!
LET GO OF ME!
YOU DON'T NEED TO SEE THIS.
WHERE'S MY DAD?!
WHERE IS HE?!
SNPP

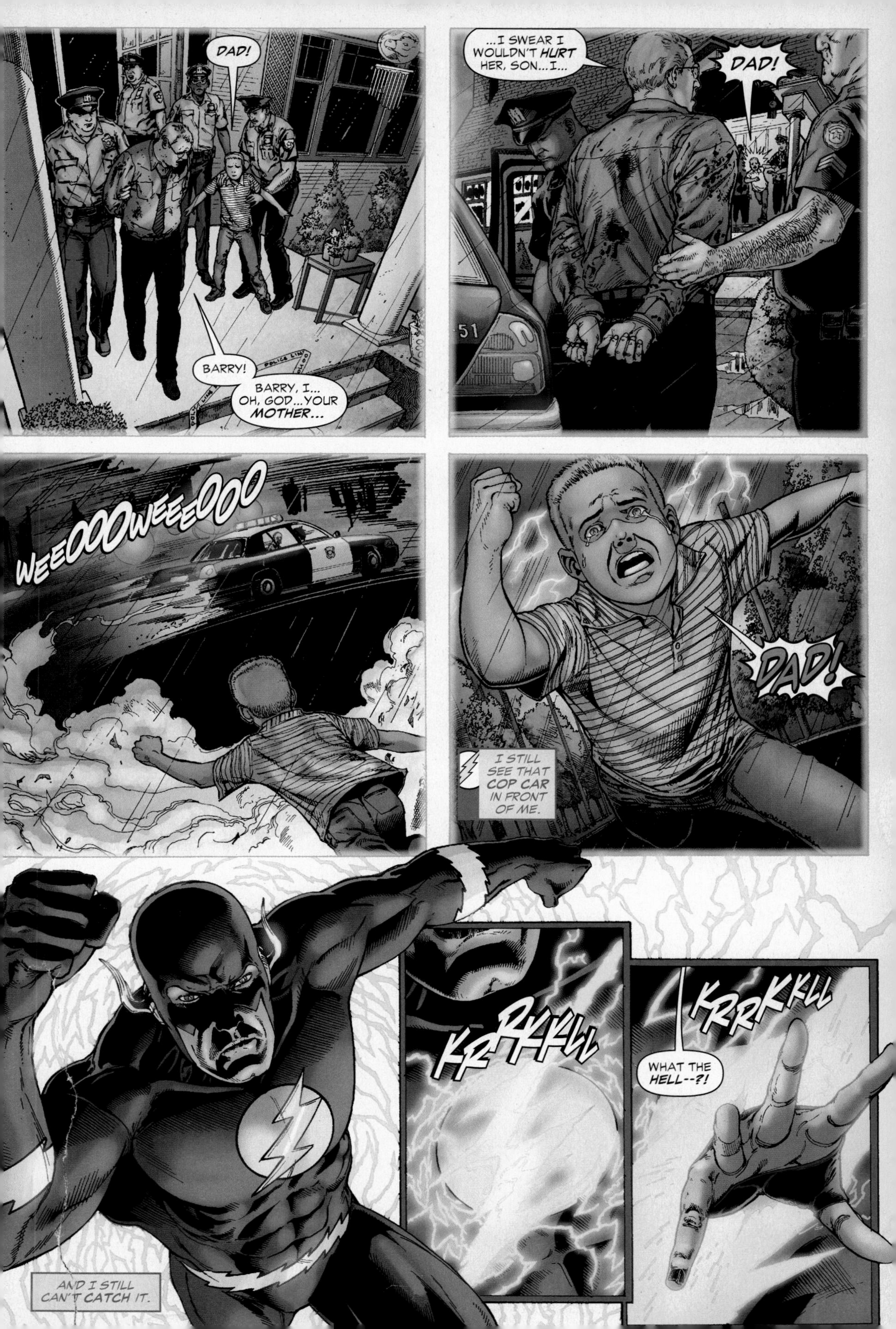
DAD!
BARRY!
BARRY, I... OH, GOD...YOUR MOTHER...
...I SWEAR I WOULDN'T HURT HER, SON...I...
DAD!
WEEOOOWEEEOOO
DAD!
I STILL SEE THAT COP CAR IN FRONT OF ME.
AND I STILL CAN'T CATCH IT.
KRRKKLL
KRRKKLL
WHAT THE HELL--?!

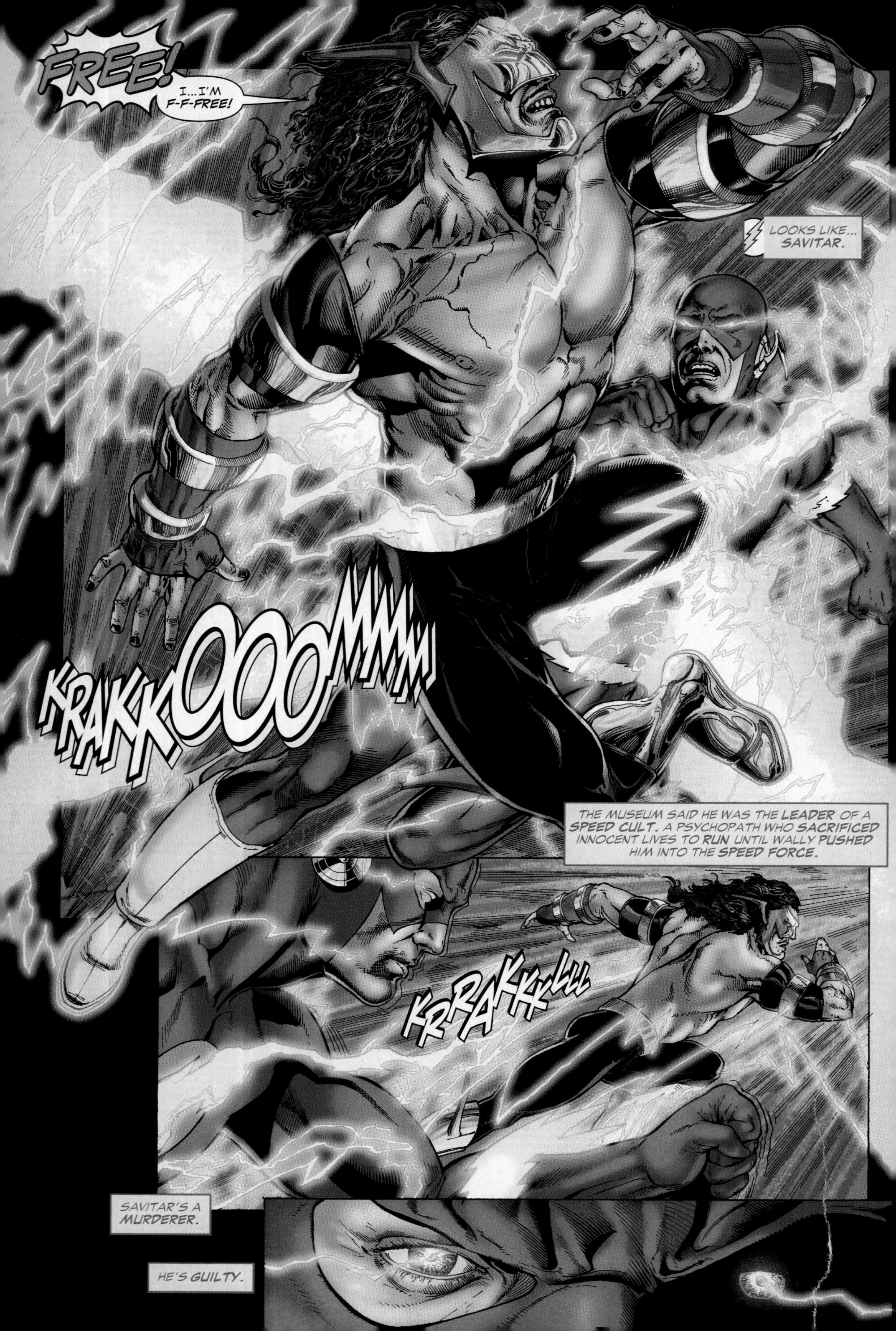
FREE!
I...I'M F-F-FREE!
LOOKS LIKE... SAVITAR.
KRAKKOOOOMMMM
THE MUSEUM SAID HE WAS THE LEADER OF A SPEED CULT. A PSYCHOPATH WHO SACRIFICED INNOCENT LIVES TO RUN UNTIL WALLY PUSHED HIM INTO THE SPEED FORCE.
KRRAKKKLLL
SAVITAR'S A MURDERER.
HE'S GUILTY.

AND HE'S ON THE RUN.

I'M NOT SURE *HOW* YOU ESCAPED, BUT YOU'RE ABOUT TO WISH YOU *HADN'T*.

STAY *AWAY* FROM ME!

WHICH ONE OF YOU IS GOING TO TAKE *RESPONSIBILITY* FOR THIS?

NOT *ME!*

YOU KNOW MY *NEPHEW*, BUT *WE* HAVEN'T MET. WHY DON'T WE *PULL OVER* AND GET ACQUAINTED?

KZK

KRRKKLL

AAAAHHH!

KRRKKLL

WALLY?!

YOU...

SOME KIND OF FEEDBACK.

I CAN'T SLOW *DOWN*.

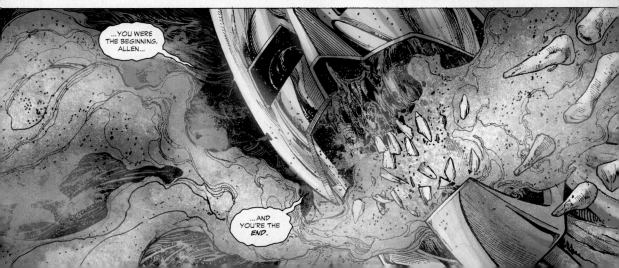

...YOU WERE THE BEGINNING, ALLEN...

...AND YOU'RE THE *END*.

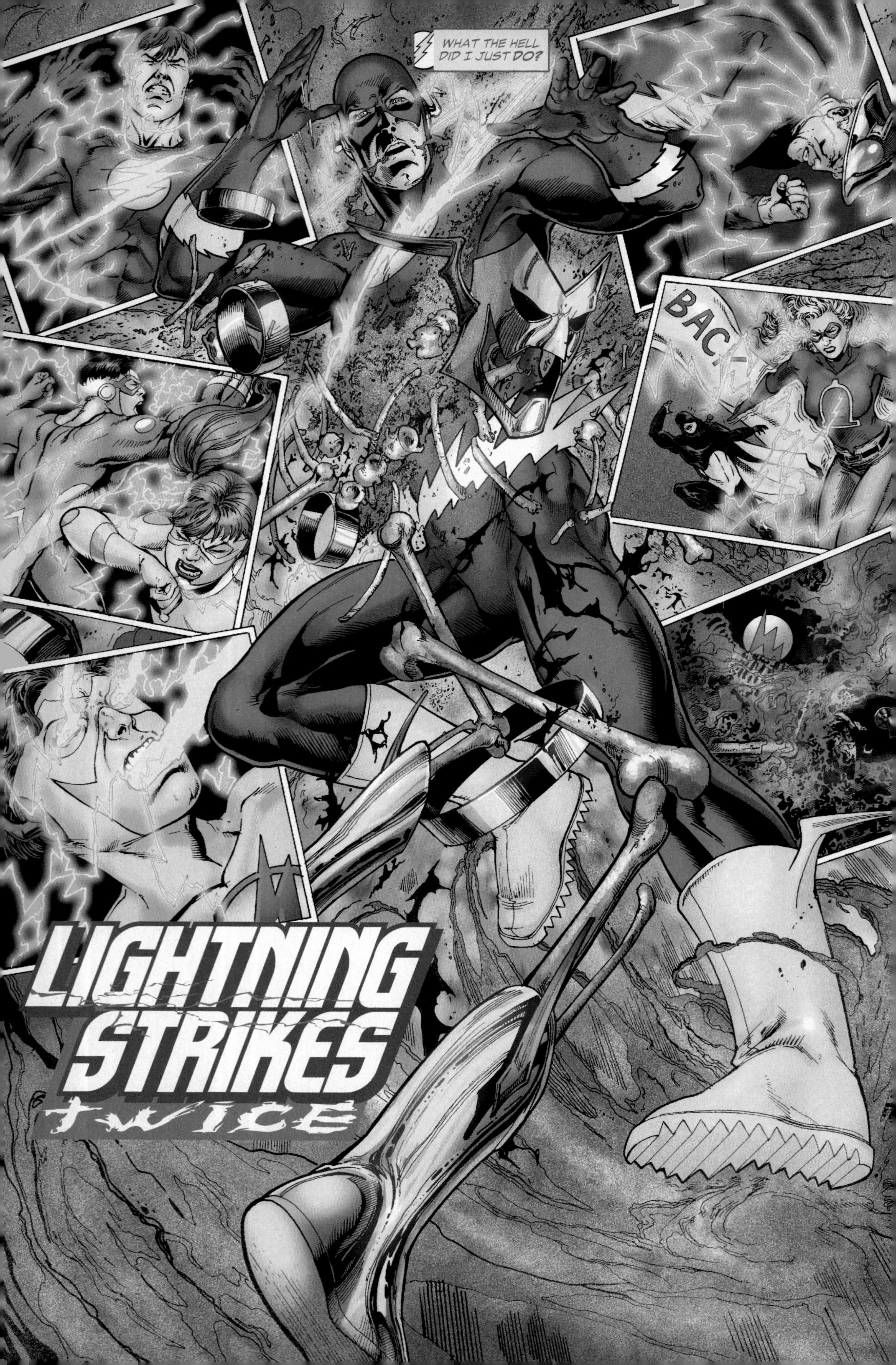
WHAT THE HELL DID I JUST DO?
BACK
LIGHTNING STRIKES TWICE

THE FLASH: REBIRTH #2
COVER BY **ETHAN VAN SCIVER** (AFTER **CARMINE INFANTINO**) WITH **ALEX SINCLAIR**

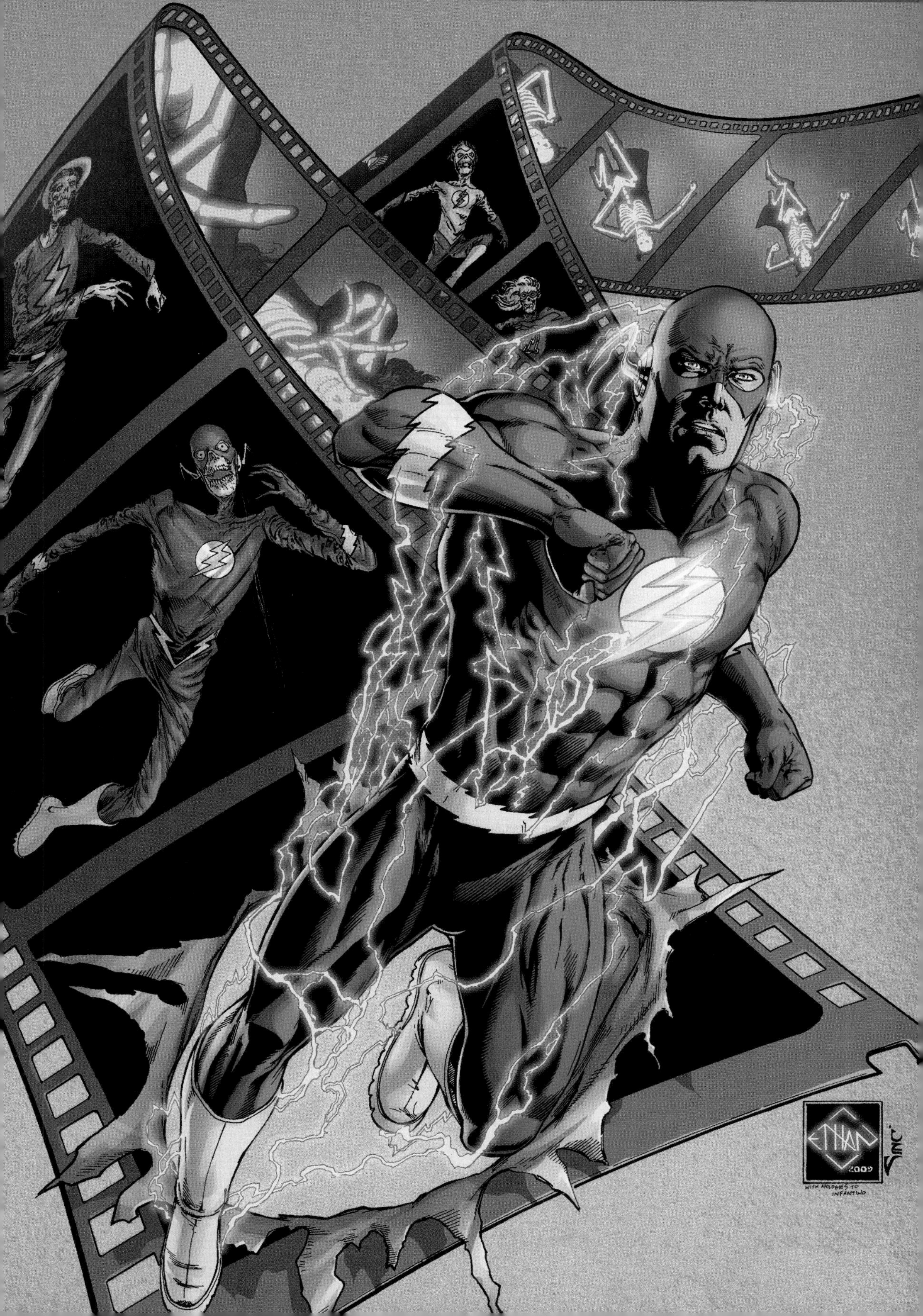
ETHAN
2009
WITH APOLOGIES TO INFANTINO

THE FLASH: REBIRTH #2 VARIANT COVER BY **ETHAN VAN SCIVER** WITH **ALEX SINCLAIR**

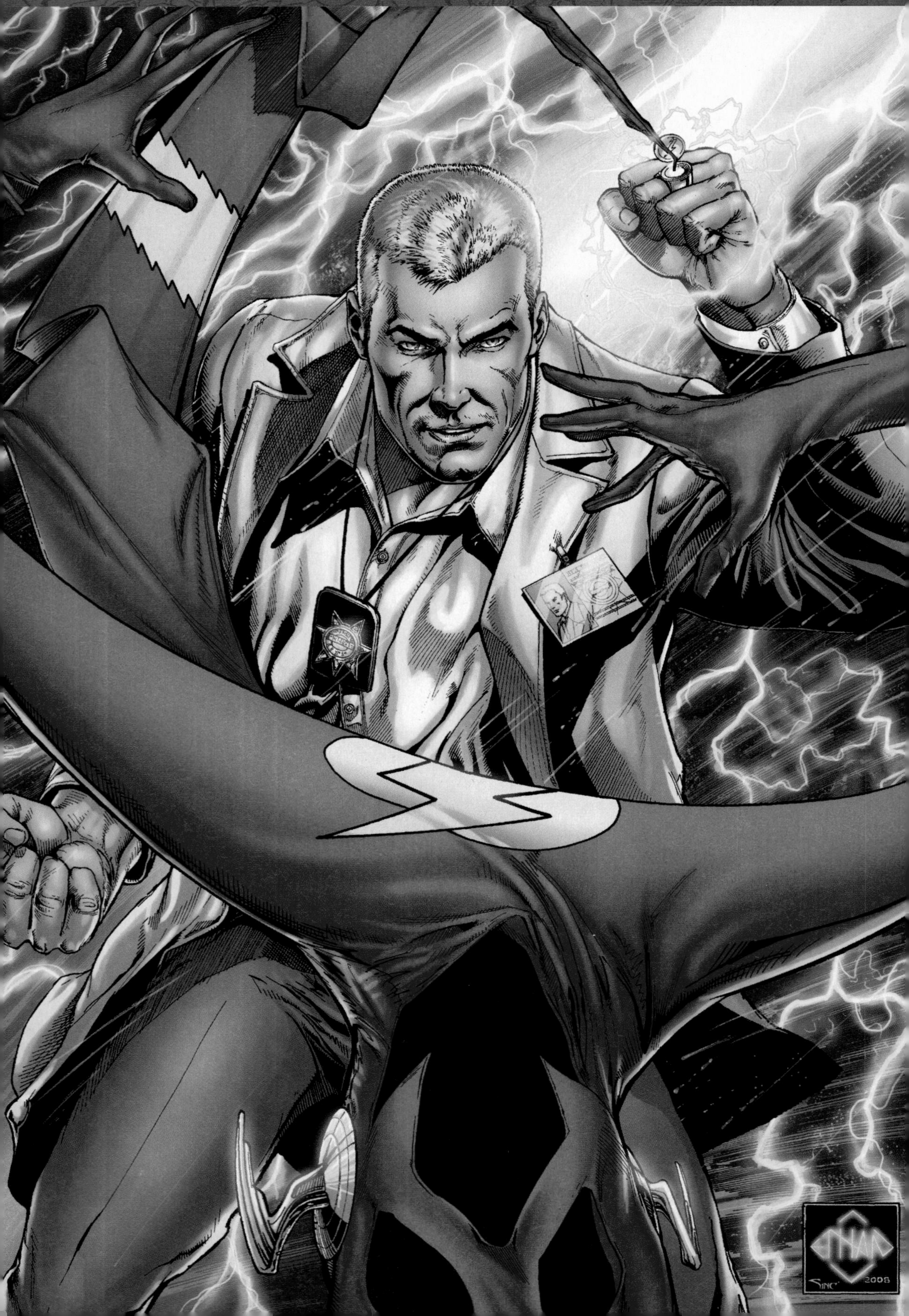

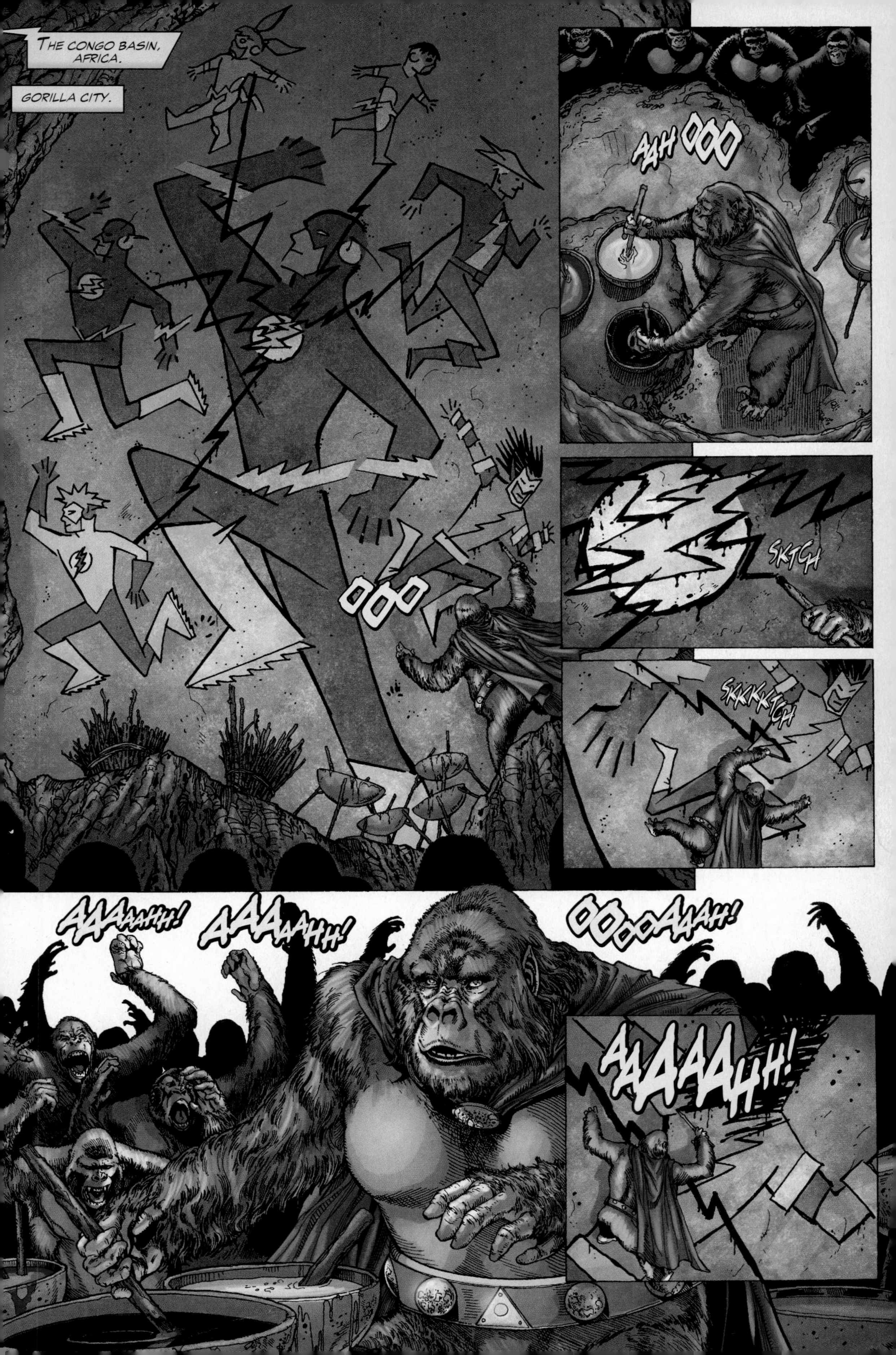
THE CONGO BASIN, AFRICA.
GORILLA CITY.
AAH OOO
OOO
SKTCH
SKKKKTCH
AAAaahh!
AAAaahh!
OOooAAAH!
AAAAAAHH!

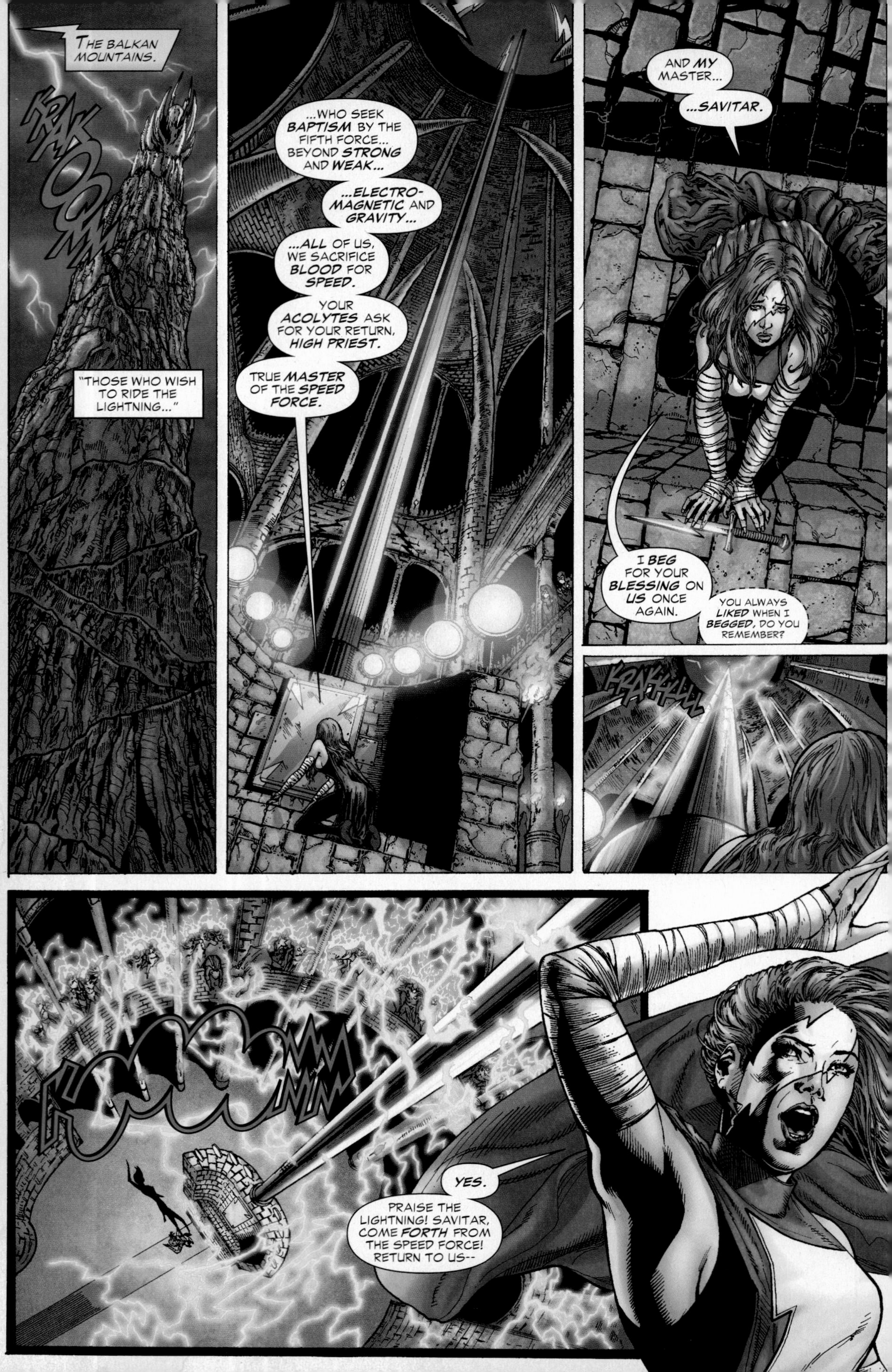
THE BALKAN MOUNTAINS.
KRAKOOOMM
"THOSE WHO WISH TO RIDE THE LIGHTNING..."
...WHO SEEK BAPTISM BY THE FIFTH FORCE... BEYOND STRONG AND WEAK...
...ELECTRO-MAGNETIC AND GRAVITY...
...ALL OF US, WE SACRIFICE BLOOD FOR SPEED.
YOUR ACOLYTES ASK FOR YOUR RETURN, HIGH PRIEST.
TRUE MASTER OF THE SPEED FORCE.
AND MY MASTER...
...SAVITAR.
I BEG FOR YOUR BLESSING ON US ONCE AGAIN.
YOU ALWAYS LIKED WHEN I BEGGED, DO YOU REMEMBER?
KRAKKALL
KOOOOMMMMM
YES.
PRAISE THE LIGHTNING! SAVITAR, COME FORTH FROM THE SPEED FORCE! RETURN TO US--

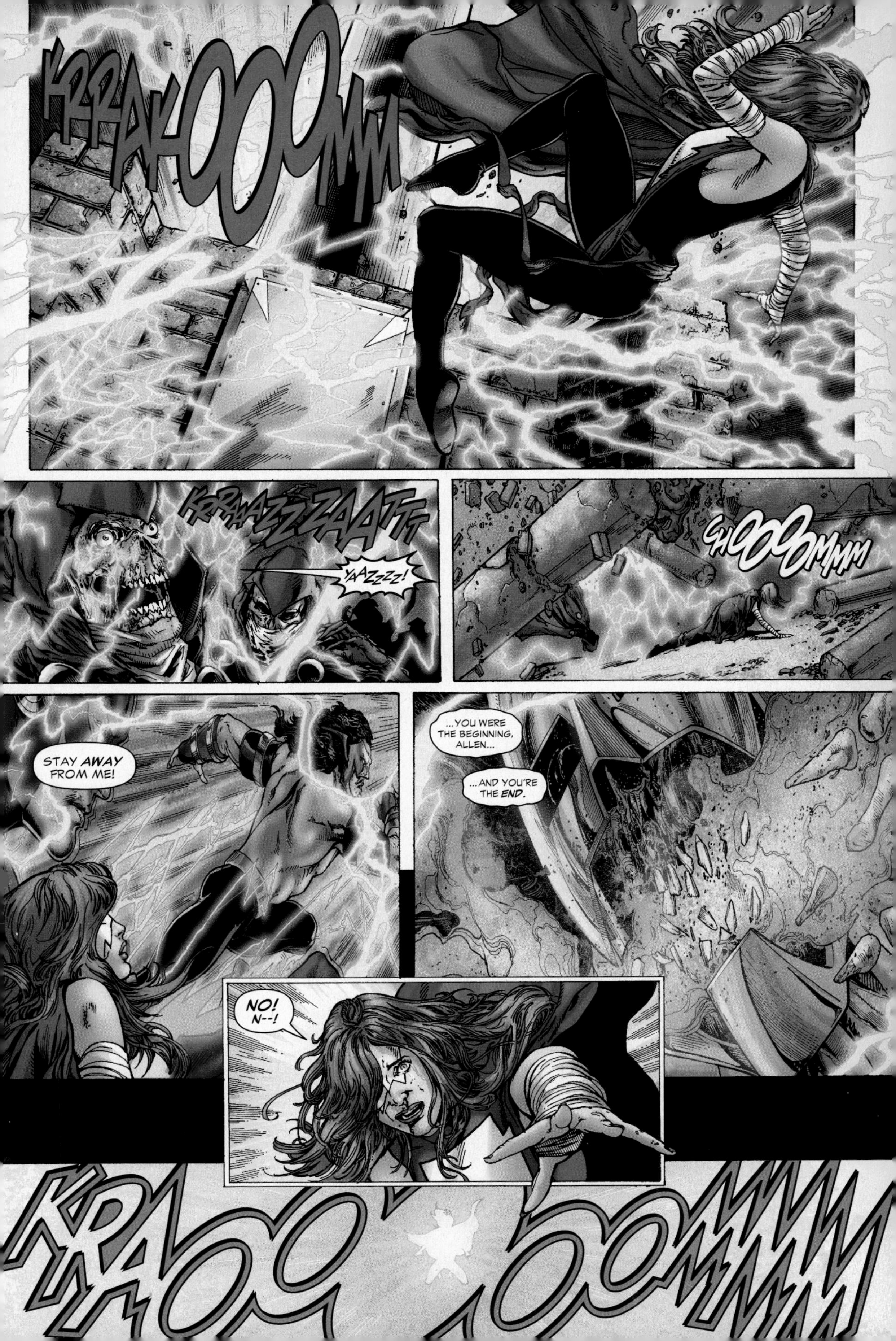

KRRAKOOOMMM
KRRAAZZZZAATTT
YAAZZZZ!
CHOOOOMMM
STAY AWAY FROM ME!
...YOU WERE THE BEGINNING, ALLEN...
...AND YOU'RE THE END.
NO! N--!
KRAOOOOOMMMM

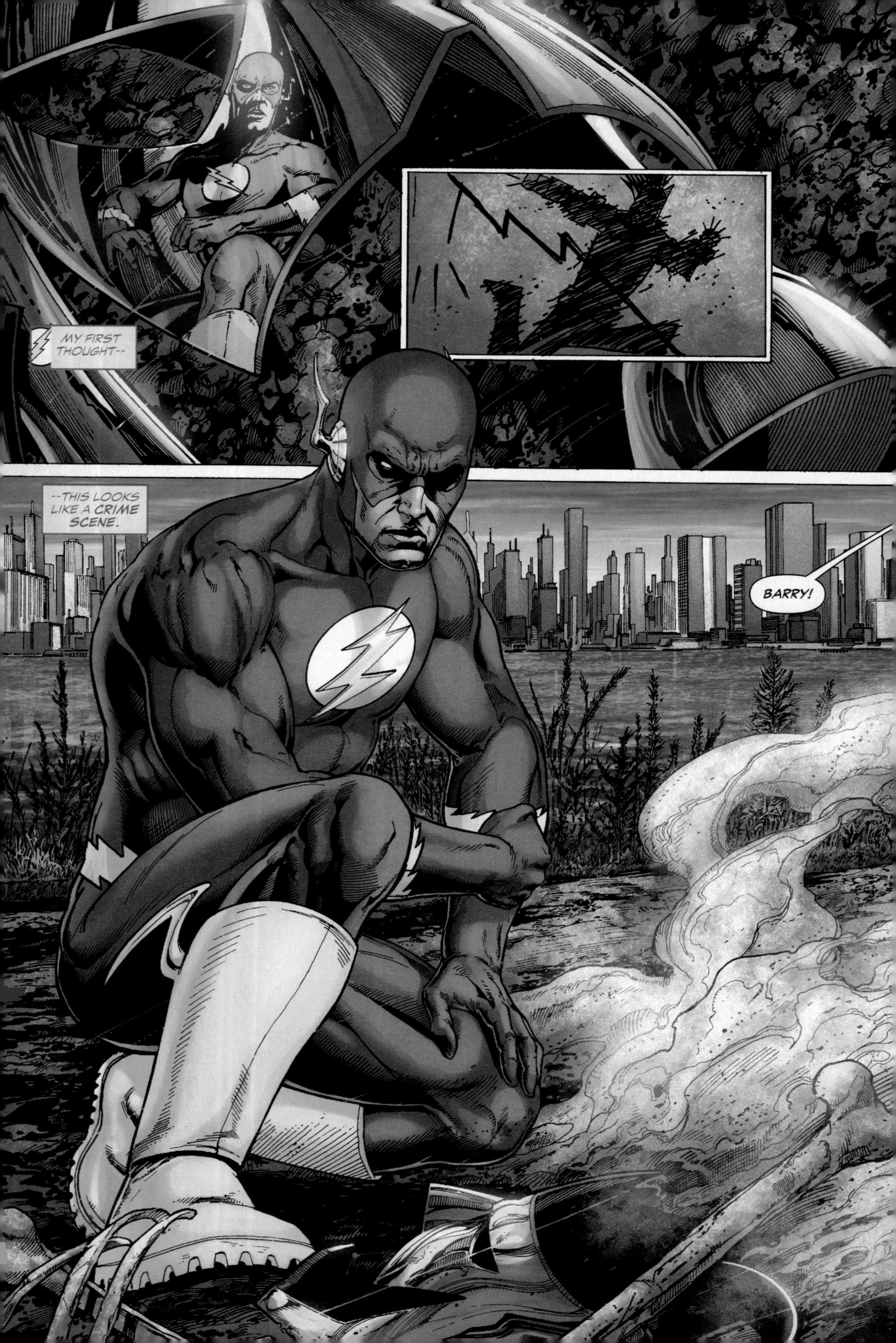
MY FIRST THOUGHT--
--THIS LOOKS LIKE A CRIME SCENE.
BARRY!

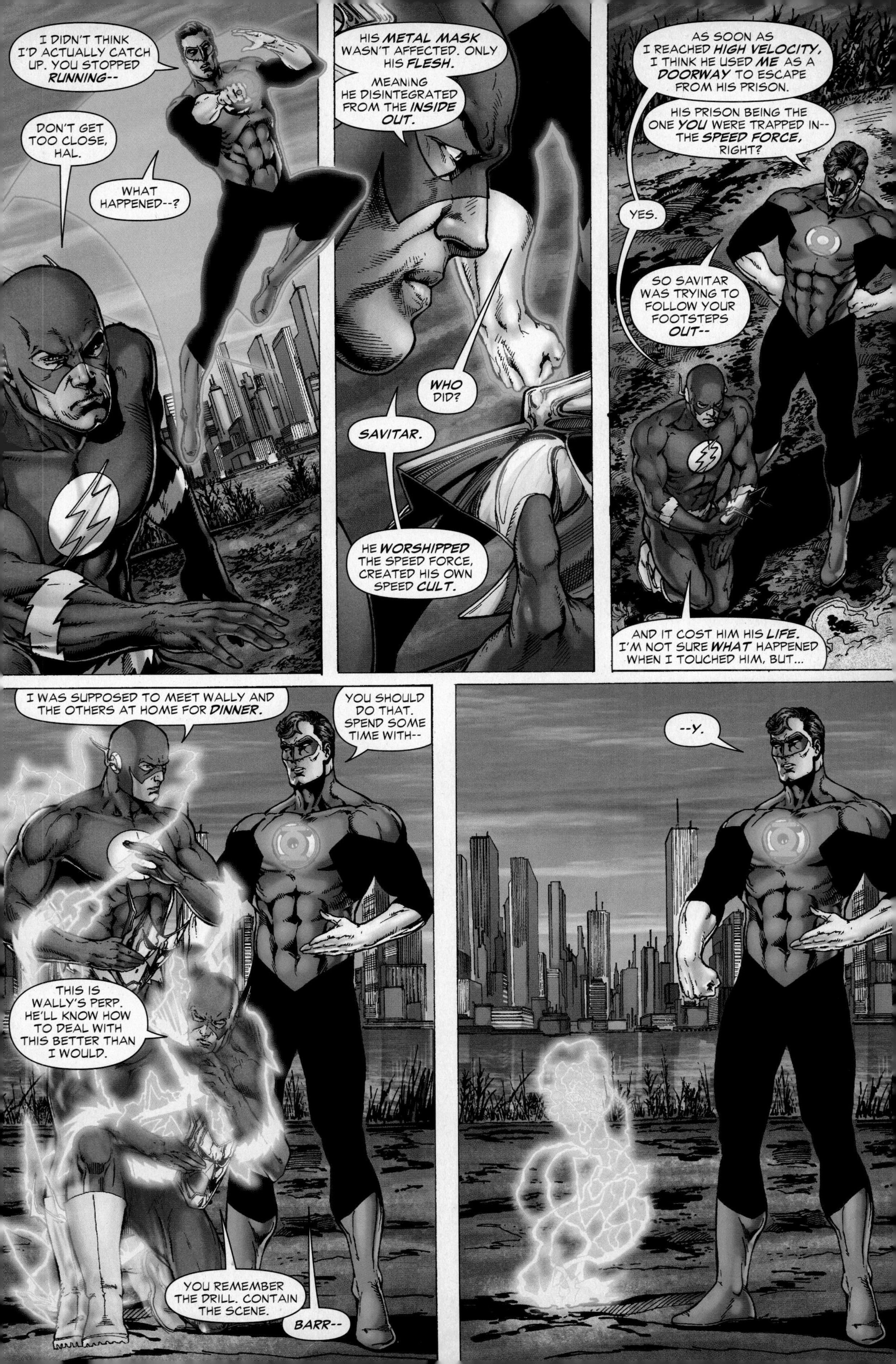
I DIDN'T THINK I'D ACTUALLY CATCH UP. YOU STOPPED RUNNING--
DON'T GET TOO CLOSE, HAL.
WHAT HAPPENED--?
HIS METAL MASK WASN'T AFFECTED. ONLY HIS FLESH.
MEANING HE DISINTEGRATED FROM THE INSIDE OUT.
WHO DID?
SAVITAR.
HE WORSHIPPED THE SPEED FORCE, CREATED HIS OWN SPEED CULT.
AS SOON AS I REACHED HIGH VELOCITY, I THINK HE USED ME AS A DOORWAY TO ESCAPE FROM HIS PRISON.
HIS PRISON BEING THE ONE YOU WERE TRAPPED IN-- THE SPEED FORCE, RIGHT?
YES.
SO SAVITAR WAS TRYING TO FOLLOW YOUR FOOTSTEPS OUT--
AND IT COST HIM HIS LIFE. I'M NOT SURE WHAT HAPPENED WHEN I TOUCHED HIM, BUT...
I WAS SUPPOSED TO MEET WALLY AND THE OTHERS AT HOME FOR DINNER.
YOU SHOULD DO THAT. SPEND SOME TIME WITH--
THIS IS WALLY'S PERP. HE'LL KNOW HOW TO DEAL WITH THIS BETTER THAN I WOULD.
YOU REMEMBER THE DRILL. CONTAIN THE SCENE.
BARR--
--Y.

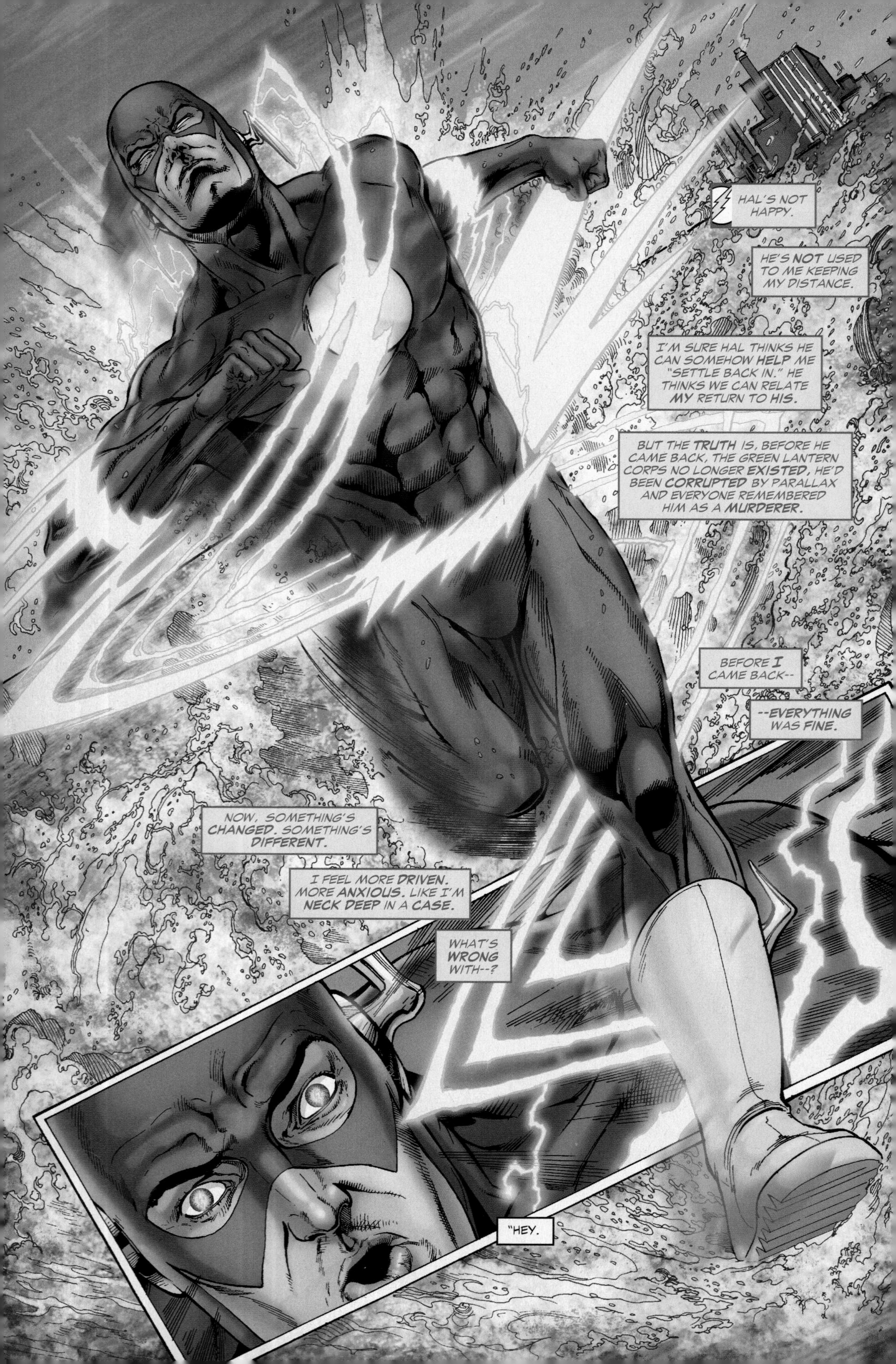
HAL'S NOT HAPPY.
HE'S NOT USED TO ME KEEPING MY DISTANCE.
I'M SURE HAL THINKS HE CAN SOMEHOW HELP ME "SETTLE BACK IN." HE THINKS WE CAN RELATE MY RETURN TO HIS.
BUT THE TRUTH IS, BEFORE HE CAME BACK, THE GREEN LANTERN CORPS NO LONGER EXISTED, HE'D BEEN CORRUPTED BY PARALLAX AND EVERYONE REMEMBERED HIM AS A MURDERER.
BEFORE I CAME BACK--
--EVERYTHING WAS FINE.
NOW, SOMETHING'S CHANGED. SOMETHING'S DIFFERENT.
I FEEL MORE DRIVEN. MORE ANXIOUS. LIKE I'M NECK DEEP IN A CASE.
WHAT'S WRONG WITH--?
"HEY.

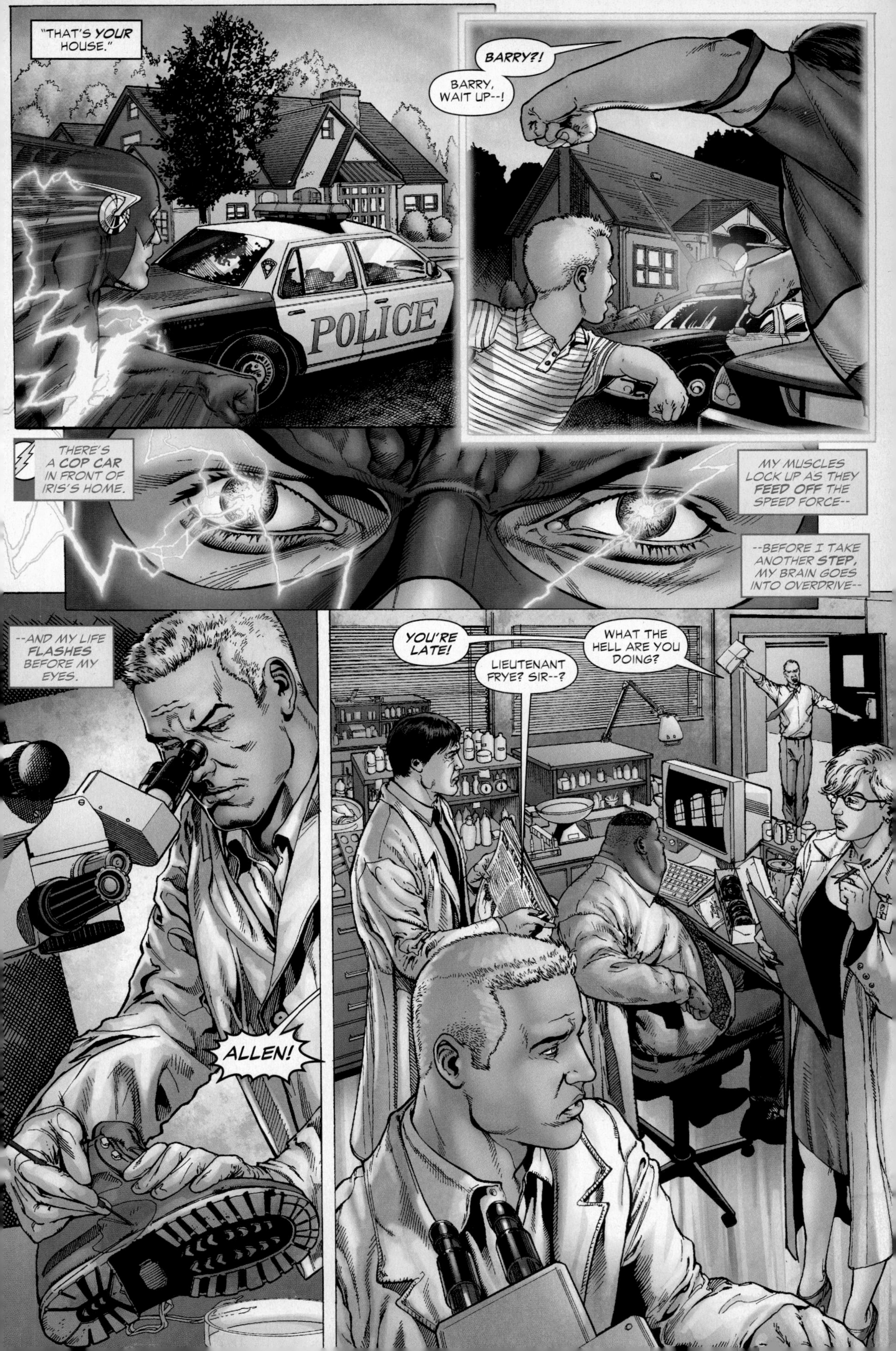
"THAT'S YOUR HOUSE."
BARRY?!
BARRY, WAIT UP--!
THERE'S A COP CAR IN FRONT OF IRIS'S HOME.
MY MUSCLES LOCK UP AS THEY FEED OFF THE SPEED FORCE--
--BEFORE I TAKE ANOTHER STEP, MY BRAIN GOES INTO OVERDRIVE--
--AND MY LIFE FLASHES BEFORE MY EYES.
ALLEN!
YOU'RE LATE!
WHAT THE HELL ARE YOU DOING?
LIEUTENANT FRYE? SIR--?
POLICE

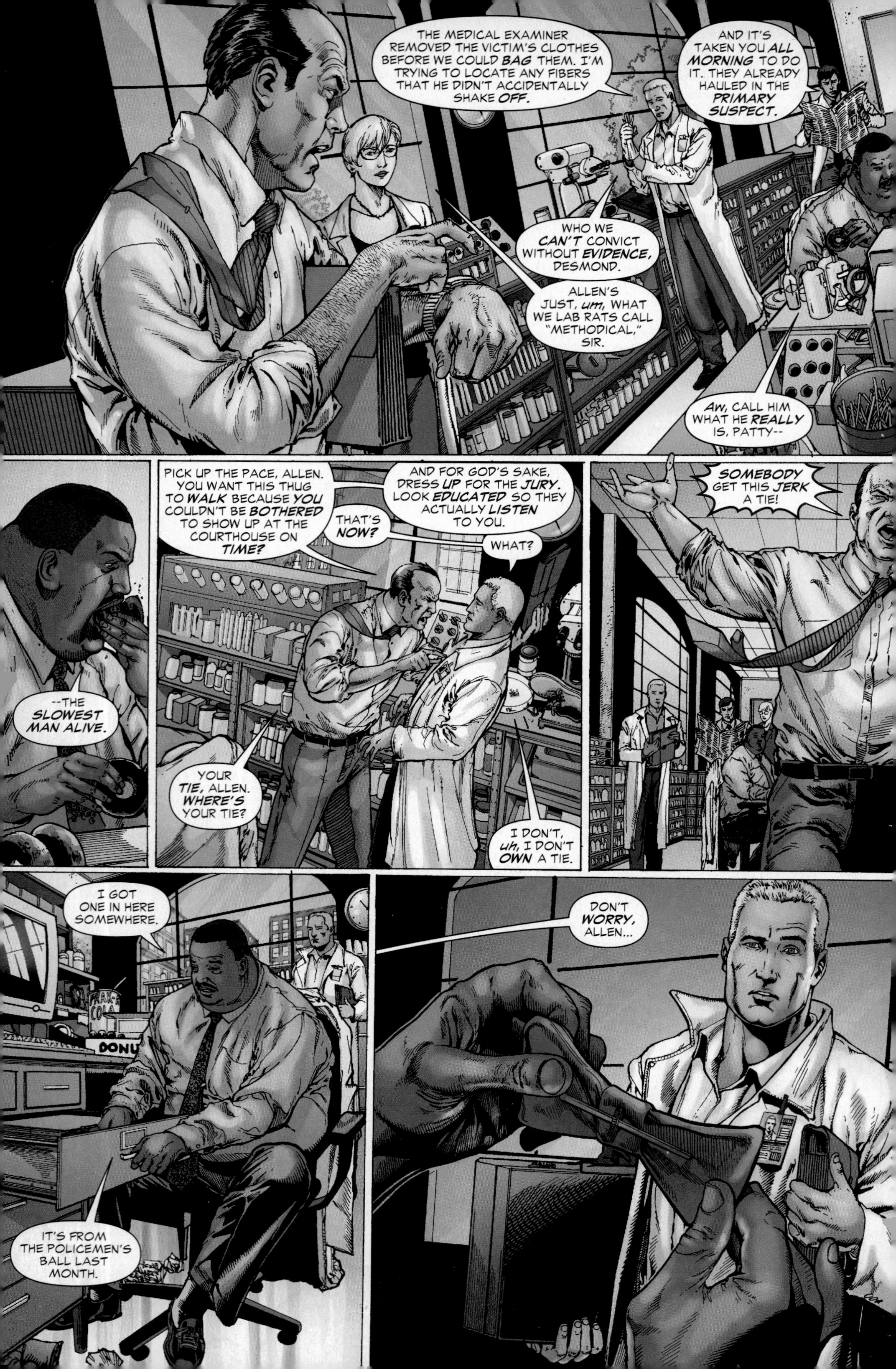
THE MEDICAL EXAMINER REMOVED THE VICTIM'S CLOTHES BEFORE WE COULD BAG THEM. I'M TRYING TO LOCATE ANY FIBERS THAT HE DIDN'T ACCIDENTALLY SHAKE OFF.
AND IT'S TAKEN YOU ALL MORNING TO DO IT. THEY ALREADY HAULED IN THE PRIMARY SUSPECT.
WHO WE CAN'T CONVICT WITHOUT EVIDENCE, DESMOND.
ALLEN'S JUST, um, WHAT WE LAB RATS CALL "METHODICAL," SIR.
AW, CALL HIM WHAT HE REALLY IS, PATTY--
--THE SLOWEST MAN ALIVE.
PICK UP THE PACE, ALLEN. YOU WANT THIS THUG TO WALK BECAUSE YOU COULDN'T BE BOTHERED TO SHOW UP AT THE COURTHOUSE ON TIME?
THAT'S NOW?
AND FOR GOD'S SAKE, DRESS UP FOR THE JURY. LOOK EDUCATED SO THEY ACTUALLY LISTEN TO YOU.
WHAT?
YOUR TIE, ALLEN. WHERE'S YOUR TIE?
I DON'T, uh, I DON'T OWN A TIE.
SOMEBODY GET THIS JERK A TIE!
I GOT ONE IN HERE SOMEWHERE.
DONU
IT'S FROM THE POLICEMEN'S BALL LAST MONTH.
DON'T WORRY, ALLEN...

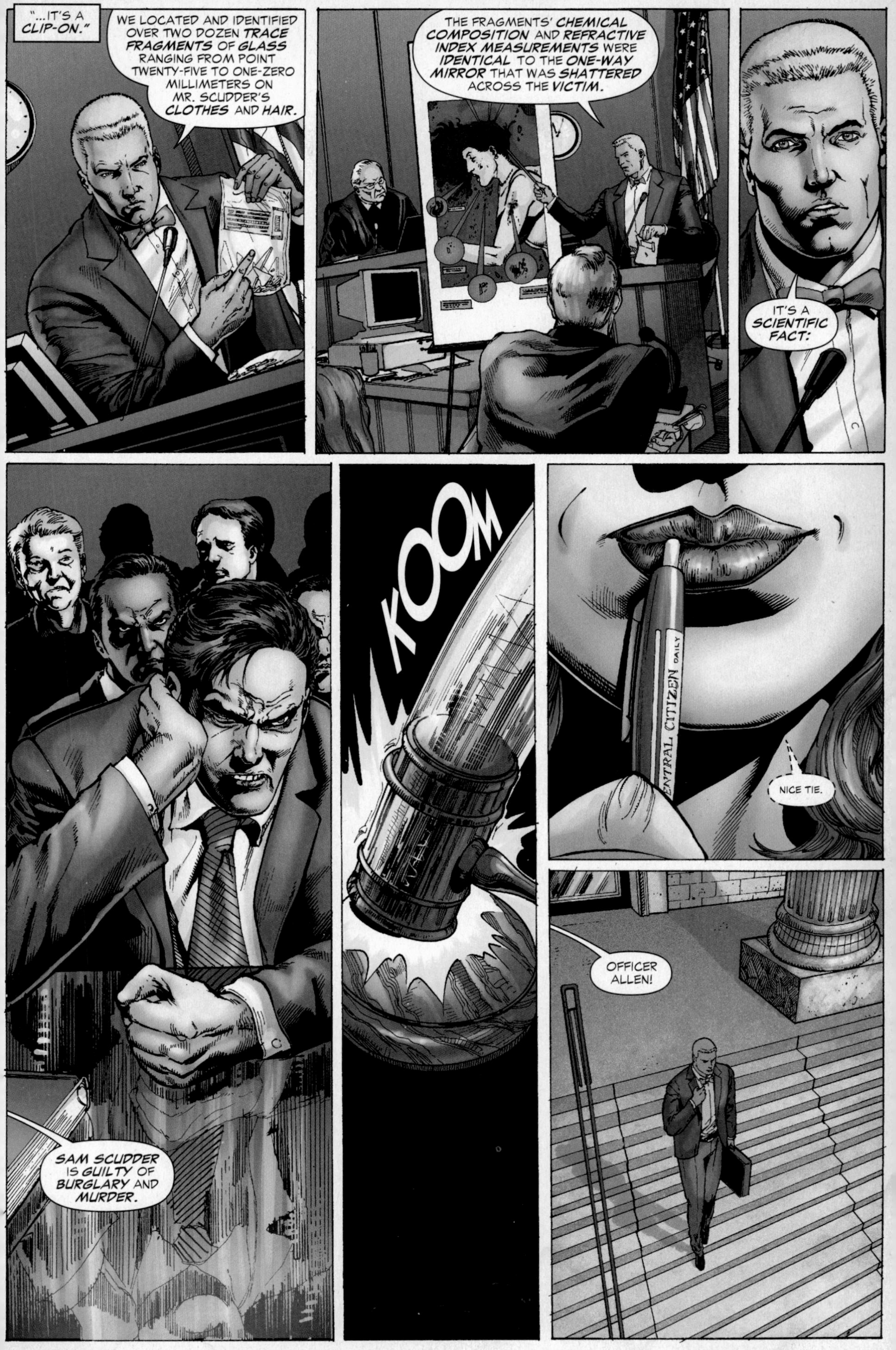
"...IT'S A CLIP-ON."
WE LOCATED AND IDENTIFIED OVER TWO DOZEN TRACE FRAGMENTS OF GLASS RANGING FROM POINT TWENTY-FIVE TO ONE-ZERO MILLIMETERS ON MR. SCUDDER'S CLOTHES AND HAIR.
THE FRAGMENTS' CHEMICAL COMPOSITION AND REFRACTIVE INDEX MEASUREMENTS WERE IDENTICAL TO THE ONE-WAY MIRROR THAT WAS SHATTERED ACROSS THE VICTIM.
IT'S A SCIENTIFIC FACT:
SAM SCUDDER IS GUILTY OF BURGLARY AND MURDER.
KOOM
ENTRAL CITIZEN DAILY
NICE TIE.
OFFICER ALLEN!

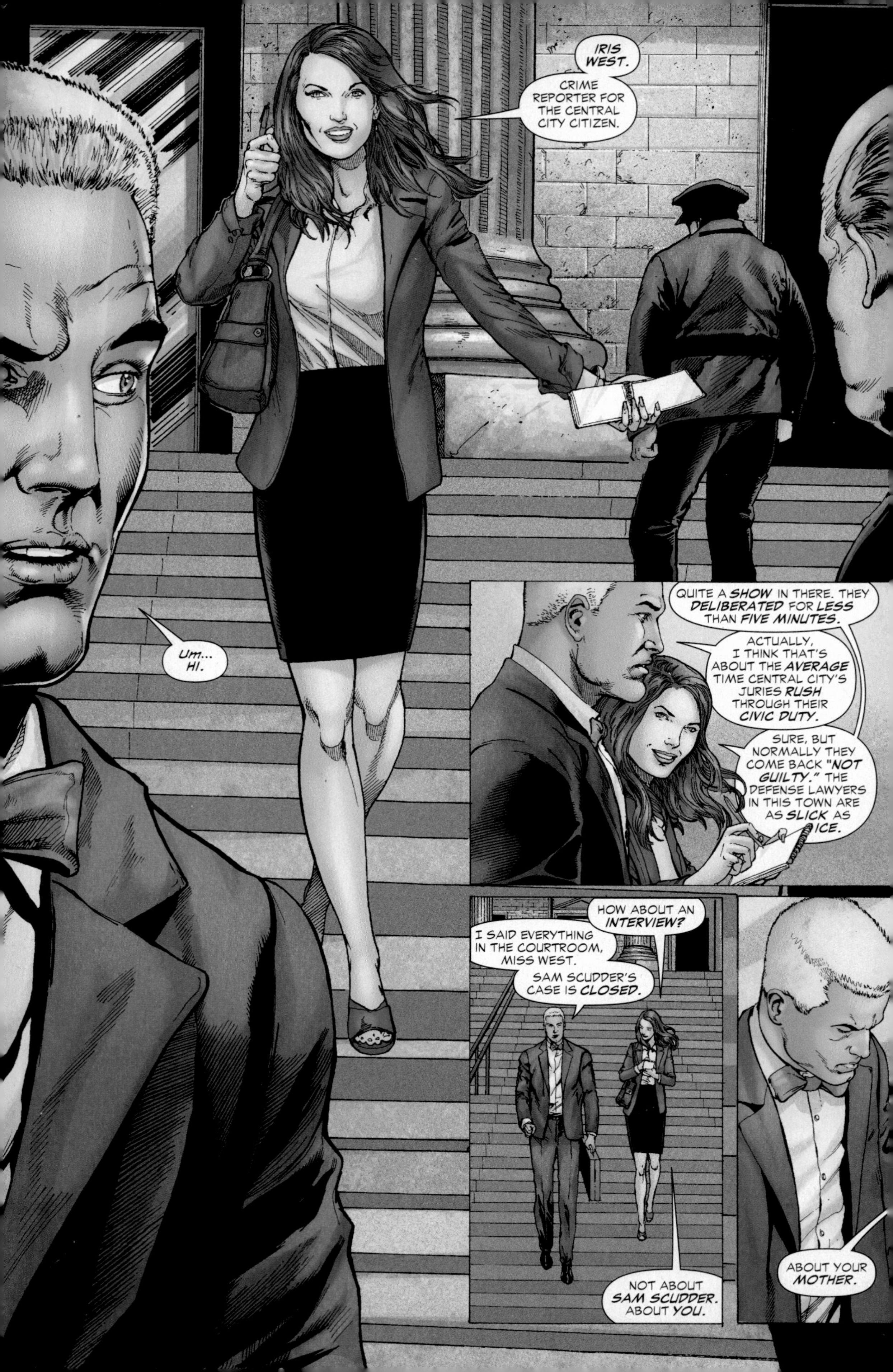
IRIS WEST.
CRIME REPORTER FOR THE CENTRAL CITY CITIZEN.
Um... HI.
QUITE A SHOW IN THERE. THEY DELIBERATED FOR LESS THAN FIVE MINUTES.
ACTUALLY, I THINK THAT'S ABOUT THE AVERAGE TIME CENTRAL CITY'S JURIES RUSH THROUGH THEIR CIVIC DUTY.
SURE, BUT NORMALLY THEY COME BACK "NOT GUILTY." THE DEFENSE LAWYERS IN THIS TOWN ARE AS SLICK AS ICE.
HOW ABOUT AN INTERVIEW?
I SAID EVERYTHING IN THE COURTROOM, MISS WEST.
SAM SCUDDER'S CASE IS CLOSED.
NOT ABOUT SAM SCUDDER. ABOUT YOU.
ABOUT YOUR MOTHER.

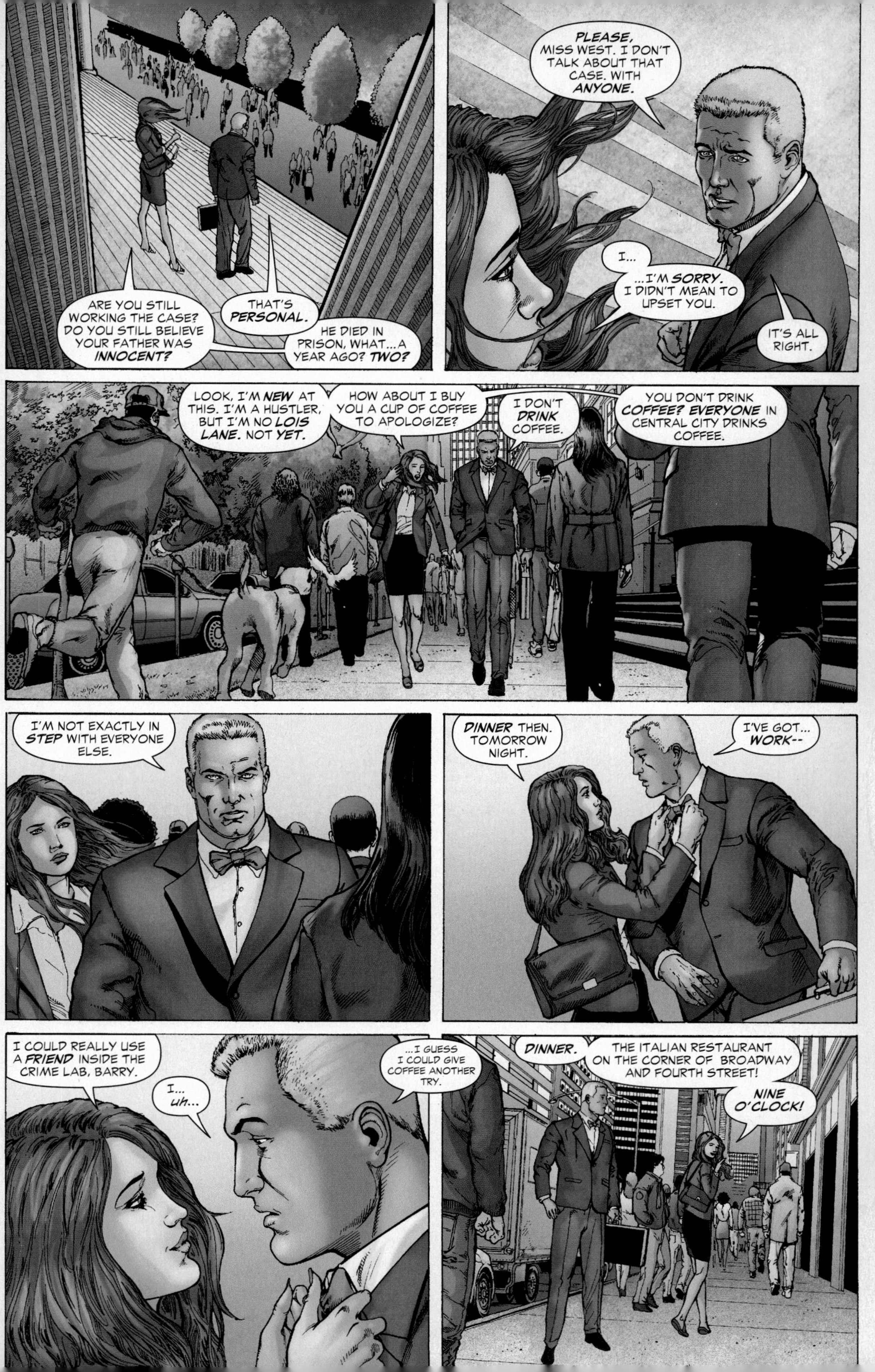
ARE YOU STILL WORKING THE CASE? DO YOU STILL BELIEVE YOUR FATHER WAS INNOCENT?
THAT'S PERSONAL.
HE DIED IN PRISON, WHAT...A YEAR AGO? TWO?
PLEASE, MISS WEST. I DON'T TALK ABOUT THAT CASE. WITH ANYONE.
I...
...I'M SORRY. I DIDN'T MEAN TO UPSET YOU.
IT'S ALL RIGHT.
LOOK, I'M NEW AT THIS. I'M A HUSTLER, BUT I'M NO LOIS LANE. NOT YET.
HOW ABOUT I BUY YOU A CUP OF COFFEE TO APOLOGIZE?
I DON'T DRINK COFFEE.
YOU DON'T DRINK COFFEE? EVERYONE IN CENTRAL CITY DRINKS COFFEE.
I'M NOT EXACTLY IN STEP WITH EVERYONE ELSE.
DINNER THEN. TOMORROW NIGHT.
I'VE GOT... WORK--
I COULD REALLY USE A FRIEND INSIDE THE CRIME LAB, BARRY.
I... uh...
...I GUESS I COULD GIVE COFFEE ANOTHER TRY.
DINNER.
THE ITALIAN RESTAURANT ON THE CORNER OF BROADWAY AND FOURTH STREET!
NINE O'CLOCK!

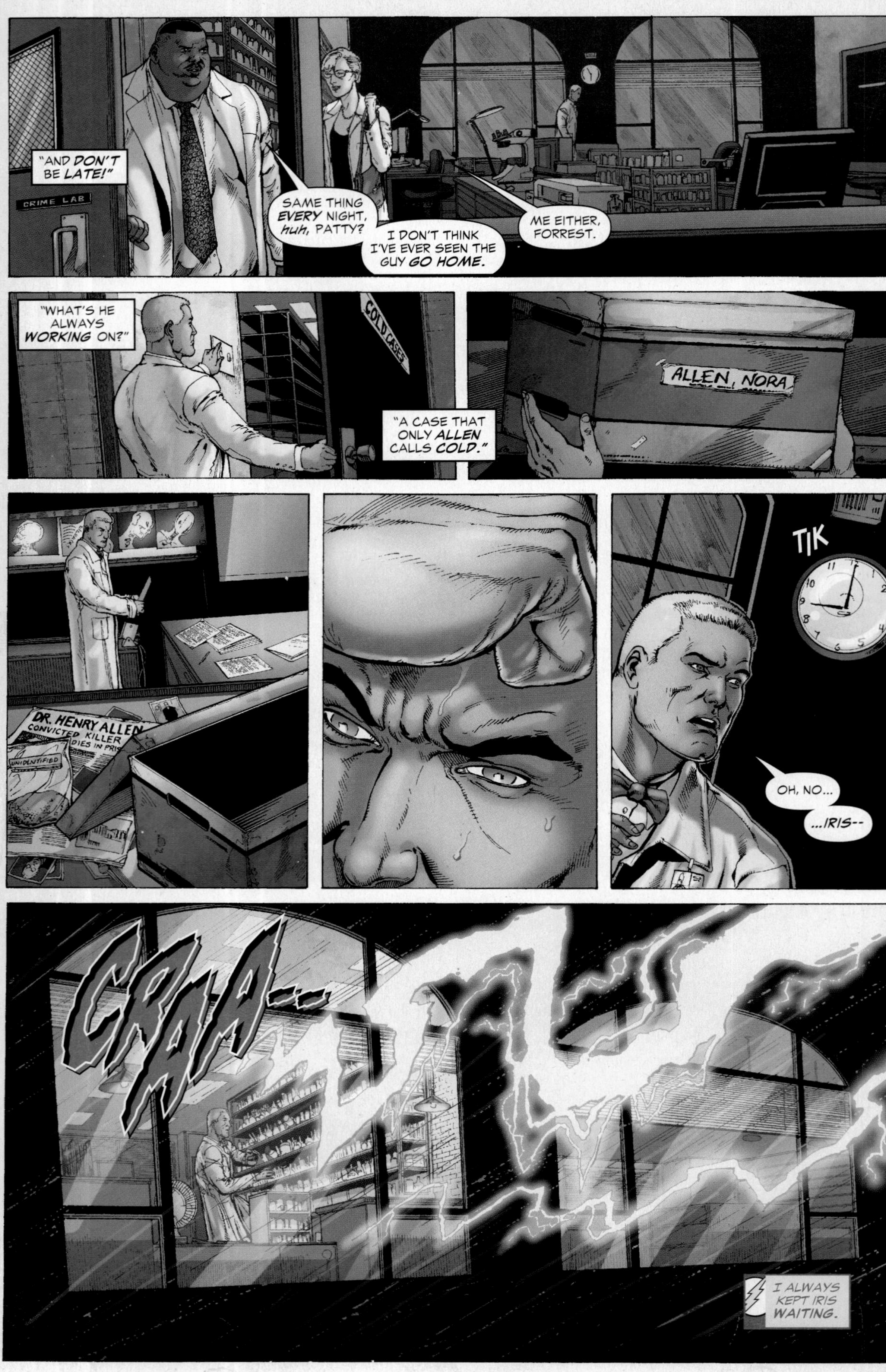
"AND DON'T BE LATE!"
CRIME LAB
SAME THING EVERY NIGHT, huh, PATTY?
I DON'T THINK I'VE EVER SEEN THE GUY GO HOME.
ME EITHER, FORREST.
"WHAT'S HE ALWAYS WORKING ON?"
COLD CASES
"A CASE THAT ONLY ALLEN CALLS COLD."
ALLEN, NORA
DR. HENRY ALLEN
CONVICTED KILLER
UNIDENTIFIED
TIK
OH, NO...
...IRIS--
CRAA--
I ALWAYS KEPT IRIS WAITING.

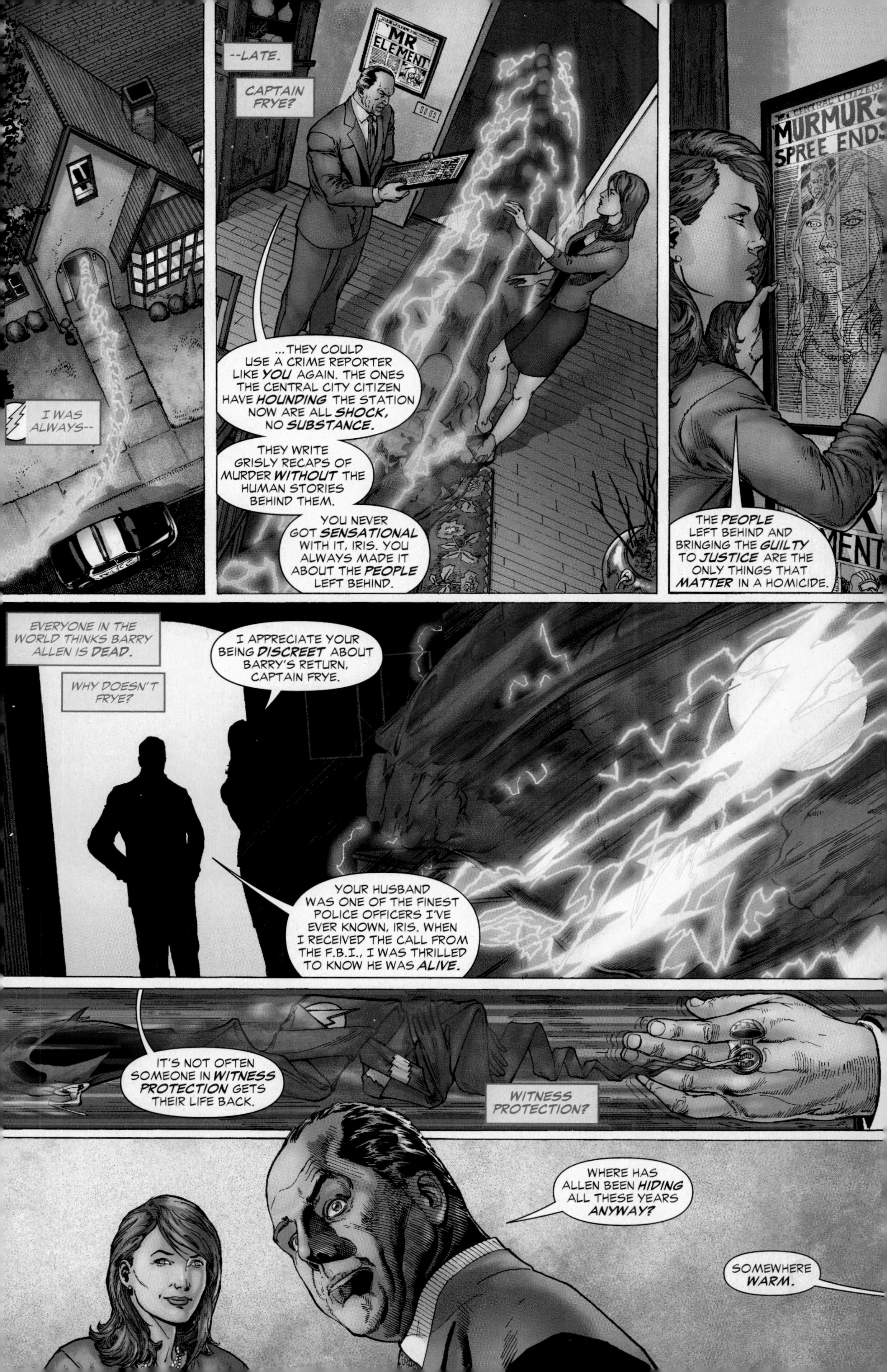
I WAS ALWAYS--
--LATE.
CAPTAIN FRYE?
MR ELEMENT
...THEY COULD USE A CRIME REPORTER LIKE YOU AGAIN. THE ONES THE CENTRAL CITY CITIZEN HAVE HOUNDING THE STATION NOW ARE ALL SHOCK, NO SUBSTANCE.
THEY WRITE GRISLY RECAPS OF MURDER WITHOUT THE HUMAN STORIES BEHIND THEM.
YOU NEVER GOT SENSATIONAL WITH IT, IRIS. YOU ALWAYS MADE IT ABOUT THE PEOPLE LEFT BEHIND.
MURMUR'S SPREE ENDS
THE PEOPLE LEFT BEHIND AND BRINGING THE GUILTY TO JUSTICE ARE THE ONLY THINGS THAT MATTER IN A HOMICIDE.
EVERYONE IN THE WORLD THINKS BARRY ALLEN IS DEAD.
WHY DOESN'T FRYE?
I APPRECIATE YOUR BEING DISCREET ABOUT BARRY'S RETURN, CAPTAIN FRYE.
YOUR HUSBAND WAS ONE OF THE FINEST POLICE OFFICERS I'VE EVER KNOWN, IRIS. WHEN I RECEIVED THE CALL FROM THE F.B.I., I WAS THRILLED TO KNOW HE WAS ALIVE.
IT'S NOT OFTEN SOMEONE IN WITNESS PROTECTION GETS THEIR LIFE BACK.
WITNESS PROTECTION?
WHERE HAS ALLEN BEEN HIDING ALL THESE YEARS ANYWAY?
SOMEWHERE WARM.

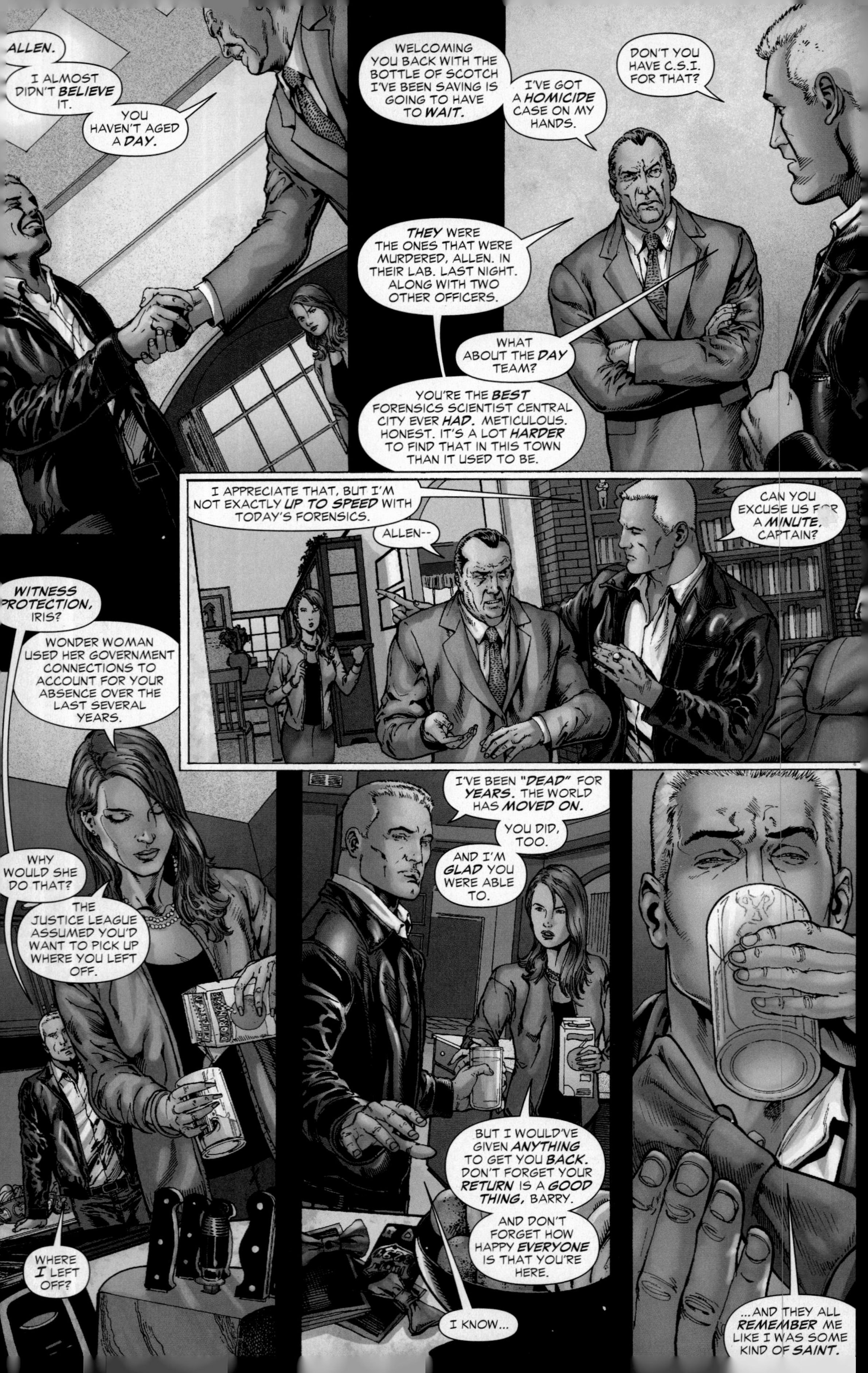
ALLEN.
I ALMOST DIDN'T BELIEVE IT.
YOU HAVEN'T AGED A DAY.
WELCOMING YOU BACK WITH THE BOTTLE OF SCOTCH I'VE BEEN SAVING IS GOING TO HAVE TO WAIT.
I'VE GOT A HOMICIDE CASE ON MY HANDS.
DON'T YOU HAVE C.S.I. FOR THAT?
THEY WERE THE ONES THAT WERE MURDERED, ALLEN. IN THEIR LAB. LAST NIGHT. ALONG WITH TWO OTHER OFFICERS.
WHAT ABOUT THE DAY TEAM?
YOU'RE THE BEST FORENSICS SCIENTIST CENTRAL CITY EVER HAD. METICULOUS. HONEST. IT'S A LOT HARDER TO FIND THAT IN THIS TOWN THAN IT USED TO BE.
I APPRECIATE THAT, BUT I'M NOT EXACTLY UP TO SPEED WITH TODAY'S FORENSICS.
ALLEN--
CAN YOU EXCUSE US FOR A MINUTE, CAPTAIN?
WITNESS PROTECTION, IRIS?
WONDER WOMAN USED HER GOVERNMENT CONNECTIONS TO ACCOUNT FOR YOUR ABSENCE OVER THE LAST SEVERAL YEARS.
WHY WOULD SHE DO THAT?
THE JUSTICE LEAGUE ASSUMED YOU'D WANT TO PICK UP WHERE YOU LEFT OFF.
WHERE I LEFT OFF?
I'VE BEEN "DEAD" FOR YEARS. THE WORLD HAS MOVED ON.
YOU DID, TOO.
AND I'M GLAD YOU WERE ABLE TO.
BUT I WOULD'VE GIVEN ANYTHING TO GET YOU BACK. DON'T FORGET YOUR RETURN IS A GOOD THING, BARRY.
AND DON'T FORGET HOW HAPPY EVERYONE IS THAT YOU'RE HERE.
I KNOW...
...AND THEY ALL REMEMBER ME LIKE I WAS SOME KIND OF SAINT.

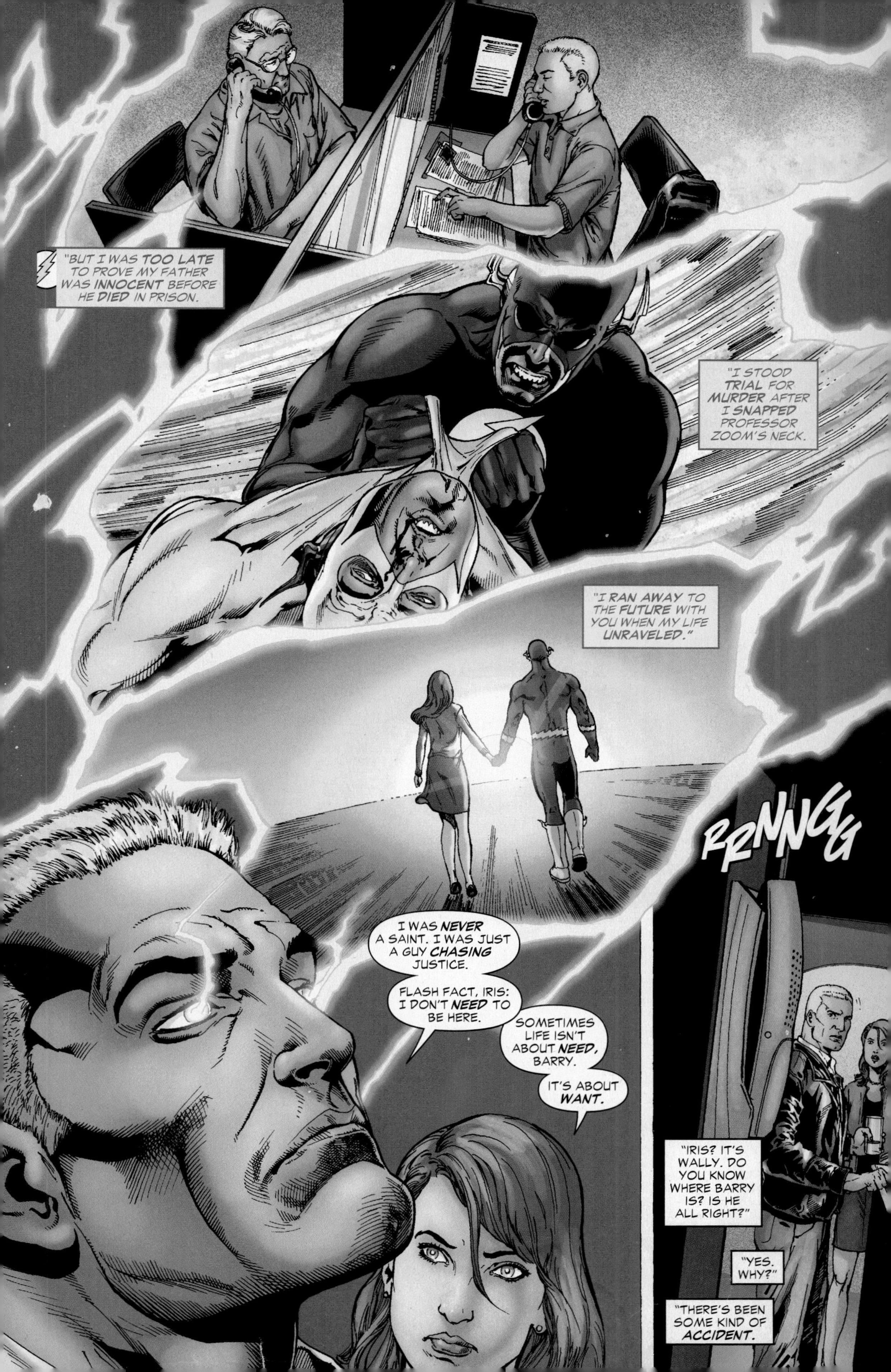
"BUT I WAS TOO LATE TO PROVE MY FATHER WAS INNOCENT BEFORE HE DIED IN PRISON.
"I STOOD TRIAL FOR MURDER AFTER I SNAPPED PROFESSOR ZOOM'S NECK.
"I RAN AWAY TO THE FUTURE WITH YOU WHEN MY LIFE UNRAVELED."
RRNNGG
I WAS NEVER A SAINT. I WAS JUST A GUY CHASING JUSTICE.
FLASH FACT, IRIS: I DON'T NEED TO BE HERE.
SOMETIMES LIFE ISN'T ABOUT NEED, BARRY.
IT'S ABOUT WANT.
"IRIS? IT'S WALLY. DO YOU KNOW WHERE BARRY IS? IS HE ALL RIGHT?"
"YES. WHY?"
"THERE'S BEEN SOME KIND OF ACCIDENT.

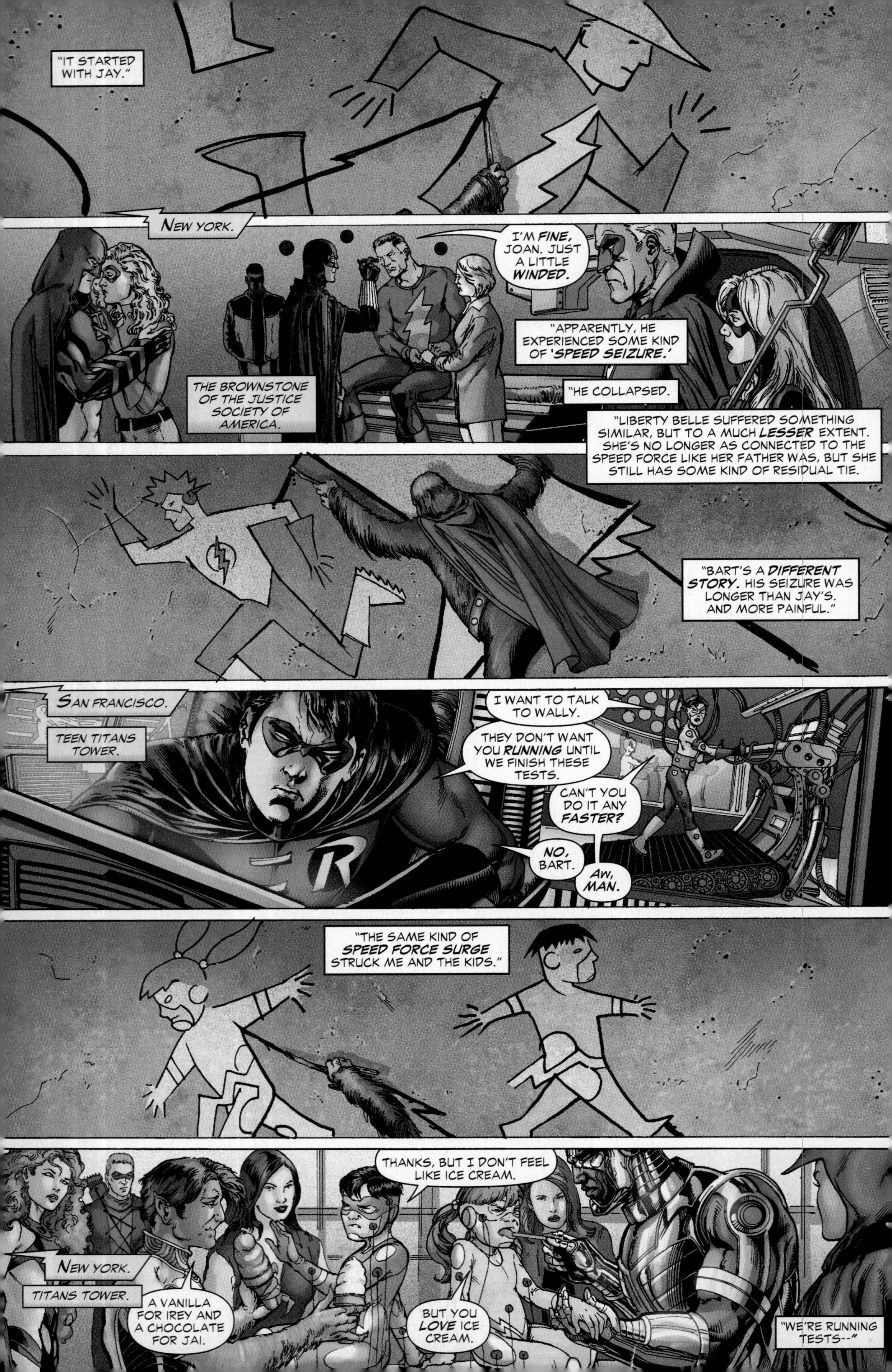
"IT STARTED WITH JAY."
NEW YORK.
I'M FINE, JOAN. JUST A LITTLE WINDED.
THE BROWNSTONE OF THE JUSTICE SOCIETY OF AMERICA.
"APPARENTLY, HE EXPERIENCED SOME KIND OF 'SPEED SEIZURE.'
"HE COLLAPSED.
"LIBERTY BELLE SUFFERED SOMETHING SIMILAR, BUT TO A MUCH LESSER EXTENT. SHE'S NO LONGER AS CONNECTED TO THE SPEED FORCE LIKE HER FATHER WAS, BUT SHE STILL HAS SOME KIND OF RESIDUAL TIE.
"BART'S A DIFFERENT STORY. HIS SEIZURE WAS LONGER THAN JAY'S. AND MORE PAINFUL."
SAN FRANCISCO.
TEEN TITANS TOWER.
I WANT TO TALK TO WALLY.
THEY DON'T WANT YOU RUNNING UNTIL WE FINISH THESE TESTS.
CAN'T YOU DO IT ANY FASTER?
NO, BART.
AW, MAN.
"THE SAME KIND OF SPEED FORCE SURGE STRUCK ME AND THE KIDS."
NEW YORK.
TITANS TOWER.
A VANILLA FOR IREY AND A CHOCOLATE FOR JAI.
THANKS, BUT I DON'T FEEL LIKE ICE CREAM.
BUT YOU LOVE ICE CREAM.
"WE'RE RUNNING TESTS--"

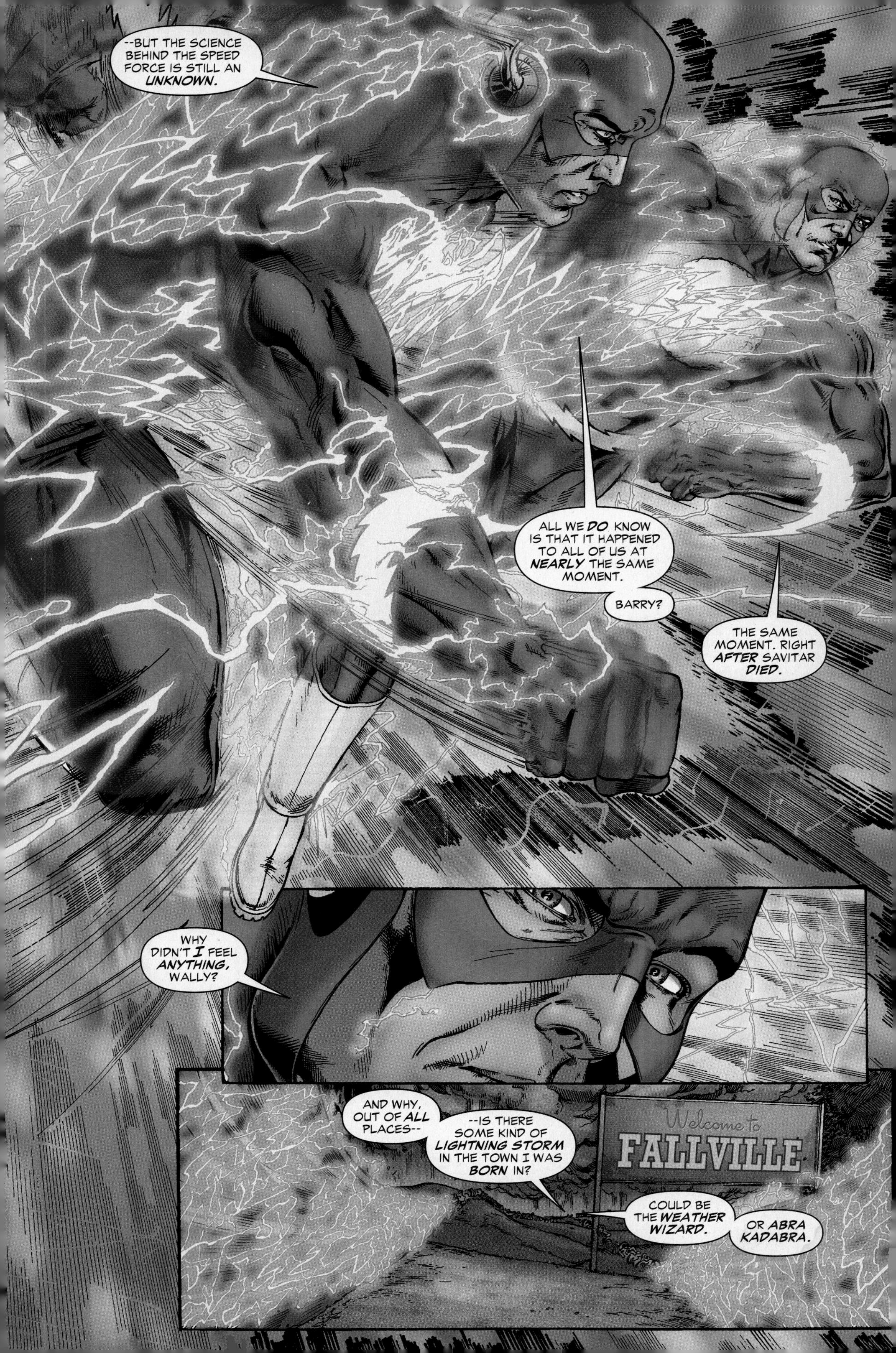
--BUT THE SCIENCE BEHIND THE SPEED FORCE IS STILL AN UNKNOWN.
ALL WE DO KNOW IS THAT IT HAPPENED TO ALL OF US AT NEARLY THE SAME MOMENT.
BARRY?
THE SAME MOMENT. RIGHT AFTER SAVITAR DIED.
WHY DIDN'T I FEEL ANYTHING, WALLY?
AND WHY, OUT OF ALL PLACES--
--IS THERE SOME KIND OF LIGHTNING STORM IN THE TOWN I WAS BORN IN?
Welcome to FALLVILLE
COULD BE THE WEATHER WIZARD.
OR ABRA KADABRA.

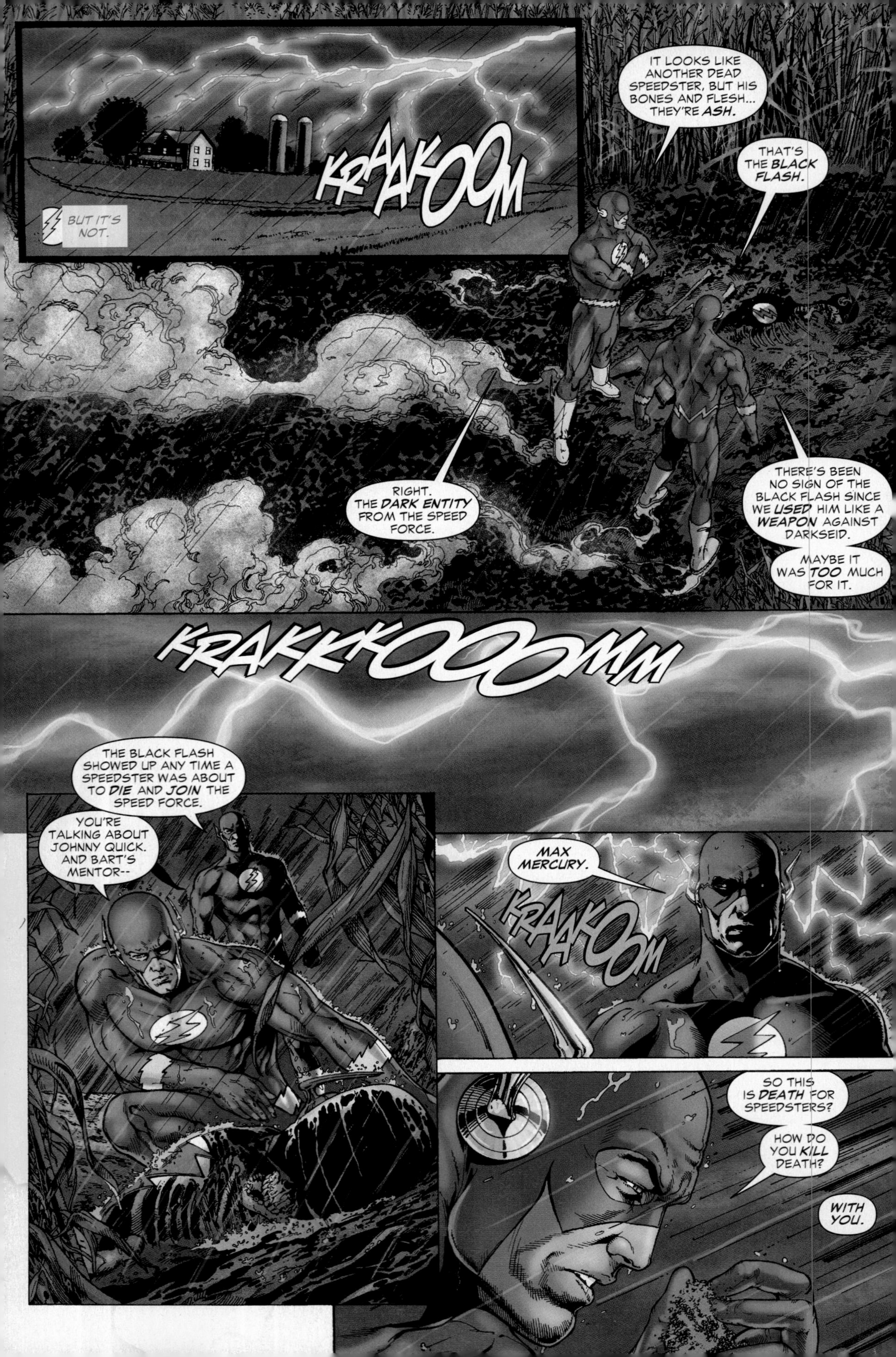

BUT IT'S NOT.
KRAAKOOM
IT LOOKS LIKE ANOTHER DEAD SPEEDSTER, BUT HIS BONES AND FLESH... THEY'RE ASH.
THAT'S THE BLACK FLASH.
RIGHT. THE DARK ENTITY FROM THE SPEED FORCE.
THERE'S BEEN NO SIGN OF THE BLACK FLASH SINCE WE USED HIM LIKE A WEAPON AGAINST DARKSEID.
MAYBE IT WAS TOO MUCH FOR IT.
KRAKKOOOOMM
THE BLACK FLASH SHOWED UP ANY TIME A SPEEDSTER WAS ABOUT TO DIE AND JOIN THE SPEED FORCE.
YOU'RE TALKING ABOUT JOHNNY QUICK. AND BART'S MENTOR--
MAX MERCURY.
KRAAKOOM
SO THIS IS DEATH FOR SPEEDSTERS?
HOW DO YOU KILL DEATH?
WITH YOU.

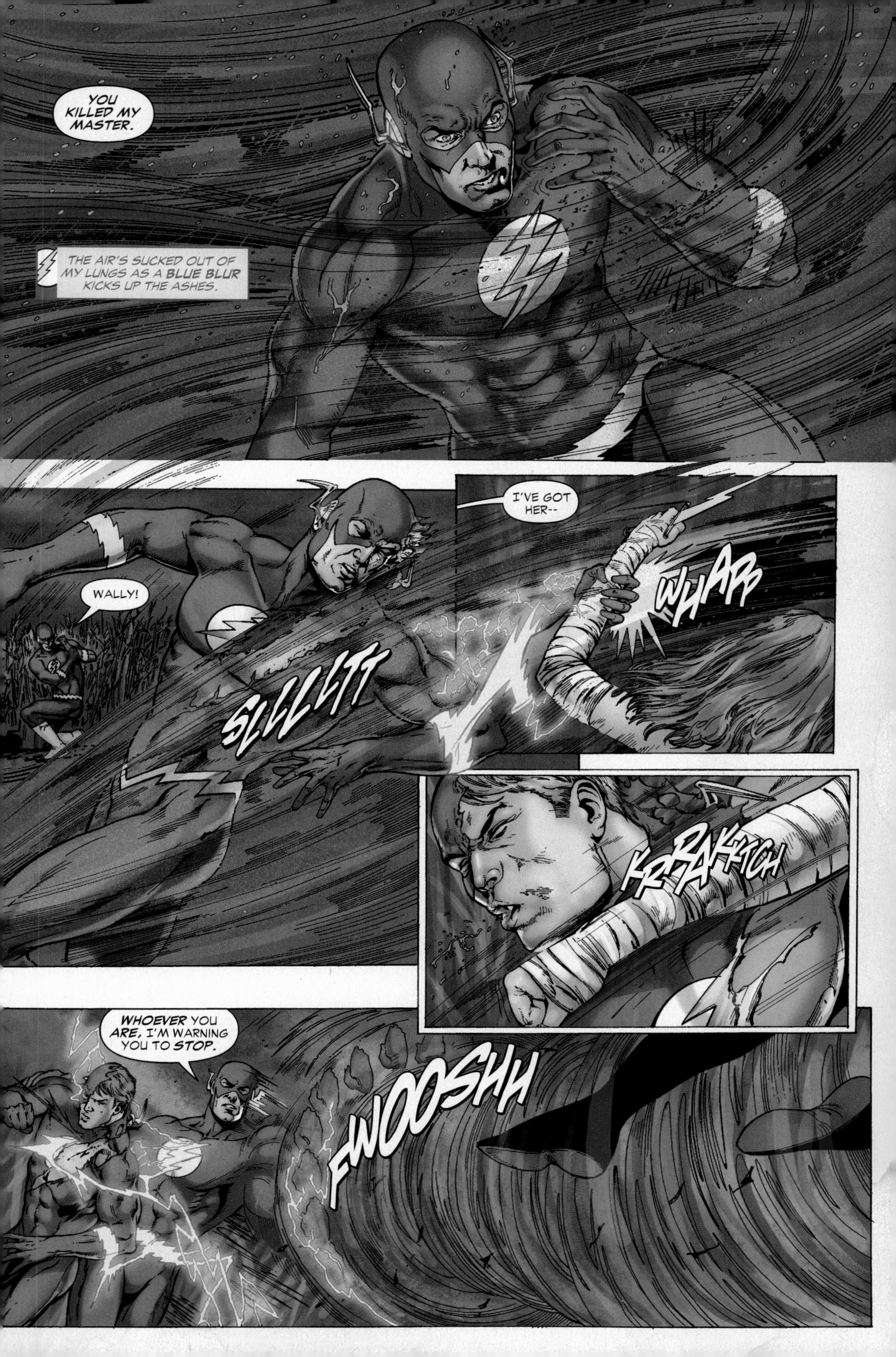
YOU KILLED MY MASTER.
THE AIR'S SUCKED OUT OF MY LUNGS AS A BLUE BLUR KICKS UP THE ASHES.
WALLY!
I'VE GOT HER--
WHAPP
SLLLLTT
KRRAKKTCH
WHOEVER YOU ARE, I'M WARNING YOU TO STOP.
FWOOSHH

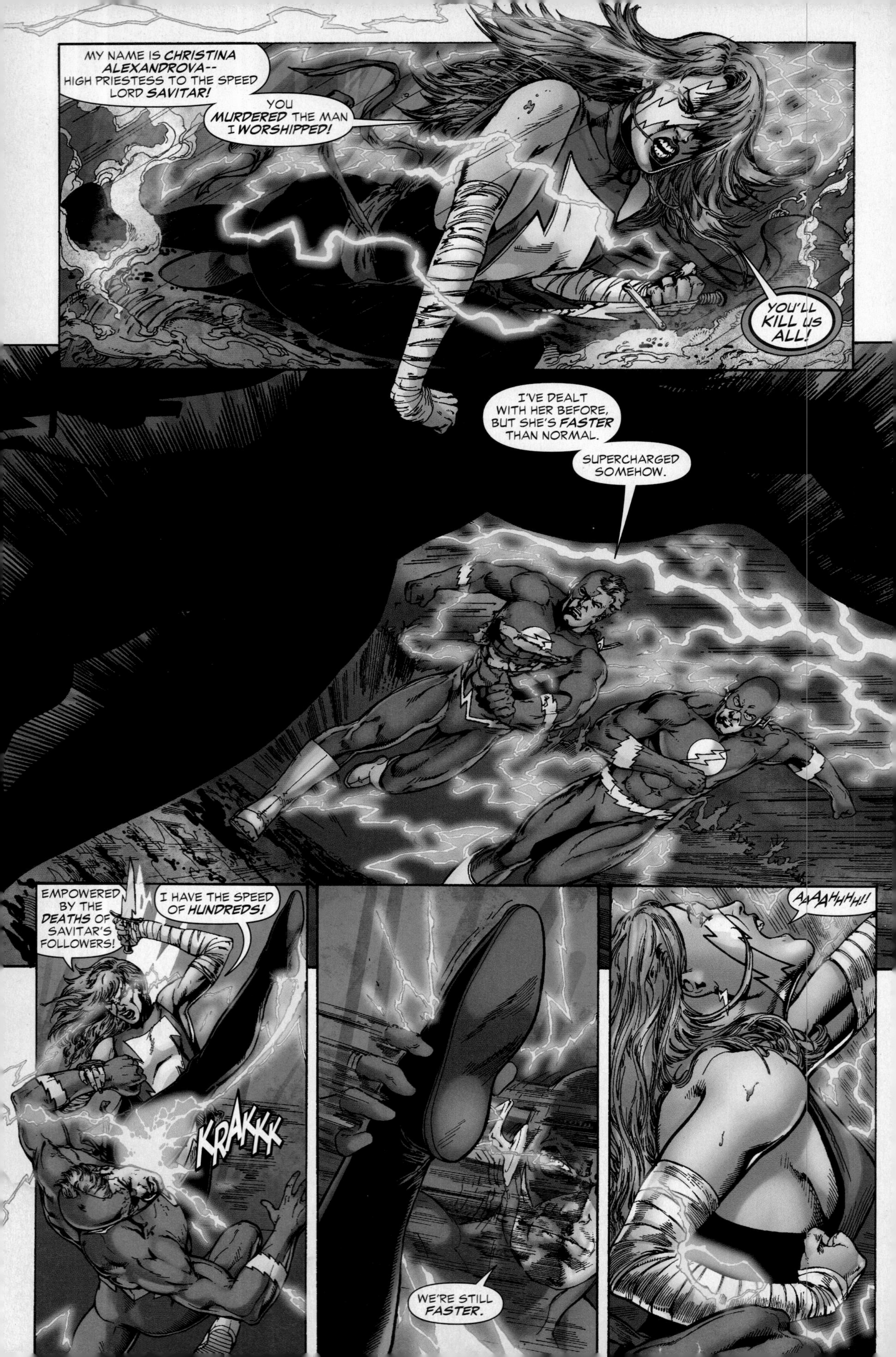
MY NAME IS CHRISTINA ALEXANDROVA-- HIGH PRIESTESS TO THE SPEED LORD SAVITAR!
YOU MURDERED THE MAN I WORSHIPPED!
YOU'LL KILL US ALL!
I'VE DEALT WITH HER BEFORE, BUT SHE'S FASTER THAN NORMAL.
SUPERCHARGED SOMEHOW.
EMPOWERED BY THE DEATHS OF SAVITAR'S FOLLOWERS!
I HAVE THE SPEED OF HUNDREDS!
KRAKKK
WE'RE STILL FASTER.
AAAAHHHH!!

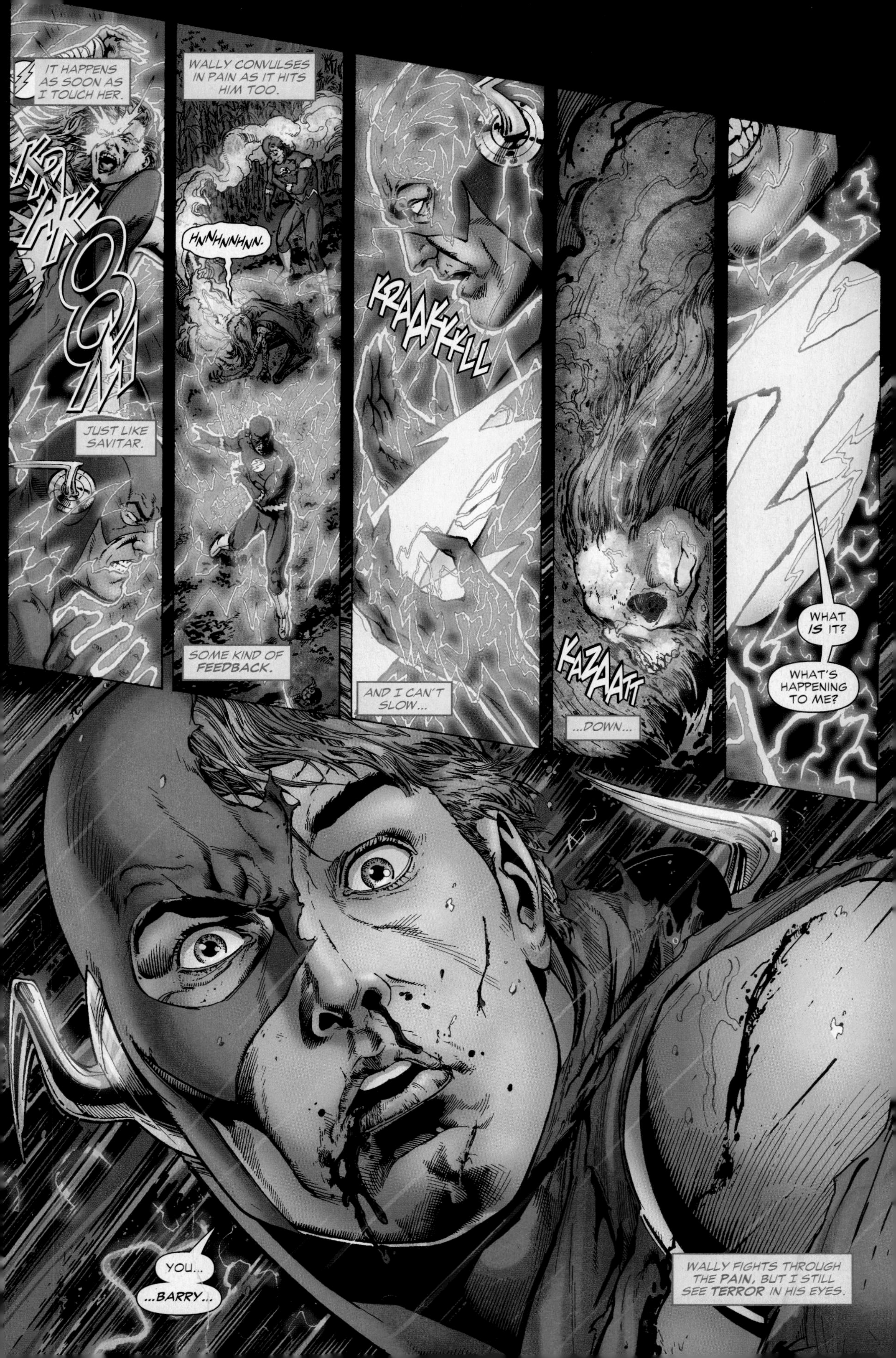

IT HAPPENS AS SOON AS I TOUCH HER.
KRAKKA-KOOM
JUST LIKE SAVITAR.
WALLY CONVULSES IN PAIN AS IT HITS HIM TOO.
HNNHNNHNN.
SOME KIND OF FEEDBACK.
KRAAKKKLL
AND I CAN'T SLOW...
KAZAAKT
...DOWN...
WHAT IS IT?
WHAT'S HAPPENING TO ME?
YOU...
...BARRY...
WALLY FIGHTS THROUGH THE PAIN, BUT I STILL SEE TERROR IN HIS EYES.

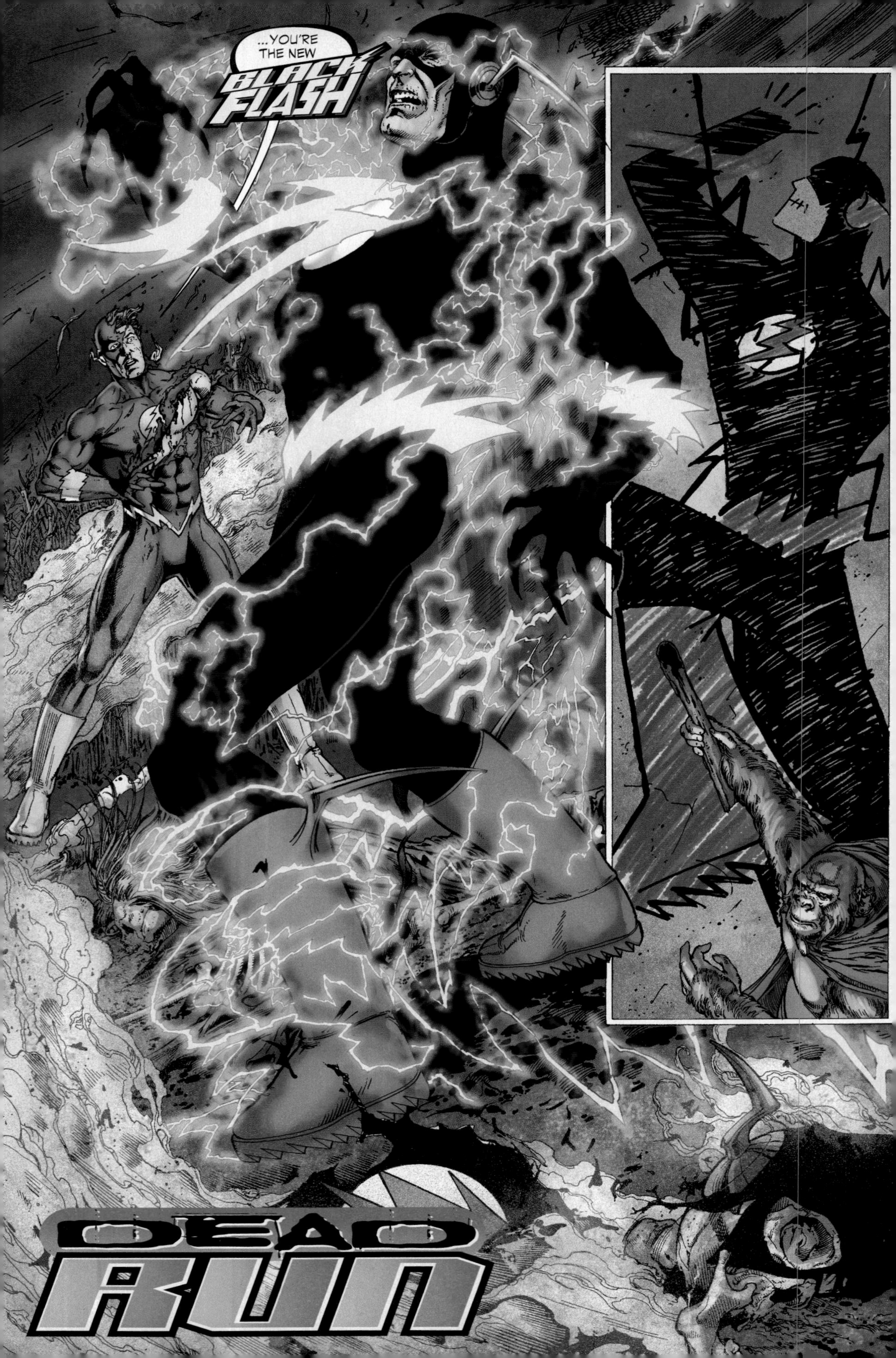
...YOU'RE THE NEW BLACK FLASH
DEAD RUN

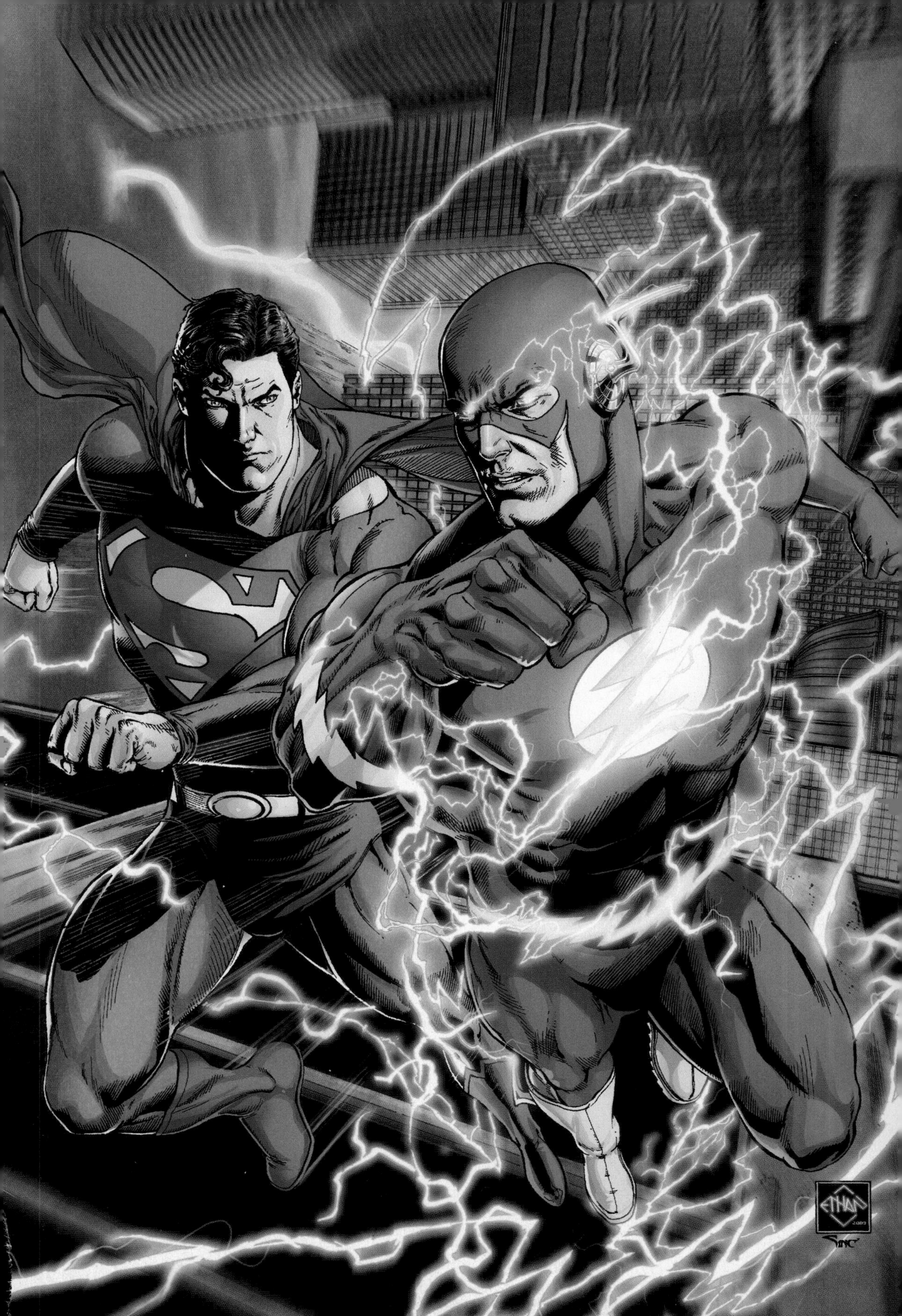

THE FLASH: REBIRTH #3 COVER BY ETHAN VAN SCIVER WITH ALEX SINCLAIR

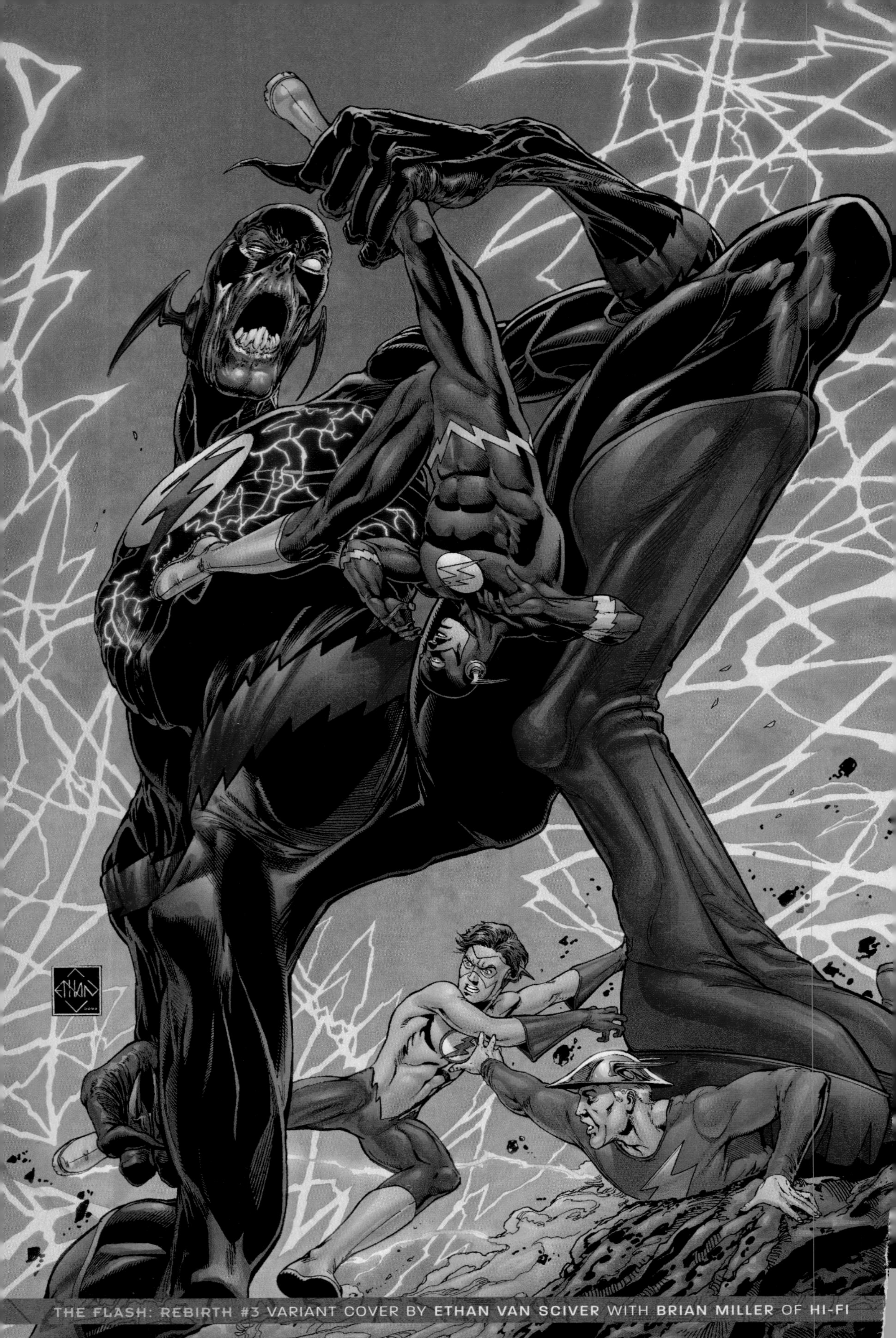
ETHAN

THE FLASH: REBIRTH #3 VARIANT COVER BY **ETHAN VAN SCIVER** WITH **BRIAN MILLER** OF **HI-FI**

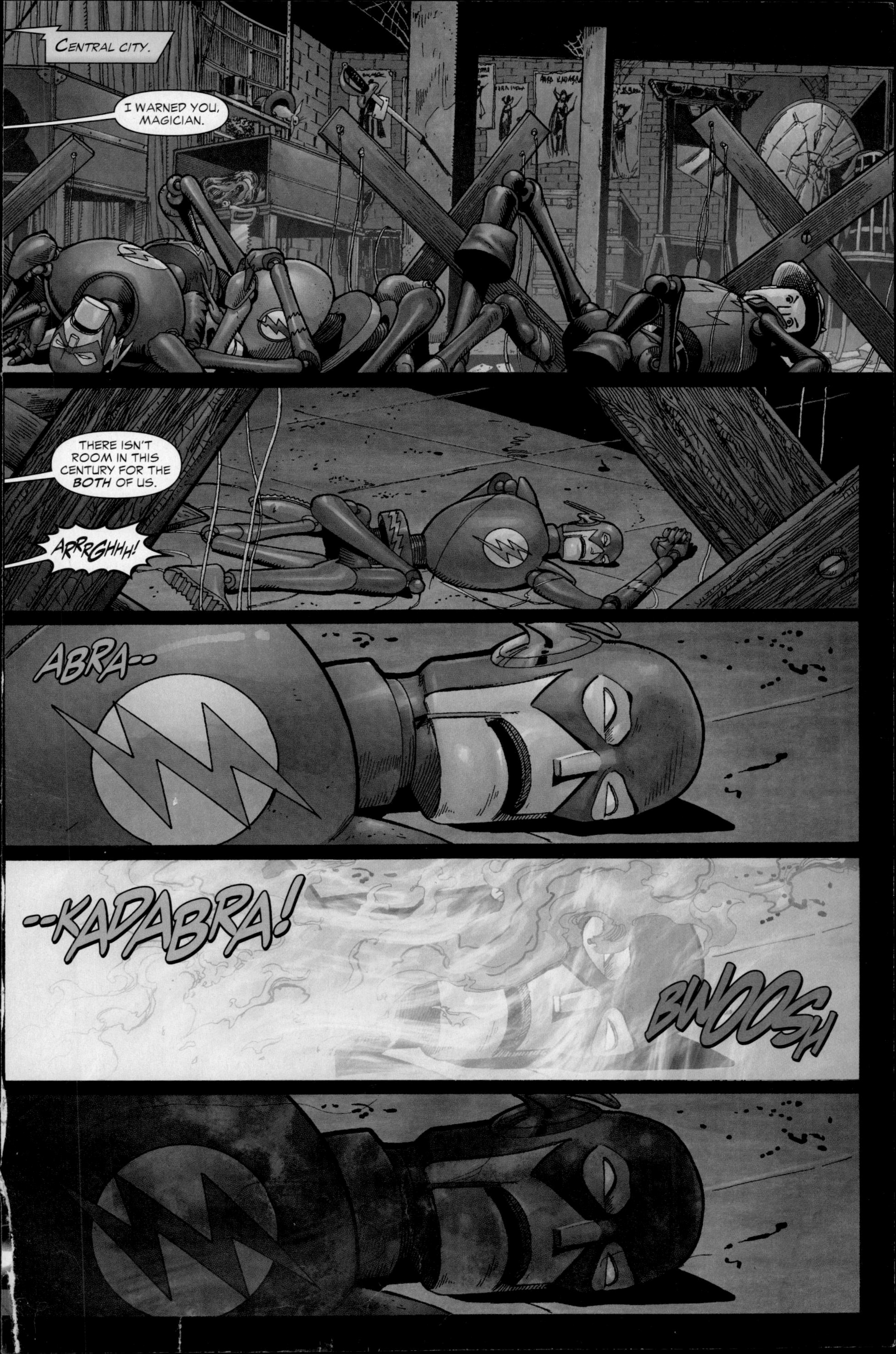
CENTRAL CITY.
I WARNED YOU, MAGICIAN.
THERE ISN'T ROOM IN THIS CENTURY FOR THE BOTH OF US.
ARRRGHHH!
ABRA--
--KADABRA!
BWOOSH

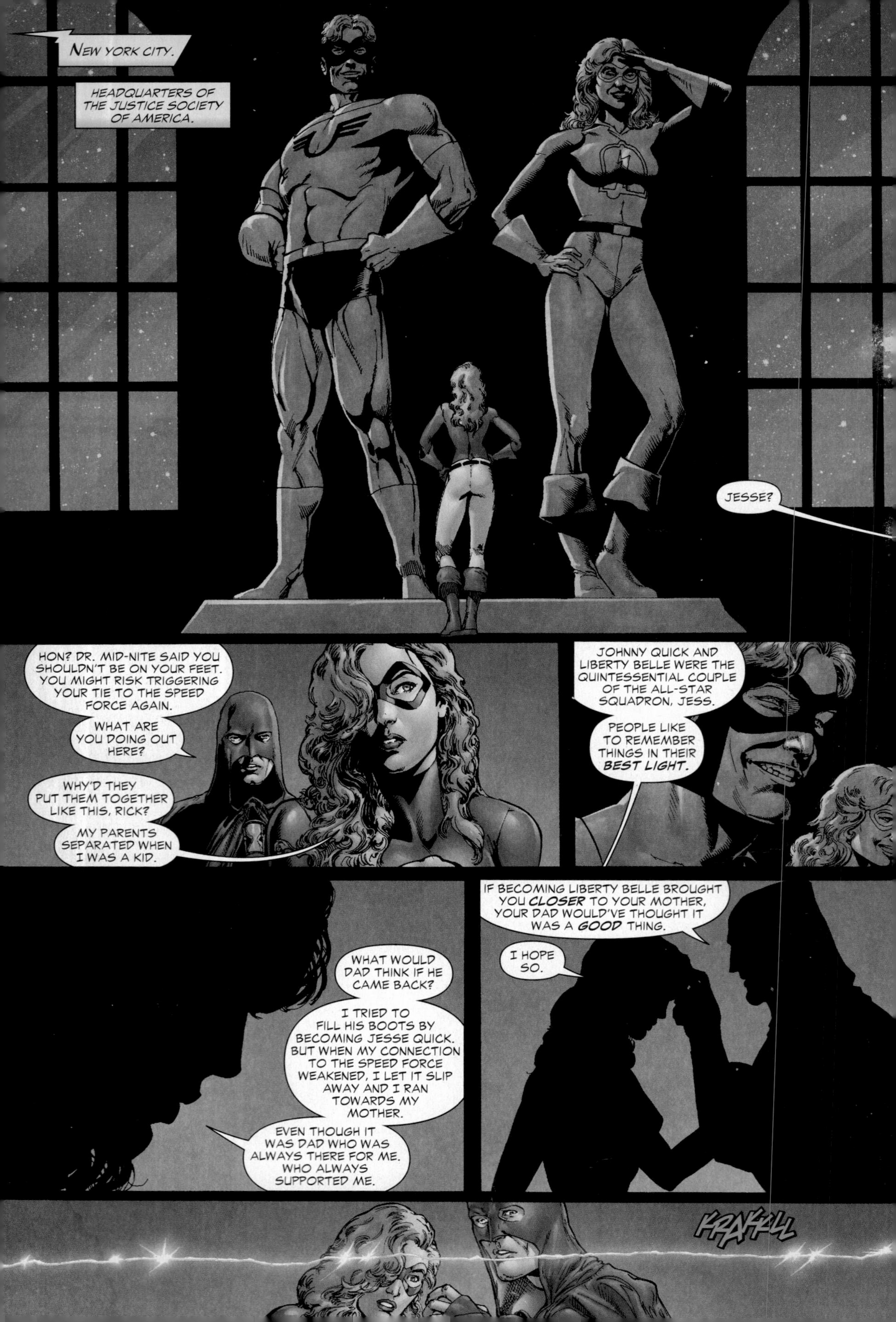
NEW YORK CITY.
HEADQUARTERS OF THE JUSTICE SOCIETY OF AMERICA.
JESSE?
HON? DR. MID-NITE SAID YOU SHOULDN'T BE ON YOUR FEET. YOU MIGHT RISK TRIGGERING YOUR TIE TO THE SPEED FORCE AGAIN.
WHAT ARE YOU DOING OUT HERE?
WHY'D THEY PUT THEM TOGETHER LIKE THIS, RICK?
MY PARENTS SEPARATED WHEN I WAS A KID.
JOHNNY QUICK AND LIBERTY BELLE WERE THE QUINTESSENTIAL COUPLE OF THE ALL-STAR SQUADRON, JESS.
PEOPLE LIKE TO REMEMBER THINGS IN THEIR BEST LIGHT.
WHAT WOULD DAD THINK IF HE CAME BACK?
I TRIED TO FILL HIS BOOTS BY BECOMING JESSE QUICK. BUT WHEN MY CONNECTION TO THE SPEED FORCE WEAKENED, I LET IT SLIP AWAY AND I RAN TOWARDS MY MOTHER.
EVEN THOUGH IT WAS DAD WHO WAS ALWAYS THERE FOR ME. WHO ALWAYS SUPPORTED ME.
IF BECOMING LIBERTY BELLE BROUGHT YOU CLOSER TO YOUR MOTHER, YOUR DAD WOULD'VE THOUGHT IT WAS A GOOD THING.
I HOPE SO.
KRAKKLL

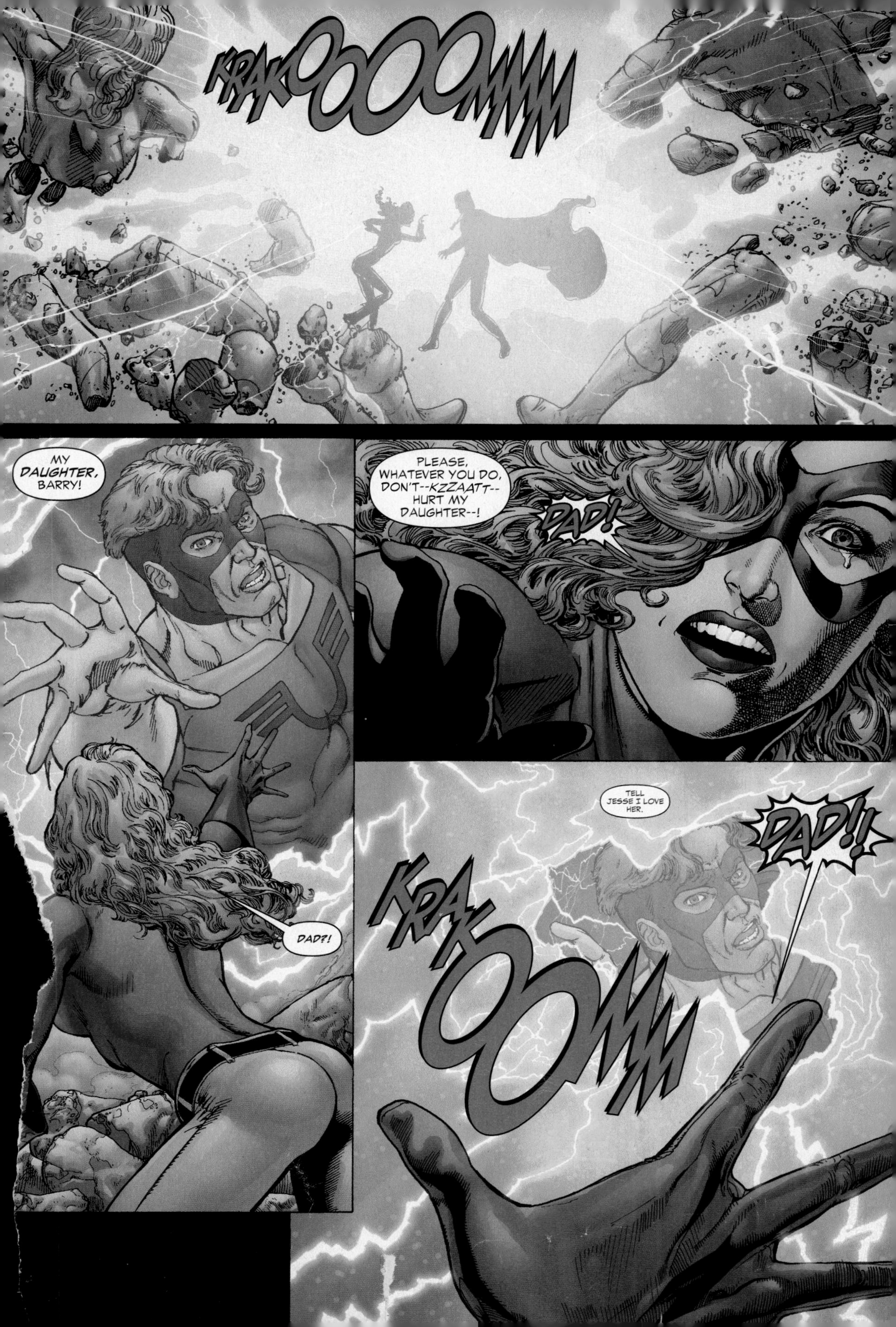
KRAKOOOOOMMMMM
MY DAUGHTER, BARRY!
PLEASE, WHATEVER YOU DO, DON'T--KZZAATT--HURT MY DAUGHTER--!
DAD!
DAD?!
TELL JESSE I LOVE HER.
DAD!!
KRAKOOMMM

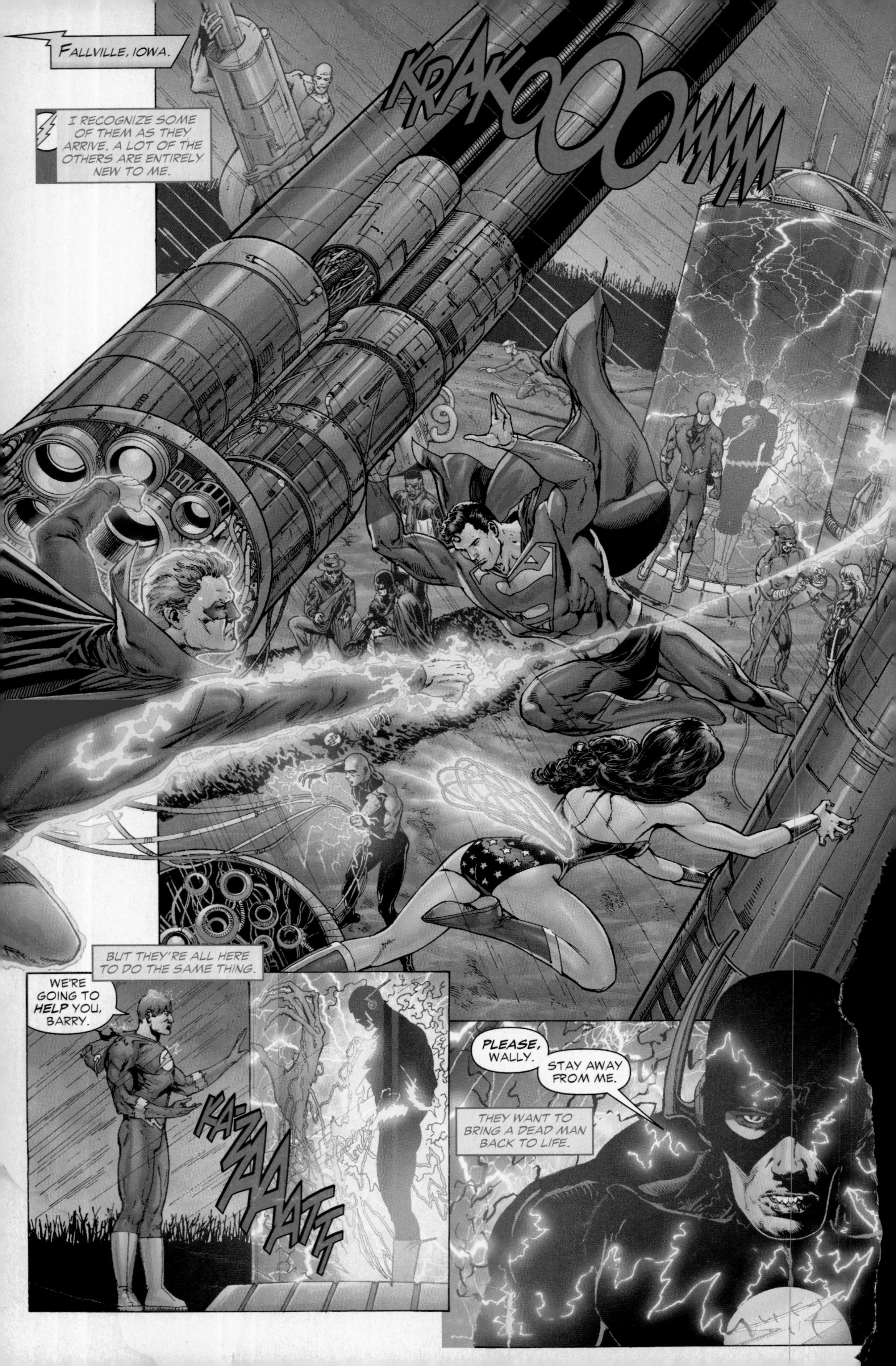
FALLVILLE, IOWA.
KRAKOOOMMM
I RECOGNIZE SOME OF THEM AS THEY ARRIVE. A LOT OF THE OTHERS ARE ENTIRELY NEW TO ME.
BUT THEY'RE ALL HERE TO DO THE SAME THING.
WE'RE GOING TO HELP YOU, BARRY.
KAZAAATT
PLEASE, WALLY.
STAY AWAY FROM ME.
THEY WANT TO BRING A DEAD MAN BACK TO LIFE.

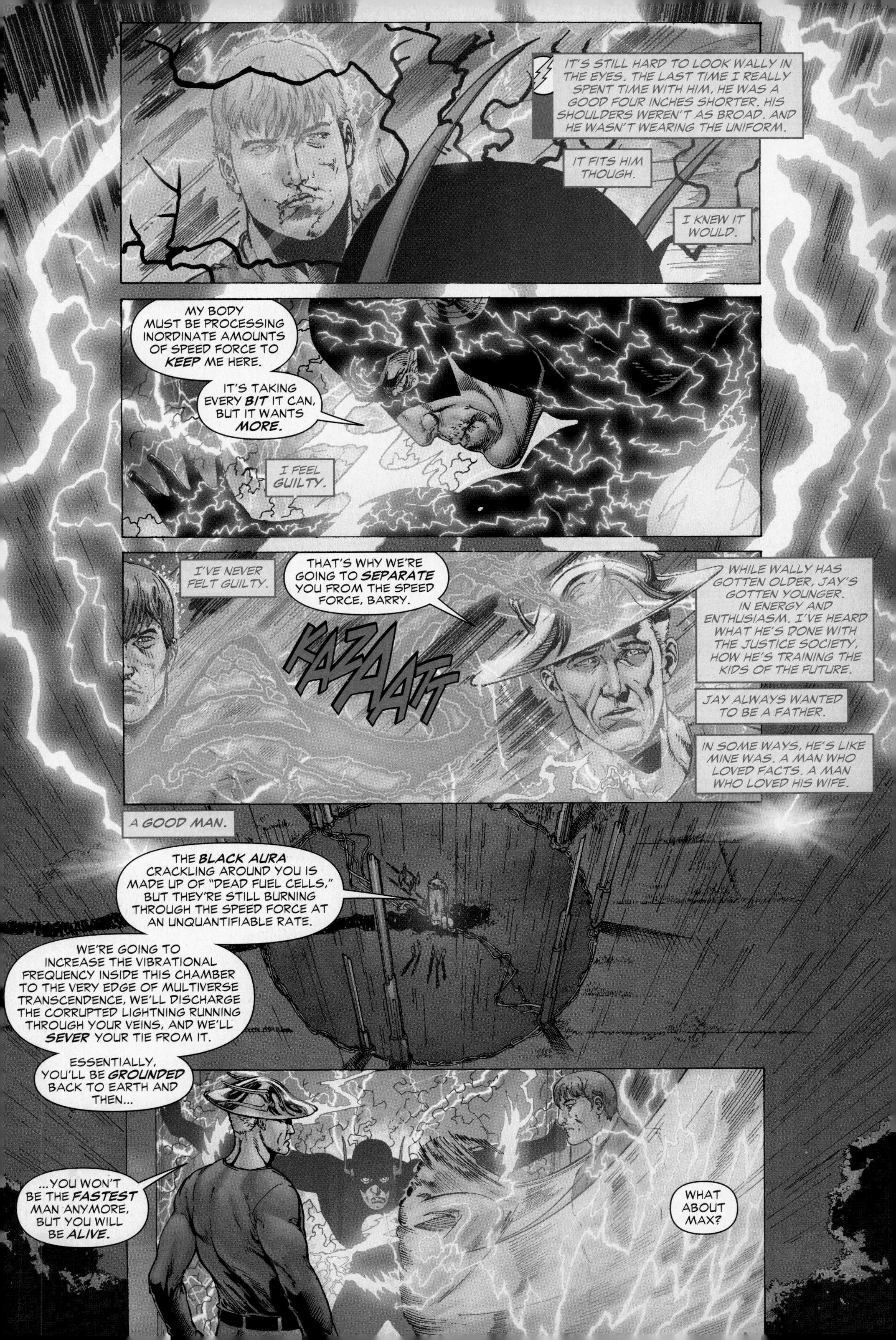
IT'S STILL HARD TO LOOK WALLY IN THE EYES. THE LAST TIME I REALLY SPENT TIME WITH HIM, HE WAS A GOOD FOUR INCHES SHORTER. HIS SHOULDERS WEREN'T AS BROAD. AND HE WASN'T WEARING THE UNIFORM.
IT FITS HIM THOUGH.
I KNEW IT WOULD.
MY BODY MUST BE PROCESSING INORDINATE AMOUNTS OF SPEED FORCE TO KEEP ME HERE.
IT'S TAKING EVERY BIT IT CAN, BUT IT WANTS MORE.
I FEEL GUILTY.
I'VE NEVER FELT GUILTY.
THAT'S WHY WE'RE GOING TO SEPARATE YOU FROM THE SPEED FORCE, BARRY.
KAZAAATT
WHILE WALLY HAS GOTTEN OLDER, JAY'S GOTTEN YOUNGER. IN ENERGY AND ENTHUSIASM. I'VE HEARD WHAT HE'S DONE WITH THE JUSTICE SOCIETY, HOW HE'S TRAINING THE KIDS OF THE FUTURE.
JAY ALWAYS WANTED TO BE A FATHER.
IN SOME WAYS, HE'S LIKE MINE WAS. A MAN WHO LOVED FACTS. A MAN WHO LOVED HIS WIFE.
A GOOD MAN.
THE BLACK AURA CRACKLING AROUND YOU IS MADE UP OF "DEAD FUEL CELLS," BUT THEY'RE STILL BURNING THROUGH THE SPEED FORCE AT AN UNQUANTIFIABLE RATE.
WE'RE GOING TO INCREASE THE VIBRATIONAL FREQUENCY INSIDE THIS CHAMBER TO THE VERY EDGE OF MULTIVERSE TRANSCENDENCE, WE'LL DISCHARGE THE CORRUPTED LIGHTNING RUNNING THROUGH YOUR VEINS, AND WE'LL SEVER YOUR TIE FROM IT.
ESSENTIALLY, YOU'LL BE GROUNDED BACK TO EARTH AND THEN...
...YOU WON'T BE THE FASTEST MAN ANYMORE, BUT YOU WILL BE ALIVE.
WHAT ABOUT MAX?

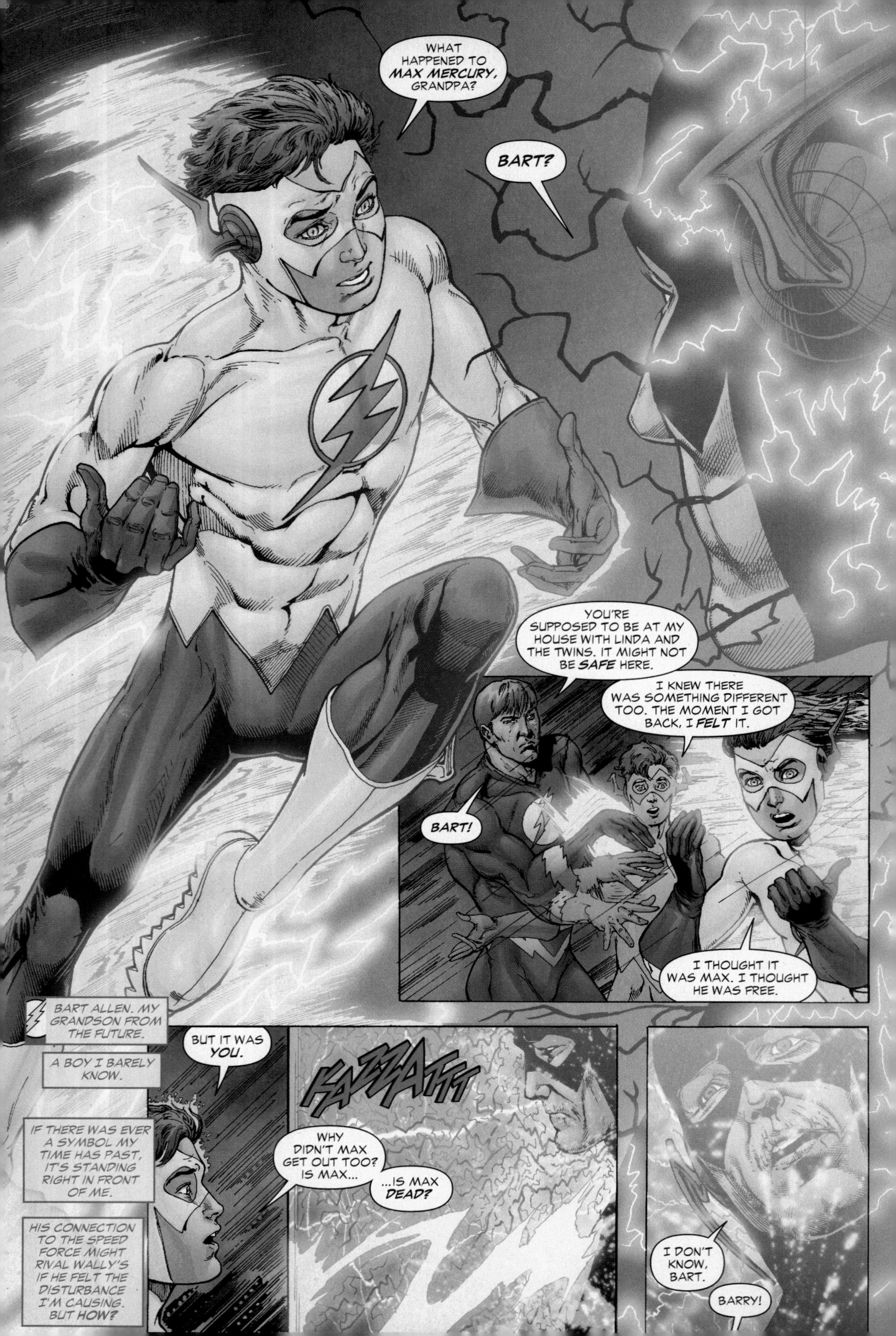

WHAT HAPPENED TO MAX MERCURY, GRANDPA?
BART?
YOU'RE SUPPOSED TO BE AT MY HOUSE WITH LINDA AND THE TWINS. IT MIGHT NOT BE SAFE HERE.
I KNEW THERE WAS SOMETHING DIFFERENT TOO. THE MOMENT I GOT BACK, I FELT IT.
BART!
I THOUGHT IT WAS MAX. I THOUGHT HE WAS FREE.
BART ALLEN. MY GRANDSON FROM THE FUTURE.
A BOY I BARELY KNOW.
BUT IT WAS YOU.
IF THERE WAS EVER A SYMBOL MY TIME HAS PAST, IT'S STANDING RIGHT IN FRONT OF ME.
HIS CONNECTION TO THE SPEED FORCE MIGHT RIVAL WALLY'S IF HE FELT THE DISTURBANCE I'M CAUSING. BUT HOW?
KAZZZATTT
WHY DIDN'T MAX GET OUT TOO? IS MAX...
...IS MAX DEAD?
I DON'T KNOW, BART.
BARRY!

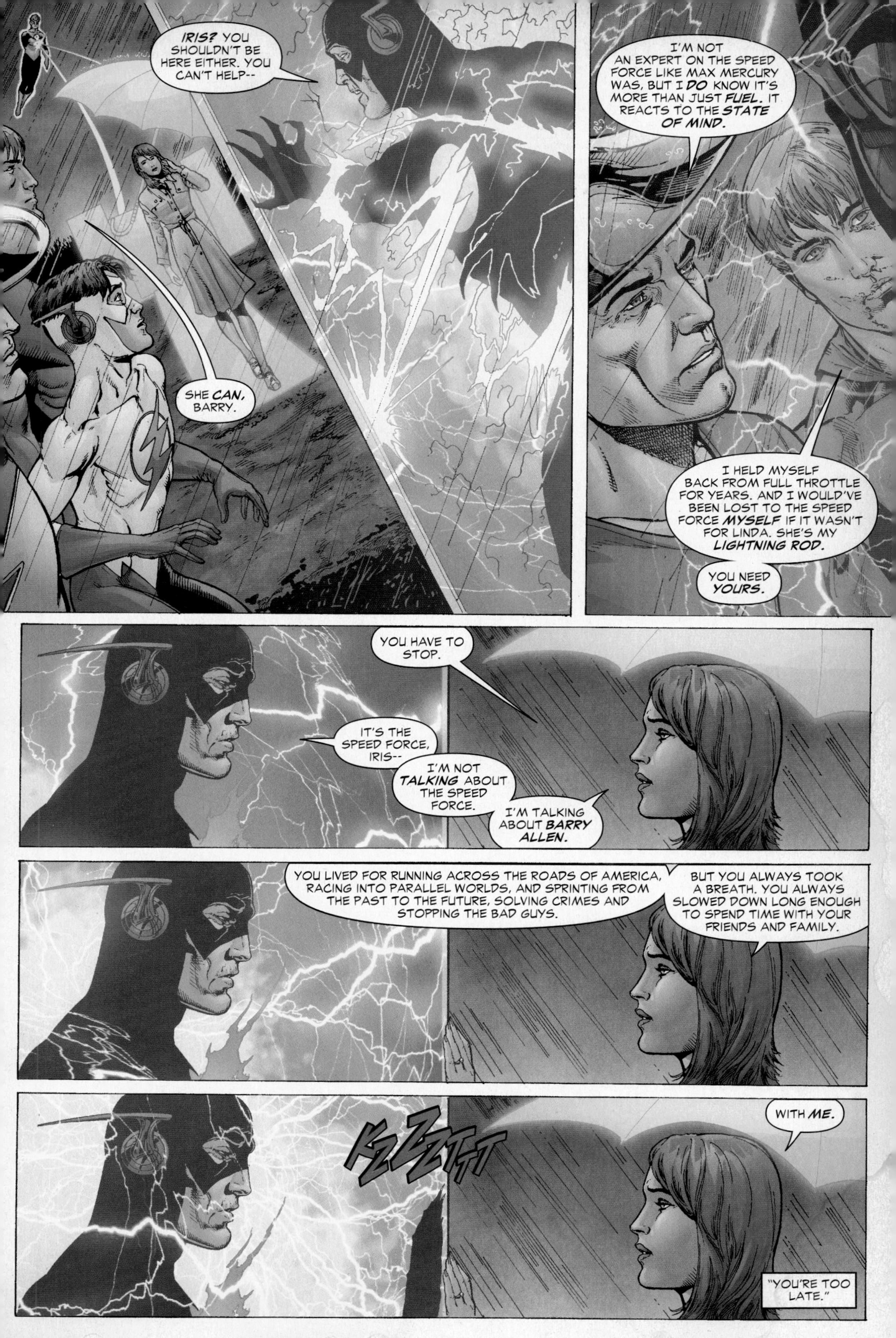
IRIS? YOU SHOULDN'T BE HERE EITHER. YOU CAN'T HELP--
SHE CAN, BARRY.
I'M NOT AN EXPERT ON THE SPEED FORCE LIKE MAX MERCURY WAS, BUT I DO KNOW IT'S MORE THAN JUST FUEL. IT REACTS TO THE STATE OF MIND.
I HELD MYSELF BACK FROM FULL THROTTLE FOR YEARS. AND I WOULD'VE BEEN LOST TO THE SPEED FORCE MYSELF IF IT WASN'T FOR LINDA. SHE'S MY LIGHTNING ROD.
YOU NEED YOURS.
YOU HAVE TO STOP.
IT'S THE SPEED FORCE, IRIS--
I'M NOT TALKING ABOUT THE SPEED FORCE.
I'M TALKING ABOUT BARRY ALLEN.
YOU LIVED FOR RUNNING ACROSS THE ROADS OF AMERICA, RACING INTO PARALLEL WORLDS, AND SPRINTING FROM THE PAST TO THE FUTURE, SOLVING CRIMES AND STOPPING THE BAD GUYS.
BUT YOU ALWAYS TOOK A BREATH. YOU ALWAYS SLOWED DOWN LONG ENOUGH TO SPEND TIME WITH YOUR FRIENDS AND FAMILY.
KZZZTTT
WITH ME.
"YOU'RE TOO LATE."

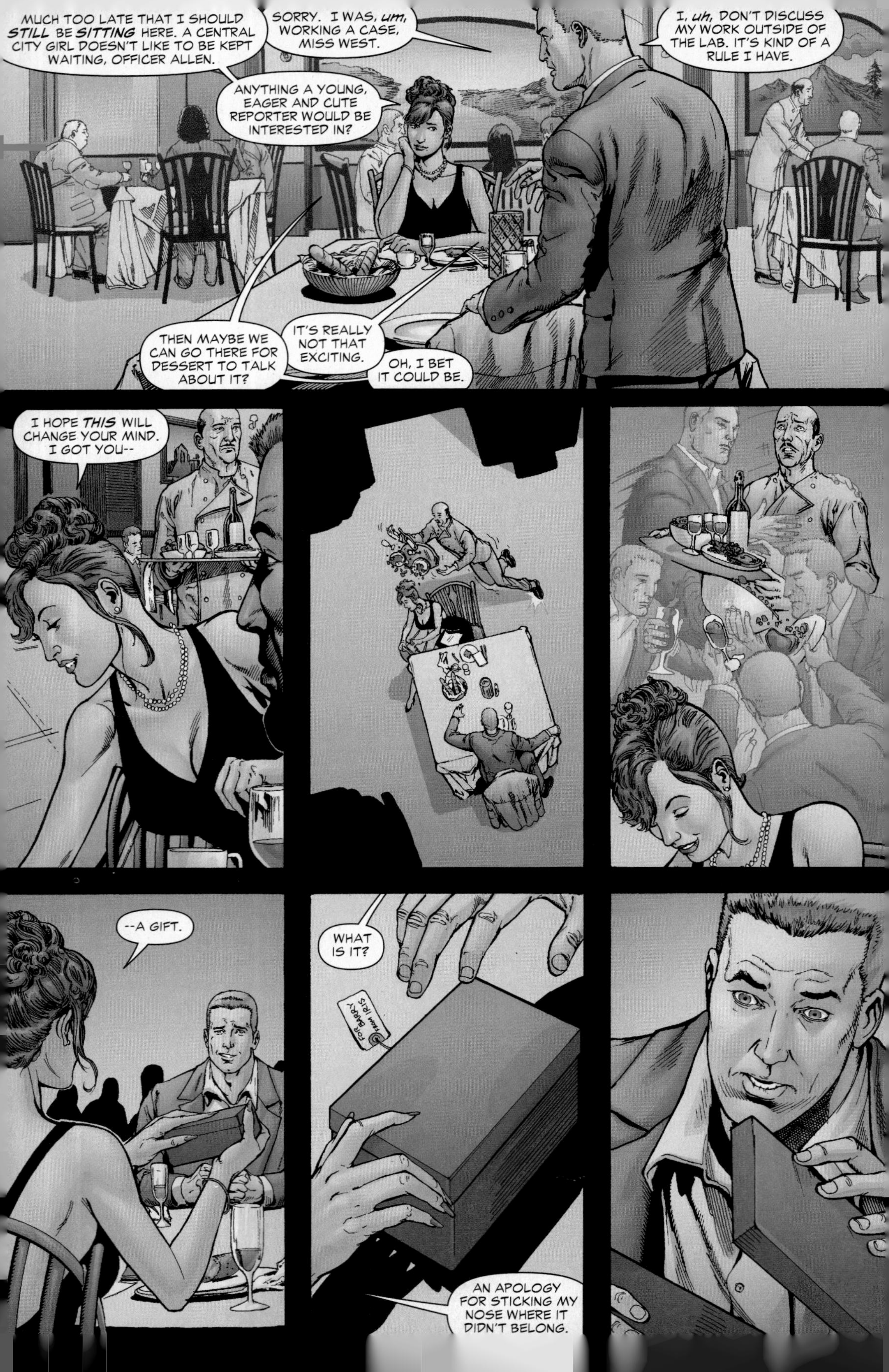

MUCH TOO LATE THAT I SHOULD STILL BE SITTING HERE. A CENTRAL CITY GIRL DOESN'T LIKE TO BE KEPT WAITING, OFFICER ALLEN.
SORRY. I WAS, um, WORKING A CASE, MISS WEST.
ANYTHING A YOUNG, EAGER AND CUTE REPORTER WOULD BE INTERESTED IN?
I, uh, DON'T DISCUSS MY WORK OUTSIDE OF THE LAB. IT'S KIND OF A RULE I HAVE.
THEN MAYBE WE CAN GO THERE FOR DESSERT TO TALK ABOUT IT?
IT'S REALLY NOT THAT EXCITING.
OH, I BET IT COULD BE.
I HOPE THIS WILL CHANGE YOUR MIND. I GOT YOU--
--A GIFT.
WHAT IS IT?
FOR BARRY FROM IRIS
AN APOLOGY FOR STICKING MY NOSE WHERE IT DIDN'T BELONG.

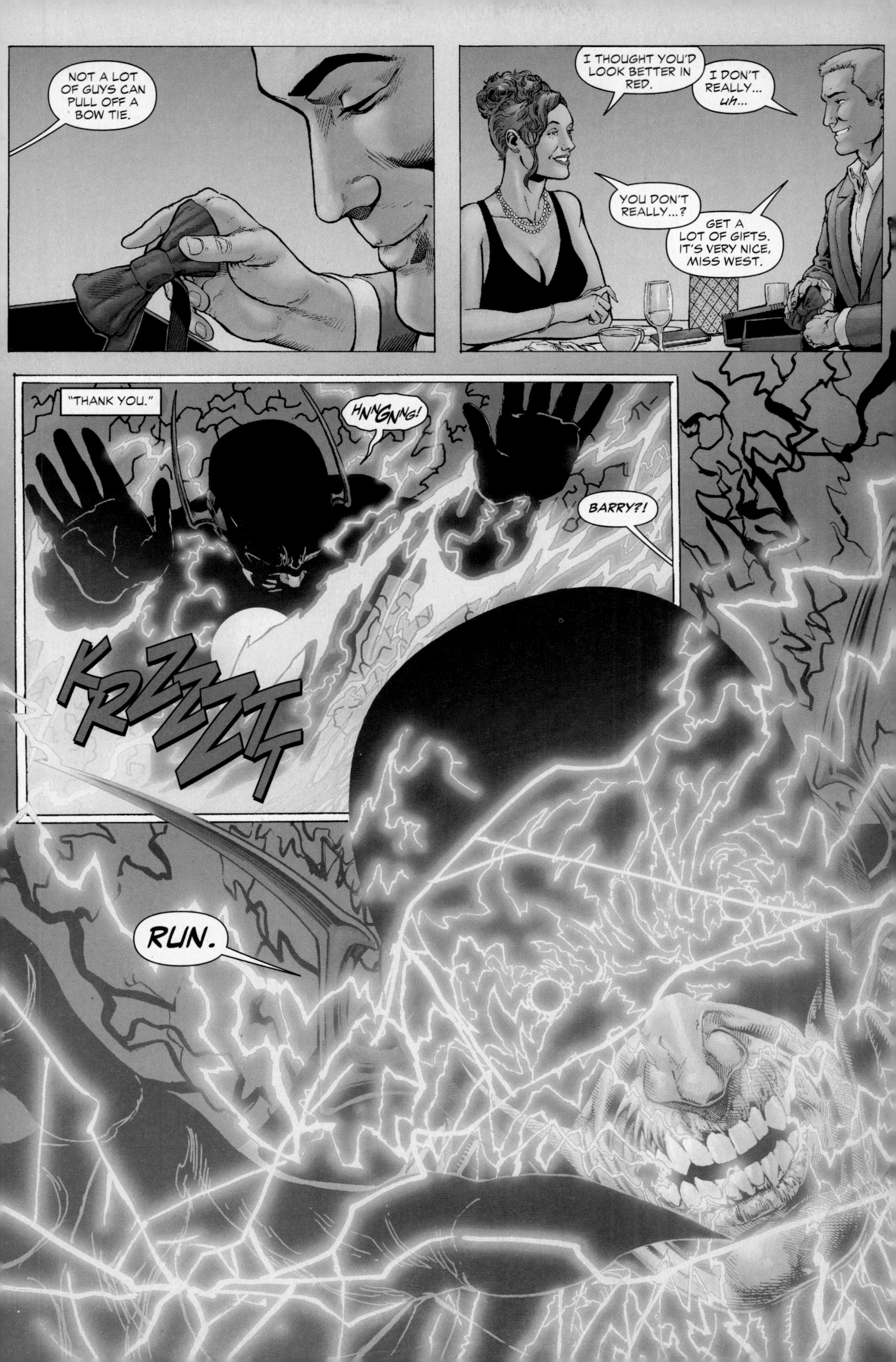
NOT A LOT OF GUYS CAN PULL OFF A BOW TIE.
I THOUGHT YOU'D LOOK BETTER IN RED.
I DON'T REALLY... uh...
YOU DON'T REALLY...?
GET A LOT OF GIFTS. IT'S VERY NICE, MISS WEST.
"THANK YOU."
HNNGNNG!
BARRY?!
KRZZZZTT
RUN.

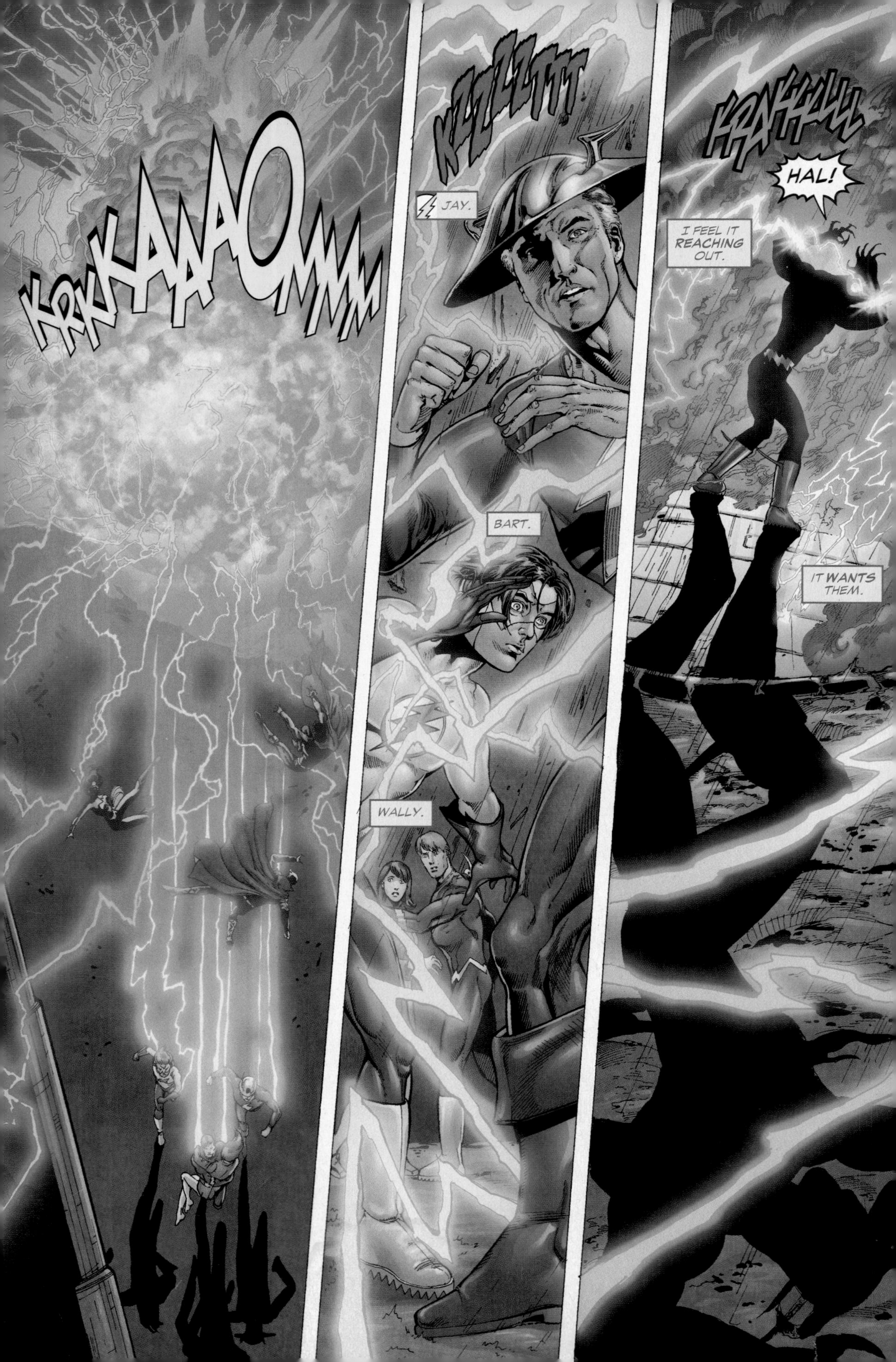

KRKKAAAOMMMM
KZZZZZTTT
JAY.
BART.
WALLY.
KRAKKLLL
HAL!
I FEEL IT REACHING OUT.
IT WANTS THEM.

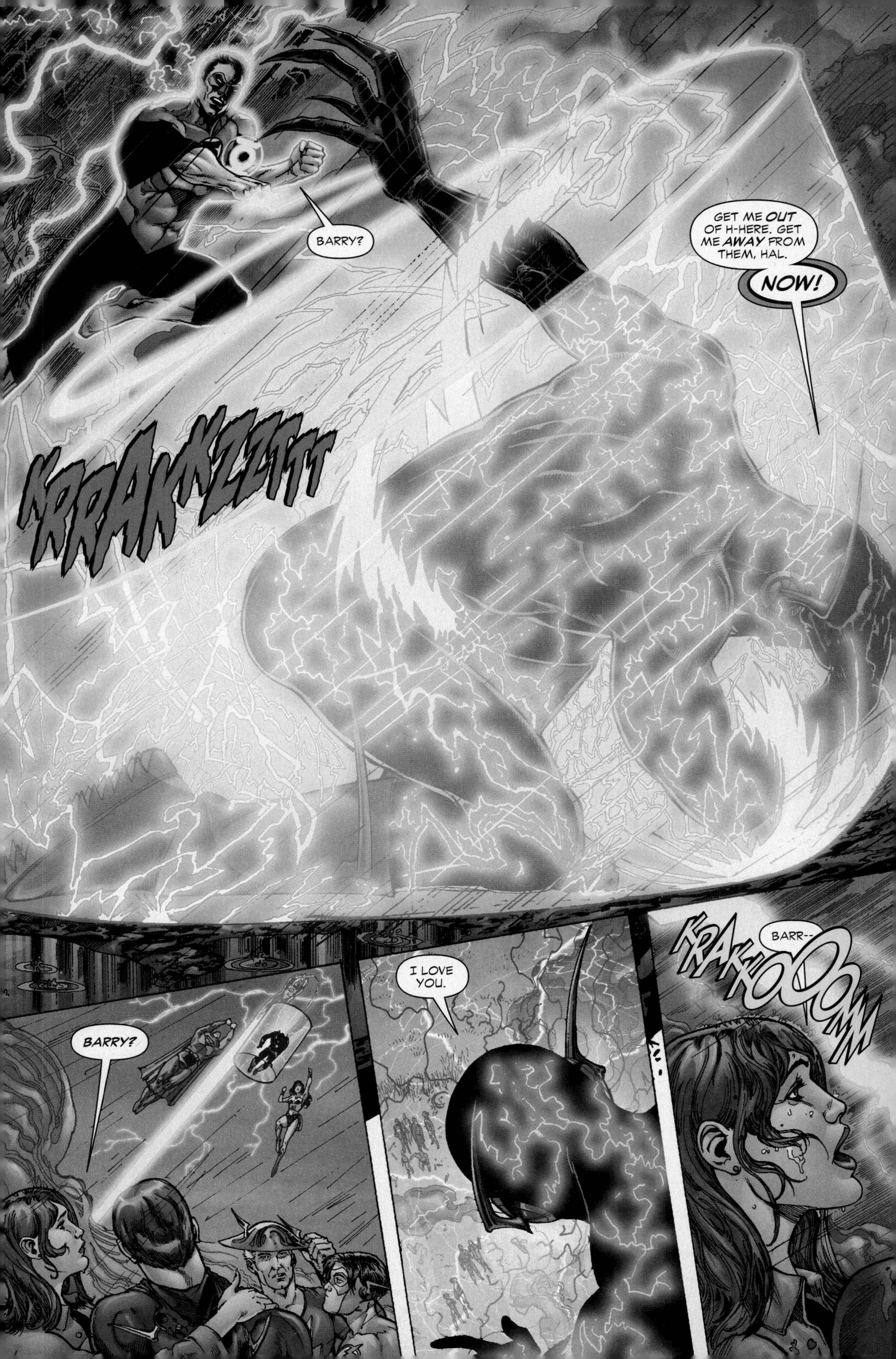
BARRY?
GET ME OUT OF H-HERE. GET ME AWAY FROM THEM, HAL.
NOW!
KRRAKKZZTTT
BARRY?
I LOVE YOU.
KRAKOOOOM
BARR--

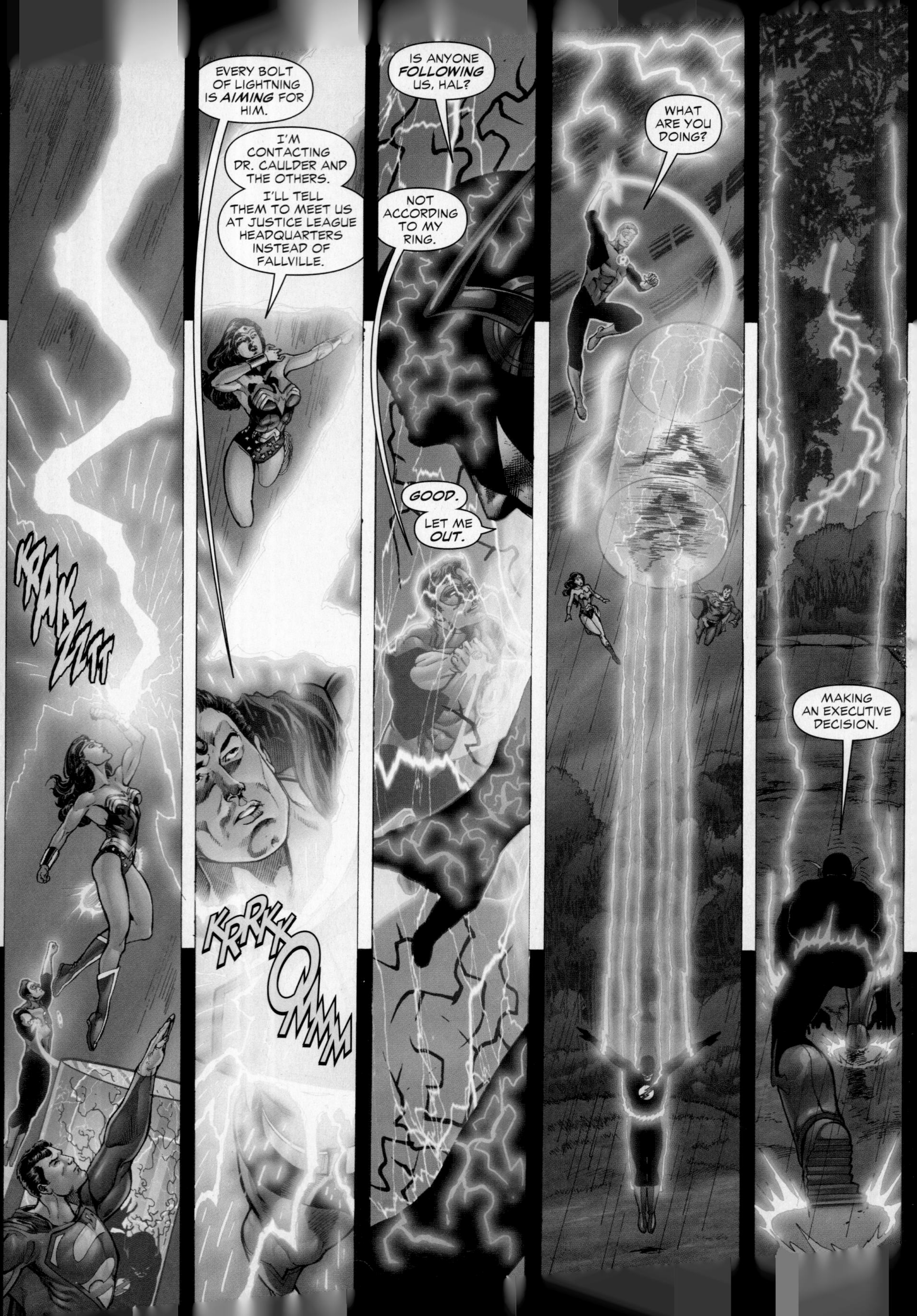
KRAKZZZTT
EVERY BOLT OF LIGHTNING IS AIMING FOR HIM.
I'M CONTACTING DR. CAULDER AND THE OTHERS.
I'LL TELL THEM TO MEET US AT JUSTICE LEAGUE HEADQUARTERS INSTEAD OF FALLVILLE.
KRRKKOMMM
IS ANYONE FOLLOWING US, HAL?
NOT ACCORDING TO MY RING.
GOOD.
LET ME OUT.
WHAT ARE YOU DOING?
MAKING AN EXECUTIVE DECISION.

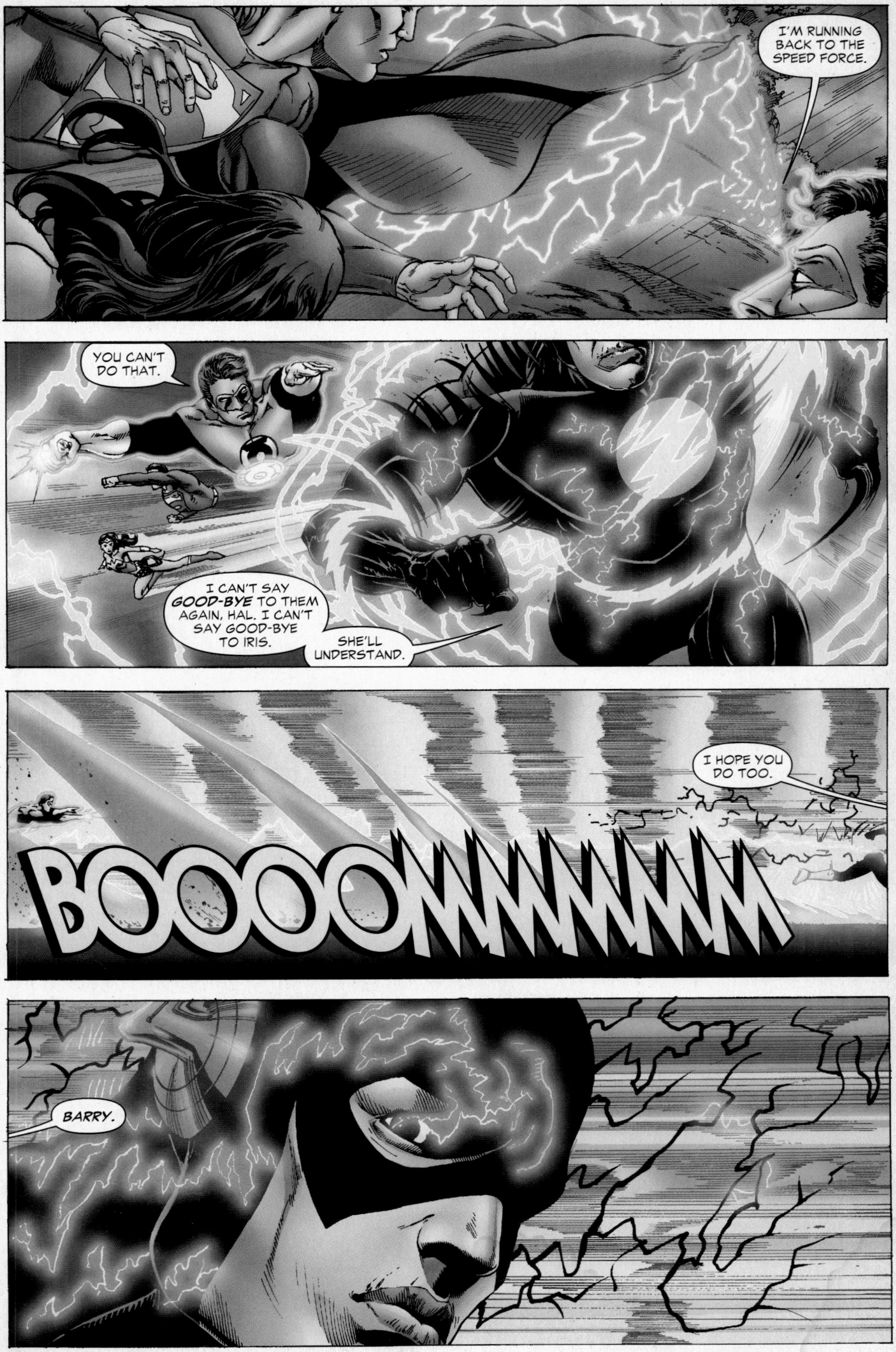
I'M RUNNING BACK TO THE SPEED FORCE.
YOU CAN'T DO THAT.
I CAN'T SAY GOOD-BYE TO THEM AGAIN, HAL. I CAN'T SAY GOOD-BYE TO IRIS.
SHE'LL UNDERSTAND.
I HOPE YOU DO TOO.
BOOOOMMMMMM
BARRY.

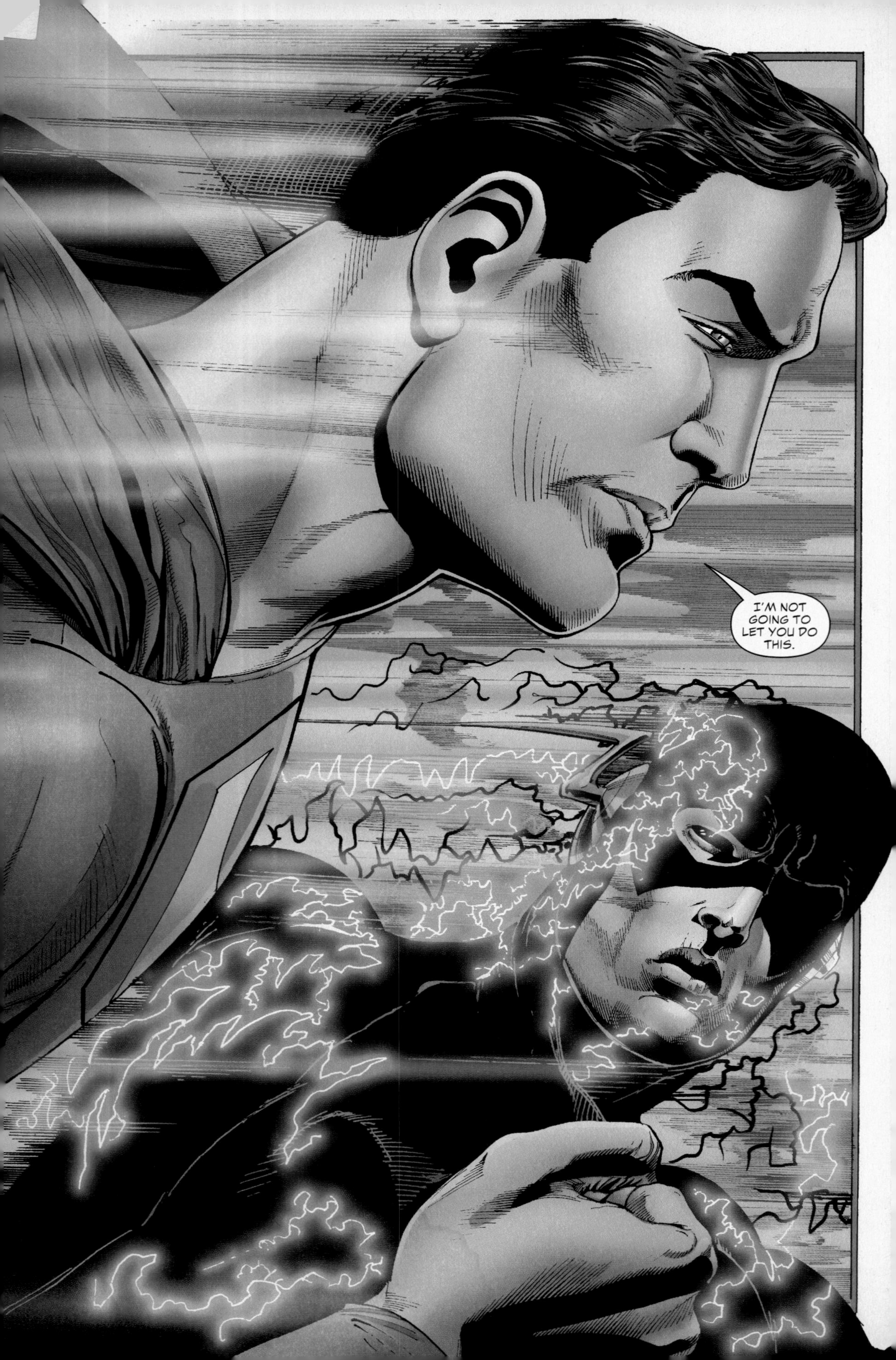
I'M NOT GOING TO LET YOU DO THIS.

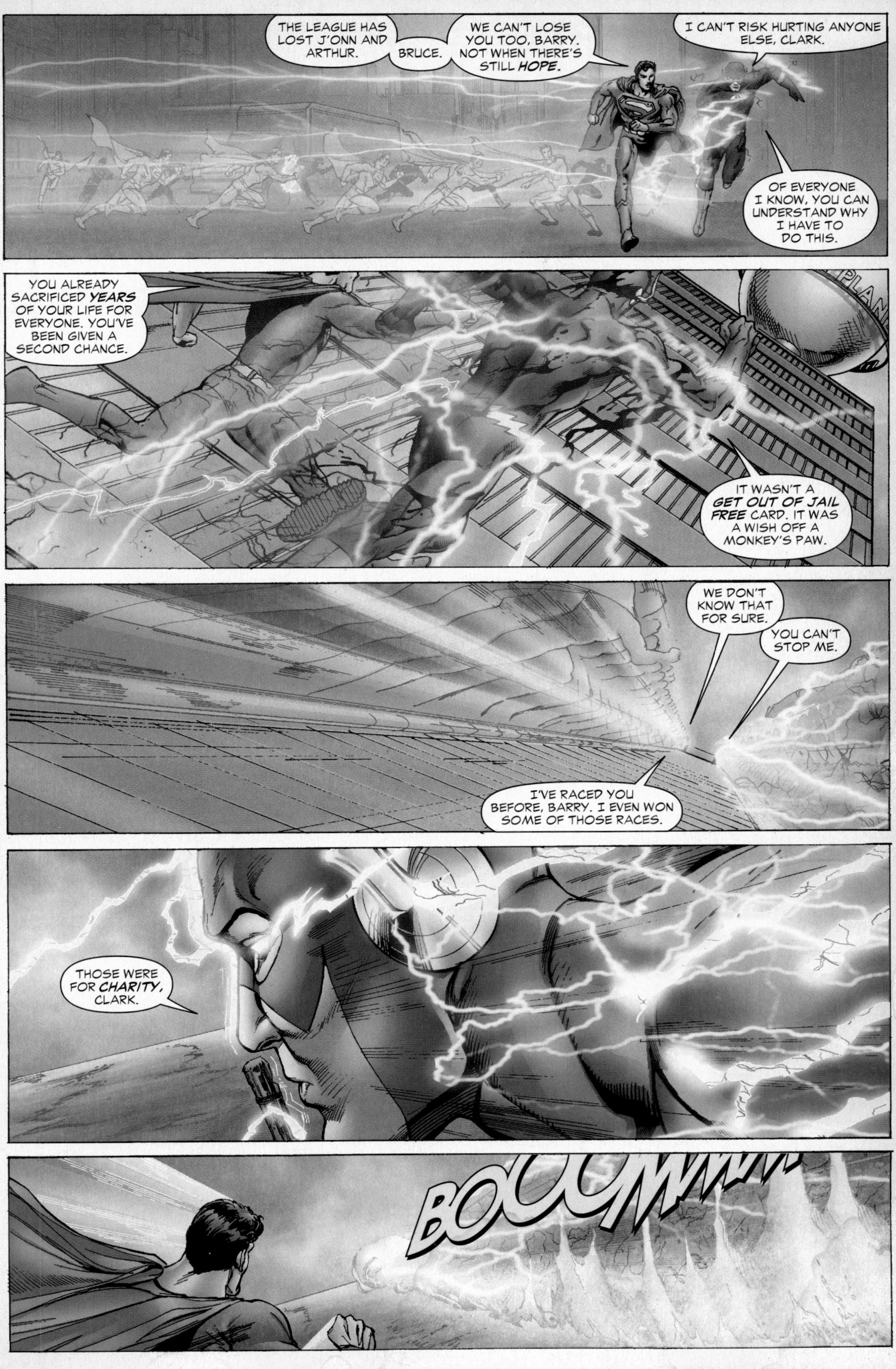
THE LEAGUE HAS LOST J'ONN AND ARTHUR.
BRUCE.
WE CAN'T LOSE YOU TOO, BARRY. NOT WHEN THERE'S STILL ***HOPE.***
I CAN'T RISK HURTING ANYONE ELSE, CLARK.
OF EVERYONE I KNOW, YOU CAN UNDERSTAND WHY I HAVE TO DO THIS.
YOU ALREADY SACRIFICED ***YEARS*** OF YOUR LIFE FOR EVERYONE. YOU'VE BEEN GIVEN A SECOND CHANCE.
IT WASN'T A ***GET OUT OF JAIL FREE*** CARD. IT WAS A WISH OFF A MONKEY'S PAW.
WE DON'T KNOW THAT FOR SURE.
YOU CAN'T STOP ME.
I'VE RACED YOU BEFORE, BARRY. I EVEN WON SOME OF THOSE RACES.
THOSE WERE FOR ***CHARITY,*** CLARK.
BOOOMMM

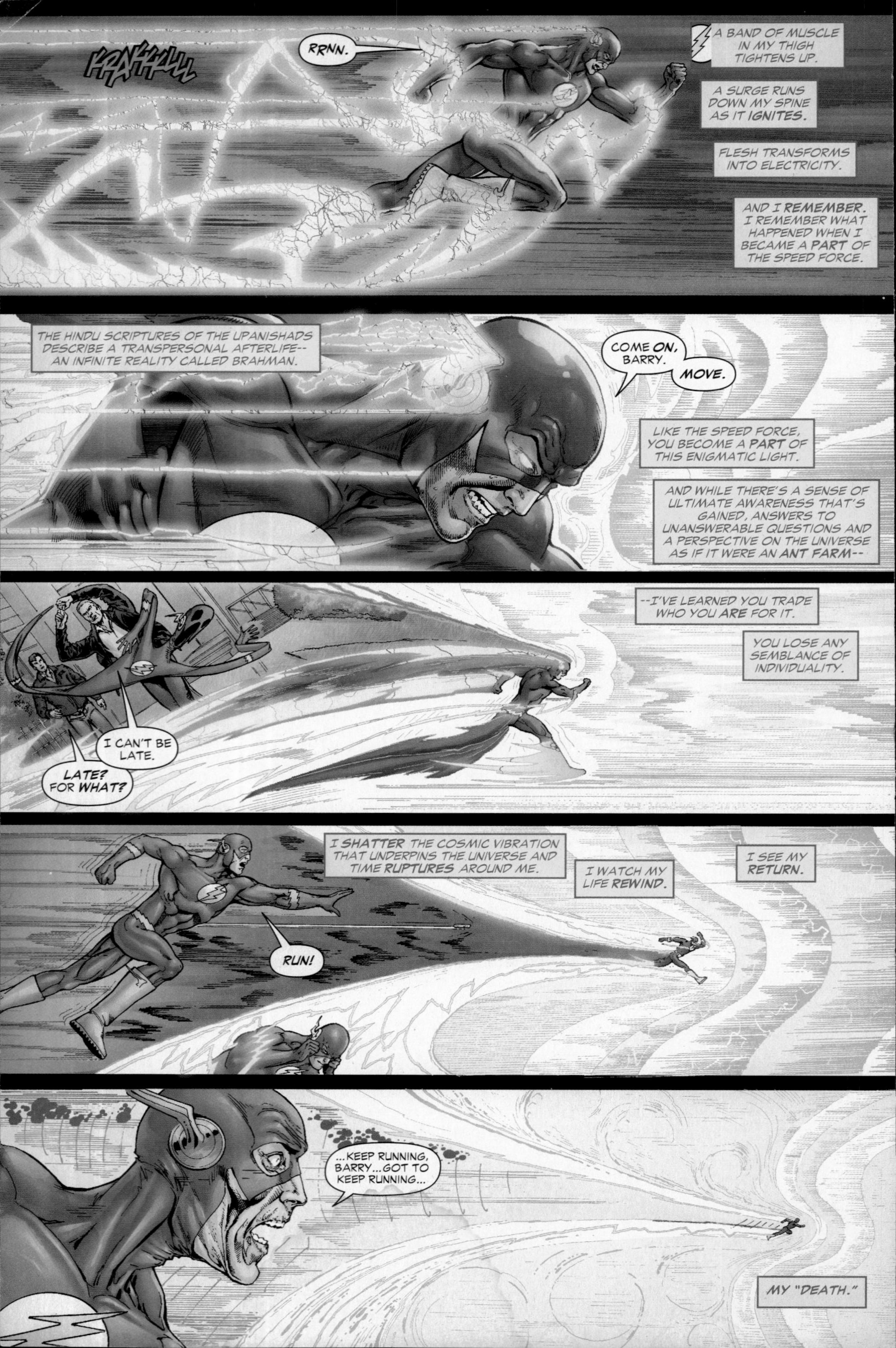
KRAKKULL
RRNN.
A BAND OF MUSCLE IN MY THIGH TIGHTENS UP.
A SURGE RUNS DOWN MY SPINE AS IT IGNITES.
FLESH TRANSFORMS INTO ELECTRICITY.
AND I REMEMBER. I REMEMBER WHAT HAPPENED WHEN I BECAME A PART OF THE SPEED FORCE.
THE HINDU SCRIPTURES OF THE UPANISHADS DESCRIBE A TRANSPERSONAL AFTERLIFE-- AN INFINITE REALITY CALLED BRAHMAN.
COME ON, BARRY.
MOVE.
LIKE THE SPEED FORCE, YOU BECOME A PART OF THIS ENIGMATIC LIGHT.
AND WHILE THERE'S A SENSE OF ULTIMATE AWARENESS THAT'S GAINED, ANSWERS TO UNANSWERABLE QUESTIONS AND A PERSPECTIVE ON THE UNIVERSE AS IF IT WERE AN ANT FARM--
--I'VE LEARNED YOU TRADE WHO YOU ARE FOR IT.
YOU LOSE ANY SEMBLANCE OF INDIVIDUALITY.
I CAN'T BE LATE.
LATE? FOR WHAT?
I SHATTER THE COSMIC VIBRATION THAT UNDERPINS THE UNIVERSE AND TIME RUPTURES AROUND ME.
I WATCH MY LIFE REWIND.
I SEE MY RETURN.
RUN!
...KEEP RUNNING, BARRY...GOT TO KEEP RUNNING...
MY "DEATH."

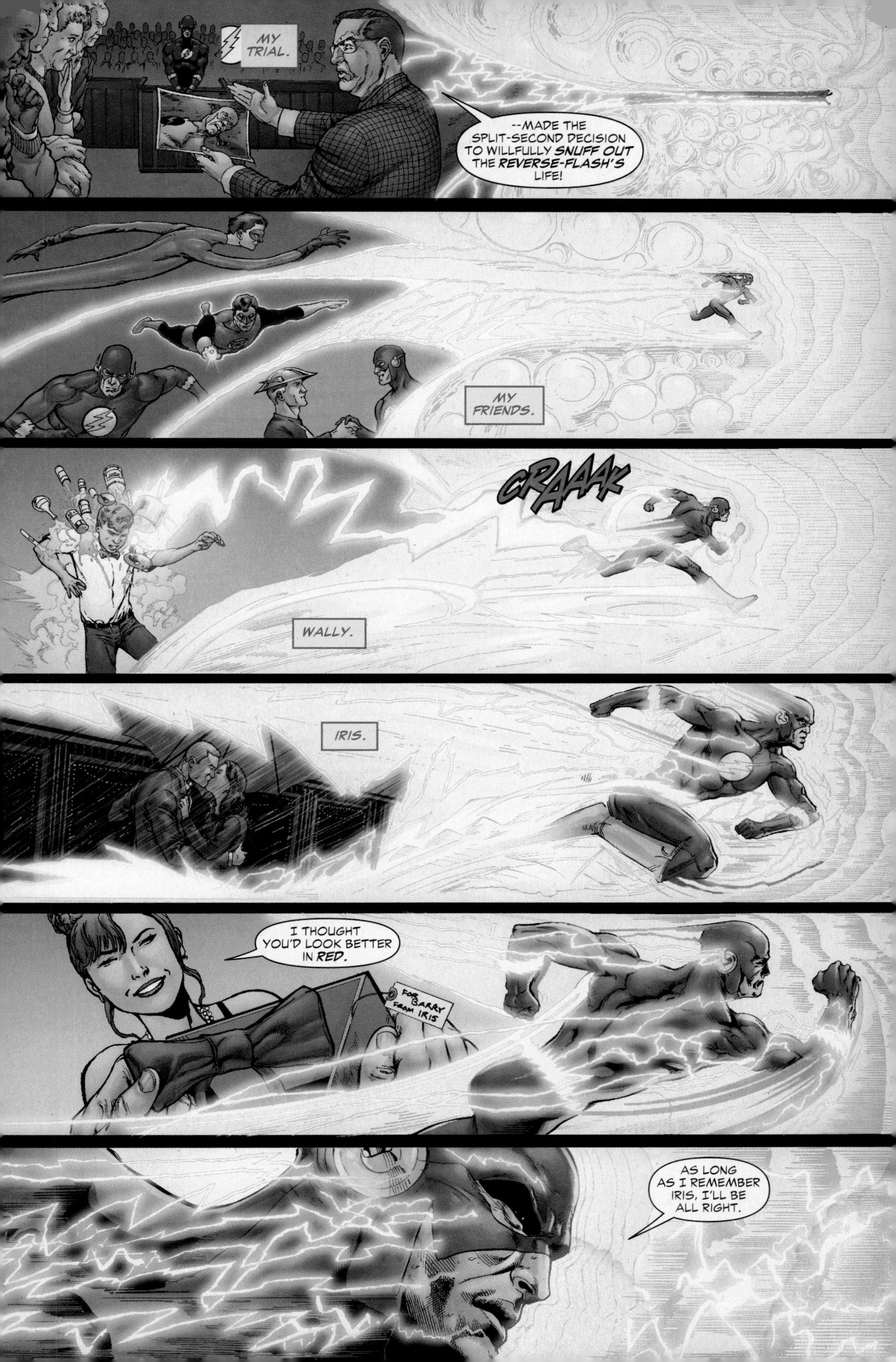
MY TRIAL.
--MADE THE SPLIT-SECOND DECISION TO WILLFULLY SNUFF OUT THE REVERSE-FLASH'S LIFE!
MY FRIENDS.
CRAAAK
WALLY.
IRIS.
I THOUGHT YOU'D LOOK BETTER IN RED.
FOR BARRY FROM IRIS
AS LONG AS I REMEMBER IRIS, I'LL BE ALL RIGHT.

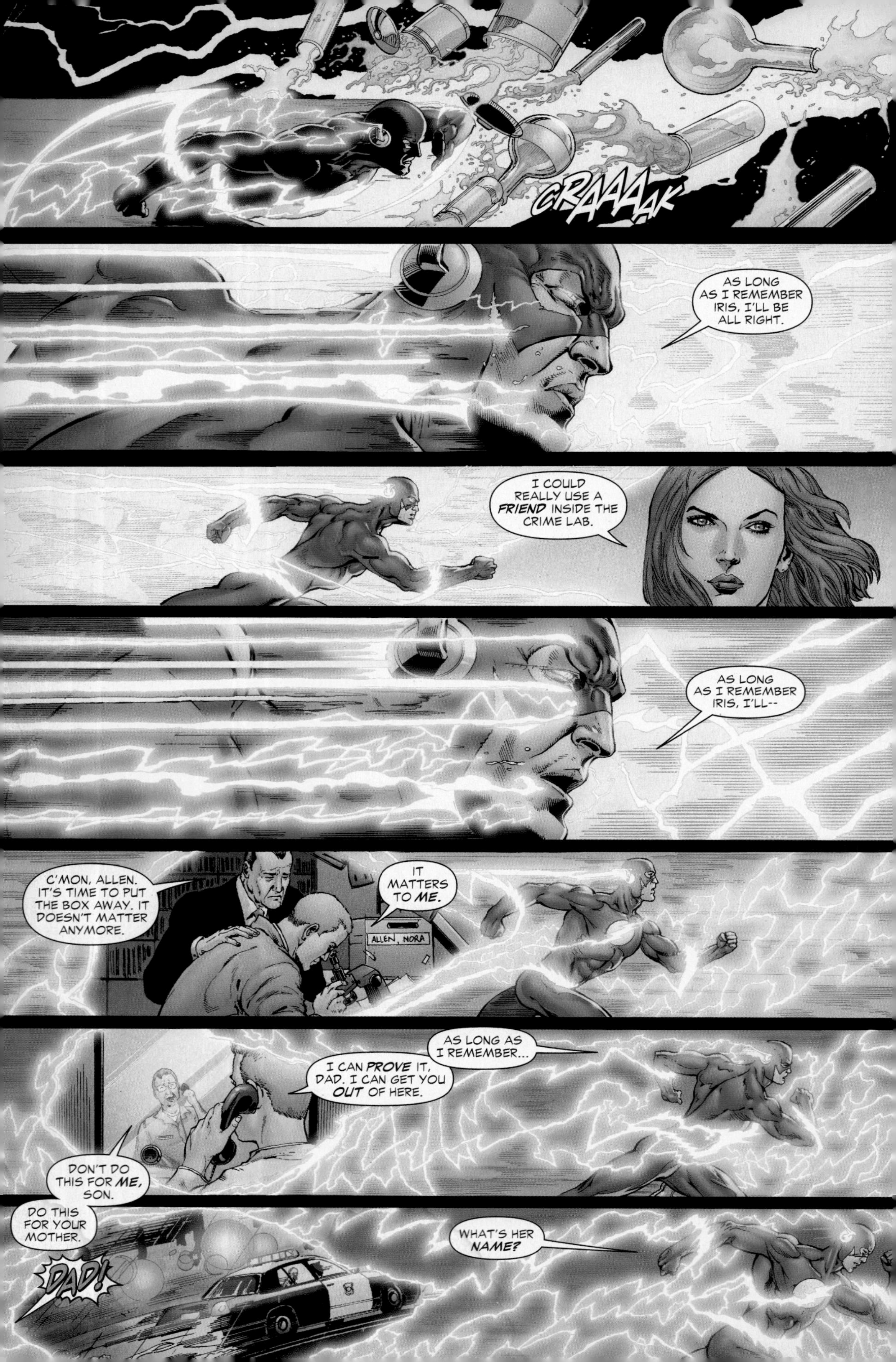
CRAAAAK
AS LONG AS I REMEMBER IRIS, I'LL BE ALL RIGHT.
I COULD REALLY USE A FRIEND INSIDE THE CRIME LAB.
AS LONG AS I REMEMBER IRIS, I'LL--
C'MON, ALLEN. IT'S TIME TO PUT THE BOX AWAY. IT DOESN'T MATTER ANYMORE.
IT MATTERS TO ME.
ALLEN, NORA
AS LONG AS I REMEMBER...
I CAN PROVE IT, DAD. I CAN GET YOU OUT OF HERE.
DON'T DO THIS FOR ME, SON.
DO THIS FOR YOUR MOTHER.
WHAT'S HER NAME?
DAD!

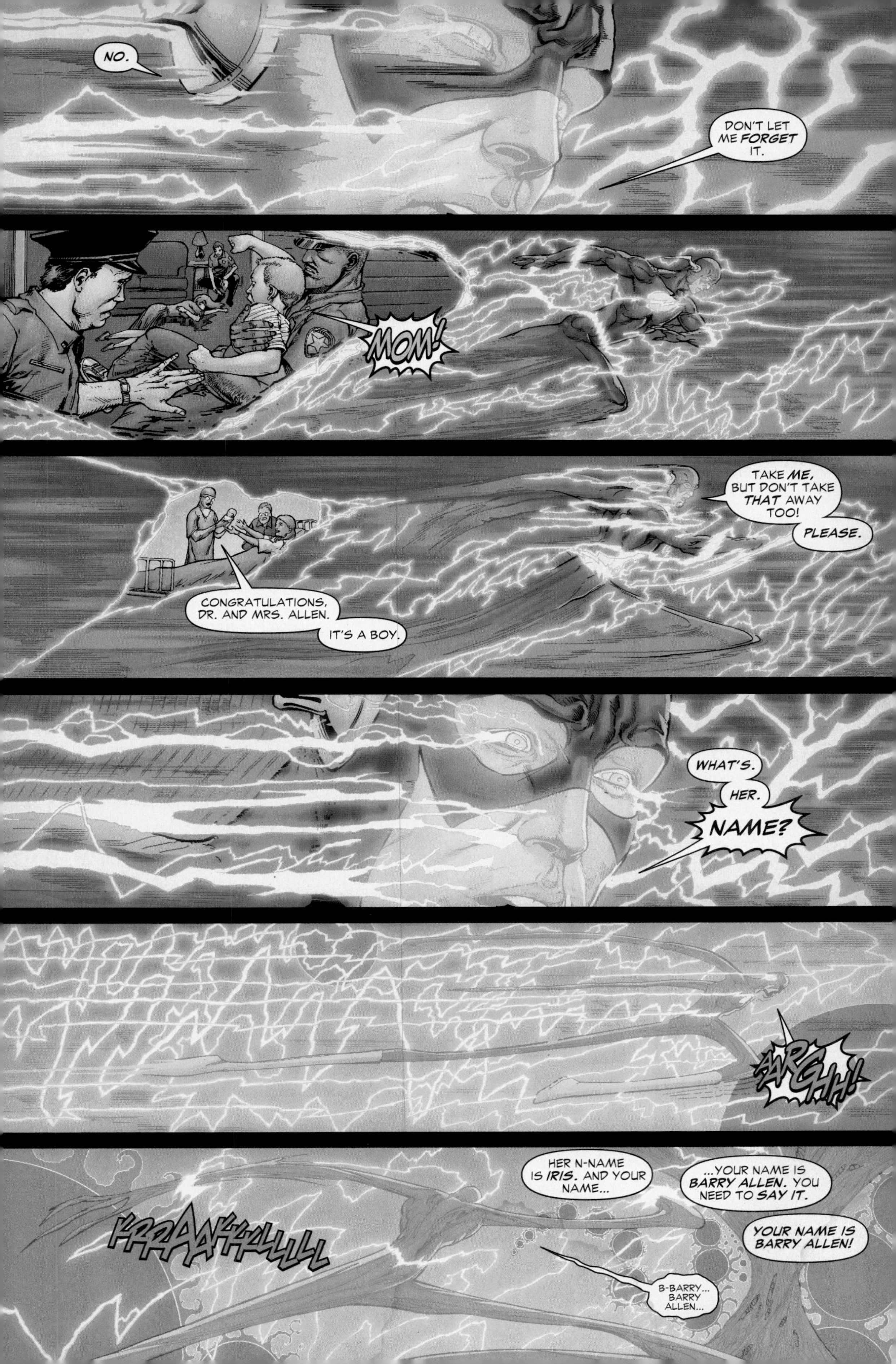
NO.
DON'T LET ME FORGET IT.
MOM!
TAKE ME, BUT DON'T TAKE THAT AWAY TOO!
PLEASE.
CONGRATULATIONS, DR. AND MRS. ALLEN.
IT'S A BOY.
WHAT'S.
HER.
NAME?
AARGHH!
KRRAAKKULLLL
HER N-NAME IS IRIS. AND YOUR NAME...
...YOUR NAME IS BARRY ALLEN. YOU NEED TO SAY IT.
YOUR NAME IS BARRY ALLEN!
B-BARRY... BARRY ALLEN...

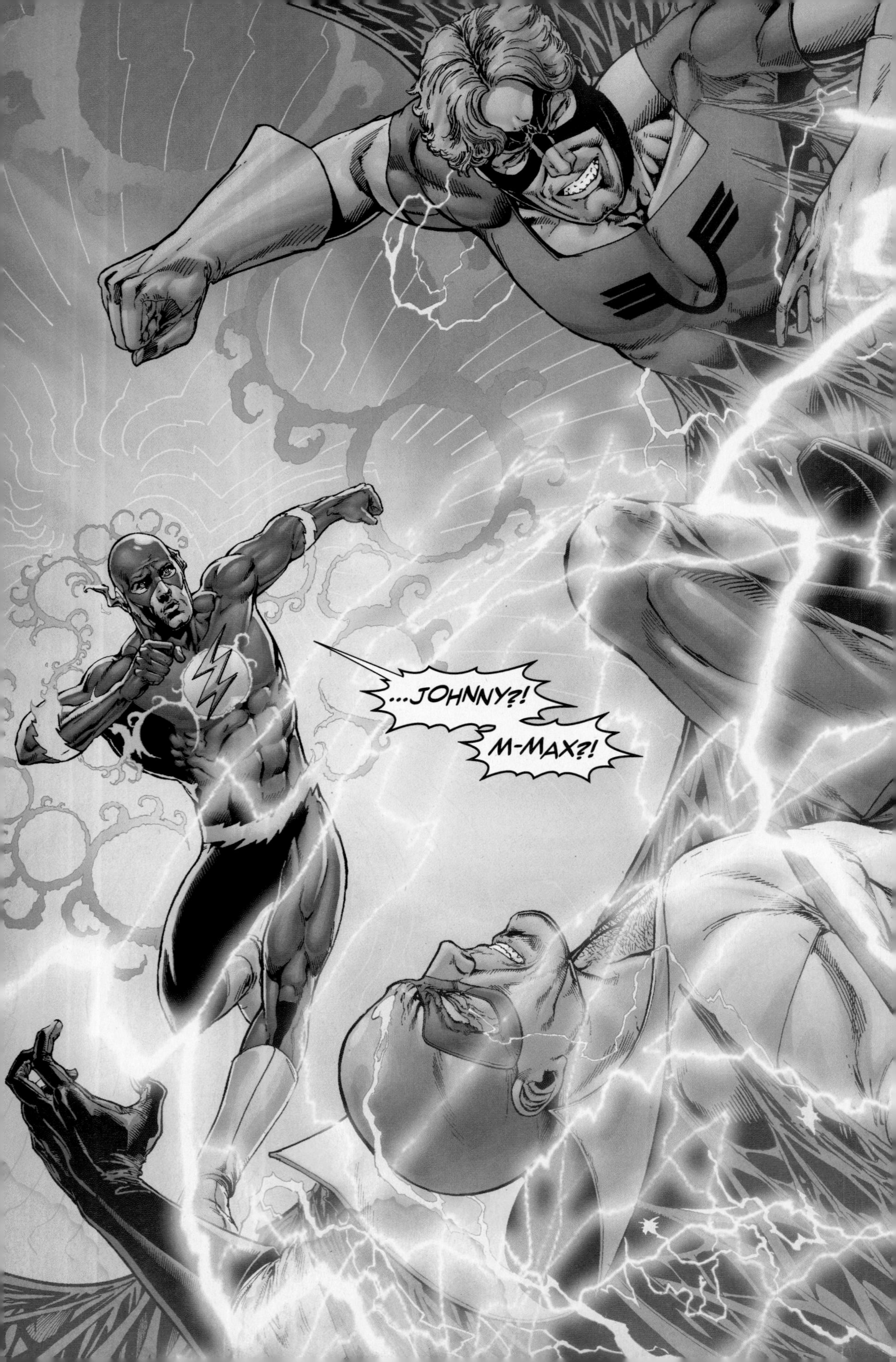
...JOHNNY?!
M-MAX?!

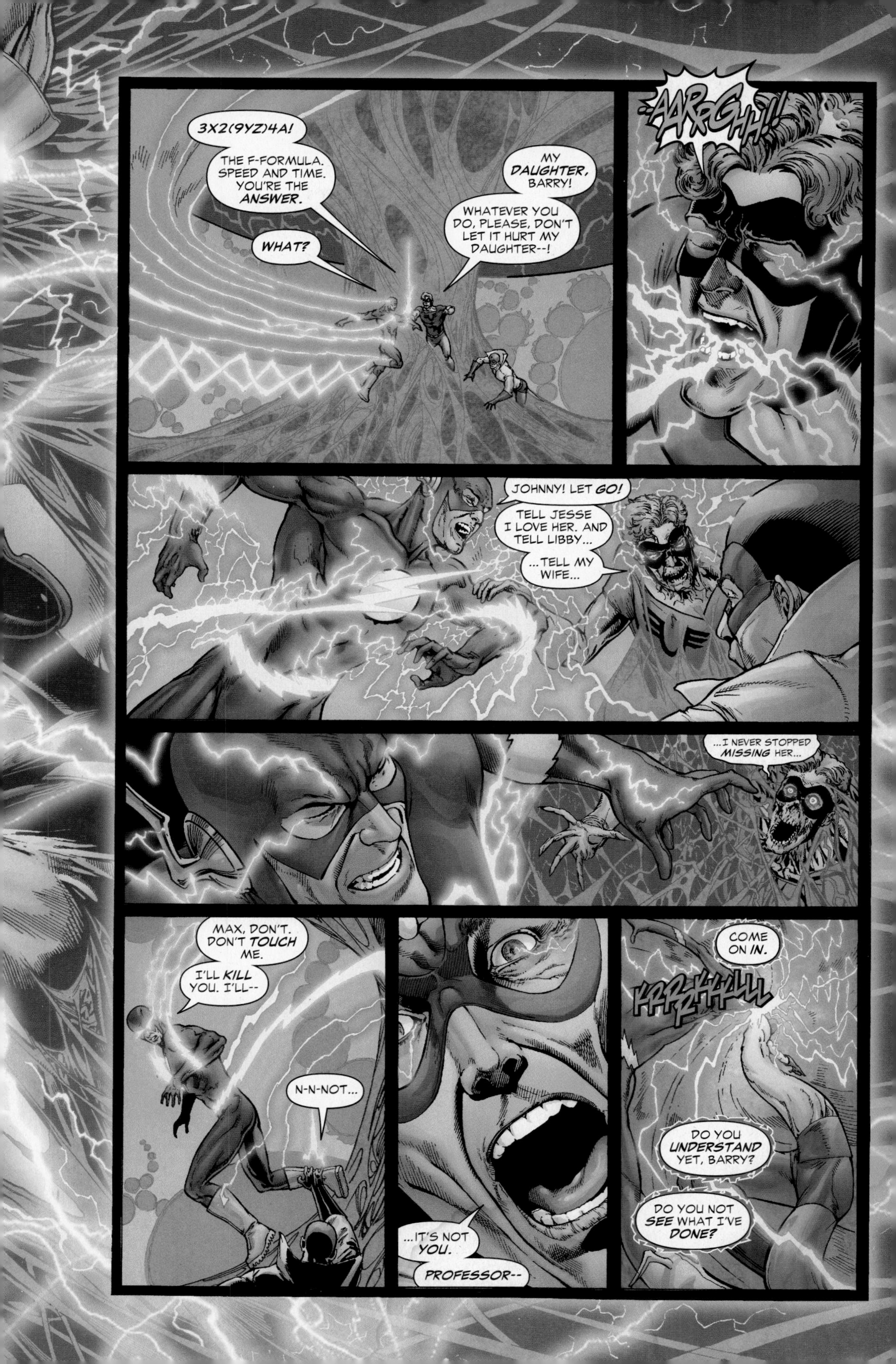
3X2(9YZ)4A!
THE F-FORMULA. SPEED AND TIME. YOU'RE THE ANSWER.
WHAT?
MY DAUGHTER, BARRY!
WHATEVER YOU DO, PLEASE, DON'T LET IT HURT MY DAUGHTER--!
AARRGHH!!
JOHNNY! LET GO!
TELL JESSE I LOVE HER. AND TELL LIBBY...
...TELL MY WIFE...
...I NEVER STOPPED MISSING HER...
MAX, DON'T. DON'T TOUCH ME.
I'LL KILL YOU. I'LL--
N-N-NOT...
...IT'S NOT YOU.
PROFESSOR--
COME ON IN.
KRRZKKLLL
DO YOU UNDERSTAND YET, BARRY?
DO YOU NOT SEE WHAT I'VE DONE?

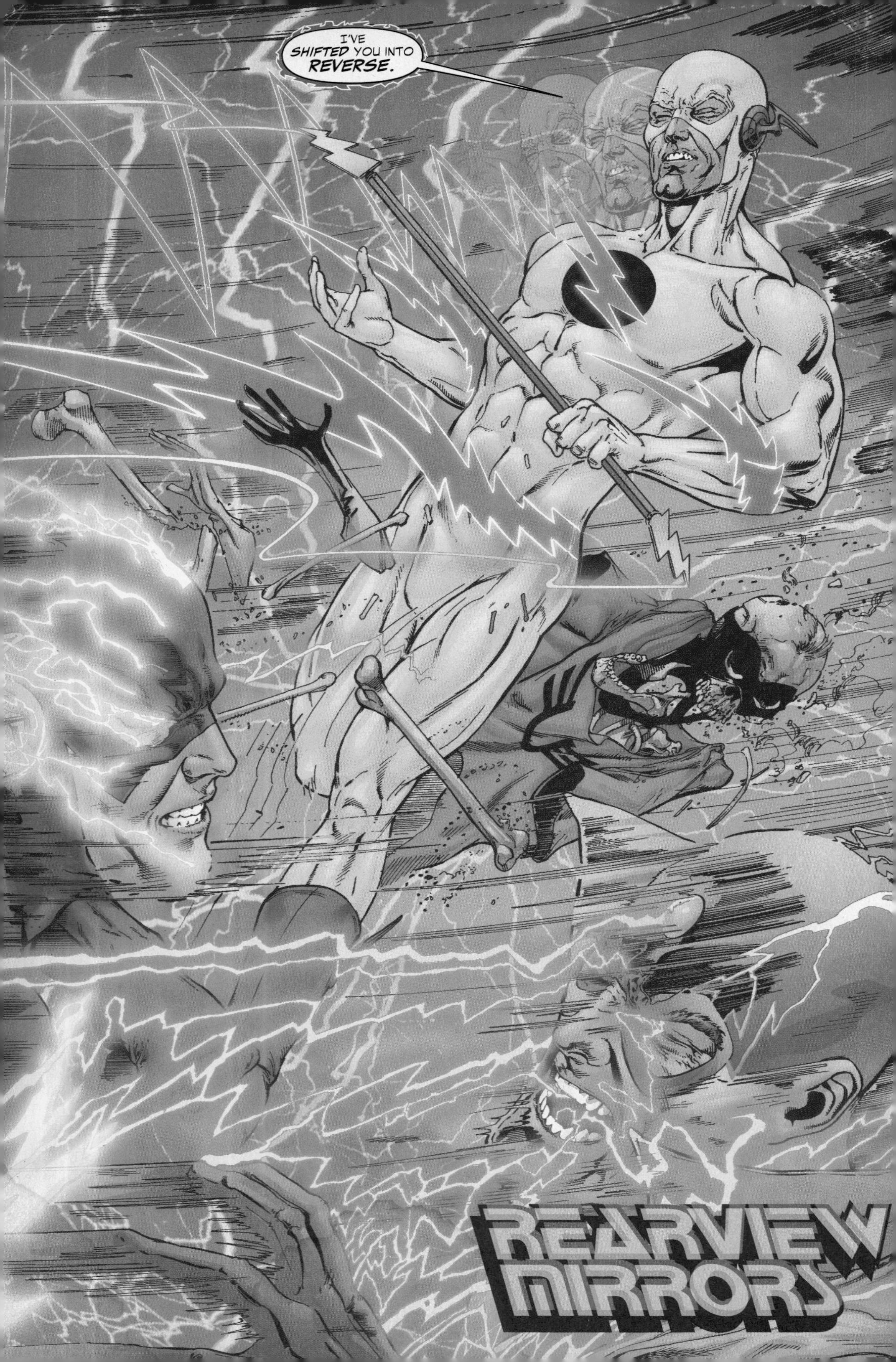
I'VE SHIFTED YOU INTO REVERSE.
REARVIEW MIRRORS

THE FLASH: REBIRTH #4 COVER BY ETHAN VAN SCIVER WITH BRIAN MILLER OF HI-FI

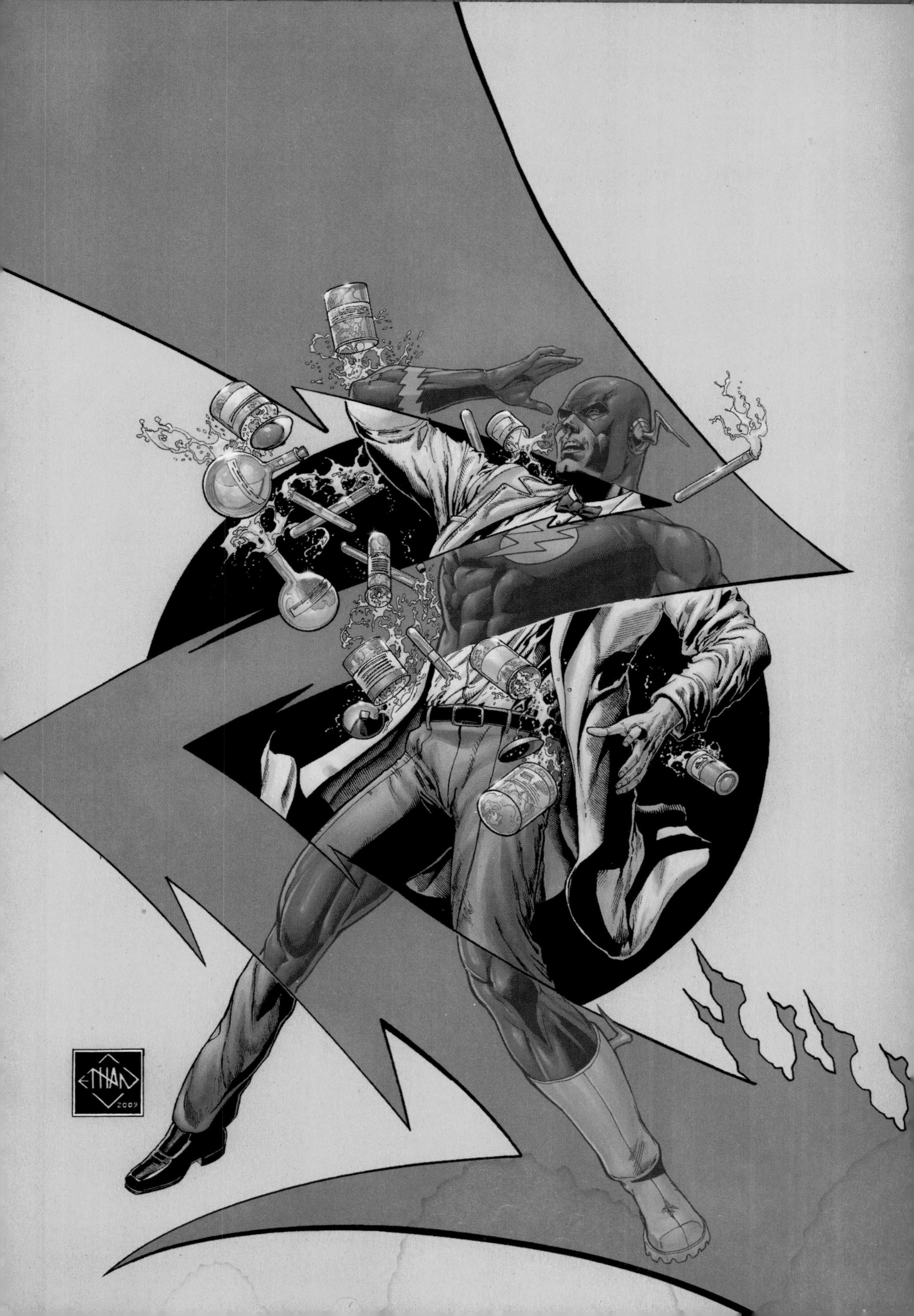
ETHAN
2009

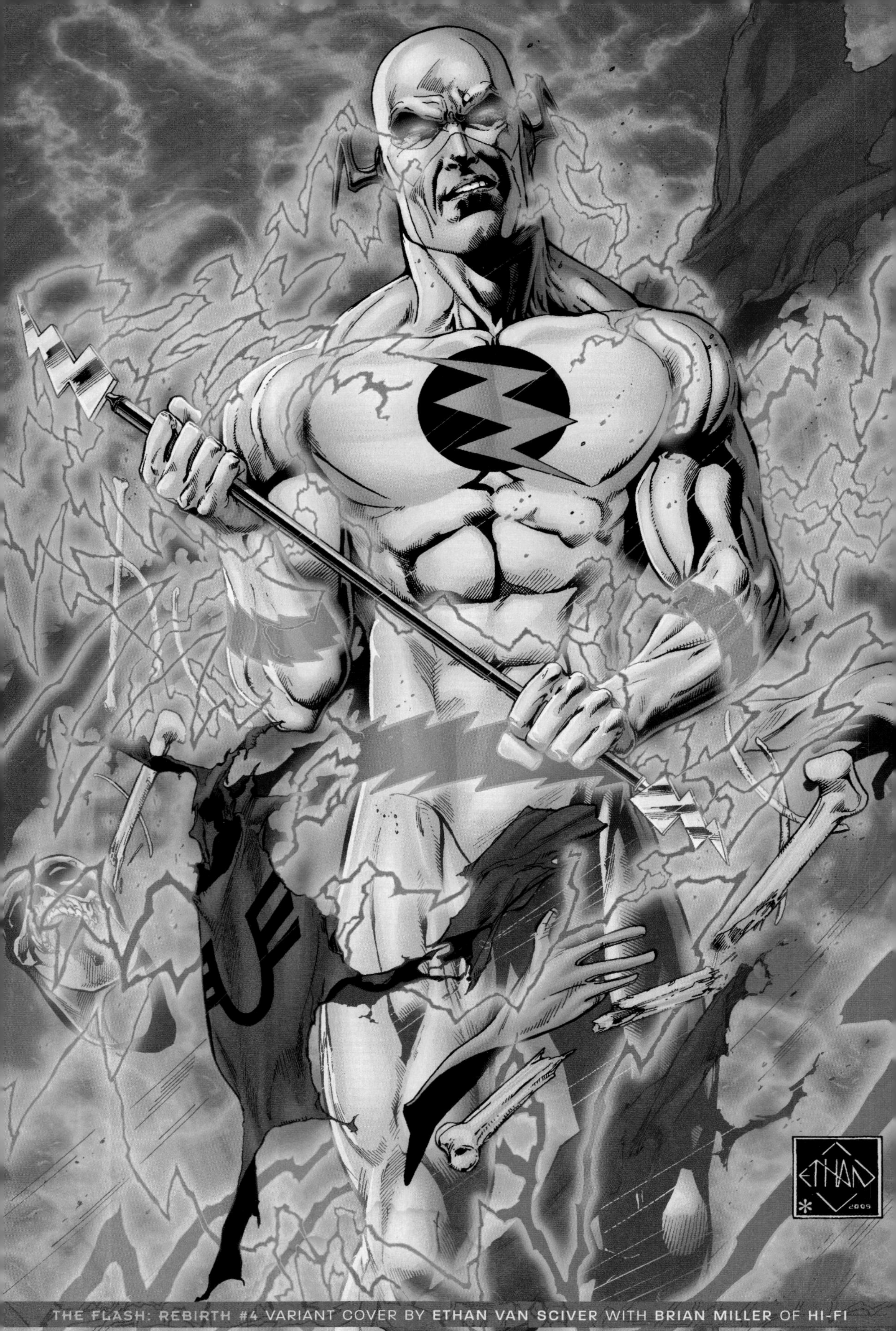
ETHAN
2009

THE FLASH: REBIRTH #4 VARIANT COVER BY **ETHAN VAN SCIVER** WITH **BRIAN MILLER** OF **HI-FI**

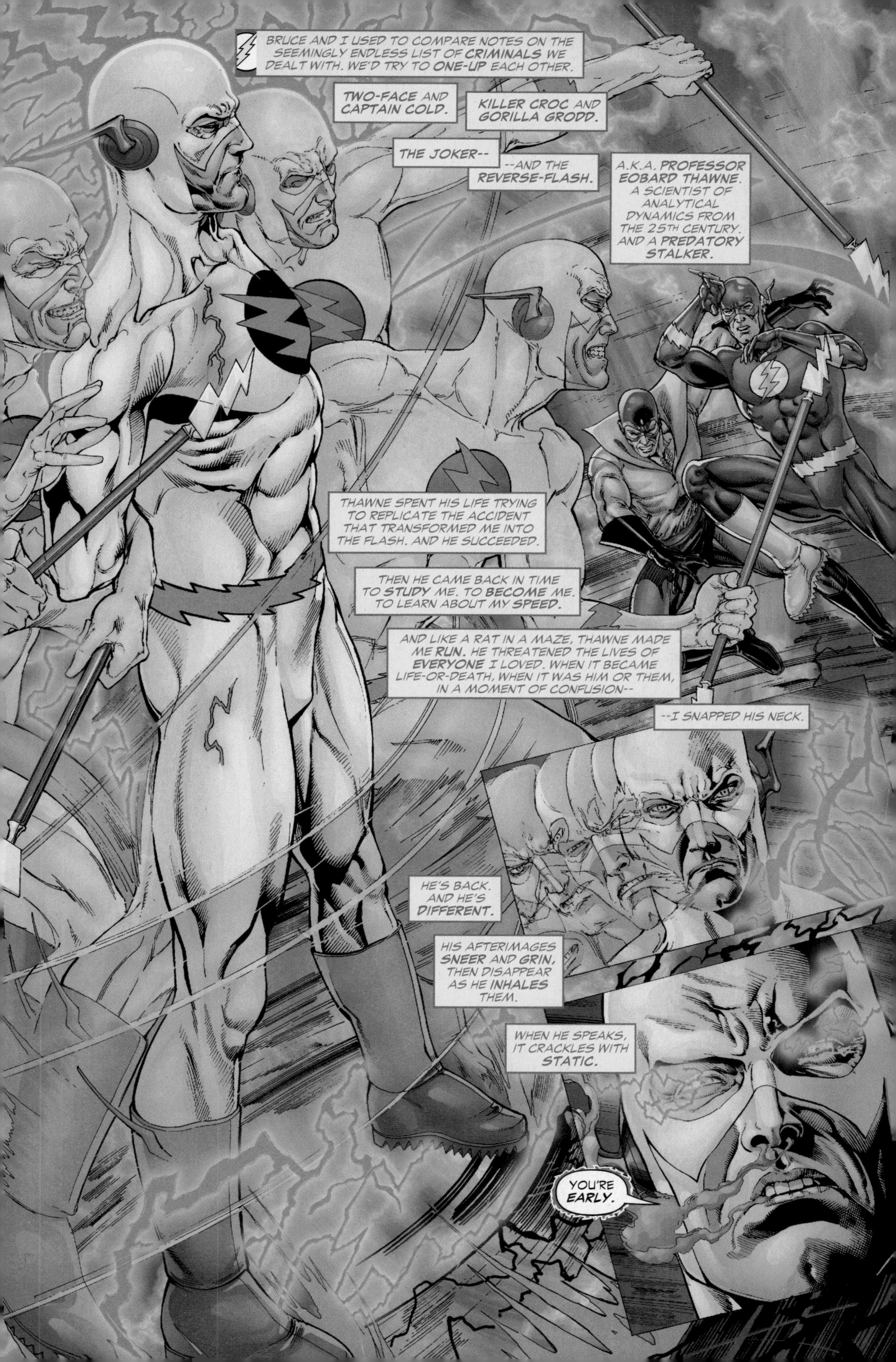
BRUCE AND I USED TO COMPARE NOTES ON THE SEEMINGLY ENDLESS LIST OF CRIMINALS WE DEALT WITH. WE'D TRY TO ONE-UP EACH OTHER.
TWO-FACE AND CAPTAIN COLD.
KILLER CROC AND GORILLA GRODD.
THE JOKER--
--AND THE REVERSE-FLASH.
A.K.A. PROFESSOR EOBARD THAWNE. A SCIENTIST OF ANALYTICAL DYNAMICS FROM THE 25TH CENTURY. AND A PREDATORY STALKER.
THAWNE SPENT HIS LIFE TRYING TO REPLICATE THE ACCIDENT THAT TRANSFORMED ME INTO THE FLASH. AND HE SUCCEEDED.
THEN HE CAME BACK IN TIME TO STUDY ME. TO BECOME ME. TO LEARN ABOUT MY SPEED.
AND LIKE A RAT IN A MAZE, THAWNE MADE ME RUN. HE THREATENED THE LIVES OF EVERYONE I LOVED. WHEN IT BECAME LIFE-OR-DEATH, WHEN IT WAS HIM OR THEM, IN A MOMENT OF CONFUSION--
--I SNAPPED HIS NECK.
HE'S BACK. AND HE'S DIFFERENT.
HIS AFTERIMAGES SNEER AND GRIN, THEN DISAPPEAR AS HE INHALES THEM.
WHEN HE SPEAKS, IT CRACKLES WITH STATIC.
YOU'RE EARLY.

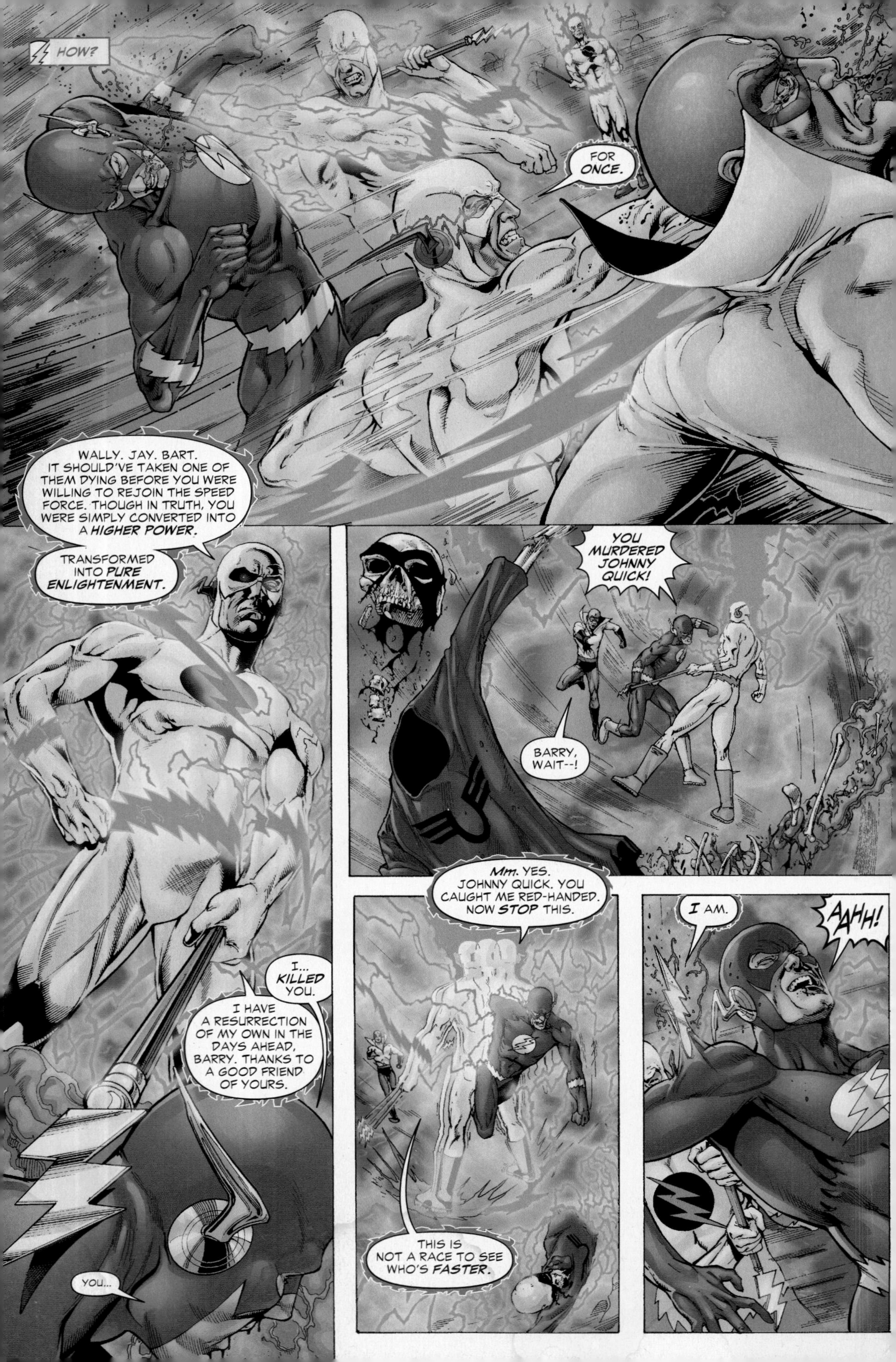
HOW?
FOR ONCE.
WALLY. JAY. BART. IT SHOULD'VE TAKEN ONE OF THEM DYING BEFORE YOU WERE WILLING TO REJOIN THE SPEED FORCE. THOUGH IN TRUTH, YOU WERE SIMPLY CONVERTED INTO A HIGHER POWER.
TRANSFORMED INTO PURE ENLIGHTENMENT.
I... KILLED YOU.
I HAVE A RESURRECTION OF MY OWN IN THE DAYS AHEAD, BARRY. THANKS TO A GOOD FRIEND OF YOURS.
YOU...
YOU MURDERED JOHNNY QUICK!
BARRY, WAIT--!
Mm. YES. JOHNNY QUICK. YOU CAUGHT ME RED-HANDED. NOW STOP THIS.
THIS IS NOT A RACE TO SEE WHO'S FASTER.
I AM.
AAHH!

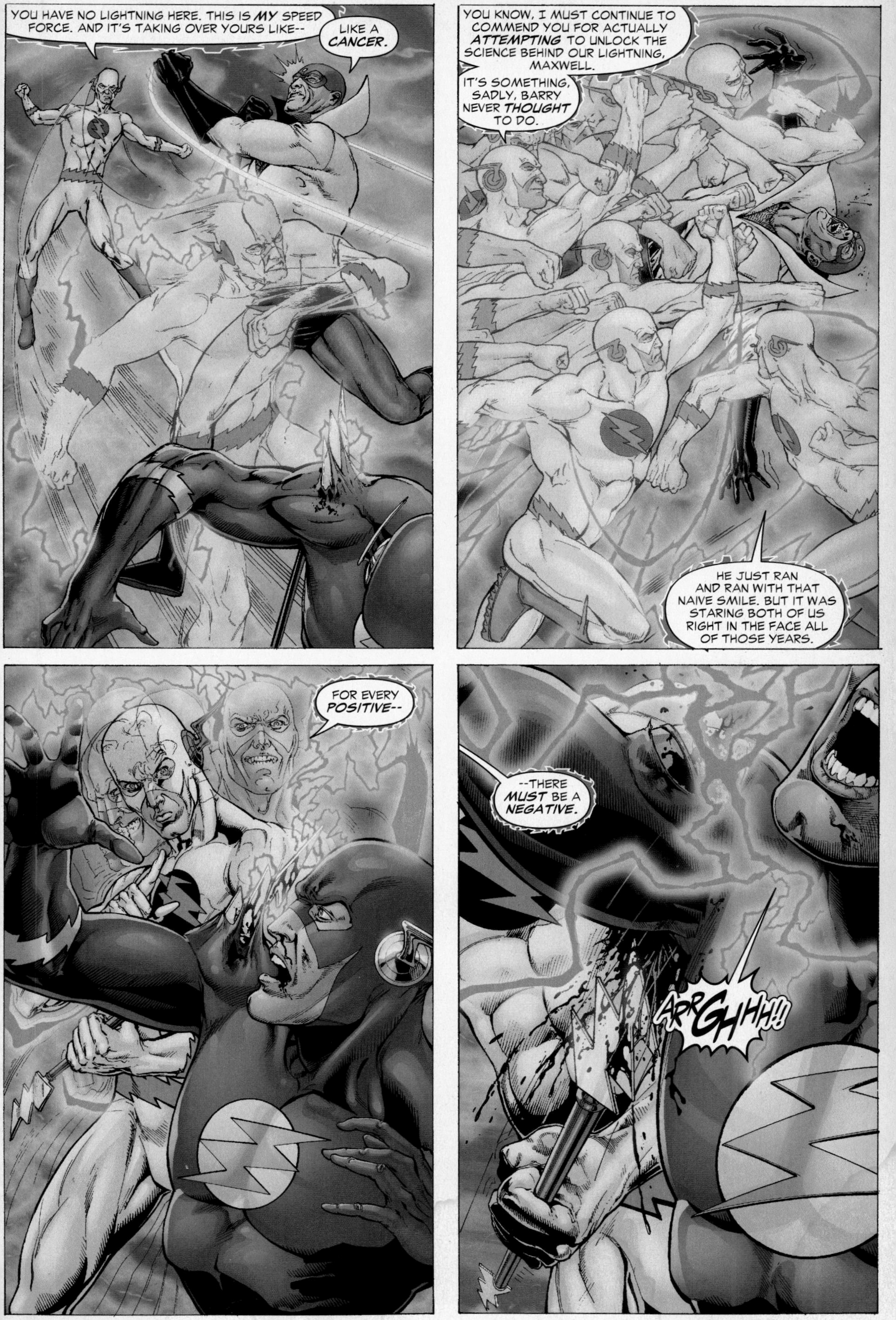

YOU HAVE NO LIGHTNING HERE. THIS IS MY SPEED FORCE. AND IT'S TAKING OVER YOURS LIKE--
LIKE A CANCER.
YOU KNOW, I MUST CONTINUE TO COMMEND YOU FOR ACTUALLY ATTEMPTING TO UNLOCK THE SCIENCE BEHIND OUR LIGHTNING, MAXWELL.
IT'S SOMETHING, SADLY, BARRY NEVER THOUGHT TO DO.
HE JUST RAN AND RAN WITH THAT NAIVE SMILE. BUT IT WAS STARING BOTH OF US RIGHT IN THE FACE ALL OF THOSE YEARS.
FOR EVERY POSITIVE--
--THERE MUST BE A NEGATIVE.
ARRGHHH!!

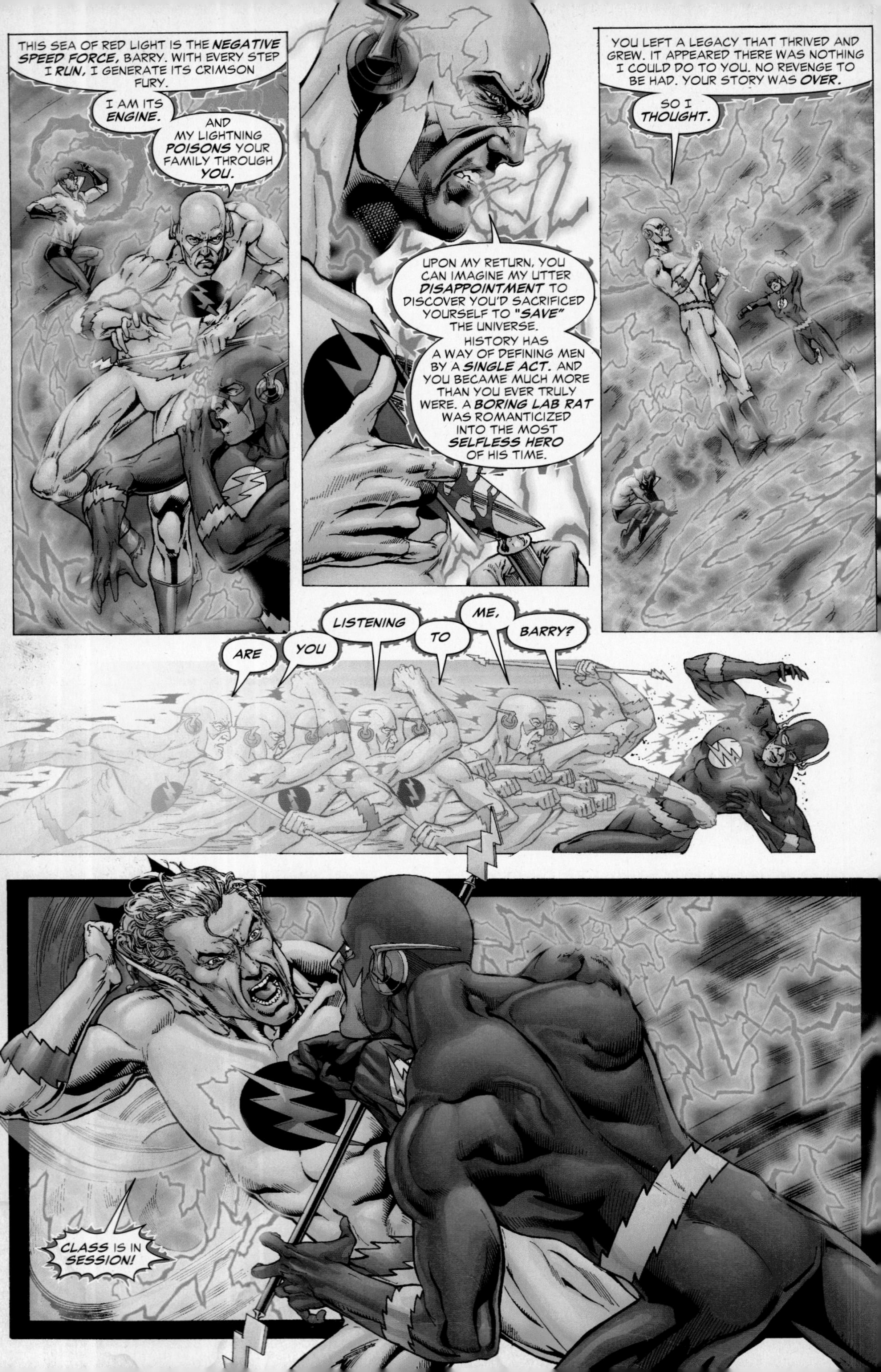
THIS SEA OF RED LIGHT IS THE NEGATIVE SPEED FORCE, BARRY. WITH EVERY STEP I RUN, I GENERATE ITS CRIMSON FURY.
I AM ITS ENGINE.
AND MY LIGHTNING POISONS YOUR FAMILY THROUGH YOU.
UPON MY RETURN, YOU CAN IMAGINE MY UTTER DISAPPOINTMENT TO DISCOVER YOU'D SACRIFICED YOURSELF TO "SAVE" THE UNIVERSE.
HISTORY HAS A WAY OF DEFINING MEN BY A SINGLE ACT. AND YOU BECAME MUCH MORE THAN YOU EVER TRULY WERE. A BORING LAB RAT WAS ROMANTICIZED INTO THE MOST SELFLESS HERO OF HIS TIME.
YOU LEFT A LEGACY THAT THRIVED AND GREW. IT APPEARED THERE WAS NOTHING I COULD DO TO YOU. NO REVENGE TO BE HAD. YOUR STORY WAS OVER.
SO I THOUGHT.
ARE
YOU
LISTENING
TO
ME,
BARRY?
CLASS IS IN SESSION!

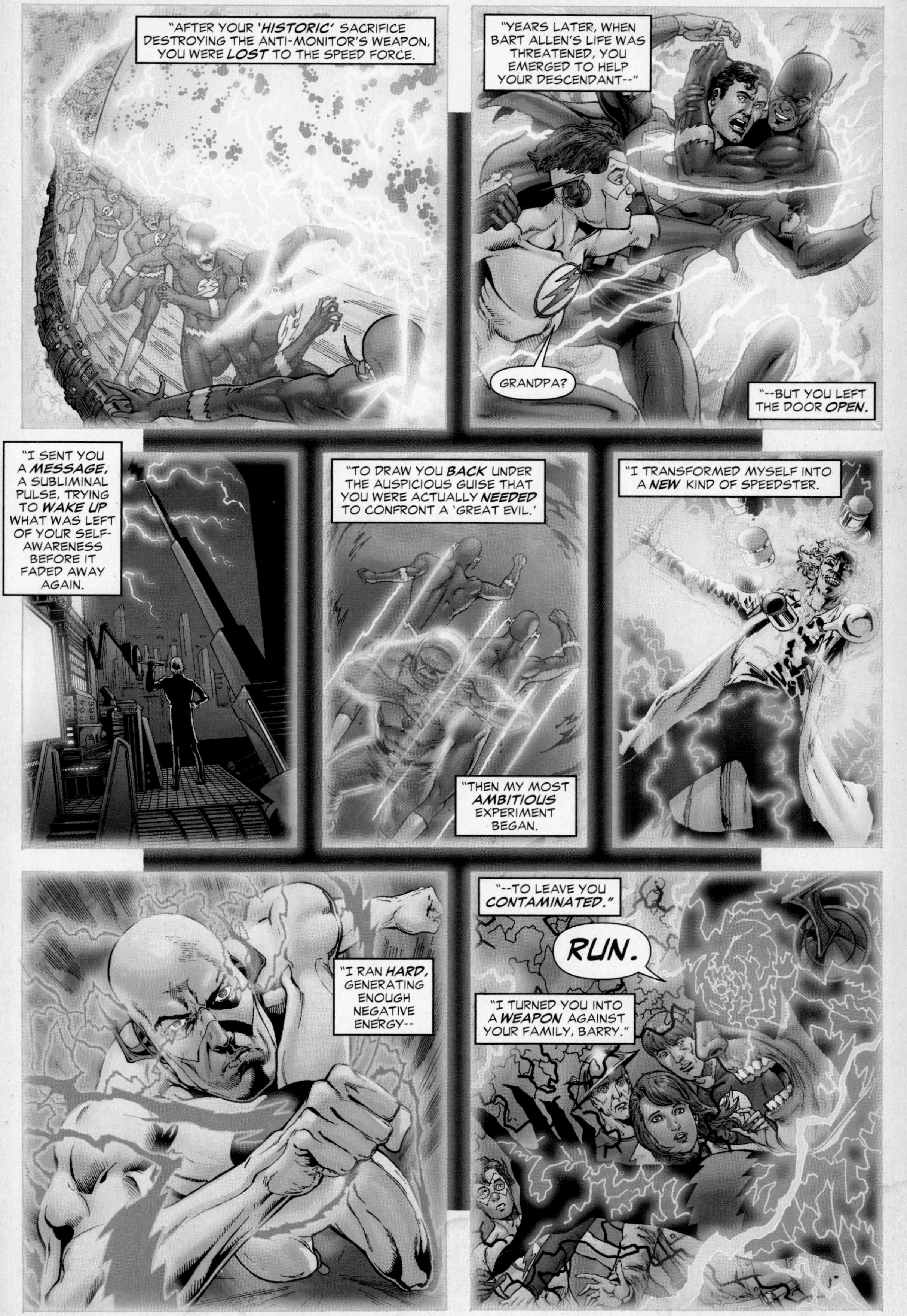
"AFTER YOUR 'HISTORIC' SACRIFICE DESTROYING THE ANTI-MONITOR'S WEAPON, YOU WERE LOST TO THE SPEED FORCE.
"YEARS LATER, WHEN BART ALLEN'S LIFE WAS THREATENED, YOU EMERGED TO HELP YOUR DESCENDANT--"
GRANDPA?
"--BUT YOU LEFT THE DOOR OPEN.
"I SENT YOU A MESSAGE, A SUBLIMINAL PULSE, TRYING TO WAKE UP WHAT WAS LEFT OF YOUR SELF-AWARENESS BEFORE IT FADED AWAY AGAIN.
"TO DRAW YOU BACK UNDER THE AUSPICIOUS GUISE THAT YOU WERE ACTUALLY NEEDED TO CONFRONT A 'GREAT EVIL.'
"THEN MY MOST AMBITIOUS EXPERIMENT BEGAN.
"I TRANSFORMED MYSELF INTO A NEW KIND OF SPEEDSTER.
"I RAN HARD, GENERATING ENOUGH NEGATIVE ENERGY--
"--TO LEAVE YOU CONTAMINATED."
RUN.
"I TURNED YOU INTO A WEAPON AGAINST YOUR FAMILY, BARRY."

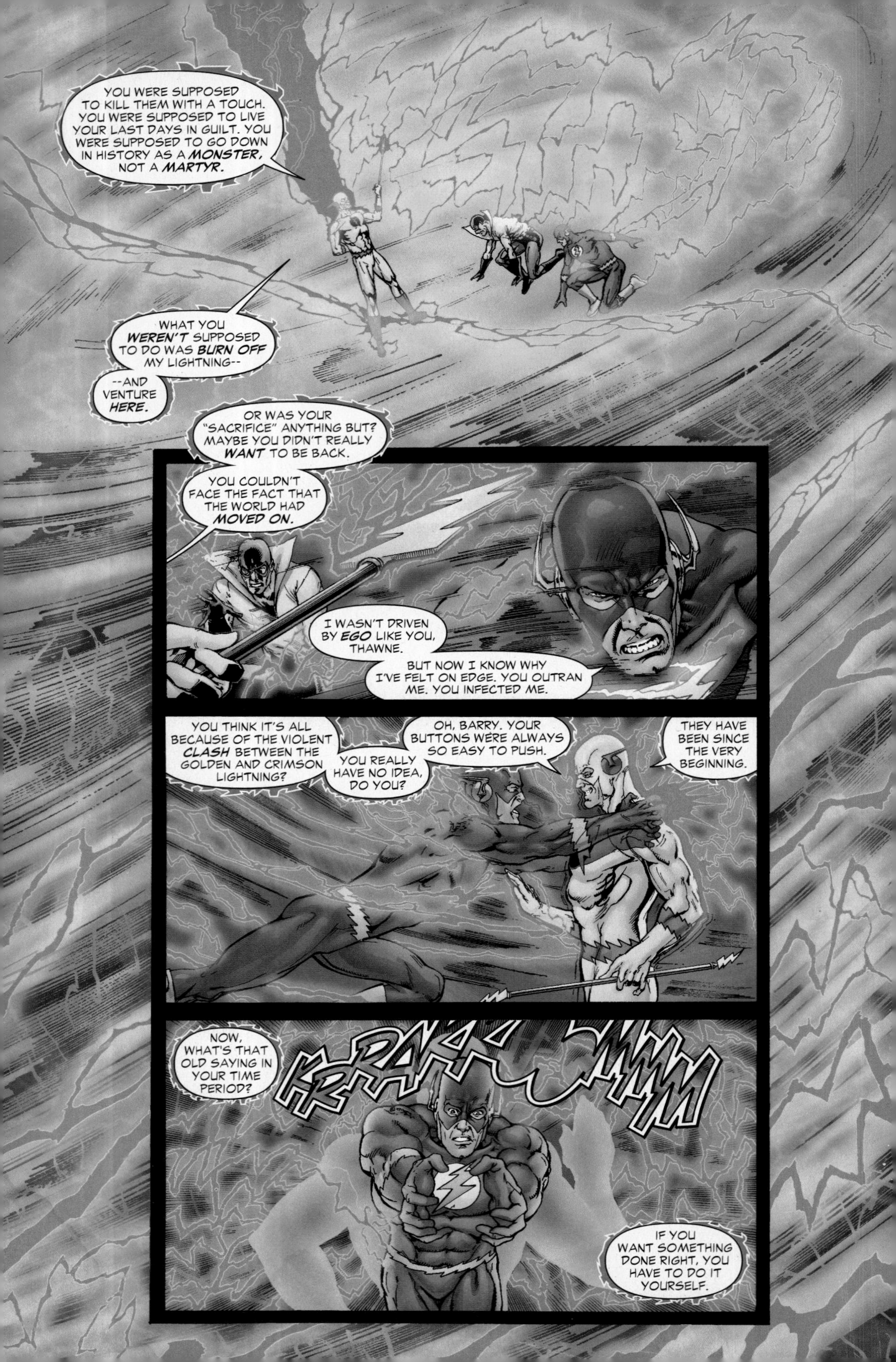
YOU WERE SUPPOSED TO KILL THEM WITH A TOUCH. YOU WERE SUPPOSED TO LIVE YOUR LAST DAYS IN GUILT. YOU WERE SUPPOSED TO GO DOWN IN HISTORY AS A MONSTER, NOT A MARTYR.
WHAT YOU WEREN'T SUPPOSED TO DO WAS BURN OFF MY LIGHTNING--
--AND VENTURE HERE.
OR WAS YOUR "SACRIFICE" ANYTHING BUT? MAYBE YOU DIDN'T REALLY WANT TO BE BACK.
YOU COULDN'T FACE THE FACT THAT THE WORLD HAD MOVED ON.
I WASN'T DRIVEN BY EGO LIKE YOU, THAWNE.
BUT NOW I KNOW WHY I'VE FELT ON EDGE. YOU OUTRAN ME. YOU INFECTED ME.
YOU THINK IT'S ALL BECAUSE OF THE VIOLENT CLASH BETWEEN THE GOLDEN AND CRIMSON LIGHTNING?
YOU REALLY HAVE NO IDEA, DO YOU?
OH, BARRY. YOUR BUTTONS WERE ALWAYS SO EASY TO PUSH.
THEY HAVE BEEN SINCE THE VERY BEGINNING.
NOW, WHAT'S THAT OLD SAYING IN YOUR TIME PERIOD?
KRAKA-VMMM
IF YOU WANT SOMETHING DONE RIGHT, YOU HAVE TO DO IT YOURSELF.

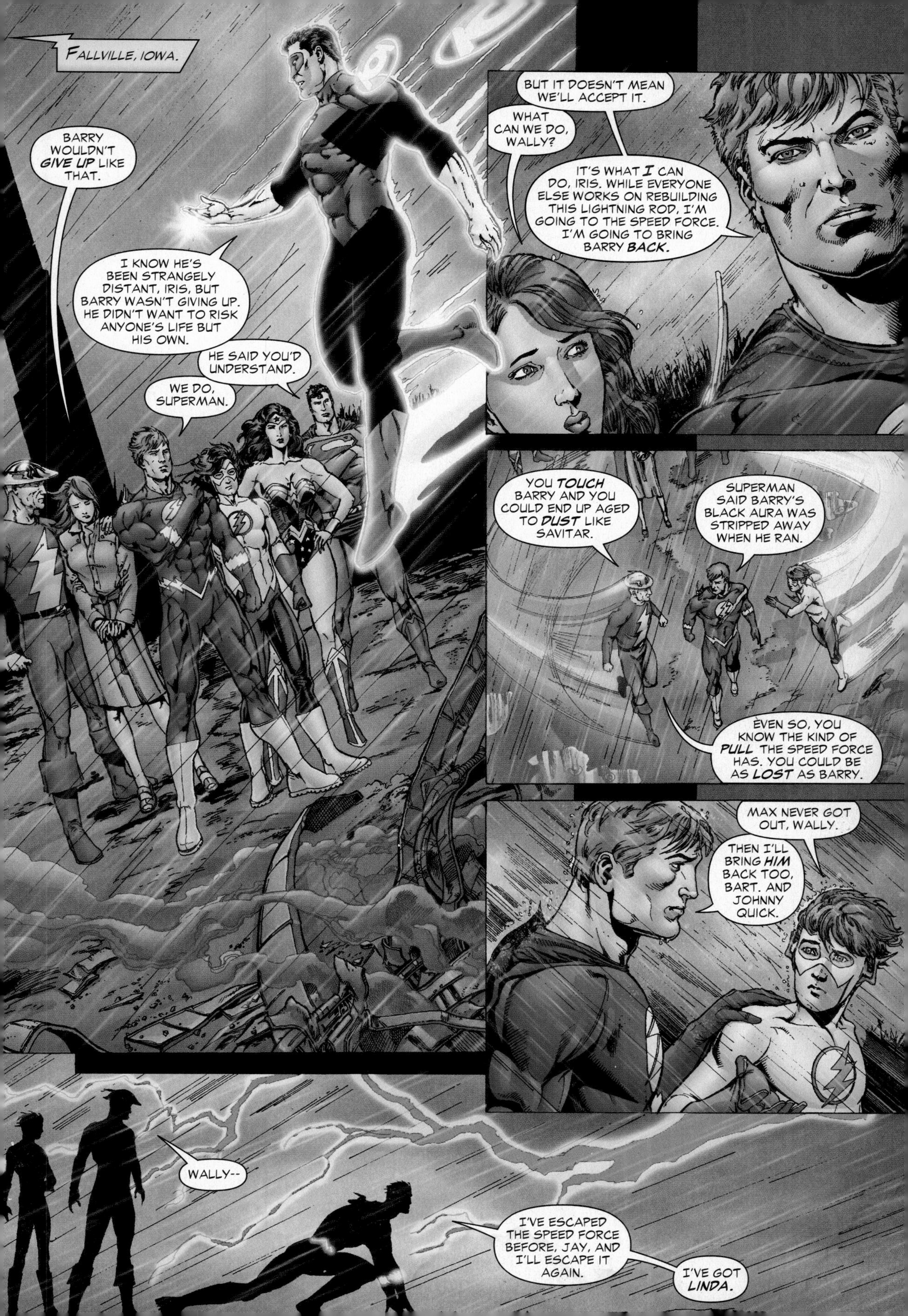

FALLVILLE, IOWA.
BARRY WOULDN'T GIVE UP LIKE THAT.
I KNOW HE'S BEEN STRANGELY DISTANT, IRIS, BUT BARRY WASN'T GIVING UP. HE DIDN'T WANT TO RISK ANYONE'S LIFE BUT HIS OWN.
HE SAID YOU'D UNDERSTAND.
WE DO, SUPERMAN.
BUT IT DOESN'T MEAN WE'LL ACCEPT IT.
WHAT CAN WE DO, WALLY?
IT'S WHAT I CAN DO, IRIS. WHILE EVERYONE ELSE WORKS ON REBUILDING THIS LIGHTNING ROD, I'M GOING TO THE SPEED FORCE. I'M GOING TO BRING BARRY BACK.
YOU TOUCH BARRY AND YOU COULD END UP AGED TO DUST LIKE SAVITAR.
SUPERMAN SAID BARRY'S BLACK AURA WAS STRIPPED AWAY WHEN HE RAN.
EVEN SO, YOU KNOW THE KIND OF PULL THE SPEED FORCE HAS. YOU COULD BE AS LOST AS BARRY.
MAX NEVER GOT OUT, WALLY.
THEN I'LL BRING HIM BACK TOO, BART. AND JOHNNY QUICK.
WALLY--
I'VE ESCAPED THE SPEED FORCE BEFORE, JAY, AND I'LL ESCAPE IT AGAIN.
I'VE GOT LINDA.

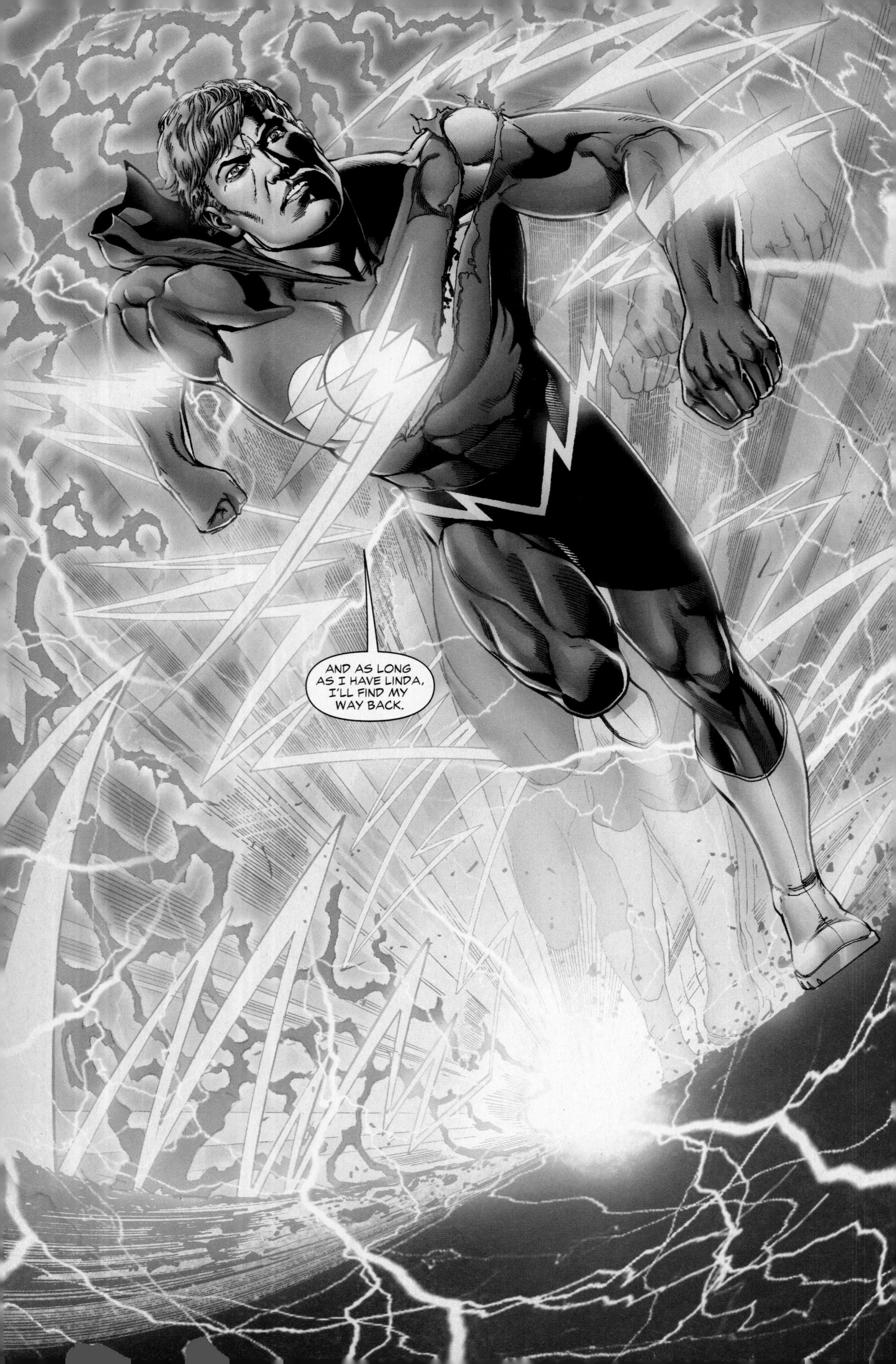
AND AS LONG AS I HAVE LINDA, I'LL FIND MY WAY BACK.

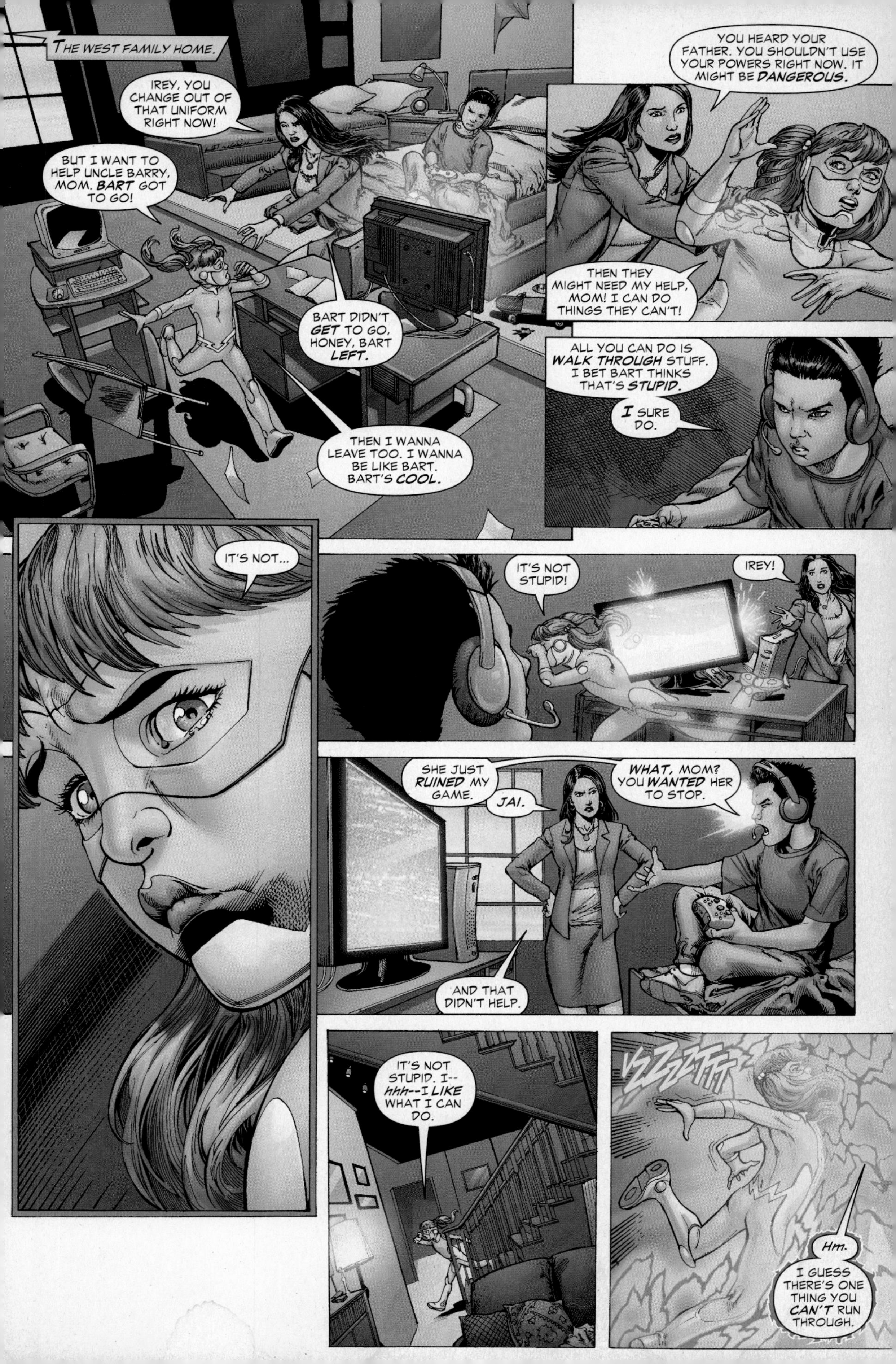
THE WEST FAMILY HOME.
IREY, YOU CHANGE OUT OF THAT UNIFORM RIGHT NOW!
BUT I WANT TO HELP UNCLE BARRY, MOM. BART GOT TO GO!
BART DIDN'T GET TO GO, HONEY, BART LEFT.
THEN I WANNA LEAVE TOO. I WANNA BE LIKE BART. BART'S COOL.
YOU HEARD YOUR FATHER. YOU SHOULDN'T USE YOUR POWERS RIGHT NOW. IT MIGHT BE DANGEROUS.
THEN THEY MIGHT NEED MY HELP, MOM! I CAN DO THINGS THEY CAN'T!
ALL YOU CAN DO IS WALK THROUGH STUFF. I BET BART THINKS THAT'S STUPID.
I SURE DO.
IT'S NOT...
IT'S NOT STUPID!
IREY!
SHE JUST RUINED MY GAME.
JAI.
WHAT, MOM? YOU WANTED HER TO STOP.
'AND THAT DIDN'T HELP.
IT'S NOT STUPID. I-- hhh--I LIKE WHAT I CAN DO.
VZZZZTTT
Hm.
I GUESS THERE'S ONE THING YOU CAN'T RUN THROUGH.

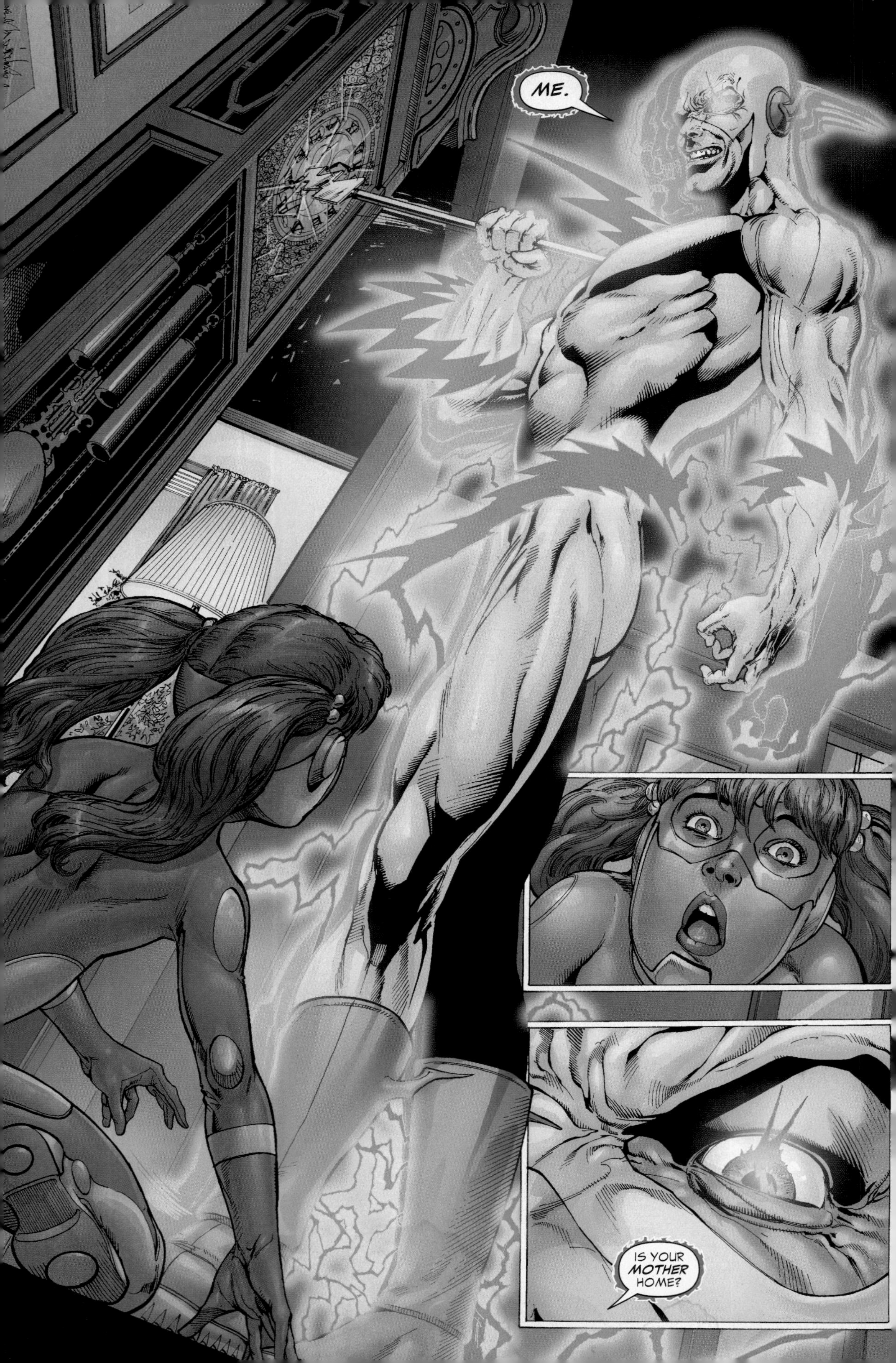
ME.
IS YOUR MOTHER HOME?

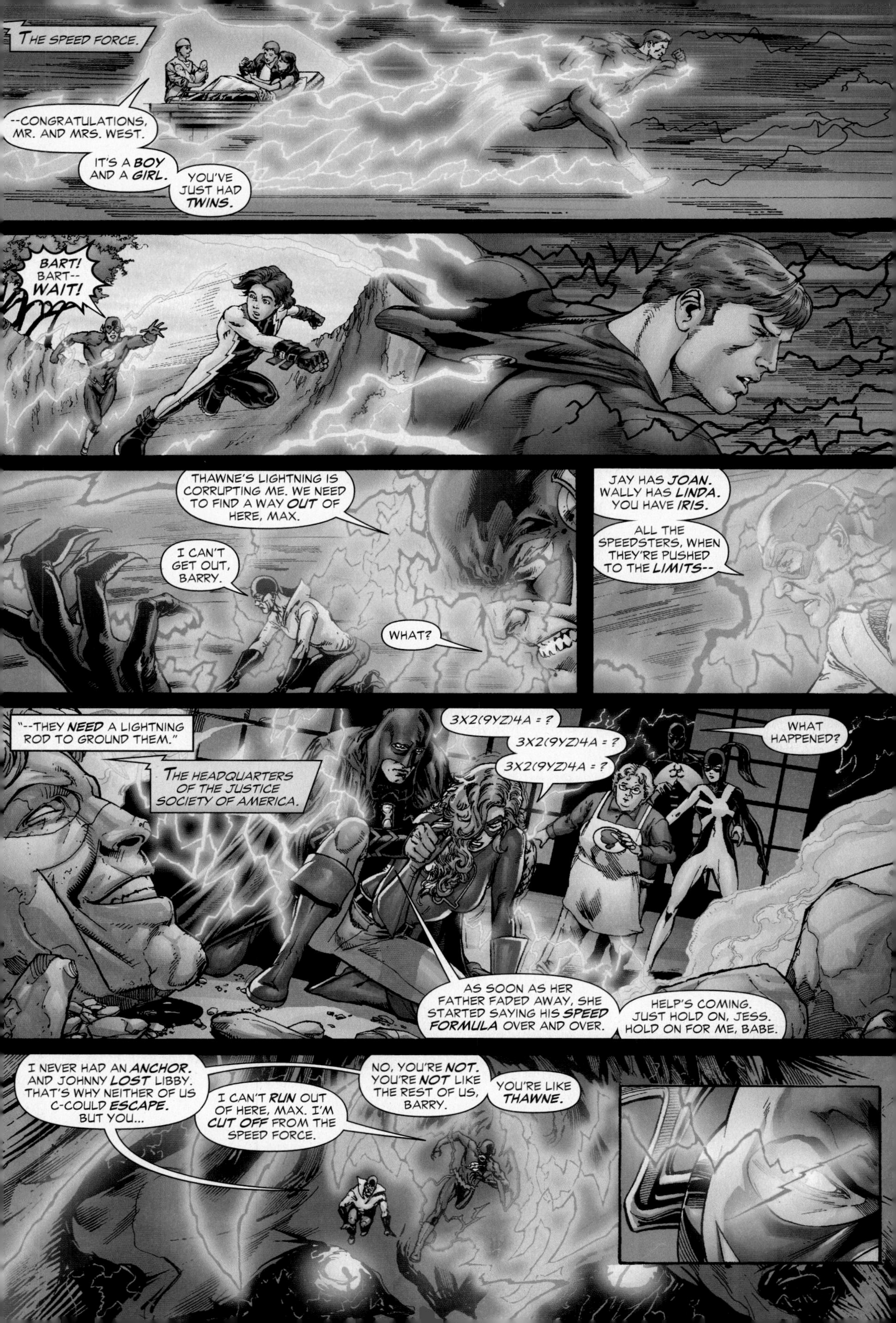
THE SPEED FORCE.
--CONGRATULATIONS, MR. AND MRS. WEST.
IT'S A BOY AND A GIRL.
YOU'VE JUST HAD TWINS.
BART! BART-- WAIT!
THAWNE'S LIGHTNING IS CORRUPTING ME. WE NEED TO FIND A WAY OUT OF HERE, MAX.
I CAN'T GET OUT, BARRY.
WHAT?
JAY HAS JOAN. WALLY HAS LINDA. YOU HAVE IRIS.
ALL THE SPEEDSTERS, WHEN THEY'RE PUSHED TO THE LIMITS--
"--THEY NEED A LIGHTNING ROD TO GROUND THEM."
THE HEADQUARTERS OF THE JUSTICE SOCIETY OF AMERICA.
3X2(9YZ)4A = ?
3X2(9YZ)4A = ?
3X2(9YZ)4A = ?
WHAT HAPPENED?
AS SOON AS HER FATHER FADED AWAY, SHE STARTED SAYING HIS SPEED FORMULA OVER AND OVER.
HELP'S COMING. JUST HOLD ON, JESS. HOLD ON FOR ME, BABE.
I NEVER HAD AN ANCHOR. AND JOHNNY LOST LIBBY. THAT'S WHY NEITHER OF US C-COULD ESCAPE. BUT YOU...
I CAN'T RUN OUT OF HERE, MAX. I'M CUT OFF FROM THE SPEED FORCE.
NO, YOU'RE NOT. YOU'RE NOT LIKE THE REST OF US, BARRY.
YOU'RE LIKE THAWNE.

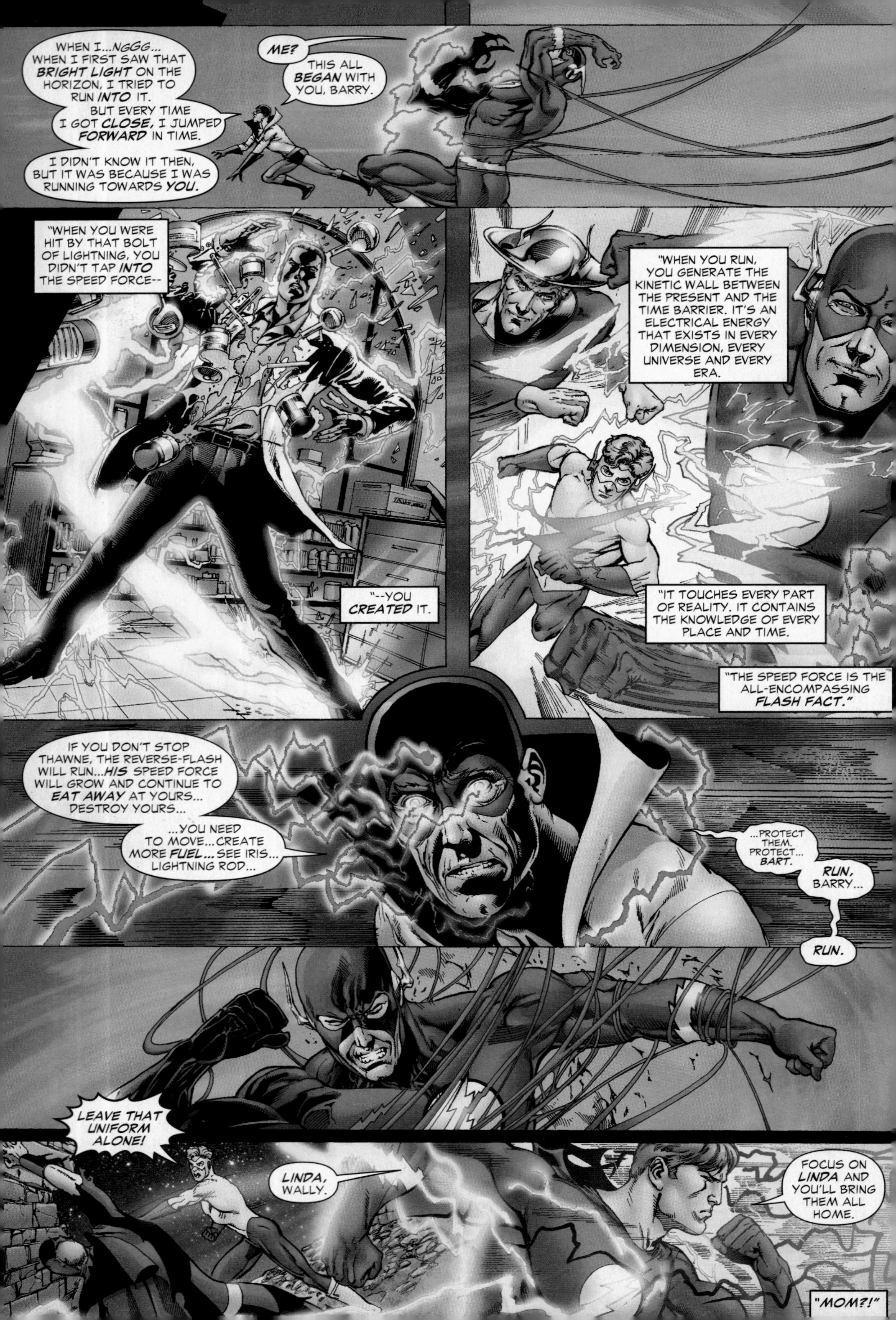
WHEN I...NGGG... WHEN I FIRST SAW THAT BRIGHT LIGHT ON THE HORIZON, I TRIED TO RUN INTO IT.
BUT EVERY TIME I GOT CLOSE, I JUMPED FORWARD IN TIME.
I DIDN'T KNOW IT THEN, BUT IT WAS BECAUSE I WAS RUNNING TOWARDS YOU.
ME?
THIS ALL BEGAN WITH YOU, BARRY.
"WHEN YOU WERE HIT BY THAT BOLT OF LIGHTNING, YOU DIDN'T TAP INTO THE SPEED FORCE--
"--YOU CREATED IT.
"WHEN YOU RUN, YOU GENERATE THE KINETIC WALL BETWEEN THE PRESENT AND THE TIME BARRIER. IT'S AN ELECTRICAL ENERGY THAT EXISTS IN EVERY DIMENSION, EVERY UNIVERSE AND EVERY ERA.
"IT TOUCHES EVERY PART OF REALITY. IT CONTAINS THE KNOWLEDGE OF EVERY PLACE AND TIME.
"THE SPEED FORCE IS THE ALL-ENCOMPASSING FLASH FACT."
IF YOU DON'T STOP THAWNE, THE REVERSE-FLASH WILL RUN...HIS SPEED FORCE WILL GROW AND CONTINUE TO EAT AWAY AT YOURS... DESTROY YOURS...
...YOU NEED TO MOVE...CREATE MORE FUEL... SEE IRIS... LIGHTNING ROD...
...PROTECT THEM. PROTECT... BART.
RUN, BARRY...
RUN.
LEAVE THAT UNIFORM ALONE!
LINDA, WALLY.
FOCUS ON LINDA AND YOU'LL BRING THEM ALL HOME.
"MOM?!"

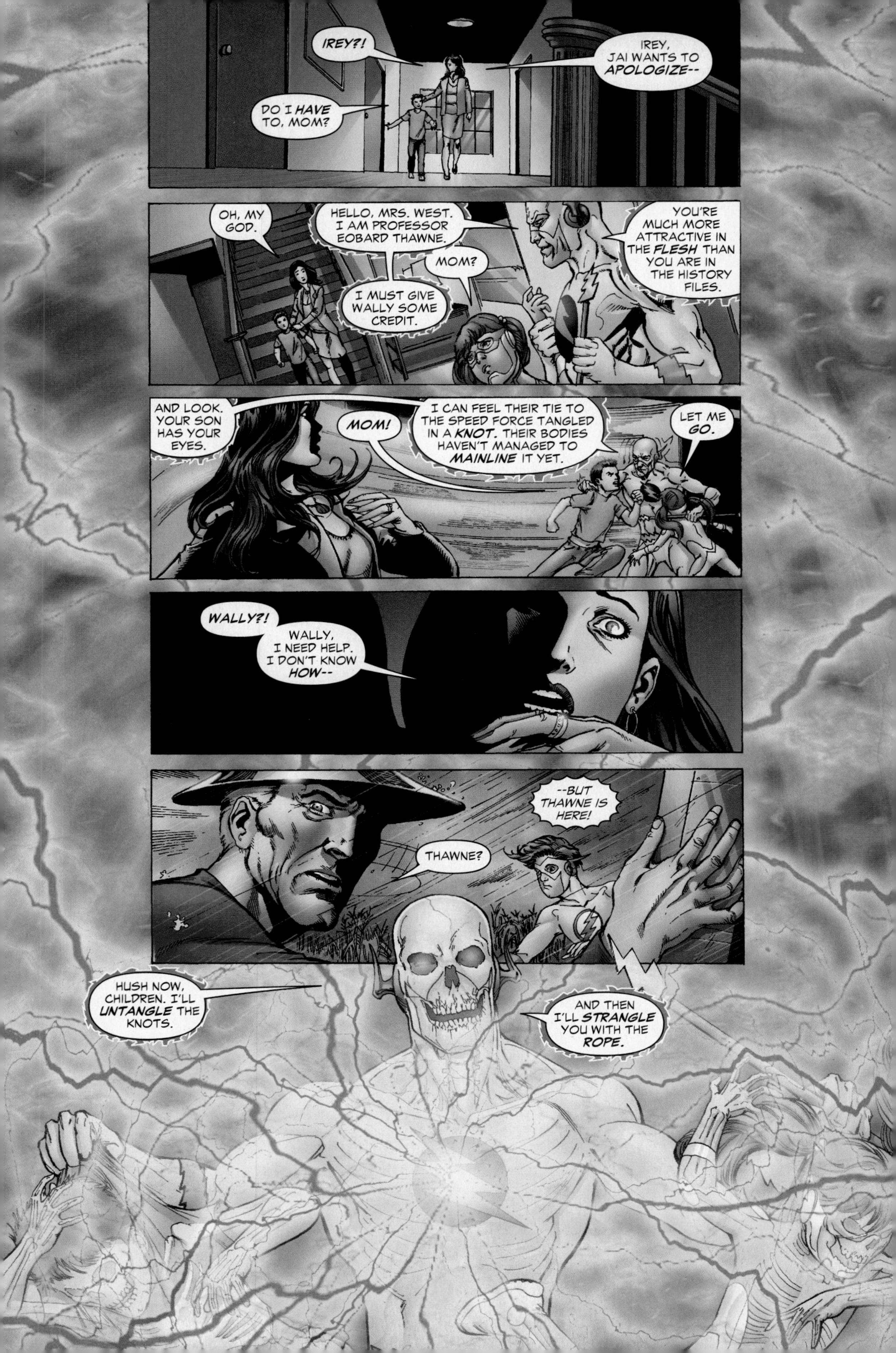
IREY?!
IREY, JAI WANTS TO APOLOGIZE--
DO I HAVE TO, MOM?
OH, MY GOD.
HELLO, MRS. WEST. I AM PROFESSOR EOBARD THAWNE.
I MUST GIVE WALLY SOME CREDIT.
MOM?
YOU'RE MUCH MORE ATTRACTIVE IN THE FLESH THAN YOU ARE IN THE HISTORY FILES.
AND LOOK. YOUR SON HAS YOUR EYES.
MOM!
I CAN FEEL THEIR TIE TO THE SPEED FORCE TANGLED IN A KNOT. THEIR BODIES HAVEN'T MANAGED TO MAINLINE IT YET.
LET ME GO.
WALLY?!
WALLY, I NEED HELP. I DON'T KNOW HOW--
--BUT THAWNE IS HERE!
THAWNE?
HUSH NOW, CHILDREN. I'LL UNTANGLE THE KNOTS.
AND THEN I'LL STRANGLE YOU WITH THE ROPE.

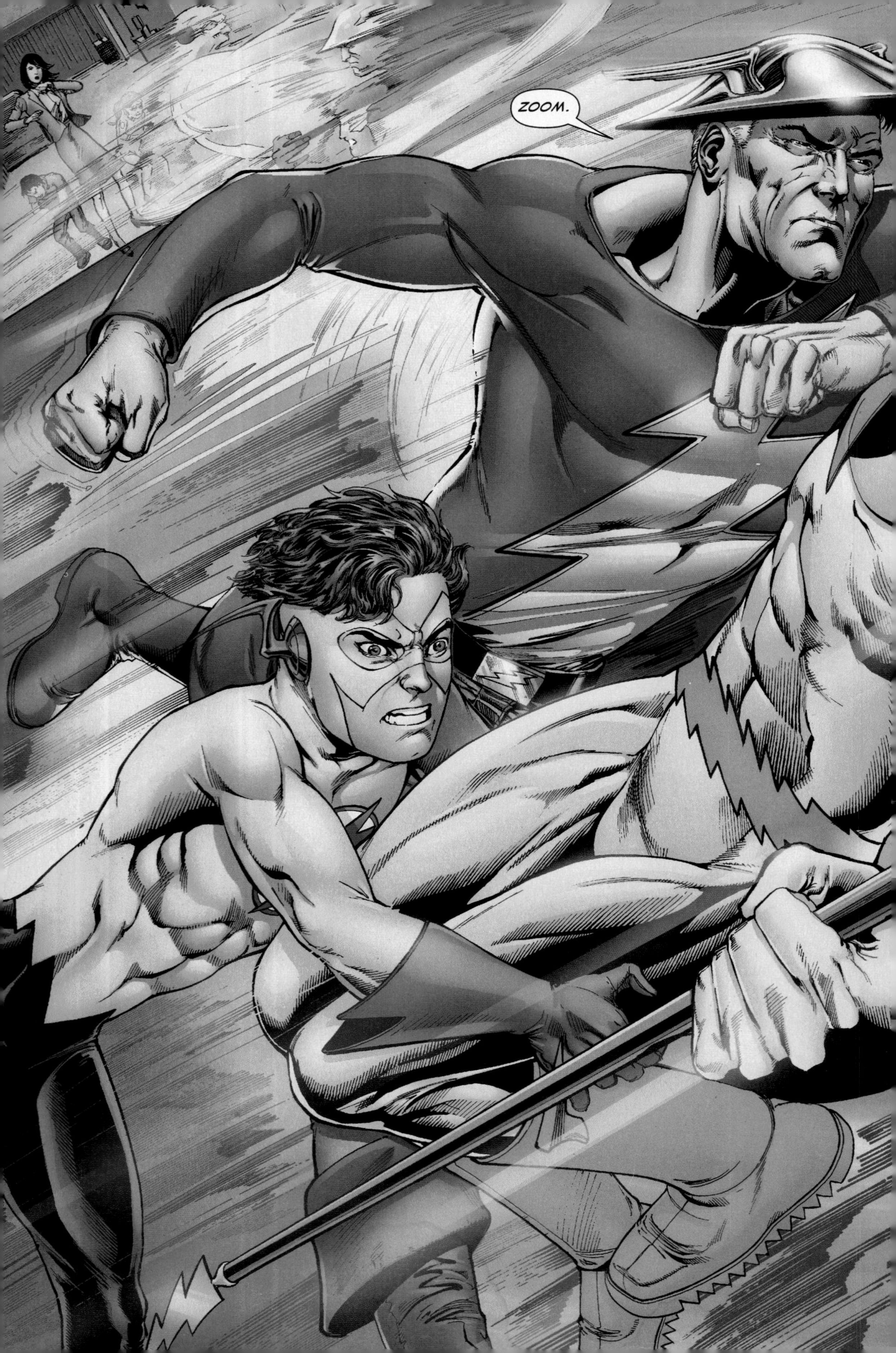
ZOOM.

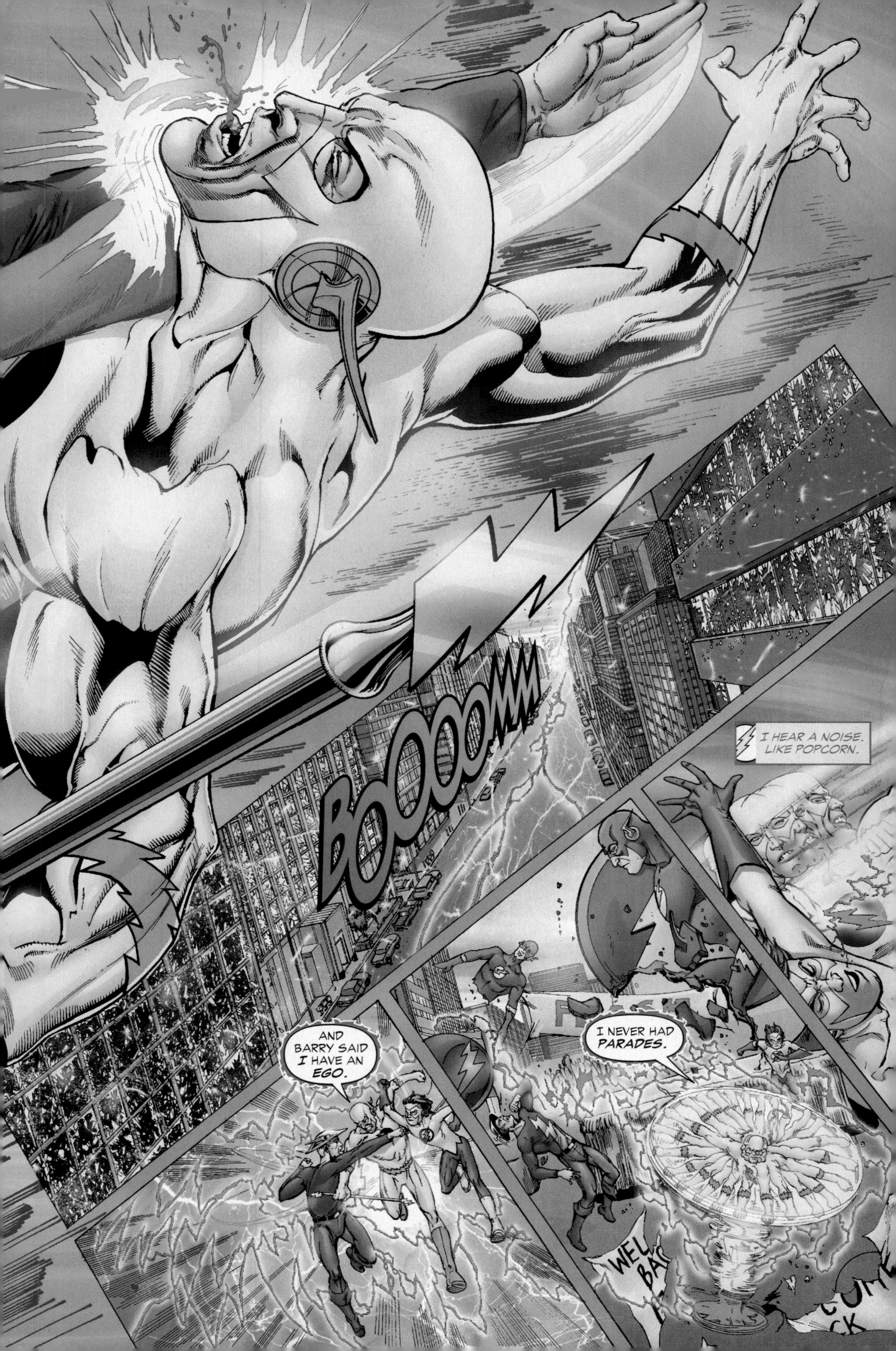

BOOOOMMM
I HEAR A NOISE. LIKE POPCORN.
AND BARRY SAID I HAVE AN EGO.
I NEVER HAD PARADES.

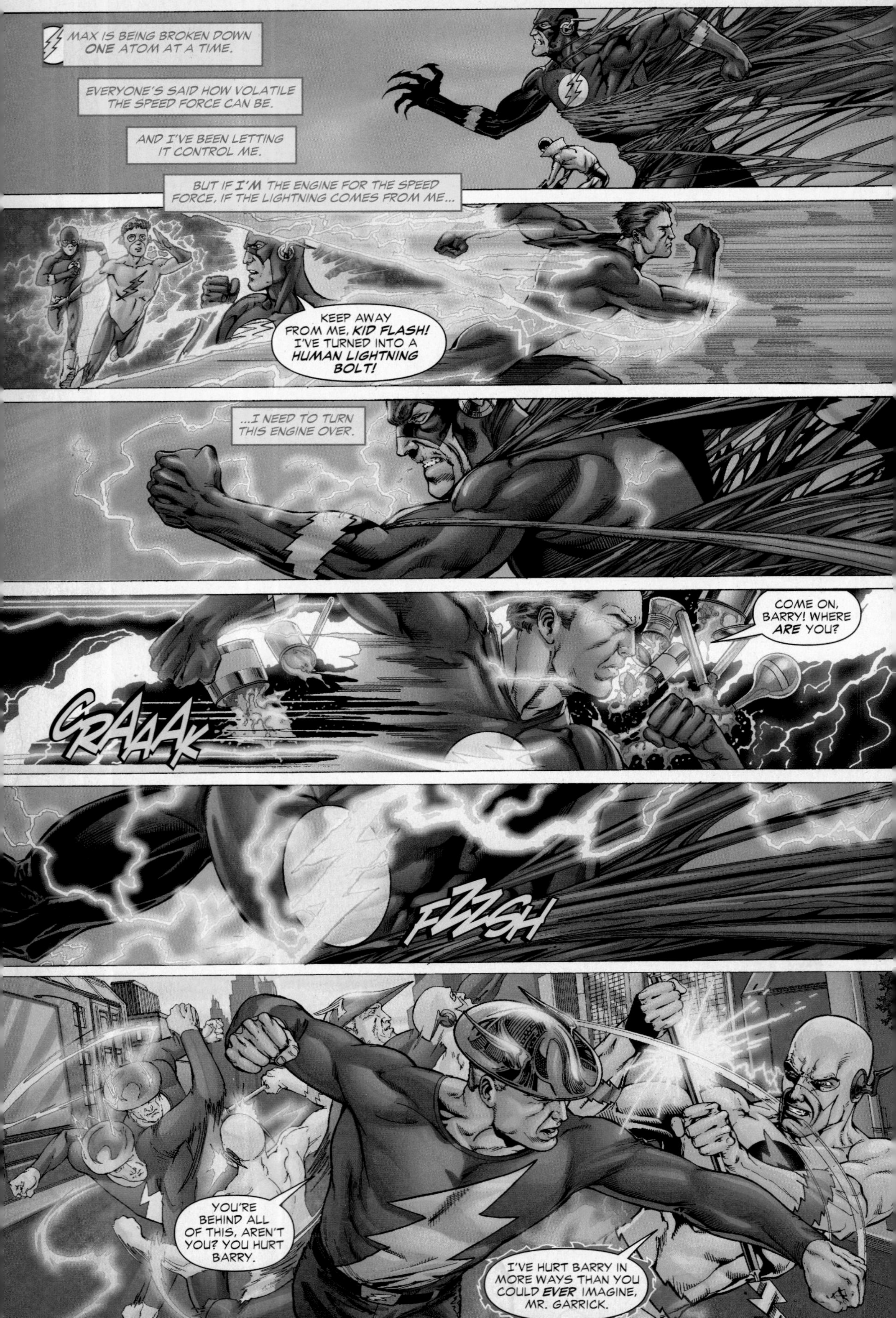
MAX IS BEING BROKEN DOWN ONE ATOM AT A TIME.
EVERYONE'S SAID HOW VOLATILE THE SPEED FORCE CAN BE.
AND I'VE BEEN LETTING IT CONTROL ME.
BUT IF I'M THE ENGINE FOR THE SPEED FORCE, IF THE LIGHTNING COMES FROM ME...
KEEP AWAY FROM ME, KID FLASH! I'VE TURNED INTO A HUMAN LIGHTNING BOLT!
...I NEED TO TURN THIS ENGINE OVER.
COME ON, BARRY! WHERE ARE YOU?
CRAAAK
FZZSH
YOU'RE BEHIND ALL OF THIS, AREN'T YOU? YOU HURT BARRY.
I'VE HURT BARRY IN MORE WAYS THAN YOU COULD EVER IMAGINE, MR. GARRICK.

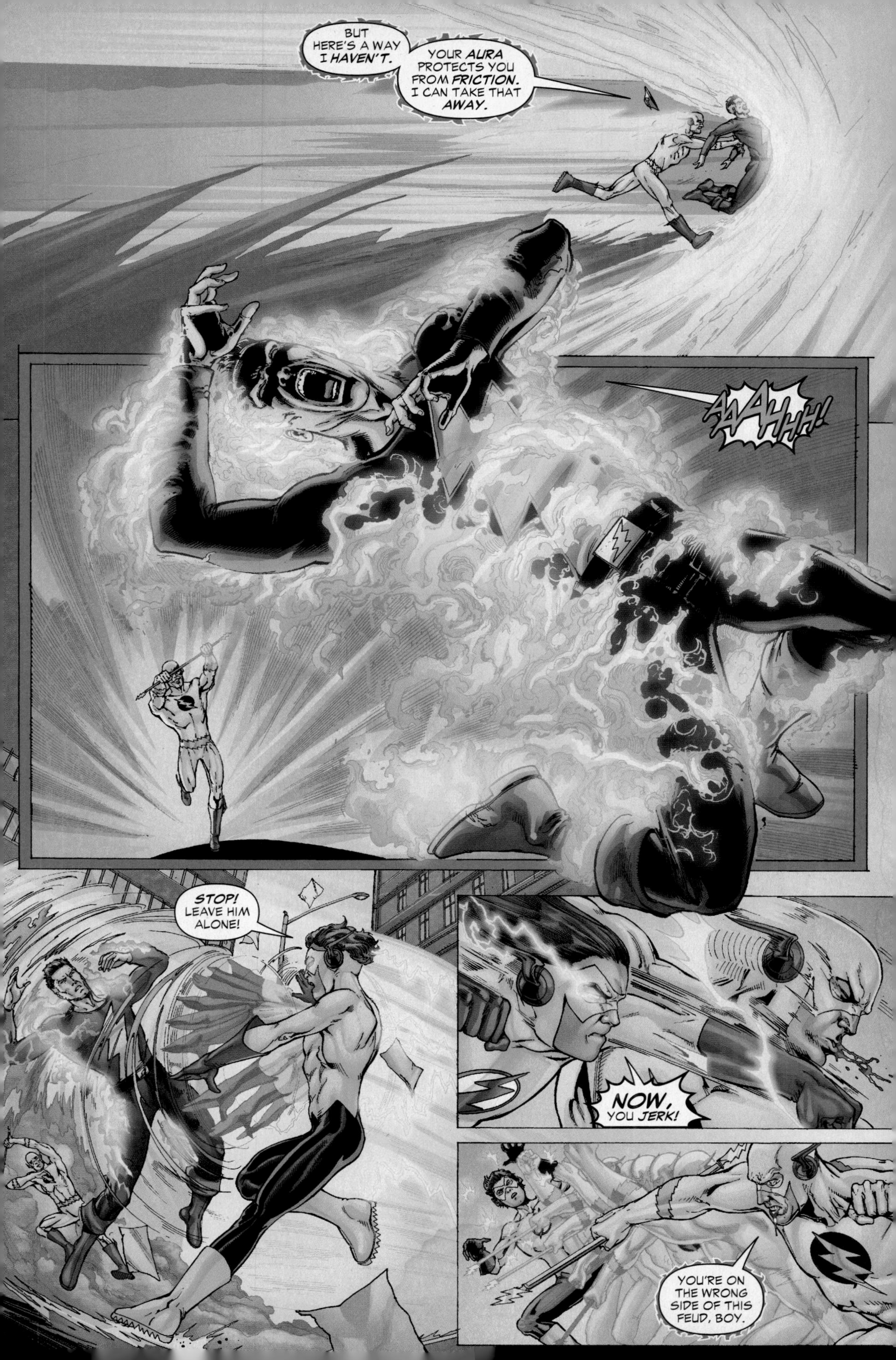

BUT HERE'S A WAY I HAVEN'T.
YOUR AURA PROTECTS YOU FROM FRICTION. I CAN TAKE THAT AWAY.
AAAHHH!
STOP! LEAVE HIM ALONE!
NOW, YOU JERK!
YOU'RE ON THE WRONG SIDE OF THIS FEUD, BOY.

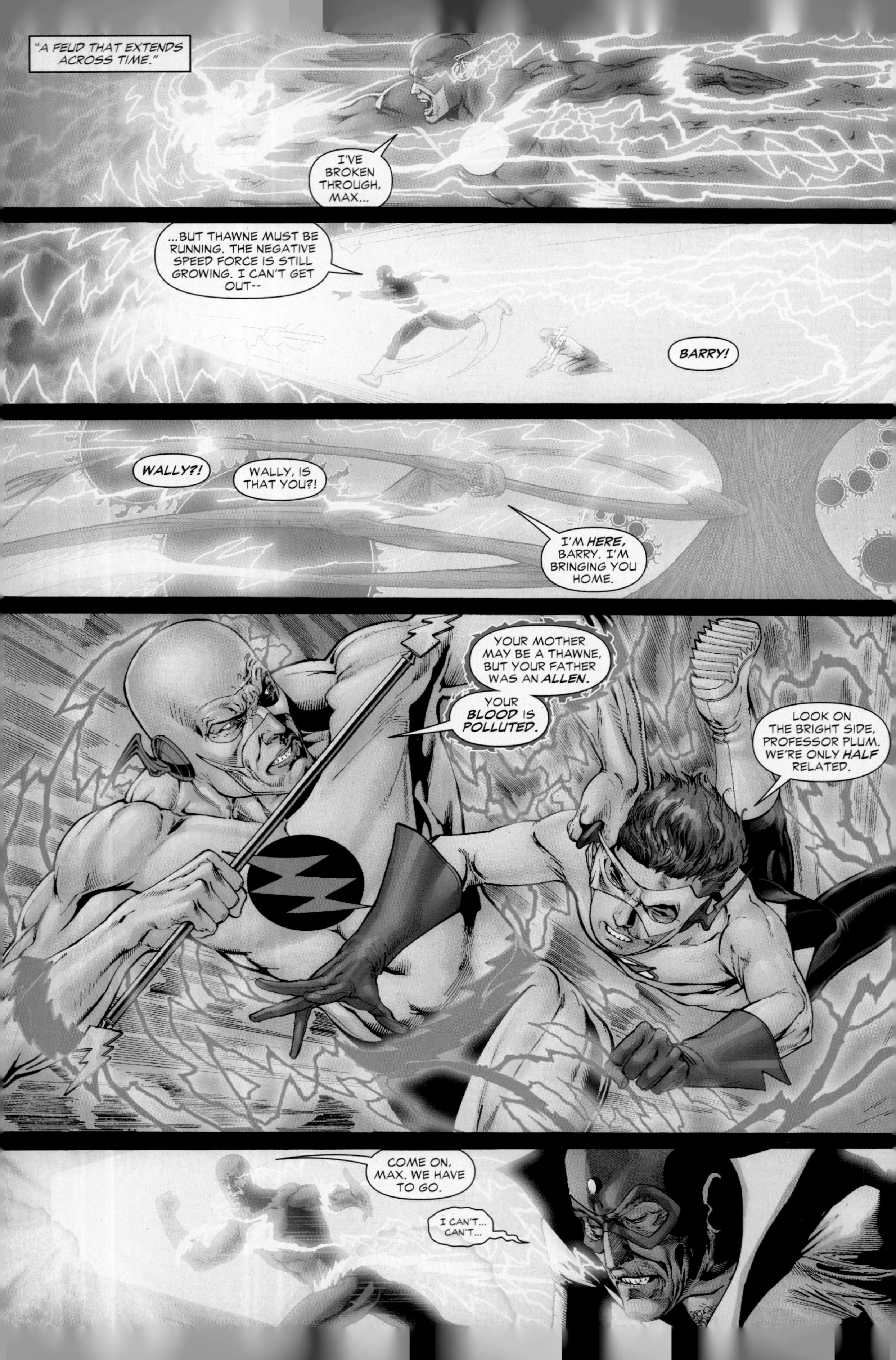

"A FEUD THAT EXTENDS ACROSS TIME."
I'VE BROKEN THROUGH, MAX...
...BUT THAWNE MUST BE RUNNING. THE NEGATIVE SPEED FORCE IS STILL GROWING. I CAN'T GET OUT--
BARRY!
WALLY?!
WALLY, IS THAT YOU?!
I'M HERE, BARRY. I'M BRINGING YOU HOME.
YOUR MOTHER MAY BE A THAWNE, BUT YOUR FATHER WAS AN ALLEN.
YOUR BLOOD IS POLLUTED.
LOOK ON THE BRIGHT SIDE, PROFESSOR PLUM. WE'RE ONLY HALF RELATED.
COME ON, MAX. WE HAVE TO GO.
I CAN'T... CAN'T...

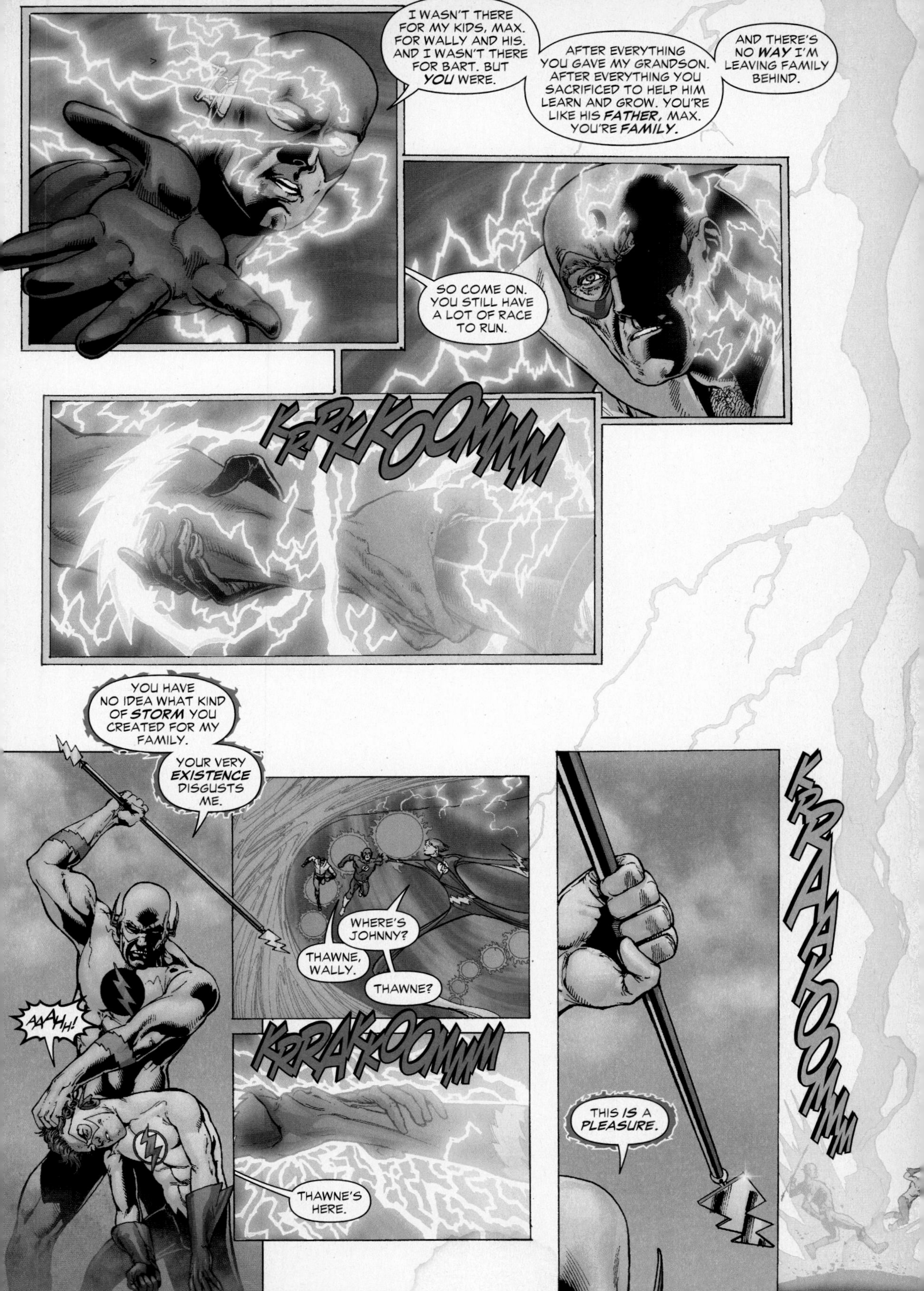
I WASN'T THERE FOR MY KIDS, MAX. FOR WALLY AND HIS. AND I WASN'T THERE FOR BART. BUT YOU WERE.
AFTER EVERYTHING YOU GAVE MY GRANDSON. AFTER EVERYTHING YOU SACRIFICED TO HELP HIM LEARN AND GROW. YOU'RE LIKE HIS FATHER, MAX. YOU'RE FAMILY.
AND THERE'S NO WAY I'M LEAVING FAMILY BEHIND.
SO COME ON. YOU STILL HAVE A LOT OF RACE TO RUN.
KRRKKOOMMM
YOU HAVE NO IDEA WHAT KIND OF STORM YOU CREATED FOR MY FAMILY.
YOUR VERY EXISTENCE DISGUSTS ME.
AAAHH!
WHERE'S JOHNNY?
THAWNE, WALLY.
THAWNE?
KRRAKOOMMM
THAWNE'S HERE.
THIS IS A PLEASURE.
KRRAAAKOOMMM

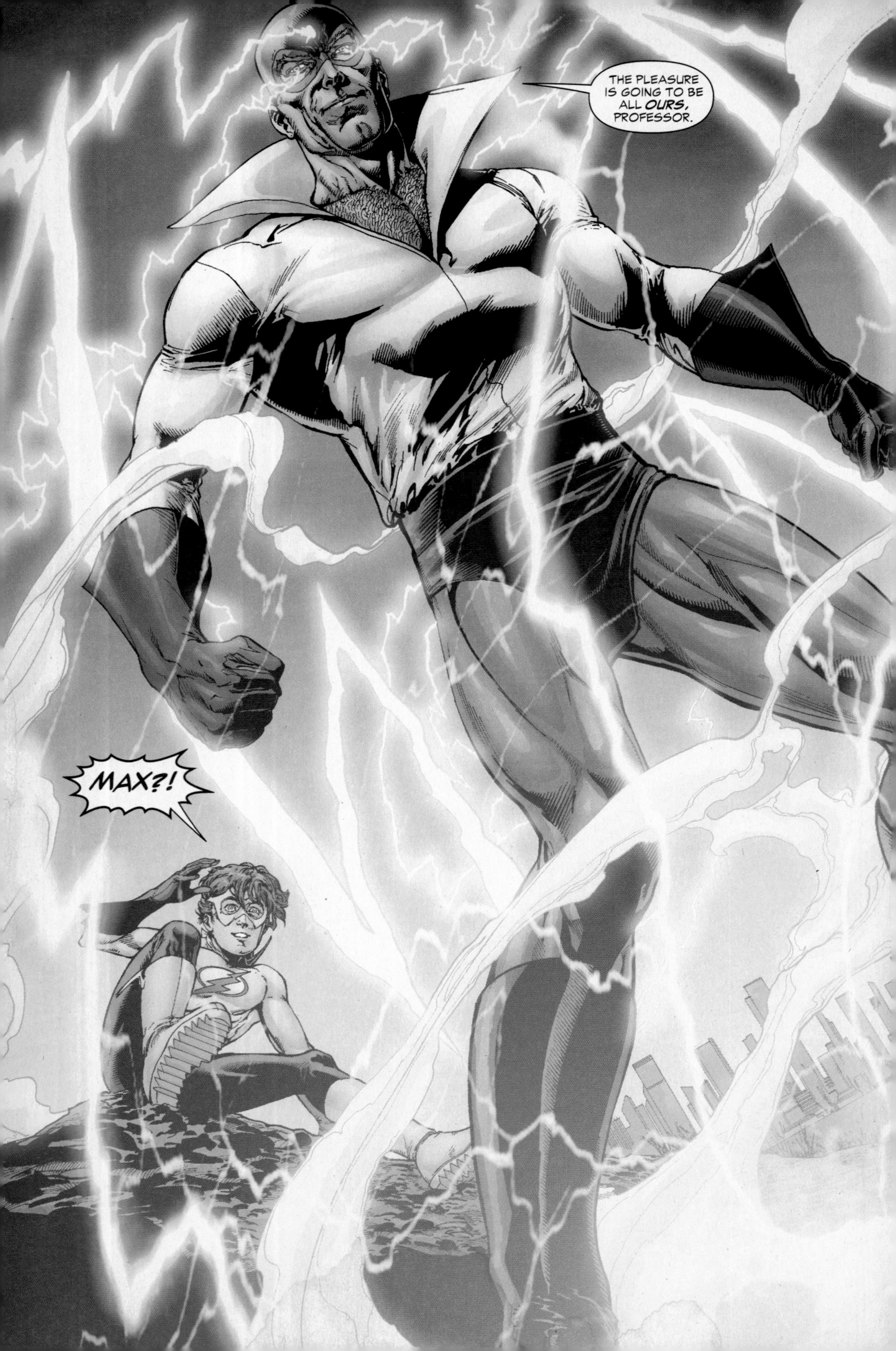
THE PLEASURE IS GOING TO BE ALL OURS, PROFESSOR.
MAX?!

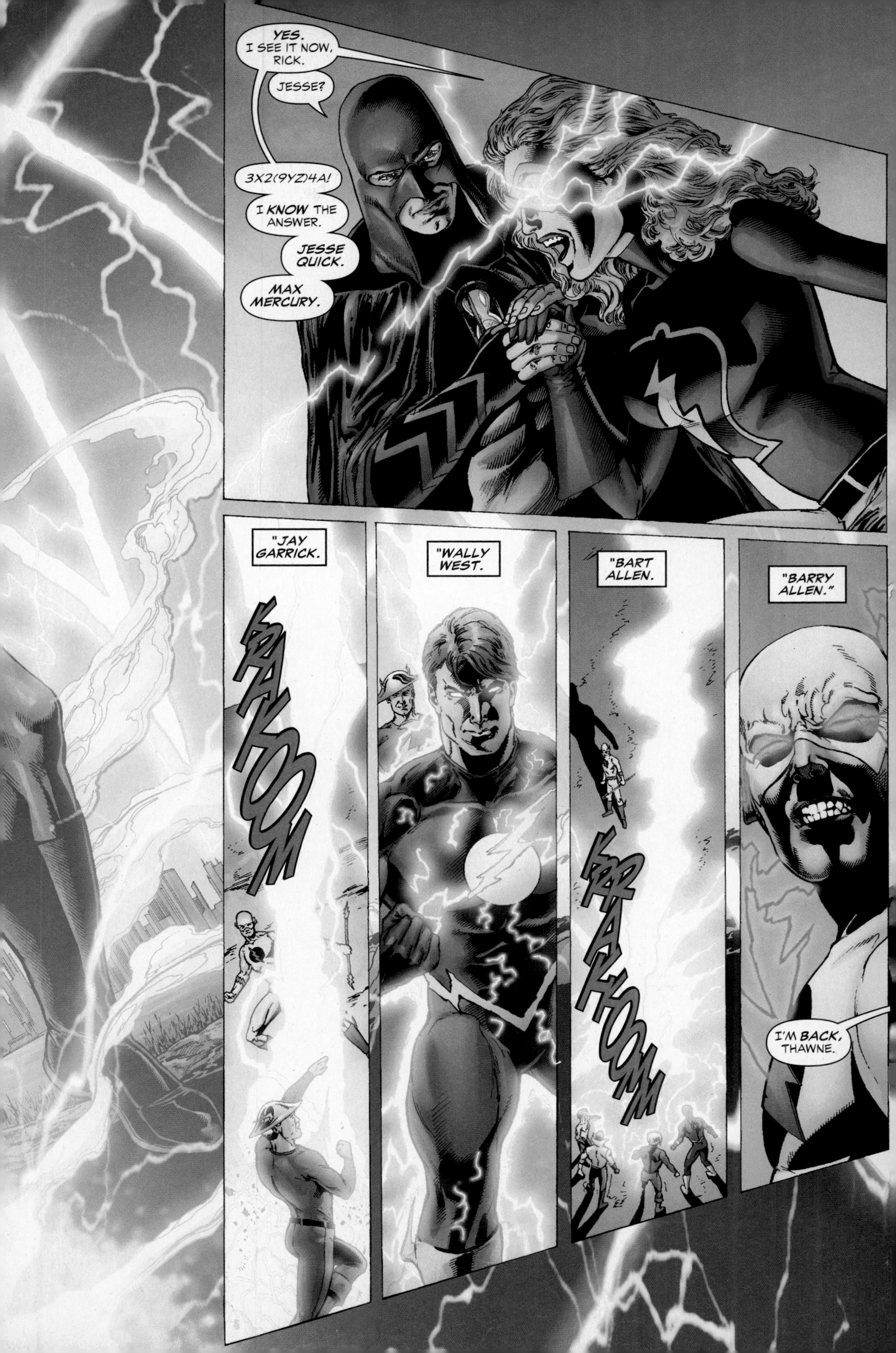

YES. I SEE IT NOW, RICK.
JESSE?
3X2(9YZ)4A!
I KNOW THE ANSWER.
JESSE QUICK.
MAX MERCURY.
"JAY GARRICK.
KRAKOOM
"WALLY WEST.
"BART ALLEN.
KRAKOOM
"BARRY ALLEN."
I'M BACK, THAWNE.

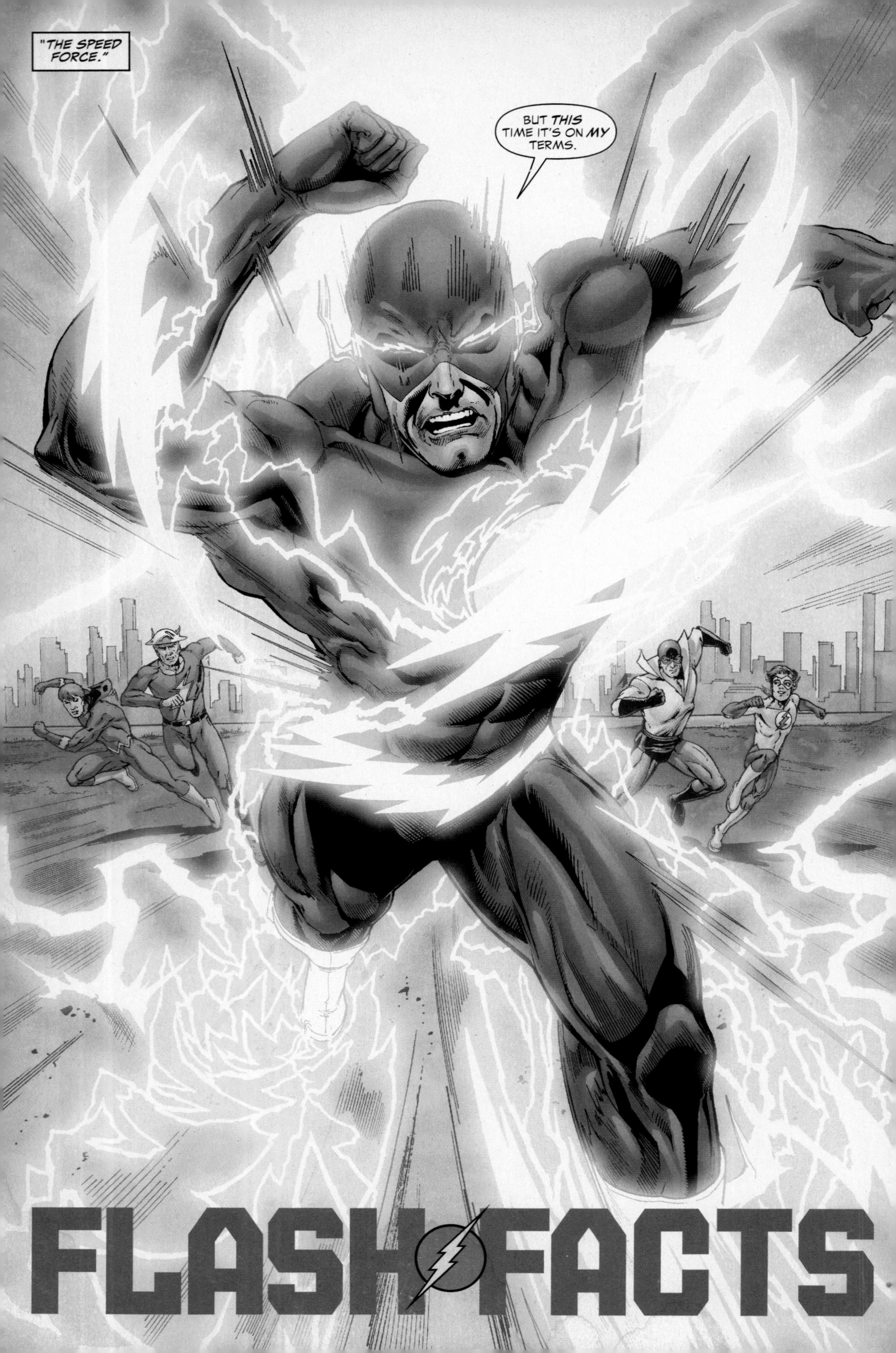
"THE SPEED FORCE."
BUT THIS TIME IT'S ON MY TERMS.
FLASH FACTS

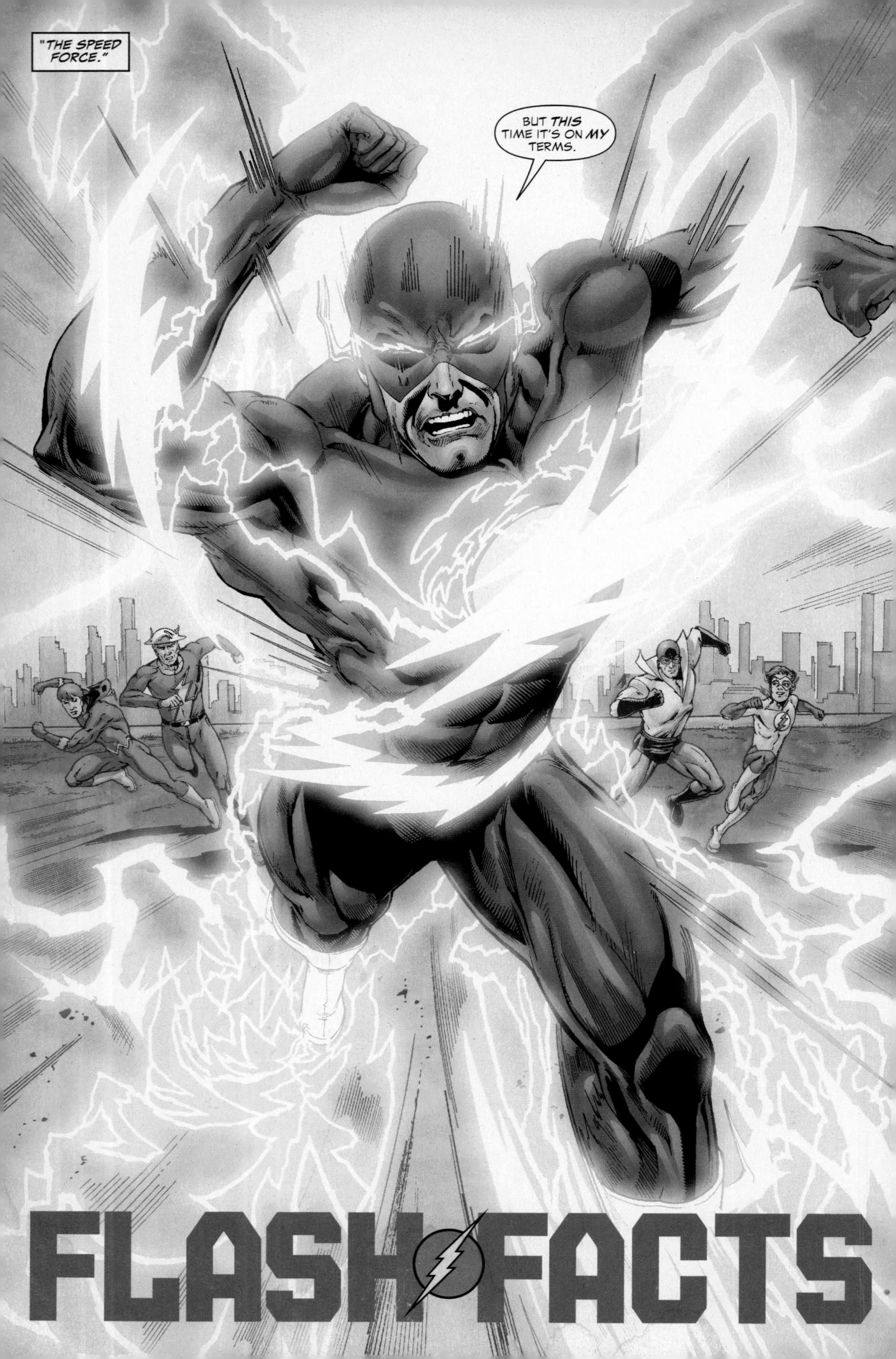
"THE SPEED FORCE."
BUT THIS TIME IT'S ON MY TERMS.
FLASH FACTS

THE FLASH: REBIRTH #5 COVER BY ETHAN VAN SCIVER (AFTER CARMINE INFANTINO) WITH BRIAN MILLER OF HI-FI

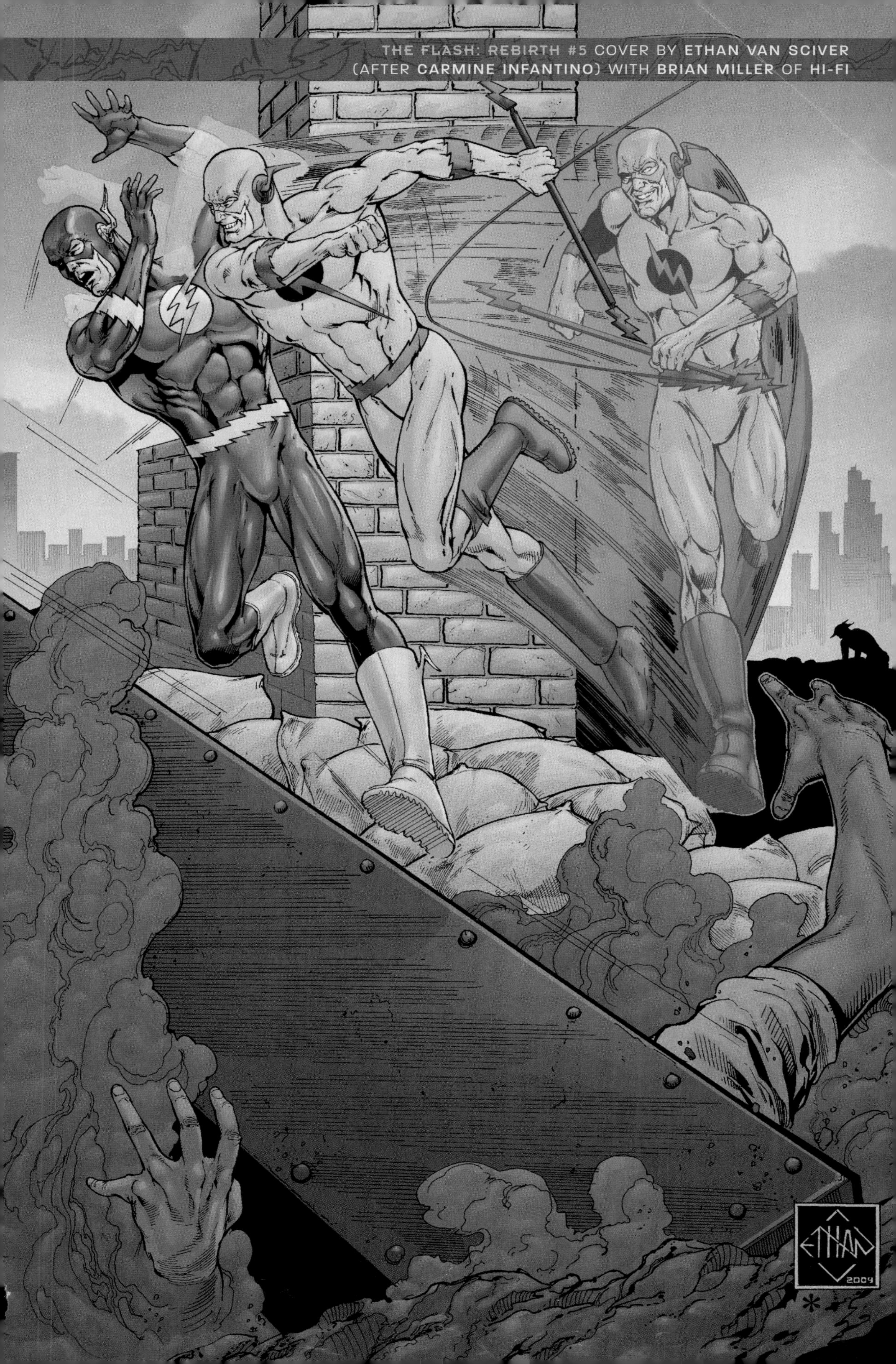
ETHAN
2009

THE FLASH: REBIRTH #5 VARIANT COVER BY ETHAN VAN SCIVER WITH BRIAN MILLER OF HI-FI

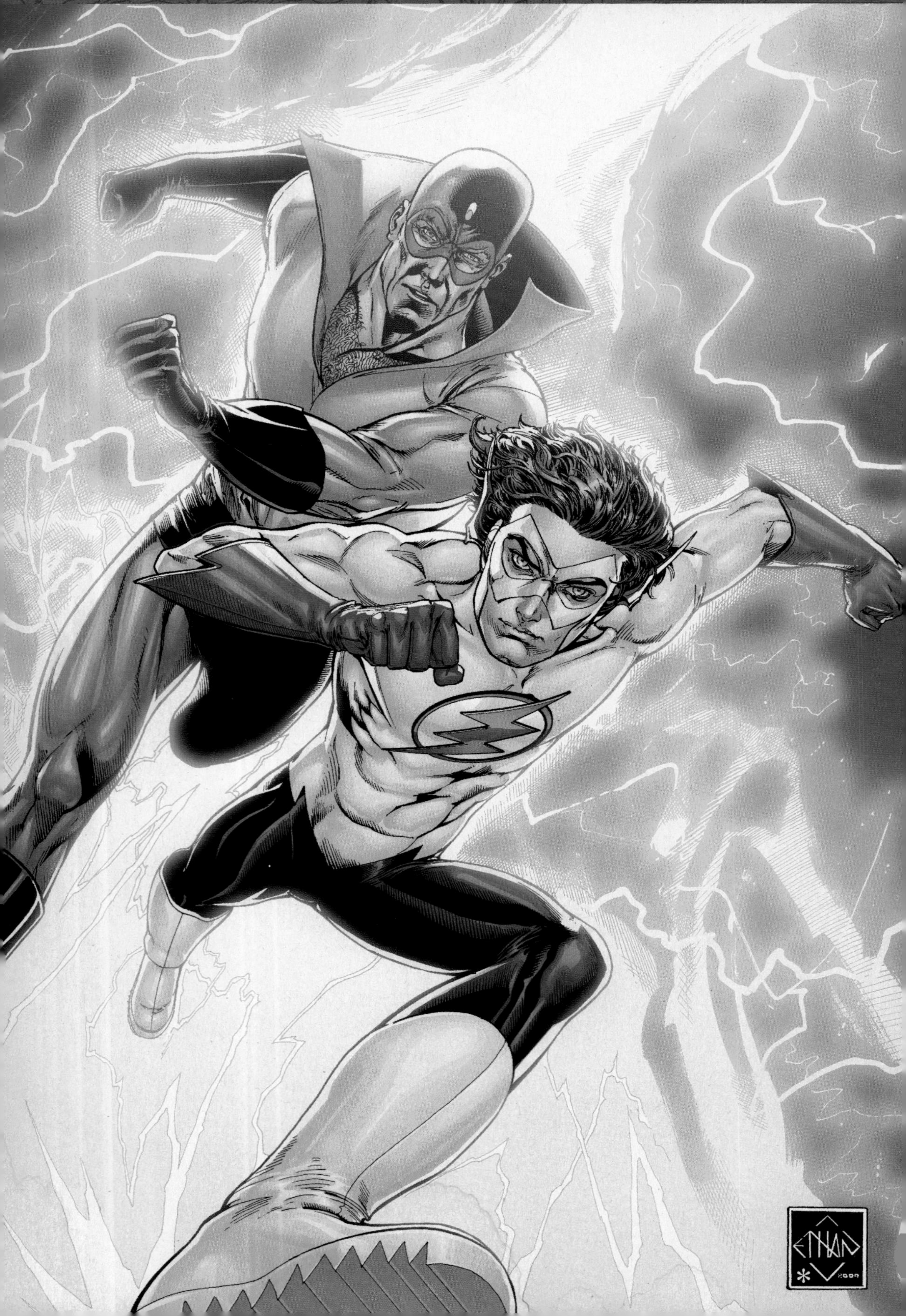
ETHAN
2009

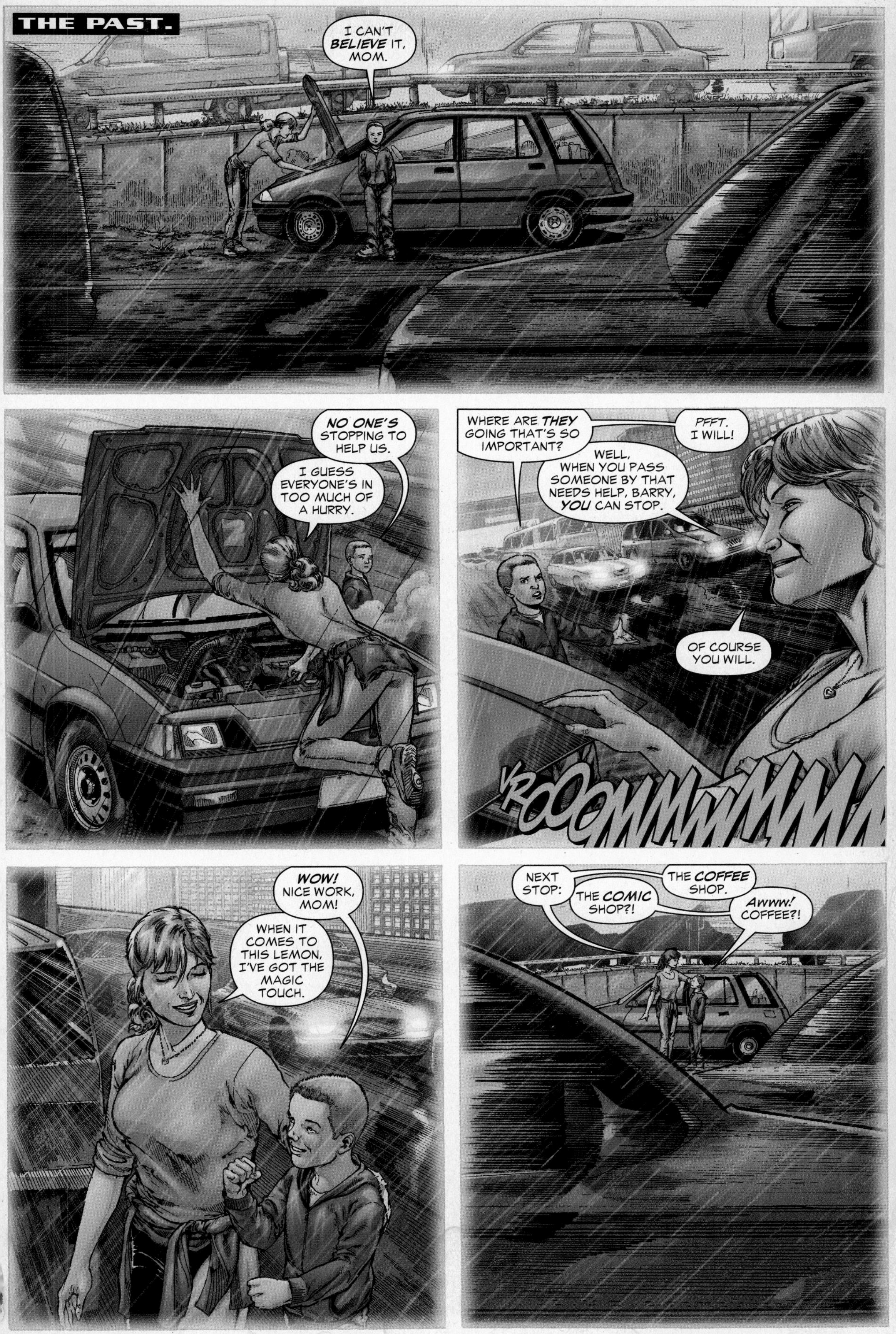
THE PAST.
I CAN'T BELIEVE IT, MOM.
NO ONE'S STOPPING TO HELP US.
I GUESS EVERYONE'S IN TOO MUCH OF A HURRY.
WHERE ARE THEY GOING THAT'S SO IMPORTANT?
WELL, WHEN YOU PASS SOMEONE BY THAT NEEDS HELP, BARRY, YOU CAN STOP.
PFFT. I WILL!
OF COURSE YOU WILL.
VROOOMMMMMMMM
WOW! NICE WORK, MOM!
WHEN IT COMES TO THIS LEMON, I'VE GOT THE MAGIC TOUCH.
NEXT STOP:
THE COFFEE SHOP.
THE COMIC SHOP?!
AWWW! COFFEE?!

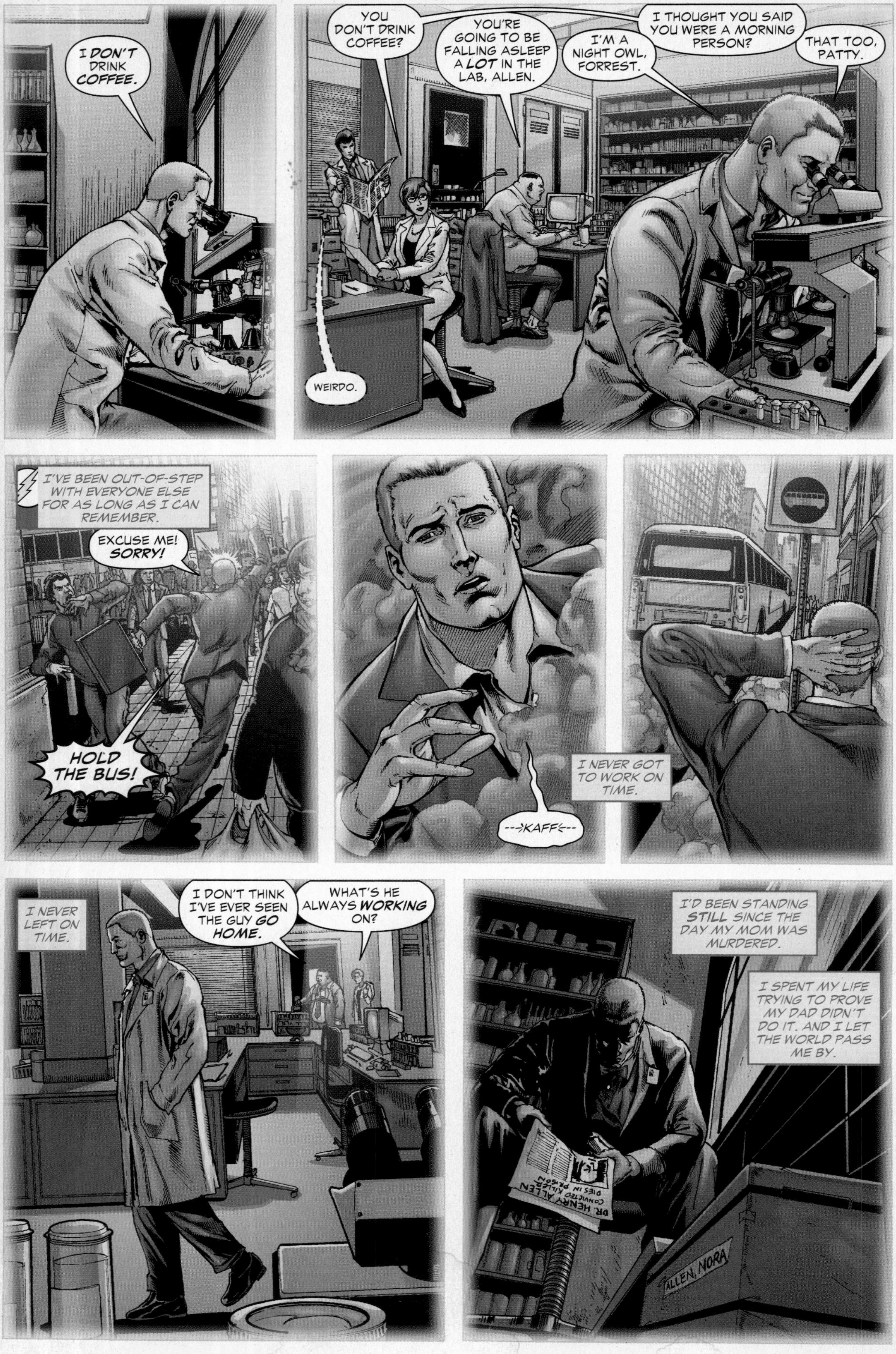

I DON'T DRINK COFFEE.
YOU DON'T DRINK COFFEE?
YOU'RE GOING TO BE FALLING ASLEEP A LOT IN THE LAB, ALLEN.
I'M A NIGHT OWL, FORREST.
I THOUGHT YOU SAID YOU WERE A MORNING PERSON?
THAT TOO, PATTY.
WEIRDO.
I'VE BEEN OUT-OF-STEP WITH EVERYONE ELSE FOR AS LONG AS I CAN REMEMBER.
EXCUSE ME! SORRY!
HOLD THE BUS!
--KAFF--
I NEVER GOT TO WORK ON TIME.
I NEVER LEFT ON TIME.
I DON'T THINK I'VE EVER SEEN THE GUY GO HOME.
WHAT'S HE ALWAYS WORKING ON?
I'D BEEN STANDING STILL SINCE THE DAY MY MOM WAS MURDERED.
I SPENT MY LIFE TRYING TO PROVE MY DAD DIDN'T DO IT. AND I LET THE WORLD PASS ME BY.
DR. HENRY ALLEN
CONVICTED KILLER DIES IN PRISON
ALLEN, NORA

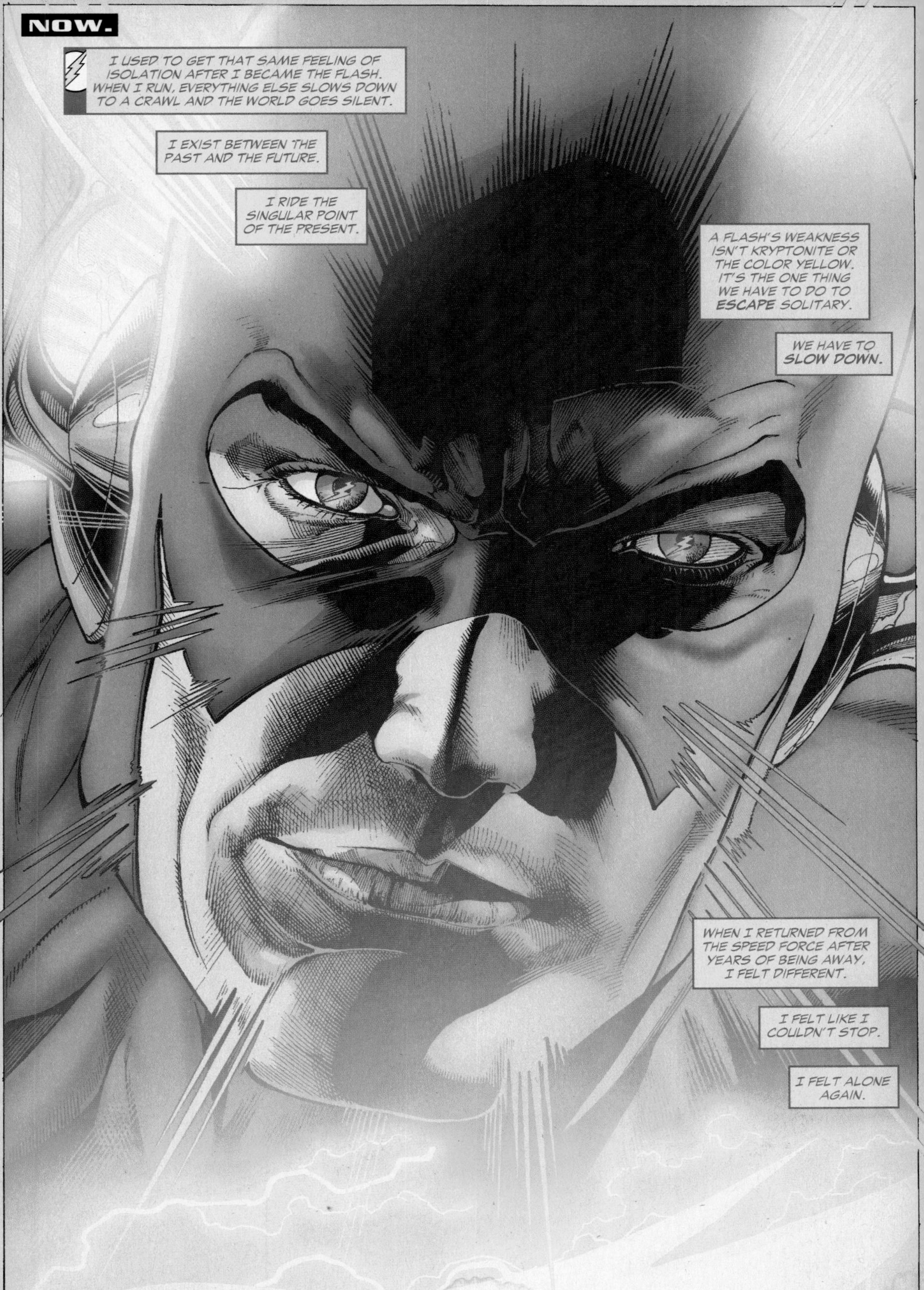
NOW.
I USED TO GET THAT SAME FEELING OF ISOLATION AFTER I BECAME THE FLASH. WHEN I RUN, EVERYTHING ELSE SLOWS DOWN TO A CRAWL AND THE WORLD GOES SILENT.
I EXIST BETWEEN THE PAST AND THE FUTURE.
I RIDE THE SINGULAR POINT OF THE PRESENT.
A FLASH'S WEAKNESS ISN'T KRYPTONITE OR THE COLOR YELLOW. IT'S THE ONE THING WE HAVE TO DO TO ESCAPE SOLITARY.
WE HAVE TO SLOW DOWN.
WHEN I RETURNED FROM THE SPEED FORCE AFTER YEARS OF BEING AWAY, I FELT DIFFERENT.
I FELT LIKE I COULDN'T STOP.
I FELT ALONE AGAIN.

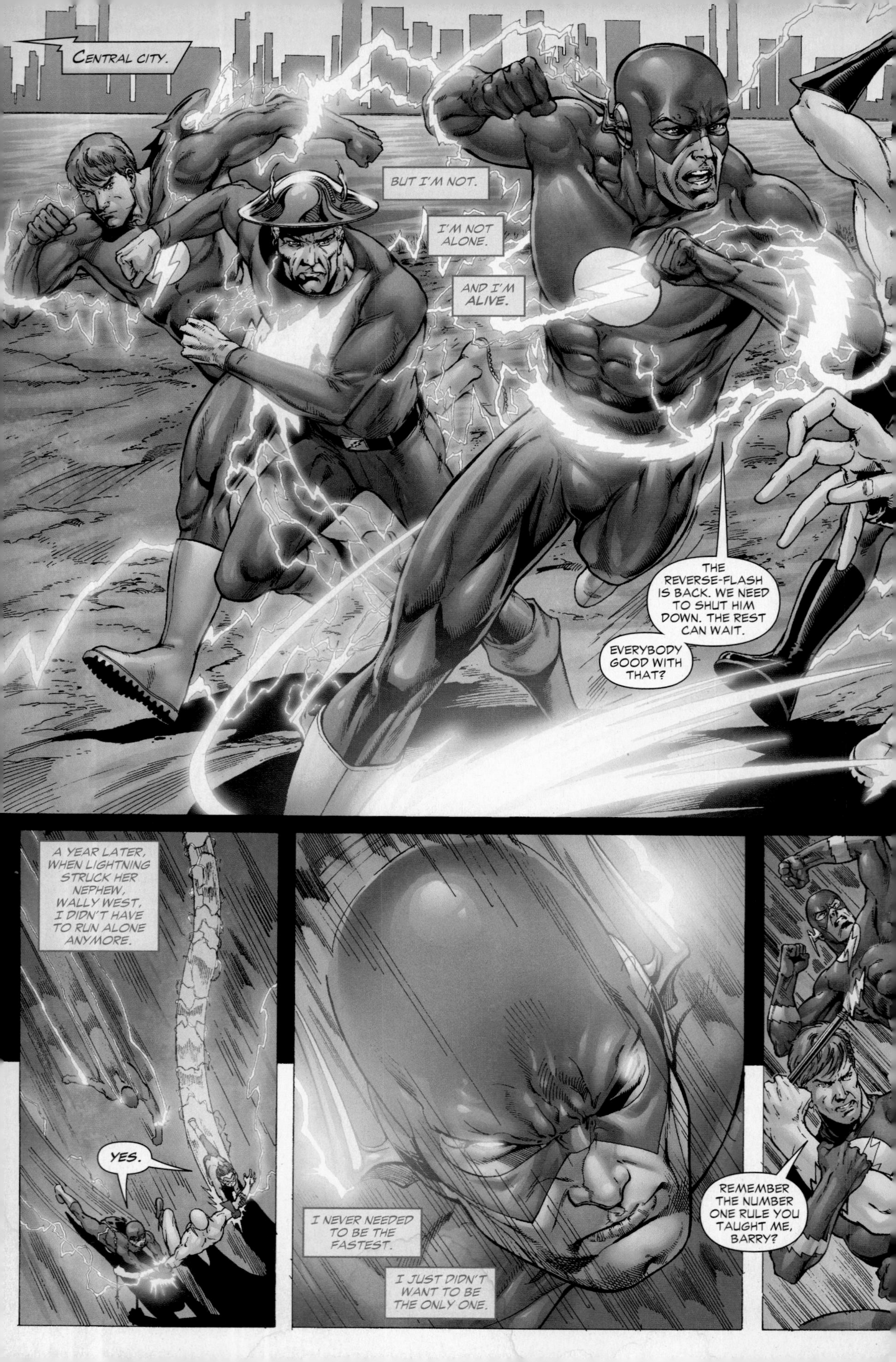
CENTRAL CITY.
BUT I'M NOT.
I'M NOT ALONE.
AND I'M ALIVE.
THE REVERSE-FLASH IS BACK. WE NEED TO SHUT HIM DOWN. THE REST CAN WAIT.
EVERYBODY GOOD WITH THAT?
A YEAR LATER, WHEN LIGHTNING STRUCK HER NEPHEW, WALLY WEST, I DIDN'T HAVE TO RUN ALONE ANYMORE.
YES.
I NEVER NEEDED TO BE THE FASTEST.
I JUST DIDN'T WANT TO BE THE ONLY ONE.
REMEMBER THE NUMBER ONE RULE YOU TAUGHT ME, BARRY?

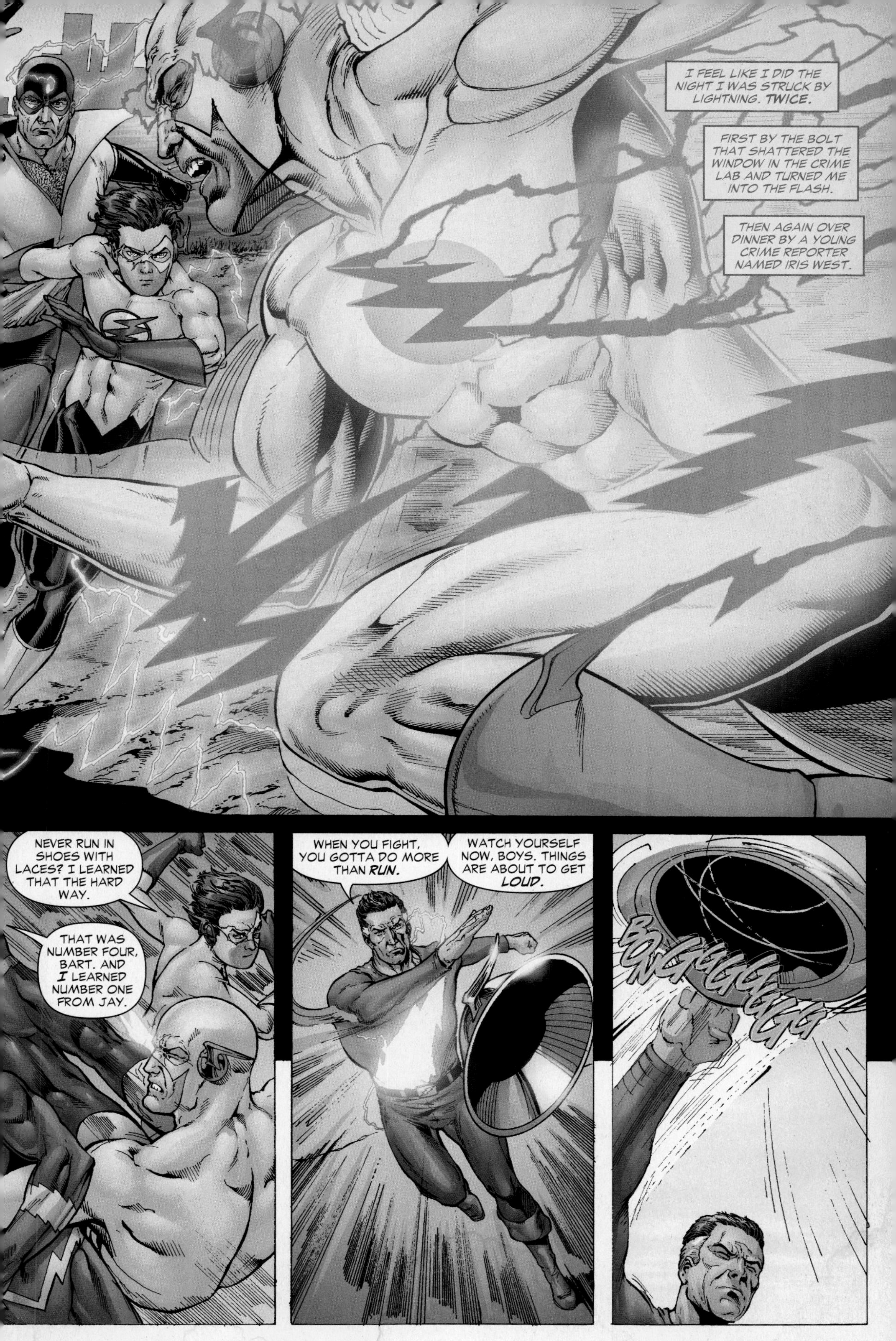
I FEEL LIKE I DID THE NIGHT I WAS STRUCK BY LIGHTNING. TWICE.
FIRST BY THE BOLT THAT SHATTERED THE WINDOW IN THE CRIME LAB AND TURNED ME INTO THE FLASH.
THEN AGAIN OVER DINNER BY A YOUNG CRIME REPORTER NAMED IRIS WEST.
NEVER RUN IN SHOES WITH LACES? I LEARNED THAT THE HARD WAY.
THAT WAS NUMBER FOUR, BART. AND I LEARNED NUMBER ONE FROM JAY.
WHEN YOU FIGHT, YOU GOTTA DO MORE THAN RUN.
WATCH YOURSELF NOW, BOYS. THINGS ARE ABOUT TO GET LOUD.
BONGGGGGGG

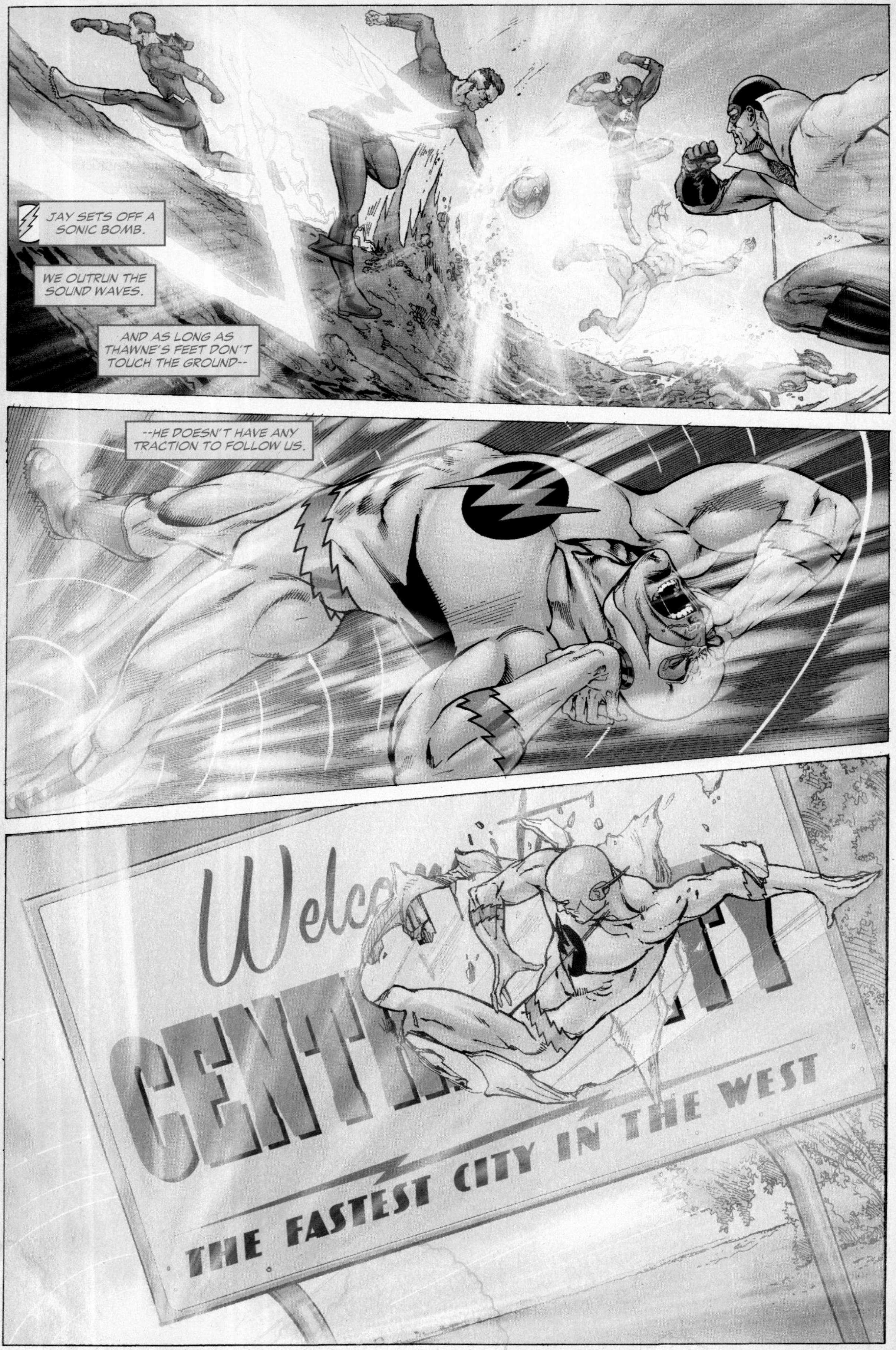
JAY SETS OFF A SONIC BOMB.
WE OUTRUN THE SOUND WAVES.
AND AS LONG AS THAWNE'S FEET DON'T TOUCH THE GROUND--
--HE DOESN'T HAVE ANY TRACTION TO FOLLOW US.
THE FASTEST CITY IN THE WEST

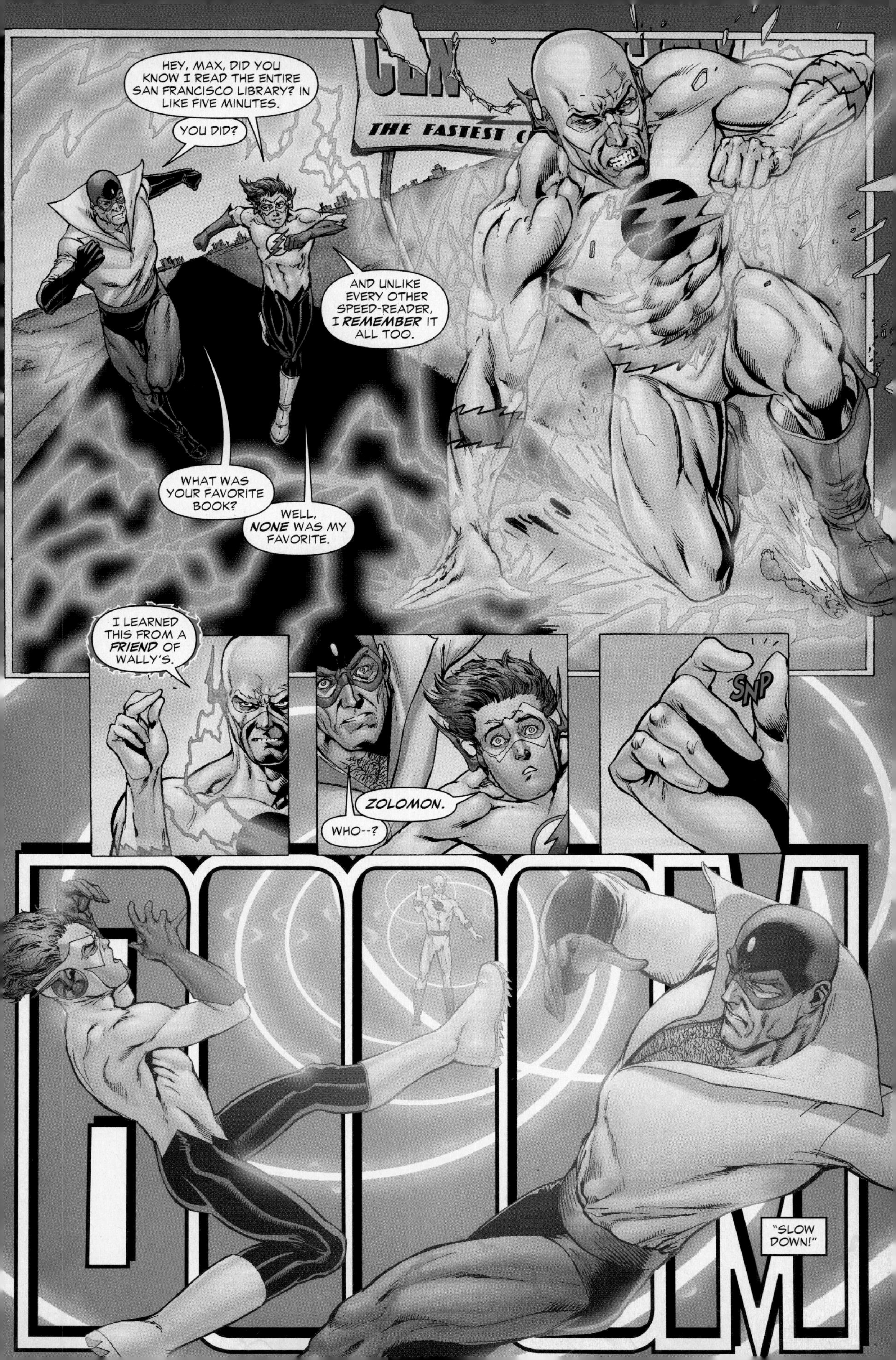
THE FASTEST
HEY, MAX, DID YOU KNOW I READ THE ENTIRE SAN FRANCISCO LIBRARY? IN LIKE FIVE MINUTES.
YOU DID?
AND UNLIKE EVERY OTHER SPEED-READER, I REMEMBER IT ALL TOO.
WHAT WAS YOUR FAVORITE BOOK?
WELL, NONE WAS MY FAVORITE.
I LEARNED THIS FROM A FRIEND OF WALLY'S.
ZOLOMON.
WHO--?
SNP
"SLOW DOWN!"

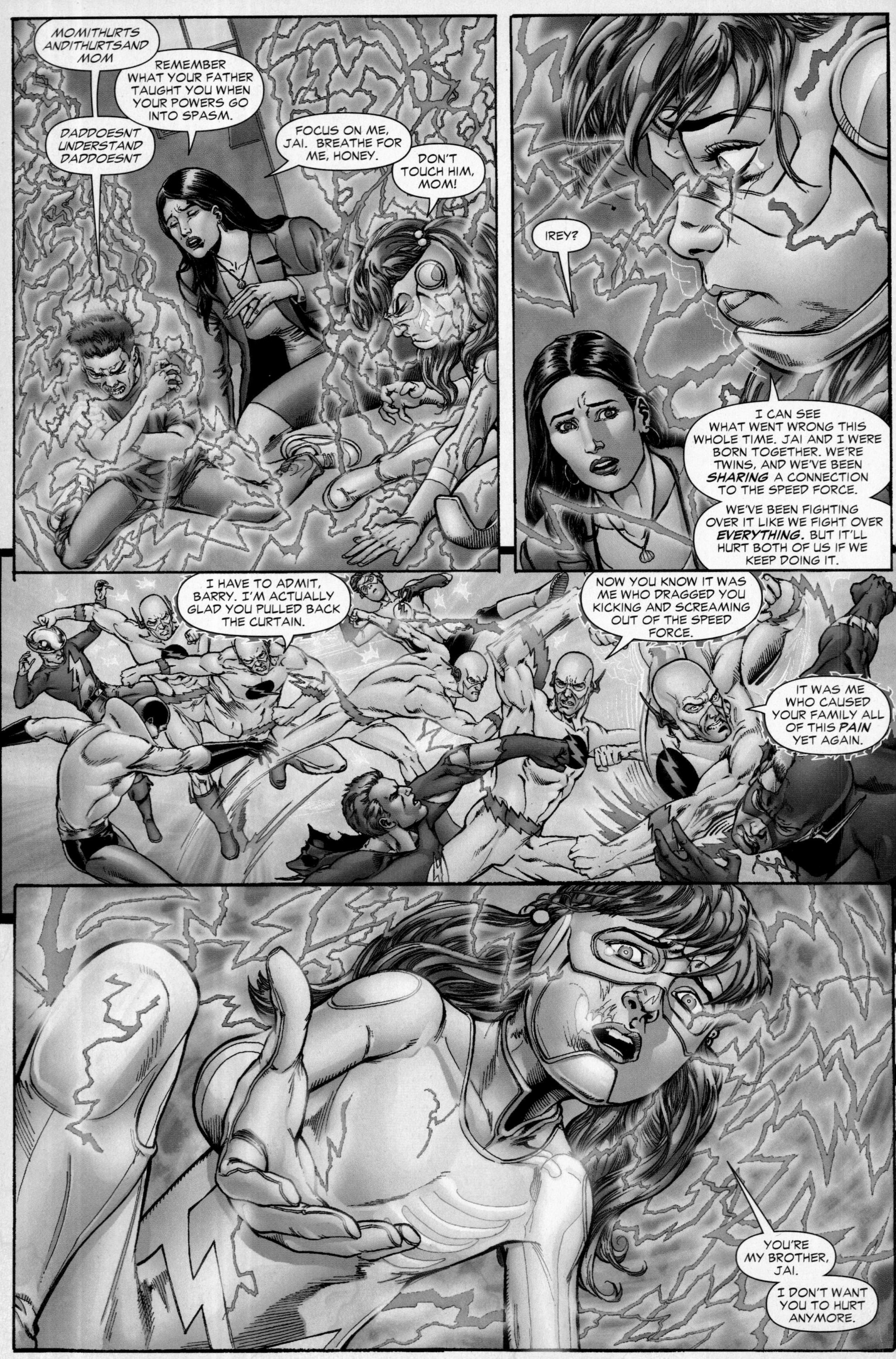
MOMITHURTS ANDITHURTSAND MOM
REMEMBER WHAT YOUR FATHER TAUGHT YOU WHEN YOUR POWERS GO INTO SPASM.
DADDOESNT UNDERSTAND DADDOESNT
FOCUS ON ME, JAI. BREATHE FOR ME, HONEY.
DON'T TOUCH HIM, MOM!
IREY?
I CAN SEE WHAT WENT WRONG THIS WHOLE TIME. JAI AND I WERE BORN TOGETHER. WE'RE TWINS, AND WE'VE BEEN SHARING A CONNECTION TO THE SPEED FORCE.
WE'VE BEEN FIGHTING OVER IT LIKE WE FIGHT OVER EVERYTHING. BUT IT'LL HURT BOTH OF US IF WE KEEP DOING IT.
I HAVE TO ADMIT, BARRY. I'M ACTUALLY GLAD YOU PULLED BACK THE CURTAIN.
NOW YOU KNOW IT WAS ME WHO DRAGGED YOU KICKING AND SCREAMING OUT OF THE SPEED FORCE.
IT WAS ME WHO CAUSED YOUR FAMILY ALL OF THIS PAIN YET AGAIN.
YOU'RE MY BROTHER, JAI.
I DON'T WANT YOU TO HURT ANYMORE.

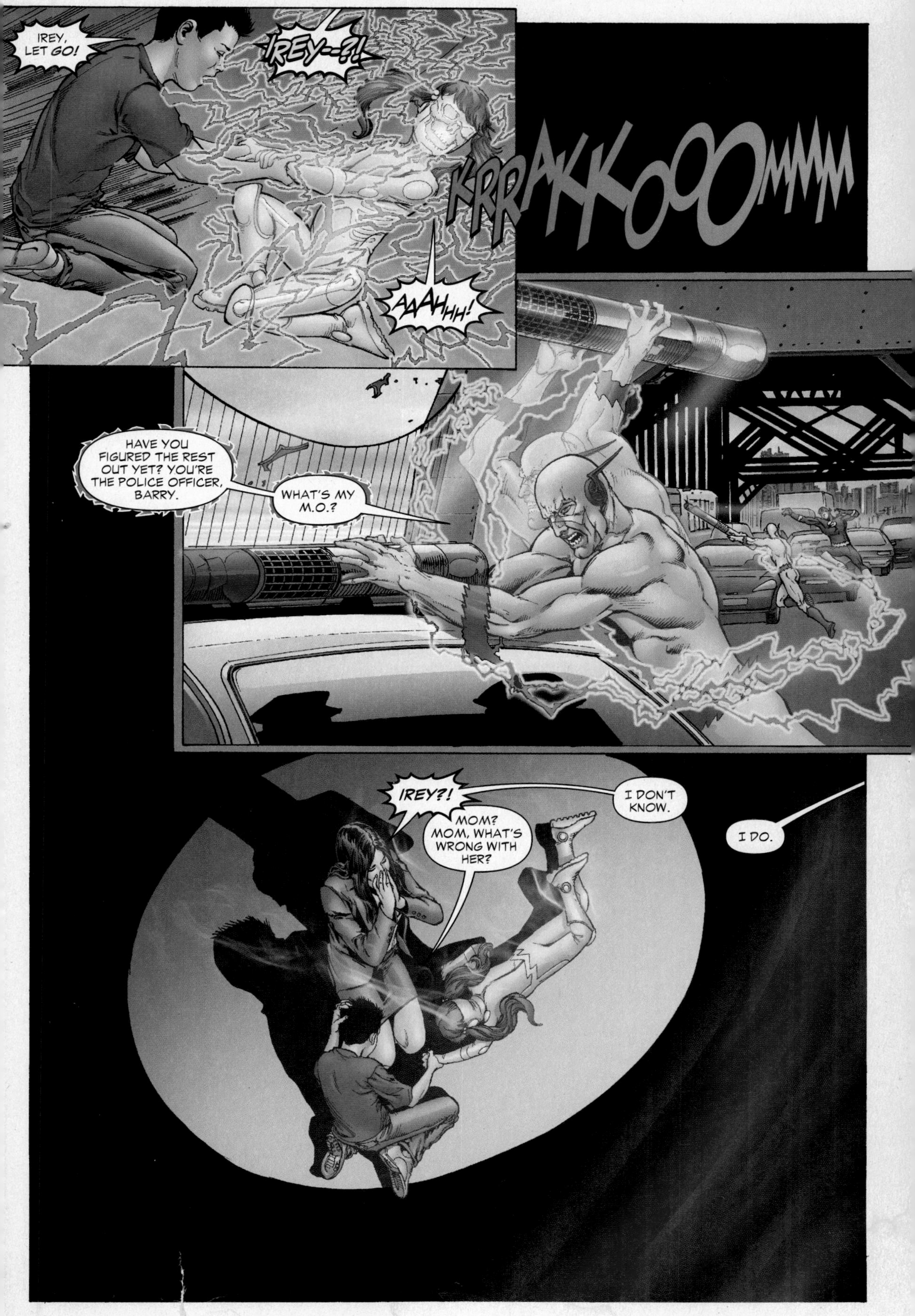
IREY, LET GO!
IREY--?!
KRRAKKOOOMMMM
AAAHHH!
HAVE YOU FIGURED THE REST OUT YET? YOU'RE THE POLICE OFFICER, BARRY.
WHAT'S MY M.O.?
IREY?!
MOM? MOM, WHAT'S WRONG WITH HER?
I DON'T KNOW.
I DO.

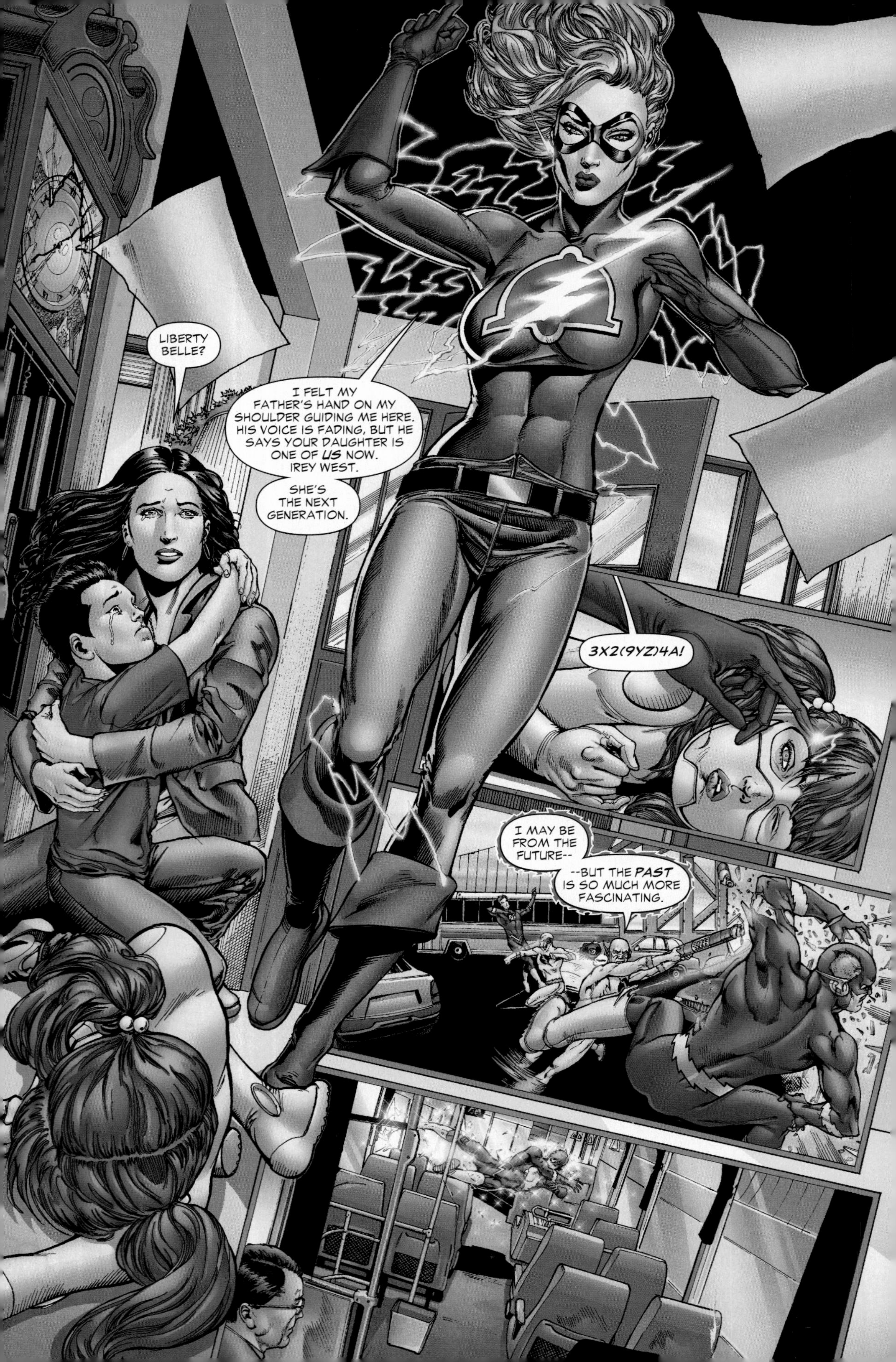
LIBERTY BELLE?
I FELT MY FATHER'S HAND ON MY SHOULDER GUIDING ME HERE. HIS VOICE IS FADING, BUT HE SAYS YOUR DAUGHTER IS ONE OF *US* NOW. IREY WEST.
SHE'S THE NEXT GENERATION.
3X2(9YZ)4A!
I MAY BE FROM THE FUTURE--
--BUT THE *PAST* IS SO MUCH MORE FASCINATING.

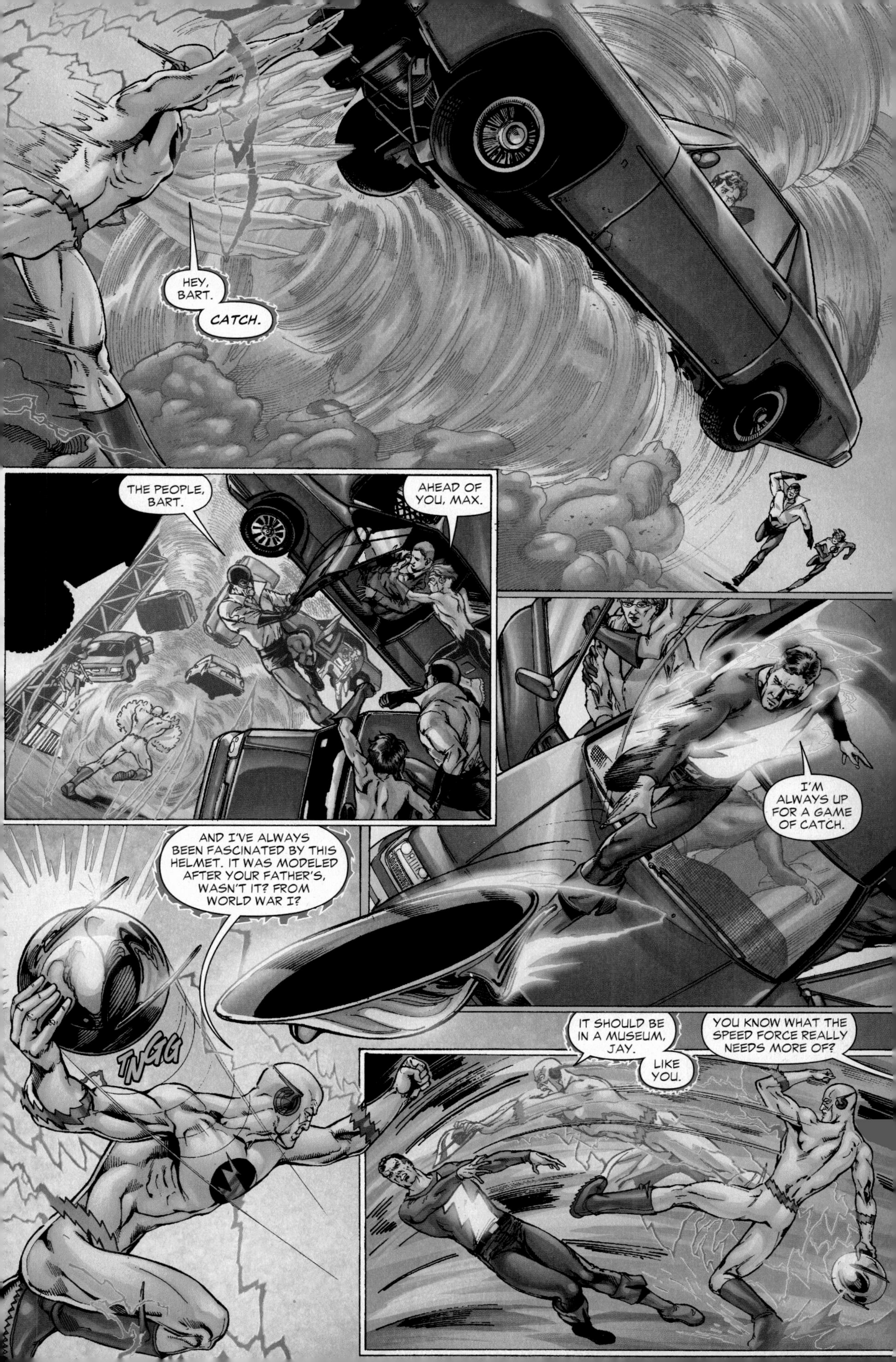
HEY, BART.
CATCH.
THE PEOPLE, BART.
AHEAD OF YOU, MAX.
I'M ALWAYS UP FOR A GAME OF CATCH.
AND I'VE ALWAYS BEEN FASCINATED BY THIS HELMET. IT WAS MODELED AFTER YOUR FATHER'S, WASN'T IT? FROM WORLD WAR I?
TNGG
IT SHOULD BE IN A MUSEUM, JAY.
LIKE YOU.
YOU KNOW WHAT THE SPEED FORCE REALLY NEEDS MORE OF?

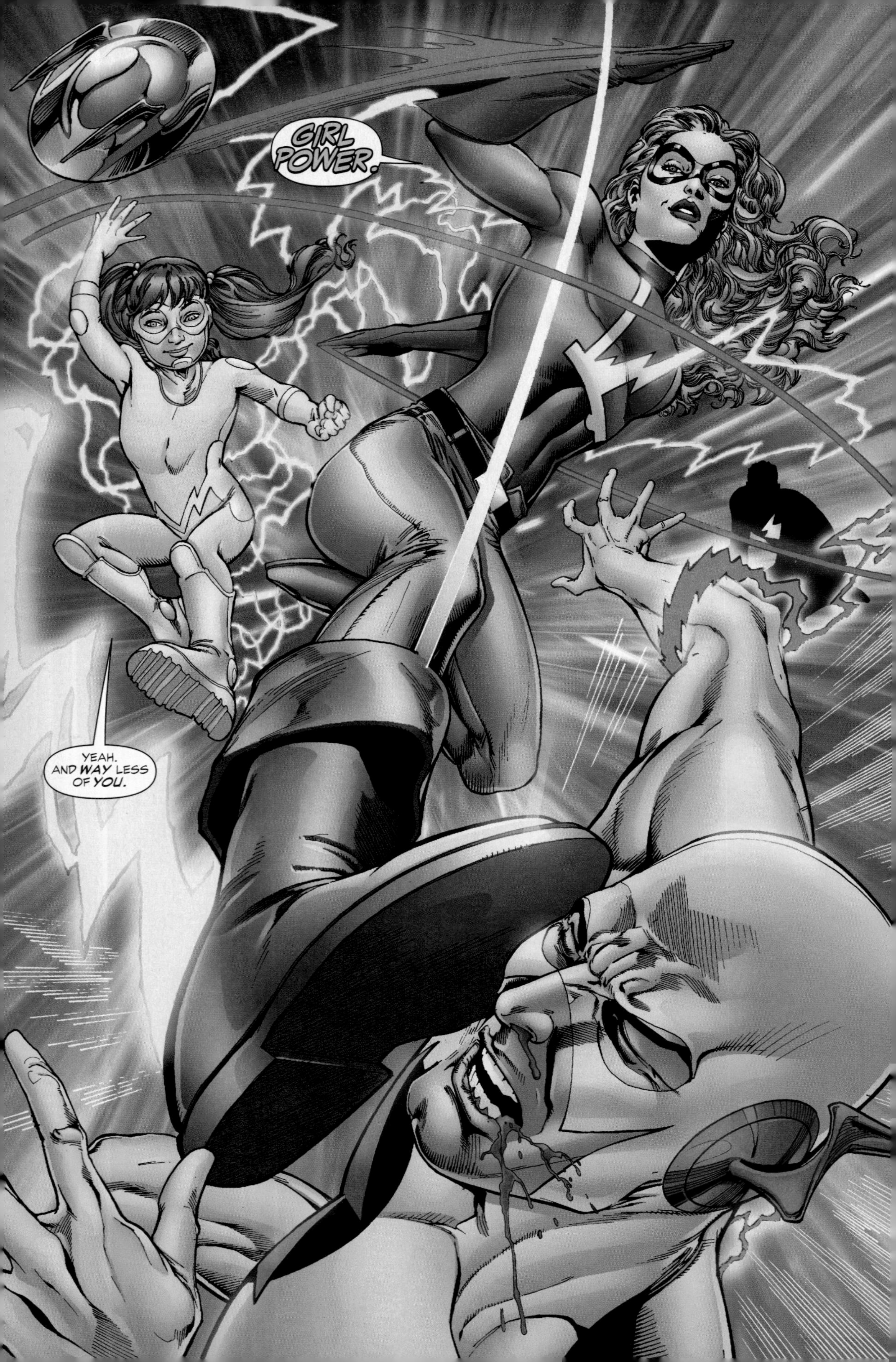
GIRL POWER.
YEAH. AND WAY LESS OF YOU.

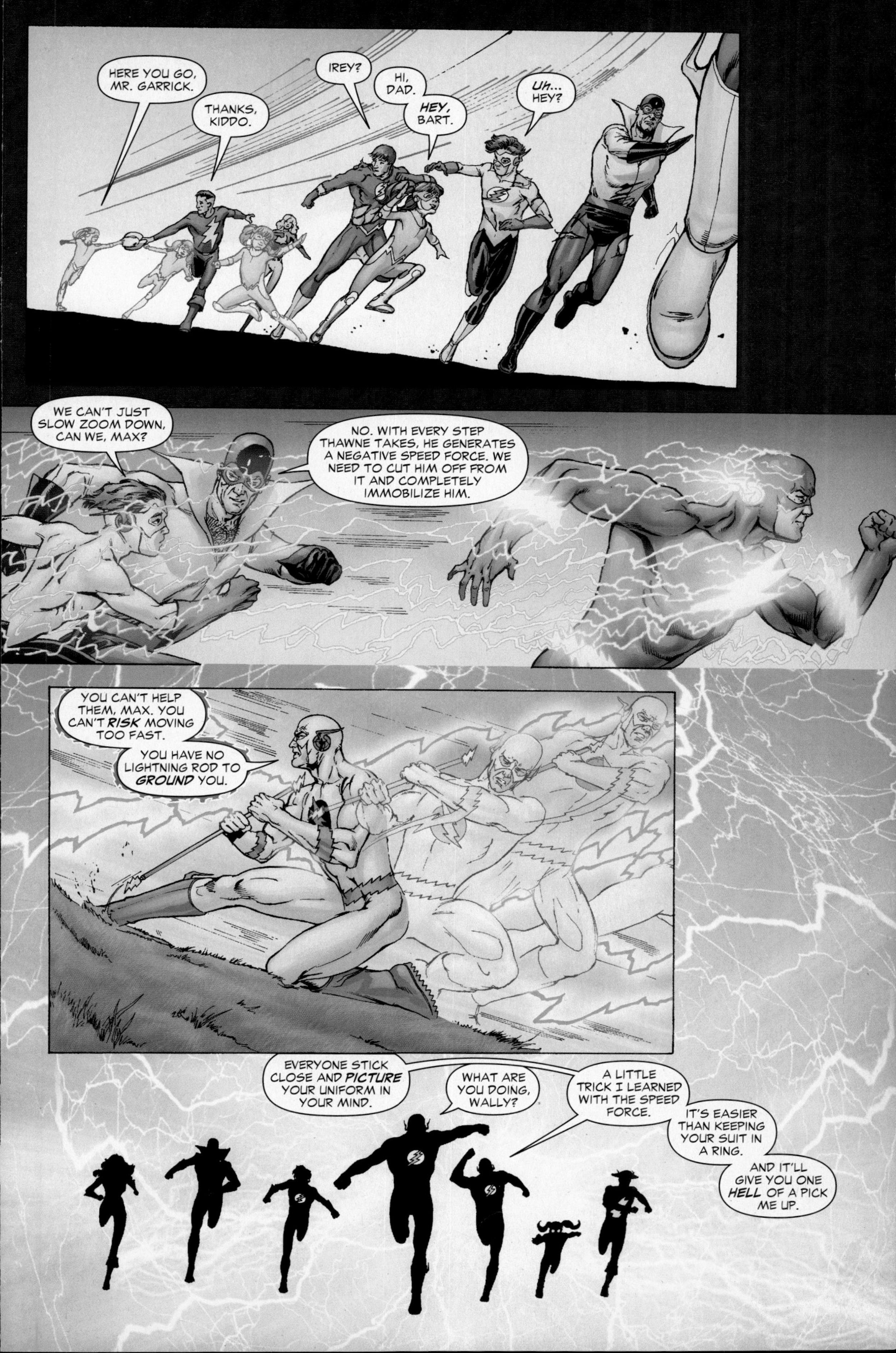
HERE YOU GO, MR. GARRICK.
THANKS, KIDDO.
IREY?
HI, DAD.
HEY, BART.
Uh... HEY?
WE CAN'T JUST SLOW ZOOM DOWN, CAN WE, MAX?
NO. WITH EVERY STEP THAWNE TAKES, HE GENERATES A NEGATIVE SPEED FORCE. WE NEED TO CUT HIM OFF FROM IT AND COMPLETELY IMMOBILIZE HIM.
YOU CAN'T HELP THEM, MAX. YOU CAN'T RISK MOVING TOO FAST.
YOU HAVE NO LIGHTNING ROD TO GROUND YOU.
EVERYONE STICK CLOSE AND PICTURE YOUR UNIFORM IN YOUR MIND.
WHAT ARE YOU DOING, WALLY?
A LITTLE TRICK I LEARNED WITH THE SPEED FORCE.
IT'S EASIER THAN KEEPING YOUR SUIT IN A RING.
AND IT'LL GIVE YOU ONE HELL OF A PICK ME UP.

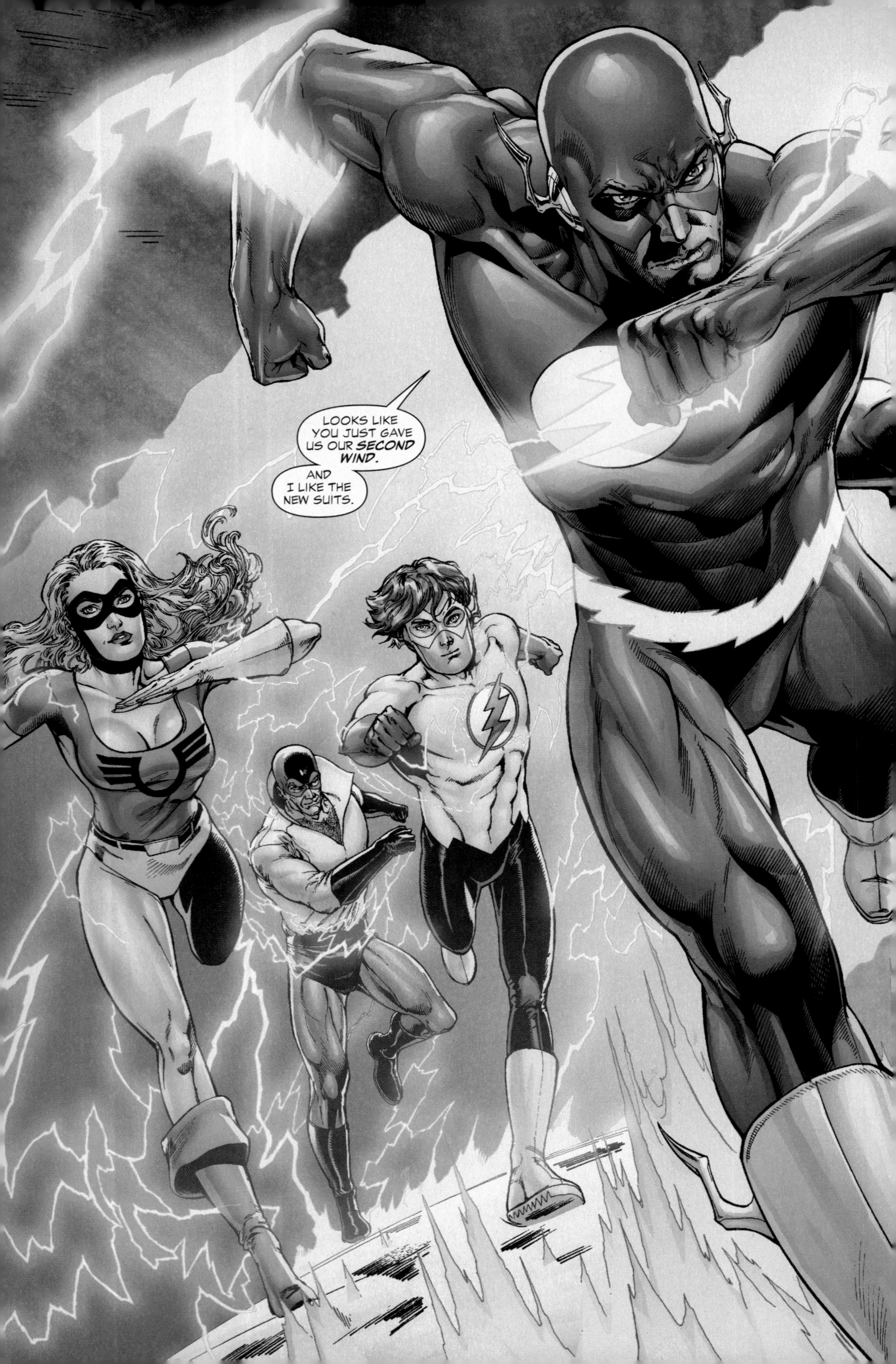
LOOKS LIKE YOU JUST GAVE US OUR SECOND WIND.
AND I LIKE THE NEW SUITS.

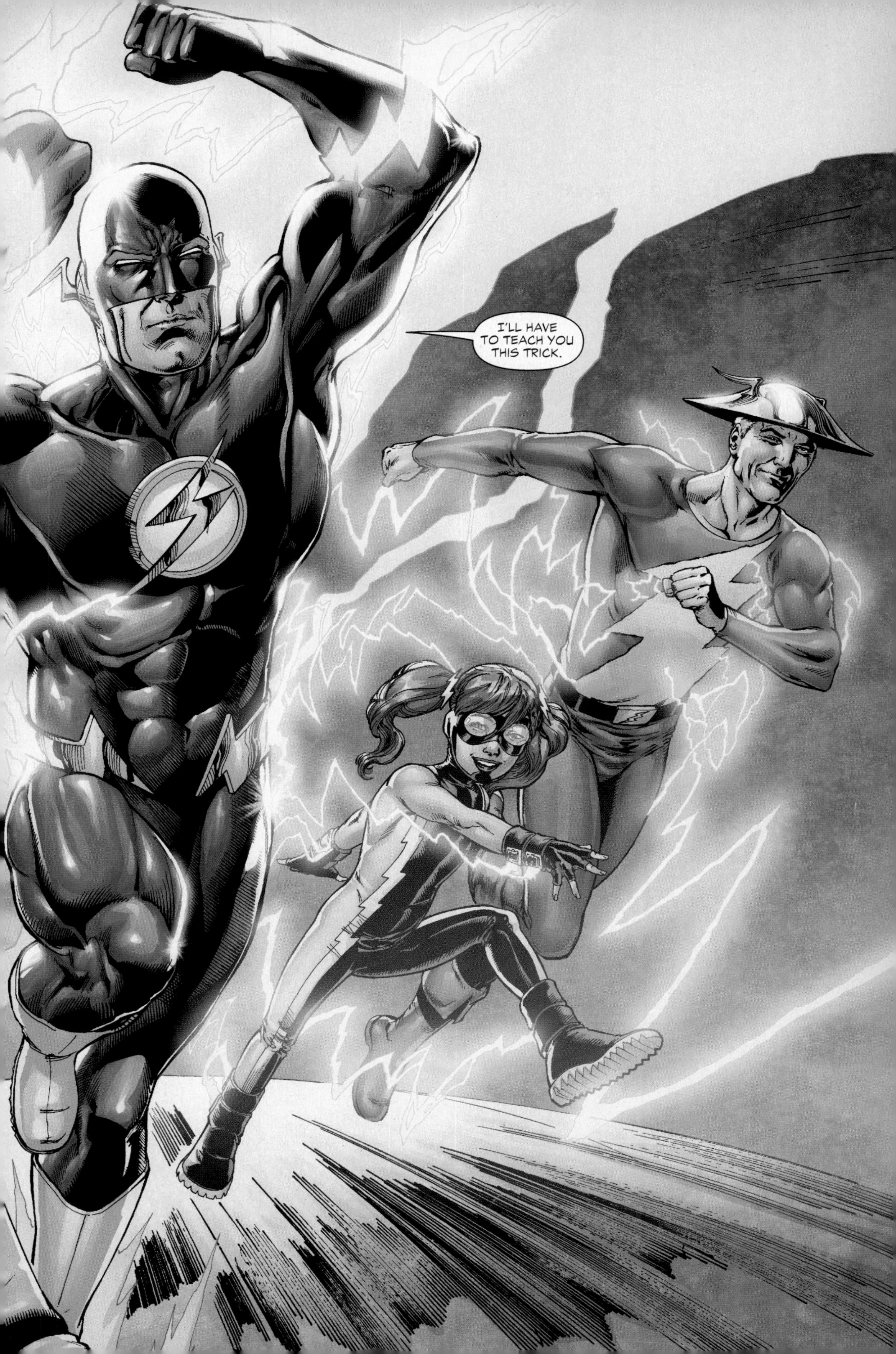
I'LL HAVE TO TEACH YOU THIS TRICK.

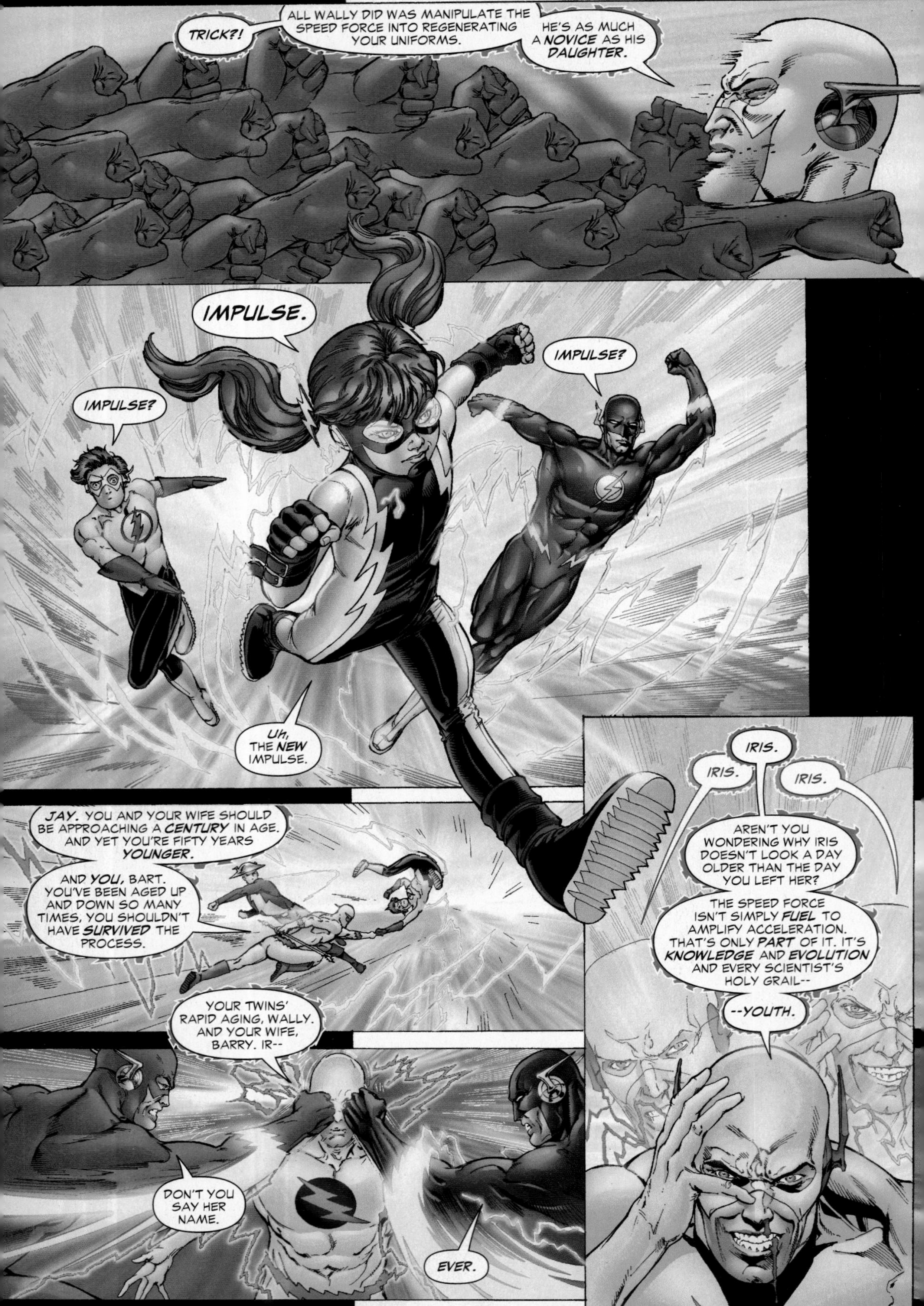
TRICK?!
ALL WALLY DID WAS MANIPULATE THE SPEED FORCE INTO REGENERATING YOUR UNIFORMS.
HE'S AS MUCH A NOVICE AS HIS DAUGHTER.
IMPULSE.
IMPULSE?
IMPULSE?
Uh, THE NEW IMPULSE.
JAY. YOU AND YOUR WIFE SHOULD BE APPROACHING A CENTURY IN AGE. AND YET YOU'RE FIFTY YEARS YOUNGER.
AND YOU, BART. YOU'VE BEEN AGED UP AND DOWN SO MANY TIMES, YOU SHOULDN'T HAVE SURVIVED THE PROCESS.
YOUR TWINS' RAPID AGING, WALLY. AND YOUR WIFE, BARRY. IR--
DON'T YOU SAY HER NAME.
EVER.
IRIS.
IRIS.
IRIS.
AREN'T YOU WONDERING WHY IRIS DOESN'T LOOK A DAY OLDER THAN THE DAY YOU LEFT HER?
THE SPEED FORCE ISN'T SIMPLY FUEL TO AMPLIFY ACCELERATION. THAT'S ONLY PART OF IT. IT'S KNOWLEDGE AND EVOLUTION AND EVERY SCIENTIST'S HOLY GRAIL--
--YOUTH.

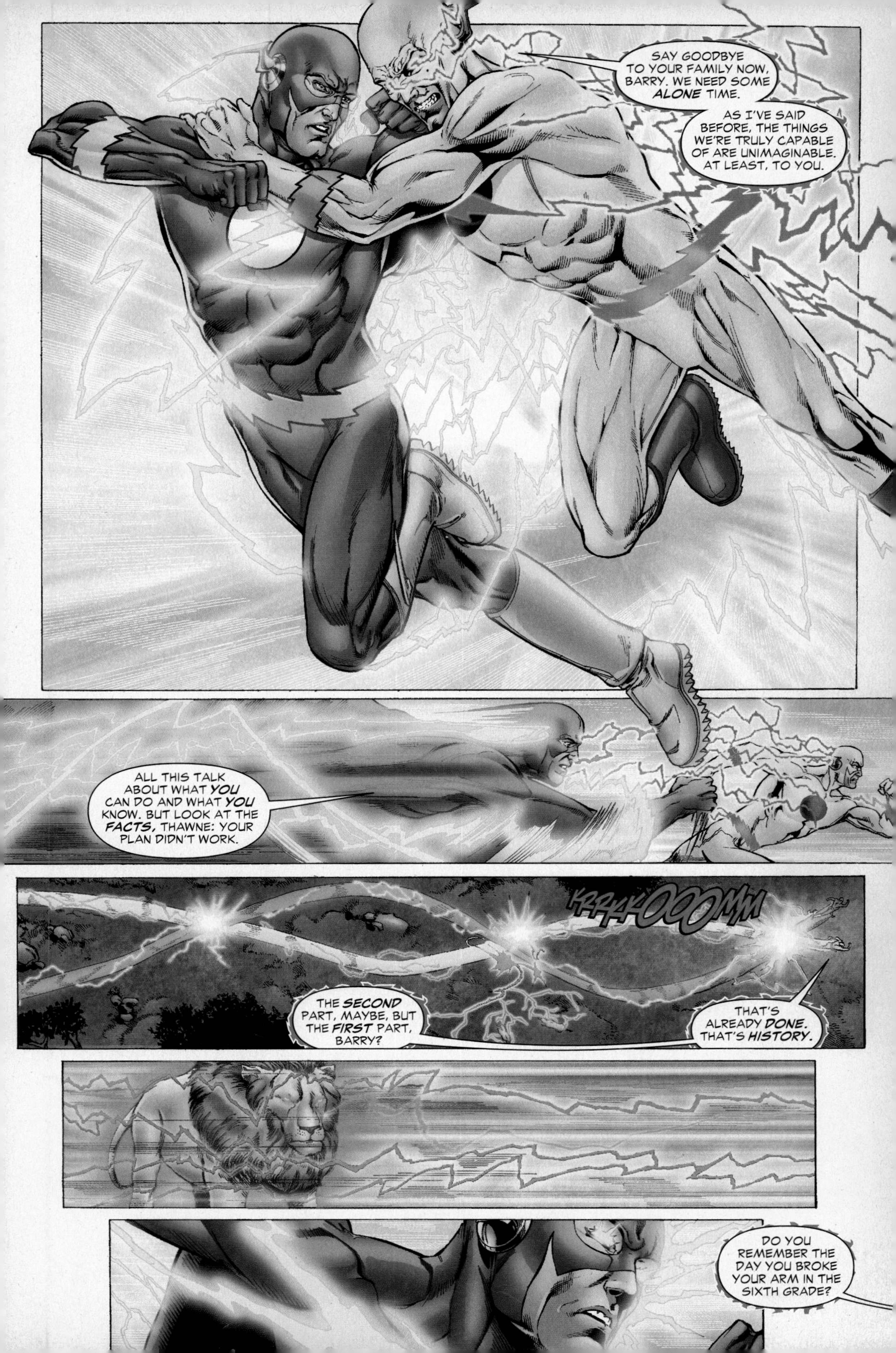
SAY GOODBYE TO YOUR FAMILY NOW, BARRY. WE NEED SOME ALONE TIME.
AS I'VE SAID BEFORE, THE THINGS WE'RE TRULY CAPABLE OF ARE UNIMAGINABLE. AT LEAST, TO YOU.
ALL THIS TALK ABOUT WHAT YOU CAN DO AND WHAT YOU KNOW. BUT LOOK AT THE FACTS, THAWNE: YOUR PLAN DIDN'T WORK.
KRRAKOOOOMM
THE SECOND PART, MAYBE, BUT THE FIRST PART, BARRY?
THAT'S ALREADY DONE. THAT'S HISTORY.
DO YOU REMEMBER THE DAY YOU BROKE YOUR ARM IN THE SIXTH GRADE?

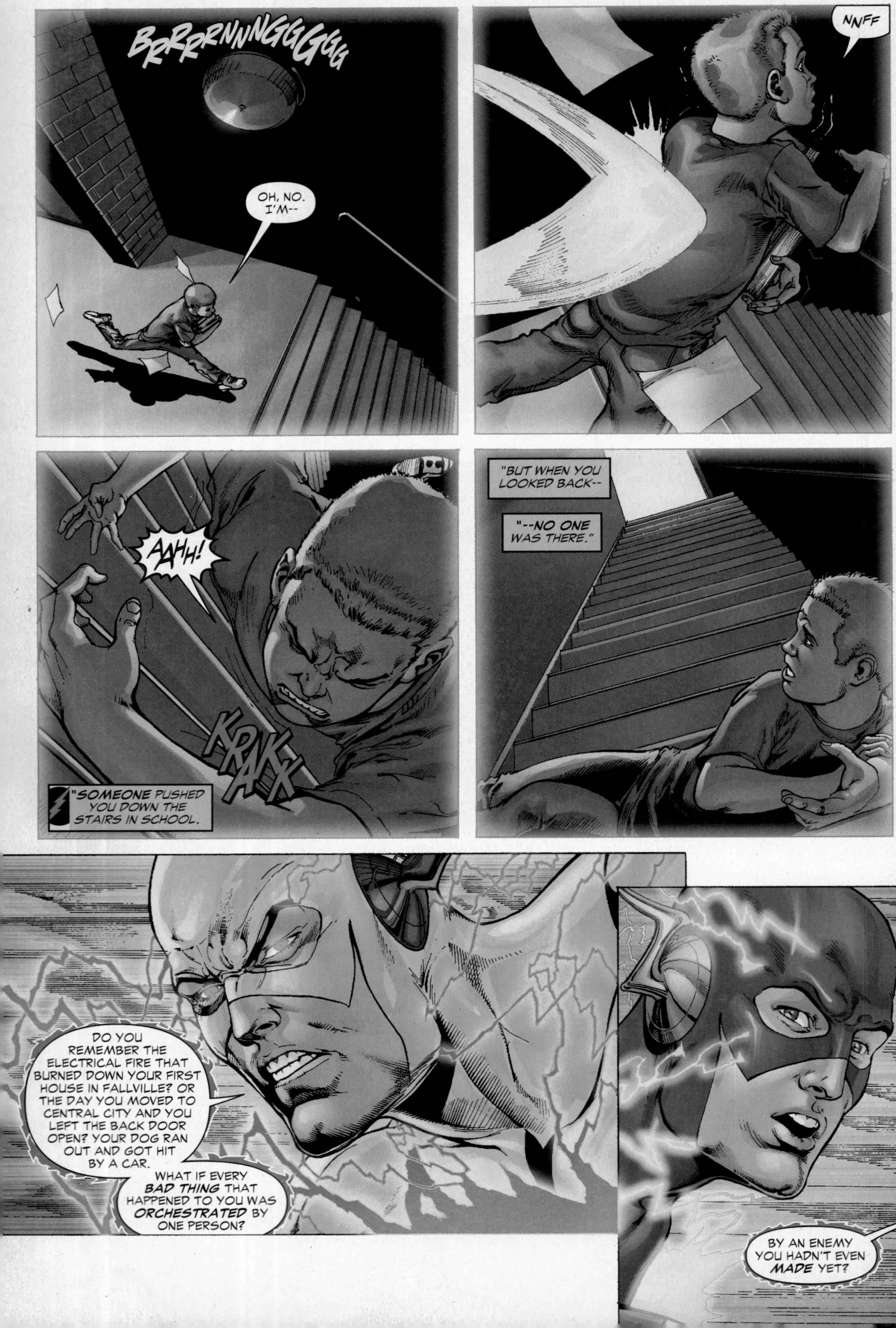
BRRRRNNNGGGGGG
OH, NO. I'M--
NNFF
AAHH!
KRAKK
"SOMEONE PUSHED YOU DOWN THE STAIRS IN SCHOOL.
"BUT WHEN YOU LOOKED BACK--
"--NO ONE WAS THERE."
DO YOU REMEMBER THE ELECTRICAL FIRE THAT BURNED DOWN YOUR FIRST HOUSE IN FALLVILLE? OR THE DAY YOU MOVED TO CENTRAL CITY AND YOU LEFT THE BACK DOOR OPEN? YOUR DOG RAN OUT AND GOT HIT BY A CAR.
WHAT IF EVERY BAD THING THAT HAPPENED TO YOU WAS ORCHESTRATED BY ONE PERSON?
BY AN ENEMY YOU HADN'T EVEN MADE YET?

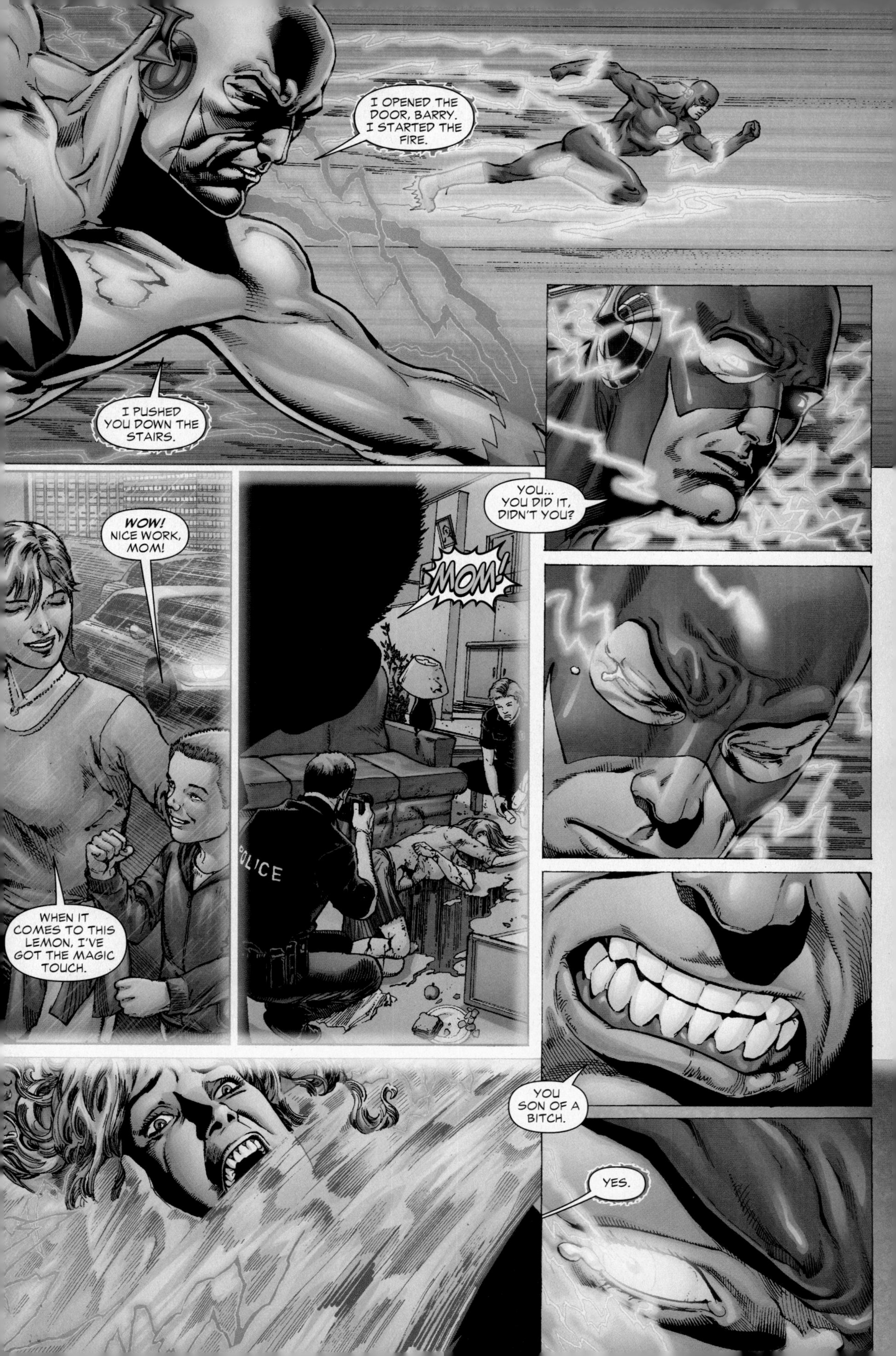
I OPENED THE DOOR, BARRY. I STARTED THE FIRE.
I PUSHED YOU DOWN THE STAIRS.
YOU... YOU DID IT, DIDN'T YOU?
WOW! NICE WORK, MOM!
WHEN IT COMES TO THIS LEMON, I'VE GOT THE MAGIC TOUCH.
MOM!
YOU SON OF A BITCH.
YES.

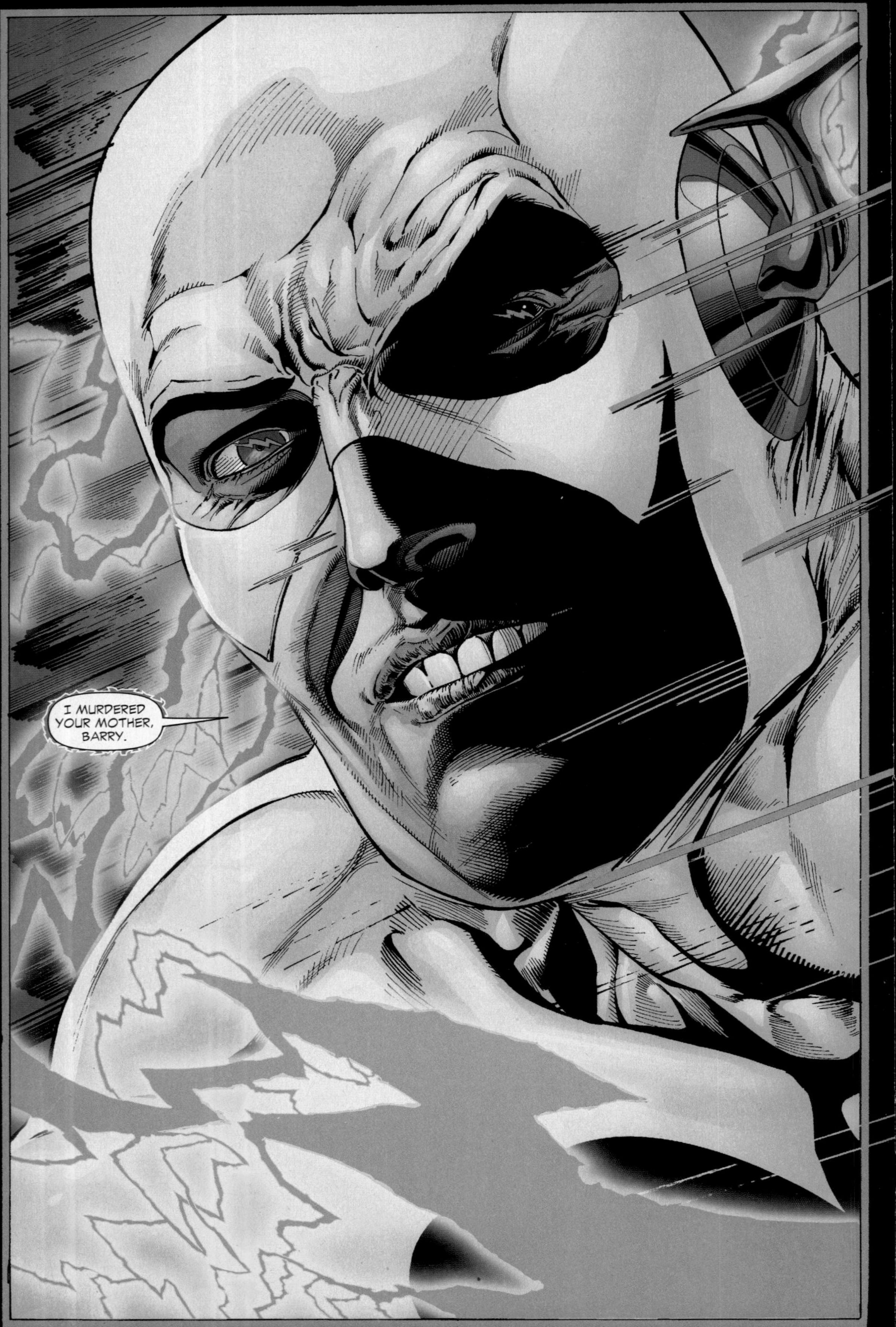
I MURDERED YOUR MOTHER, BARRY.

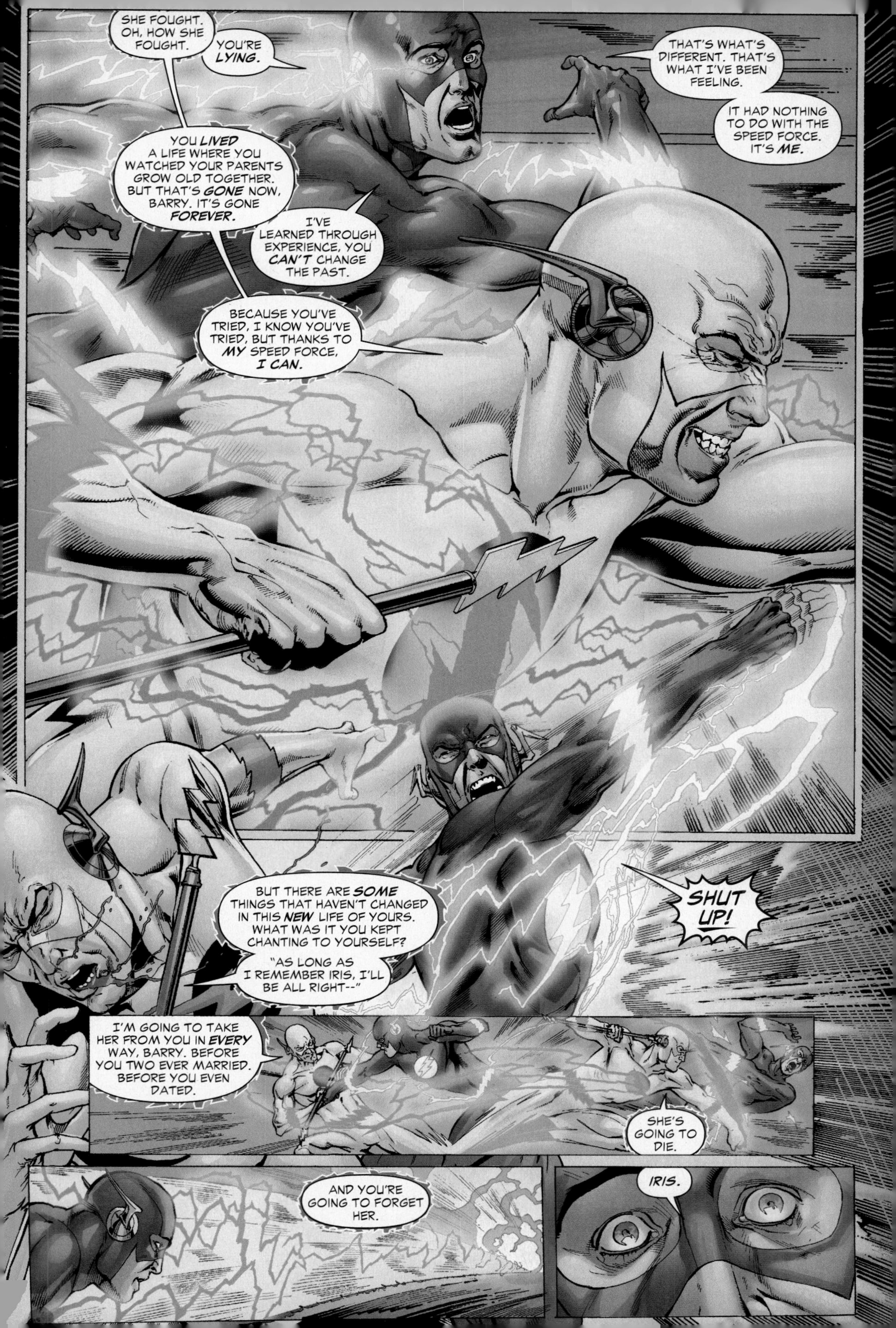
SHE FOUGHT. OH, HOW SHE FOUGHT.
YOU'RE LYING.
YOU LIVED A LIFE WHERE YOU WATCHED YOUR PARENTS GROW OLD TOGETHER. BUT THAT'S GONE NOW, BARRY. IT'S GONE FOREVER.
THAT'S WHAT'S DIFFERENT. THAT'S WHAT I'VE BEEN FEELING.
IT HAD NOTHING TO DO WITH THE SPEED FORCE. IT'S ME.
I'VE LEARNED THROUGH EXPERIENCE, YOU CAN'T CHANGE THE PAST.
BECAUSE YOU'VE TRIED, I KNOW YOU'VE TRIED, BUT THANKS TO MY SPEED FORCE, I CAN.
BUT THERE ARE SOME THINGS THAT HAVEN'T CHANGED IN THIS NEW LIFE OF YOURS. WHAT WAS IT YOU KEPT CHANTING TO YOURSELF?
"AS LONG AS I REMEMBER IRIS, I'LL BE ALL RIGHT--"
SHUT UP!
I'M GOING TO TAKE HER FROM YOU IN EVERY WAY, BARRY. BEFORE YOU TWO EVER MARRIED. BEFORE YOU EVEN DATED.
SHE'S GOING TO DIE.
AND YOU'RE GOING TO FORGET HER.
IRIS.

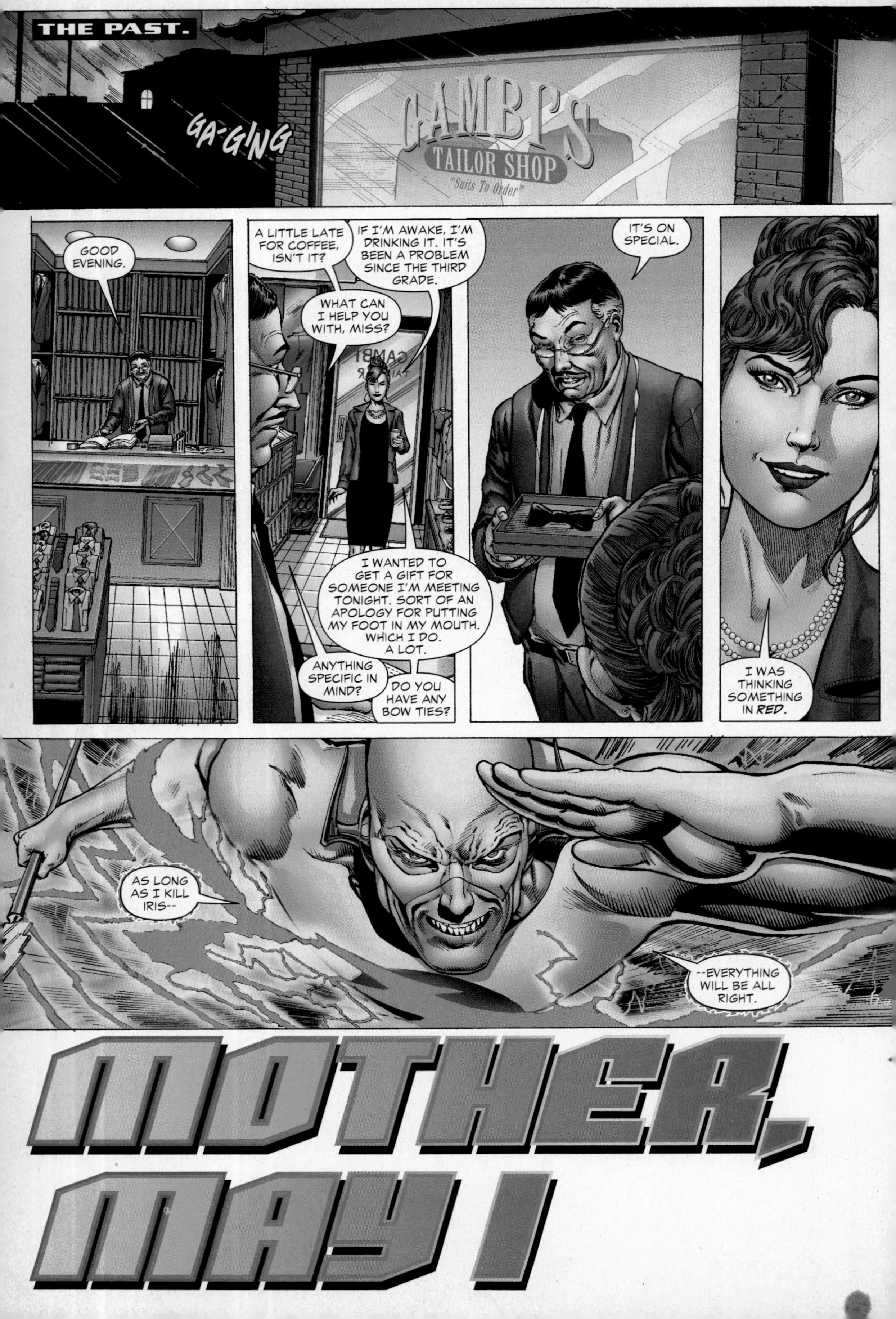
THE PAST.
GA-GING
GAMBI'S TAILOR SHOP
"Suits To Order"
GOOD EVENING.
A LITTLE LATE FOR COFFEE, ISN'T IT?
IF I'M AWAKE, I'M DRINKING IT. IT'S BEEN A PROBLEM SINCE THE THIRD GRADE.
WHAT CAN I HELP YOU WITH, MISS?
I WANTED TO GET A GIFT FOR SOMEONE I'M MEETING TONIGHT. SORT OF AN APOLOGY FOR PUTTING MY FOOT IN MY MOUTH. WHICH I DO. A LOT.
ANYTHING SPECIFIC IN MIND?
DO YOU HAVE ANY BOW TIES?
IT'S ON SPECIAL.
I WAS THINKING SOMETHING IN *RED*.
AS LONG AS I KILL IRIS--
--EVERYTHING WILL BE ALL RIGHT.
MOTHER, MAY I

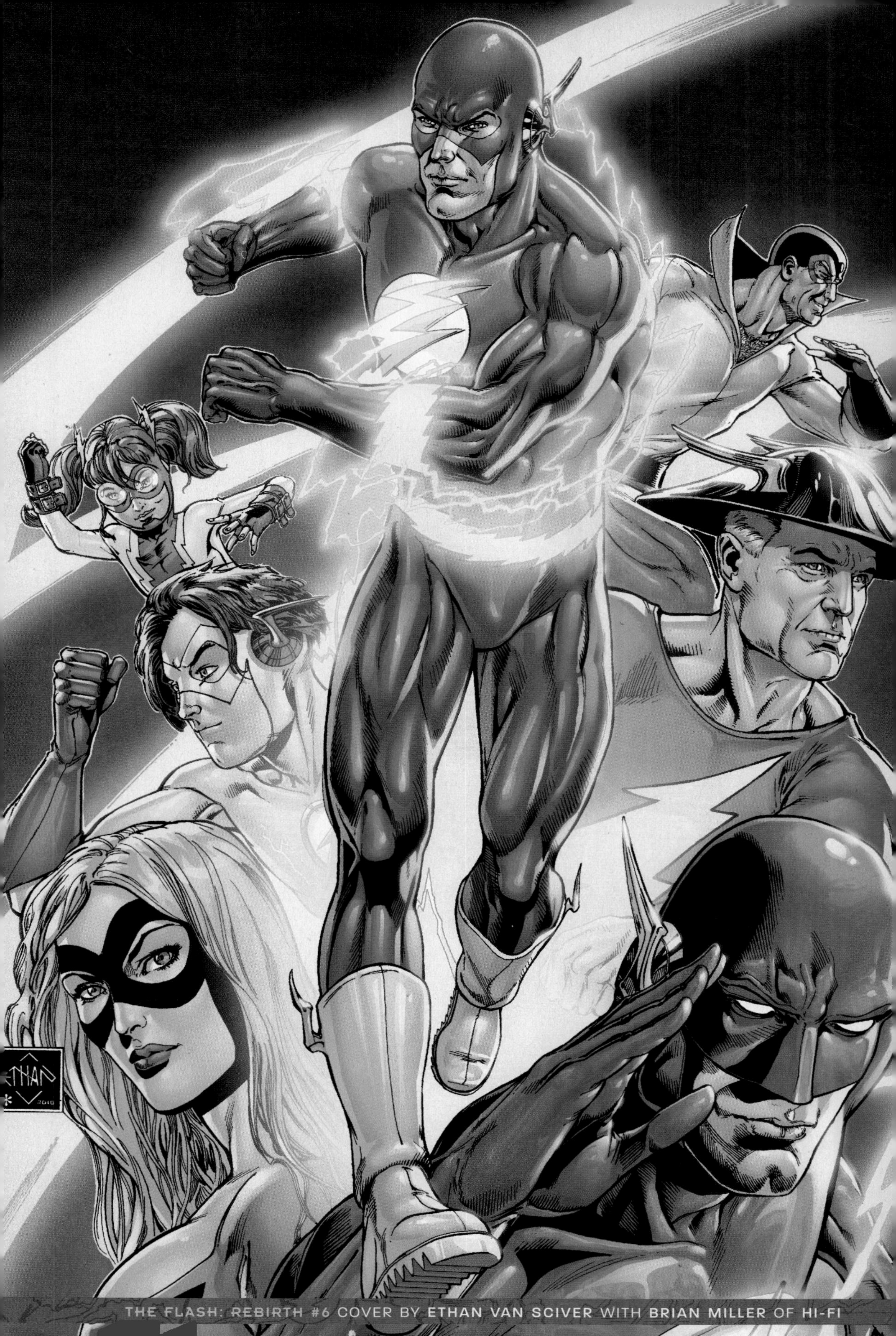
ETHAN 2010

THE FLASH: REBIRTH #6 COVER BY ETHAN VAN SCIVER WITH BRIAN MILLER OF HI-FI

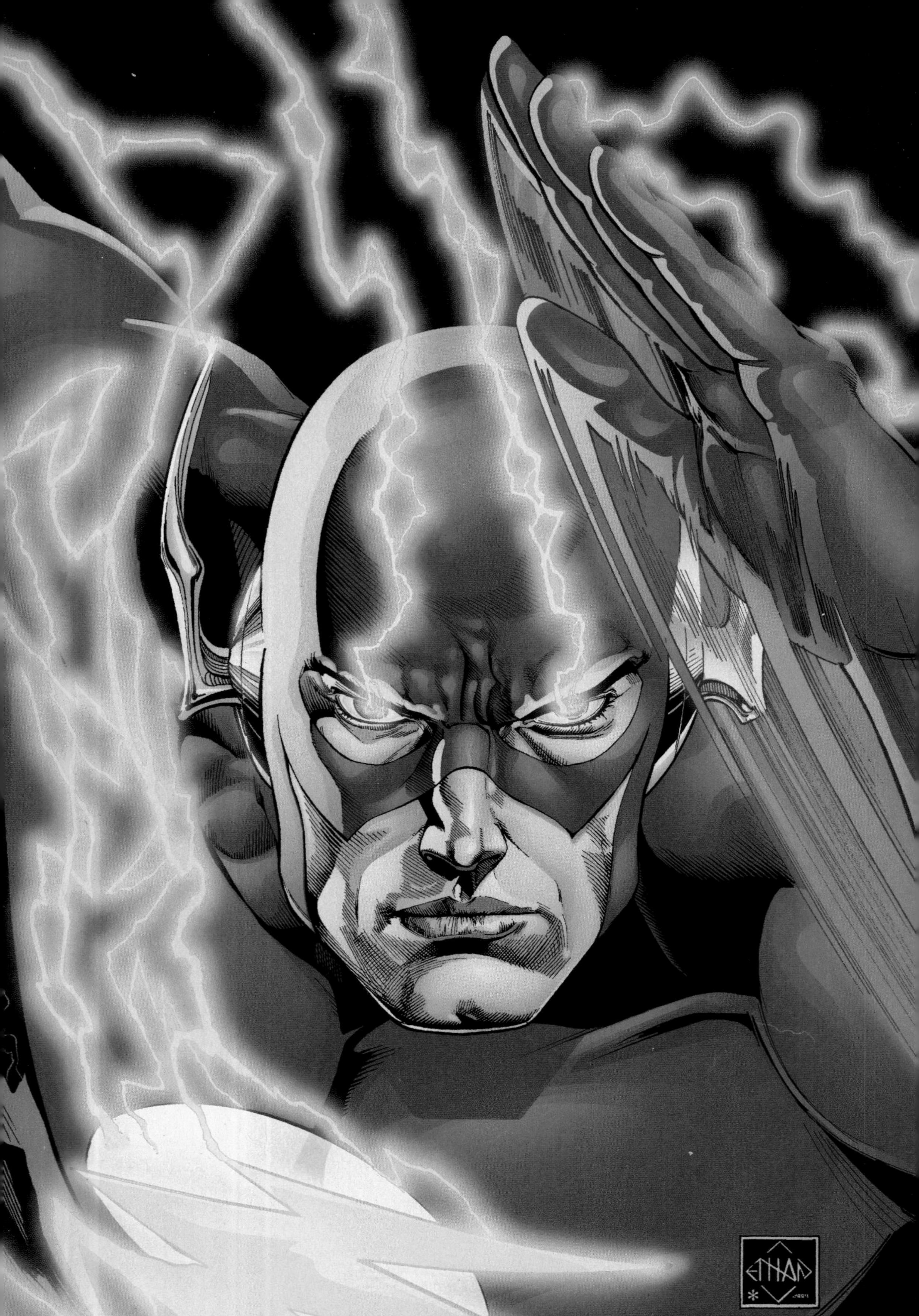
ETHAN

THE FLASH: REBIRTH #6 VARIANT COVER BY **ETHAN VAN SCIVER** WITH **BRIAN MILLER** OF **HI-FI**

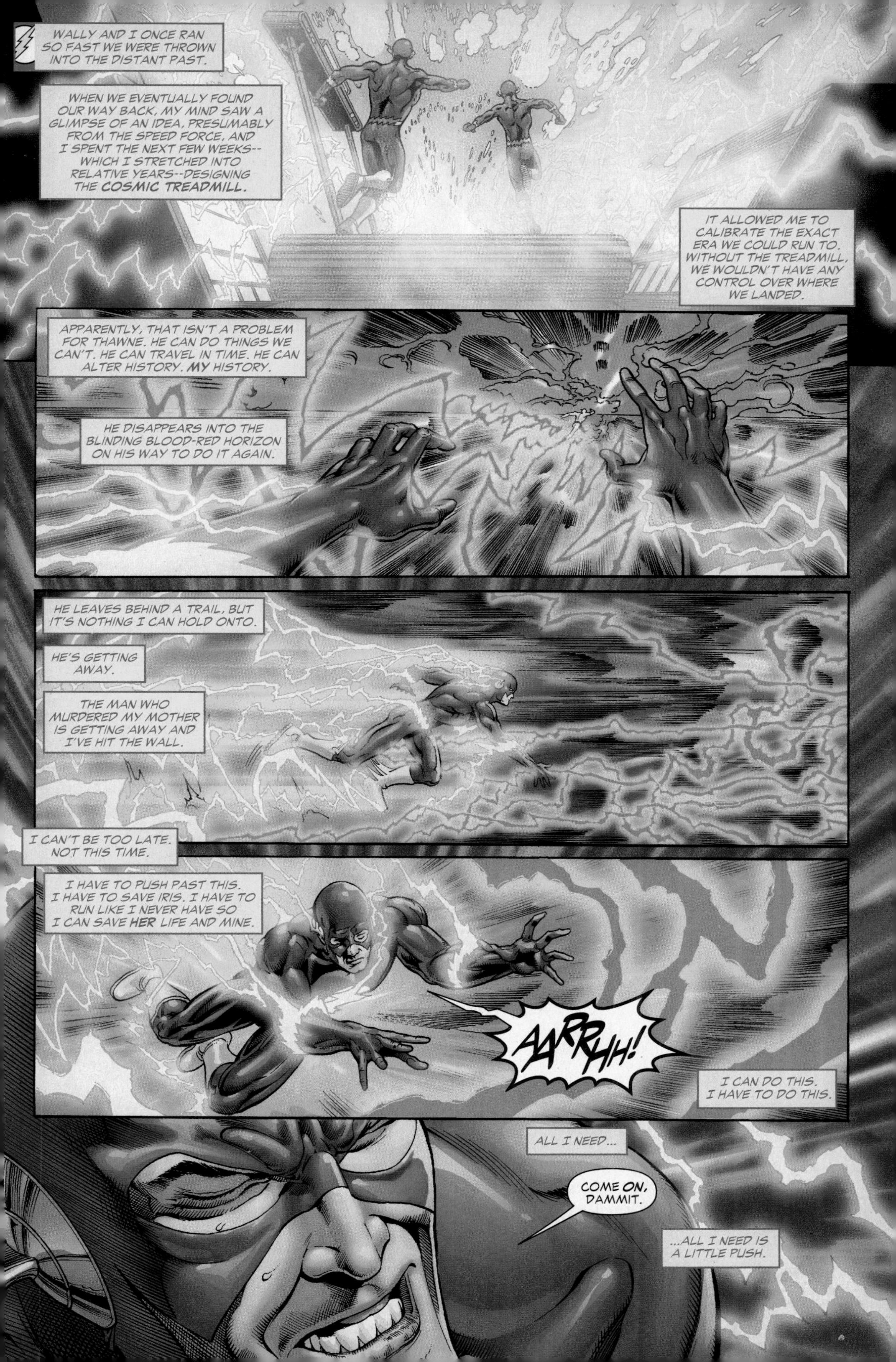
WALLY AND I ONCE RAN SO FAST WE WERE THROWN INTO THE DISTANT PAST.
WHEN WE EVENTUALLY FOUND OUR WAY BACK, MY MIND SAW A GLIMPSE OF AN IDEA, PRESUMABLY FROM THE SPEED FORCE, AND I SPENT THE NEXT FEW WEEKS--WHICH I STRETCHED INTO RELATIVE YEARS--DESIGNING THE COSMIC TREADMILL.
IT ALLOWED ME TO CALIBRATE THE EXACT ERA WE COULD RUN TO. WITHOUT THE TREADMILL, WE WOULDN'T HAVE ANY CONTROL OVER WHERE WE LANDED.
APPARENTLY, THAT ISN'T A PROBLEM FOR THAWNE. HE CAN DO THINGS WE CAN'T. HE CAN TRAVEL IN TIME. HE CAN ALTER HISTORY. MY HISTORY.
HE DISAPPEARS INTO THE BLINDING BLOOD-RED HORIZON ON HIS WAY TO DO IT AGAIN.
HE LEAVES BEHIND A TRAIL, BUT IT'S NOTHING I CAN HOLD ONTO.
HE'S GETTING AWAY.
THE MAN WHO MURDERED MY MOTHER IS GETTING AWAY AND I'VE HIT THE WALL.
I CAN'T BE TOO LATE. NOT THIS TIME.
I HAVE TO PUSH PAST THIS. I HAVE TO SAVE IRIS. I HAVE TO RUN LIKE I NEVER HAVE SO I CAN SAVE HER LIFE AND MINE.
AARRHH!
I CAN DO THIS. I HAVE TO DO THIS.
ALL I NEED...
COME ON, DAMMIT.
...ALL I NEED IS A LITTLE PUSH.

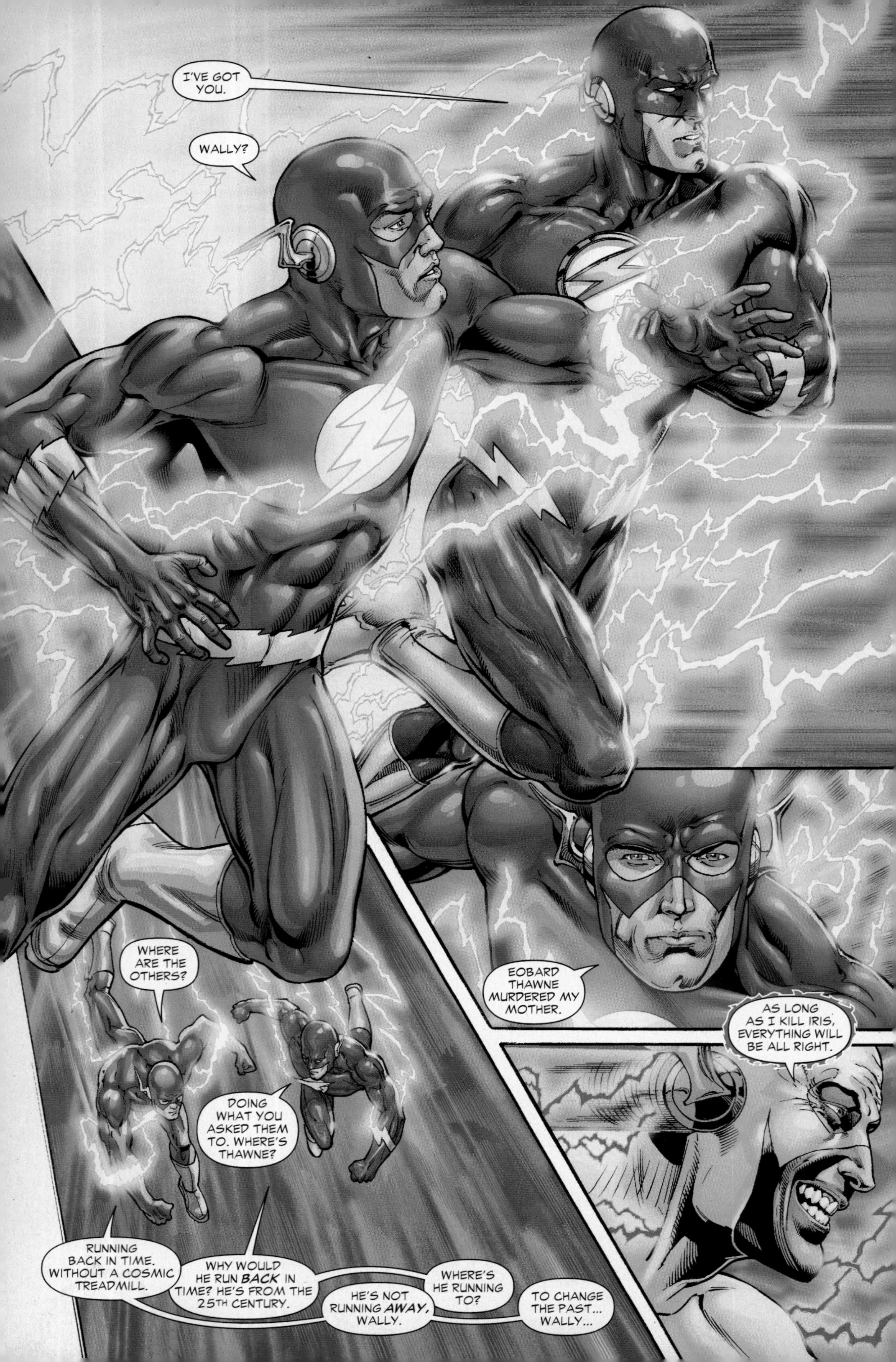
I'VE GOT YOU.
WALLY?
EOBARD THAWNE MURDERED MY MOTHER.
AS LONG AS I KILL IRIS, EVERYTHING WILL BE ALL RIGHT.
WHERE ARE THE OTHERS?
DOING WHAT YOU ASKED THEM TO. WHERE'S THAWNE?
RUNNING BACK IN TIME. WITHOUT A COSMIC TREADMILL.
WHY WOULD HE RUN BACK IN TIME? HE'S FROM THE 25TH CENTURY.
HE'S NOT RUNNING AWAY, WALLY.
WHERE'S HE RUNNING TO?
TO CHANGE THE PAST... WALLY...

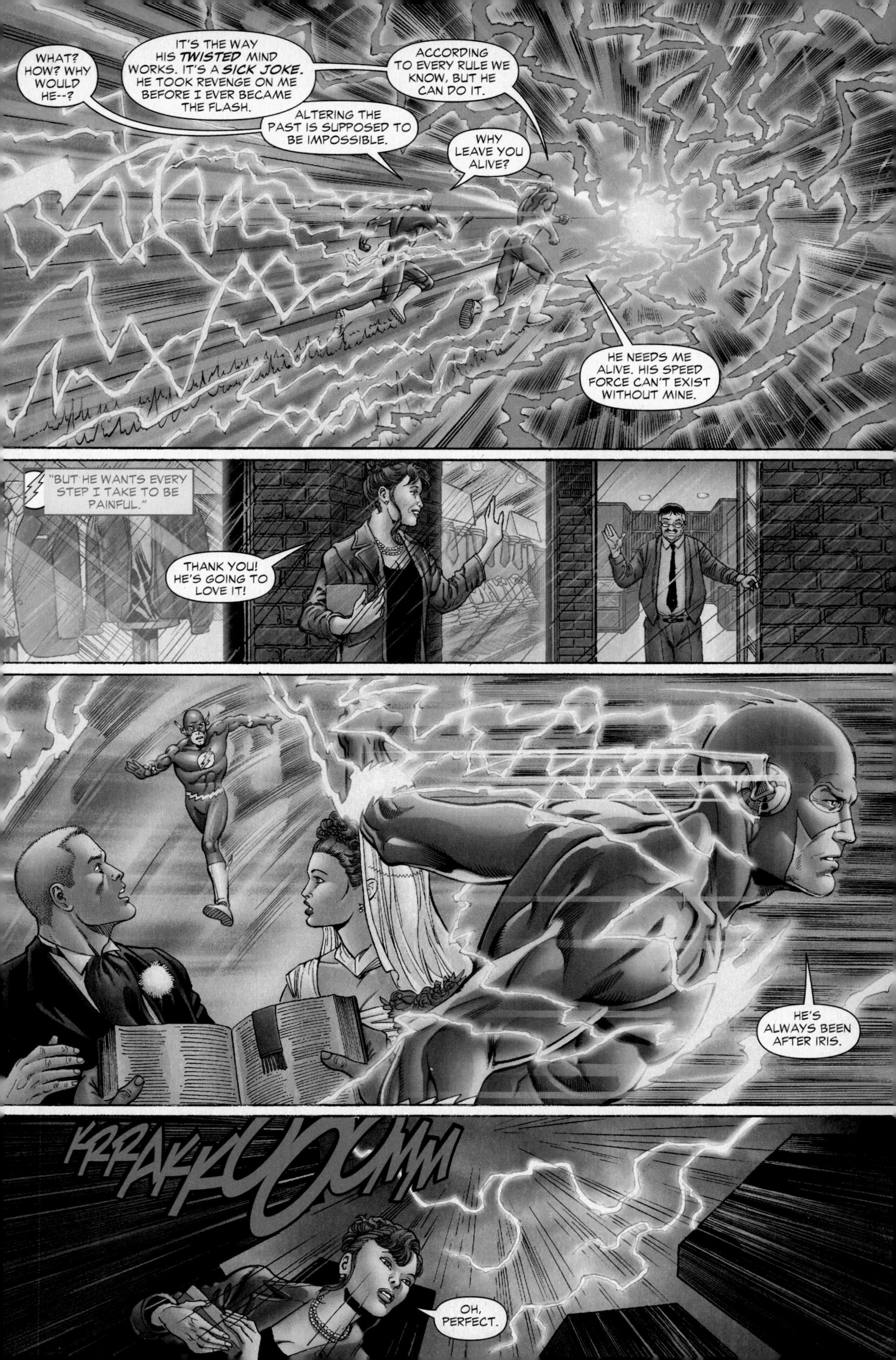
WHAT? HOW? WHY WOULD HE--?
IT'S THE WAY HIS TWISTED MIND WORKS. IT'S A SICK JOKE. HE TOOK REVENGE ON ME BEFORE I EVER BECAME THE FLASH.
ALTERING THE PAST IS SUPPOSED TO BE IMPOSSIBLE.
ACCORDING TO EVERY RULE WE KNOW, BUT HE CAN DO IT.
WHY LEAVE YOU ALIVE?
HE NEEDS ME ALIVE. HIS SPEED FORCE CAN'T EXIST WITHOUT MINE.
"BUT HE WANTS EVERY STEP I TAKE TO BE PAINFUL."
THANK YOU! HE'S GOING TO LOVE IT!
HE'S ALWAYS BEEN AFTER IRIS.
KRRAKKOOOMM
OH, PERFECT.

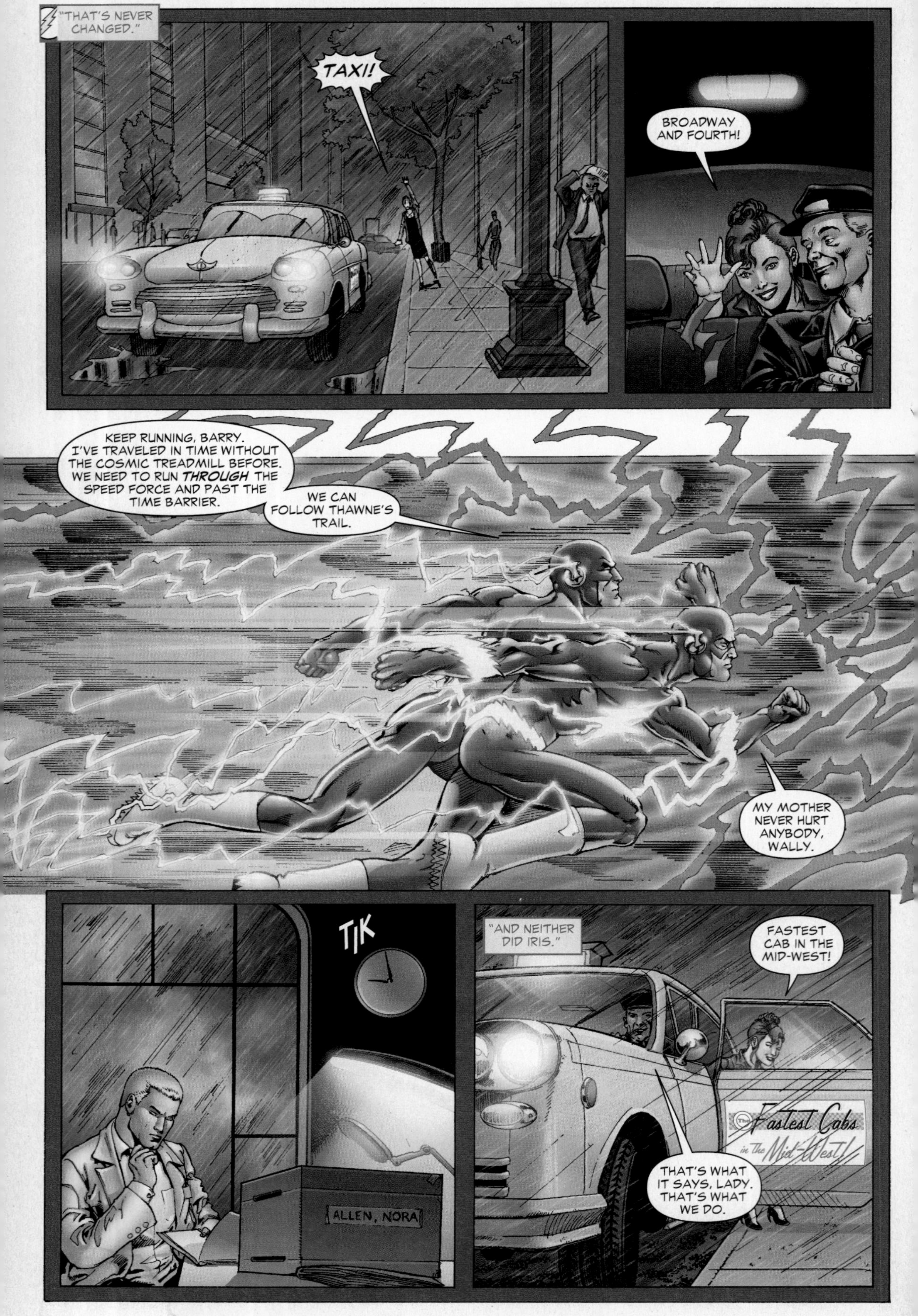
"THAT'S NEVER CHANGED."
TAXI!
BROADWAY AND FOURTH!
KEEP RUNNING, BARRY. I'VE TRAVELED IN TIME WITHOUT THE COSMIC TREADMILL BEFORE. WE NEED TO RUN *THROUGH* THE SPEED FORCE AND PAST THE TIME BARRIER.
WE CAN FOLLOW THAWNE'S TRAIL.
MY MOTHER NEVER HURT ANYBODY, WALLY.
TIK
ALLEN, NORA
"AND NEITHER DID IRIS."
FASTEST CAB IN THE MID-WEST!
The Fastest Cabs in The Mid-West!
THAT'S WHAT IT SAYS, LADY. THAT'S WHAT WE DO.

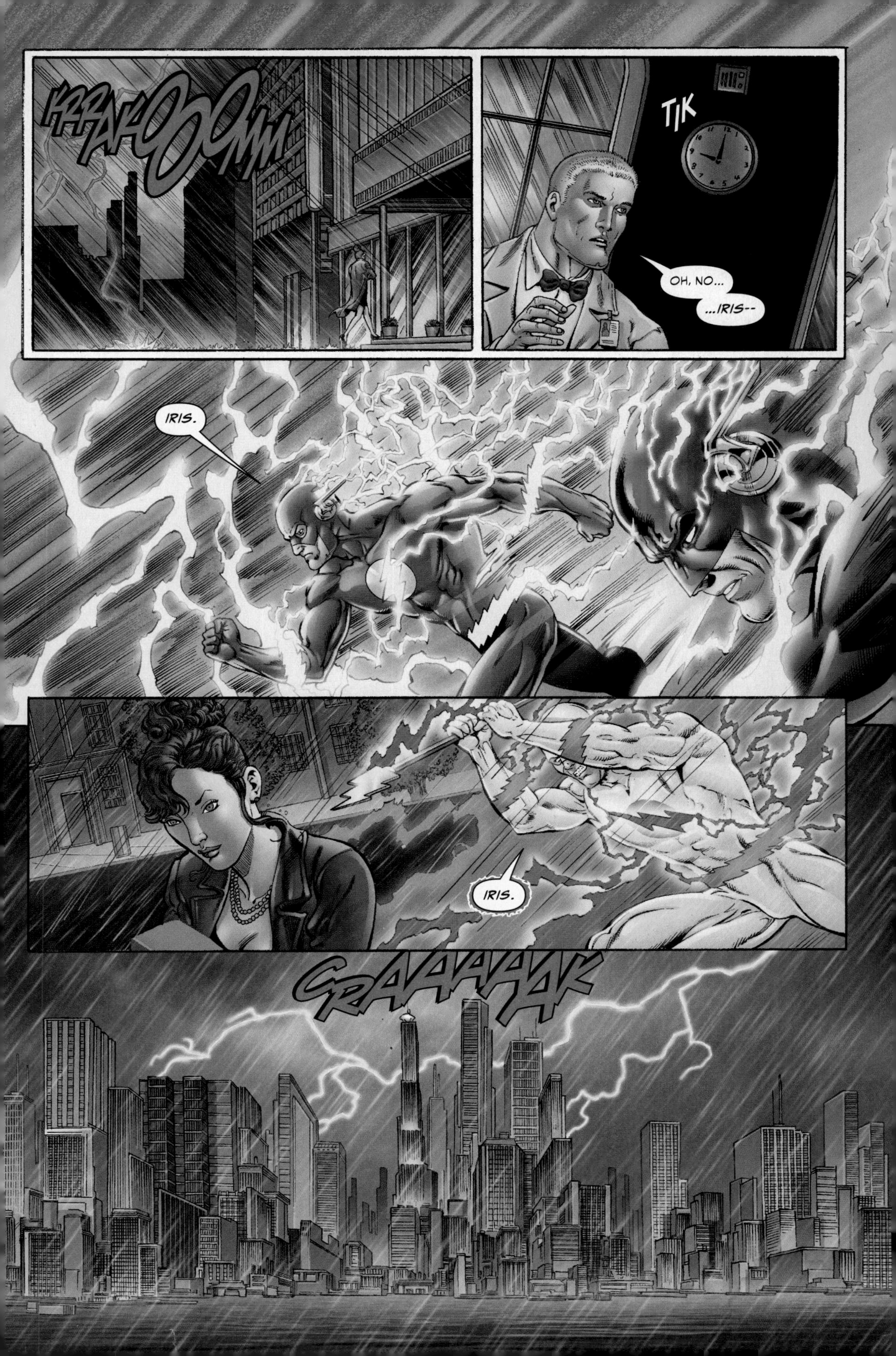
KRRAKOOOMMM
TIK
OH, NO...
...IRIS--
IRIS.
IRIS.
CRAAAAAK

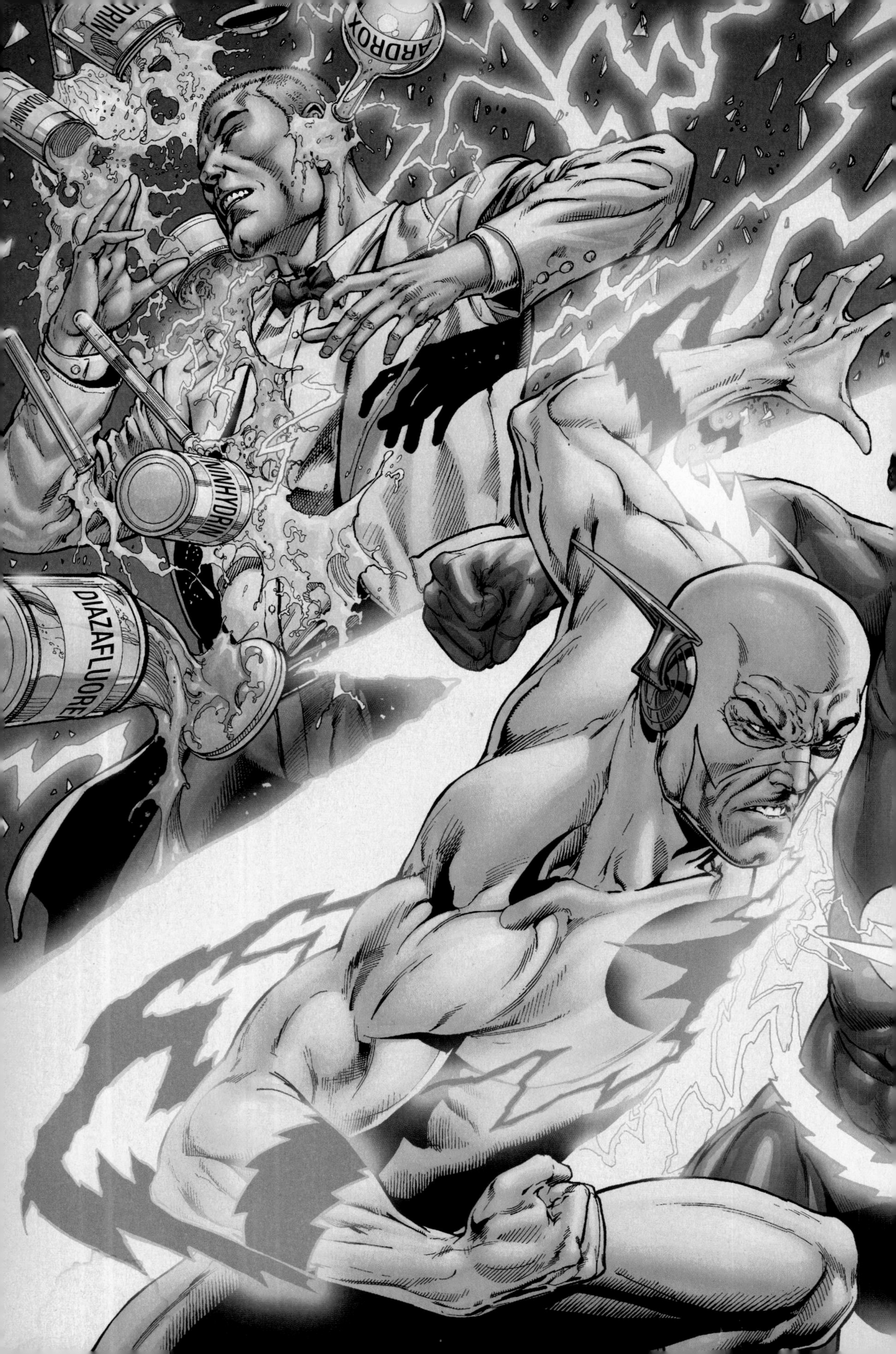
ARDROX
NINHYDRIN
DIAZAFLUORE

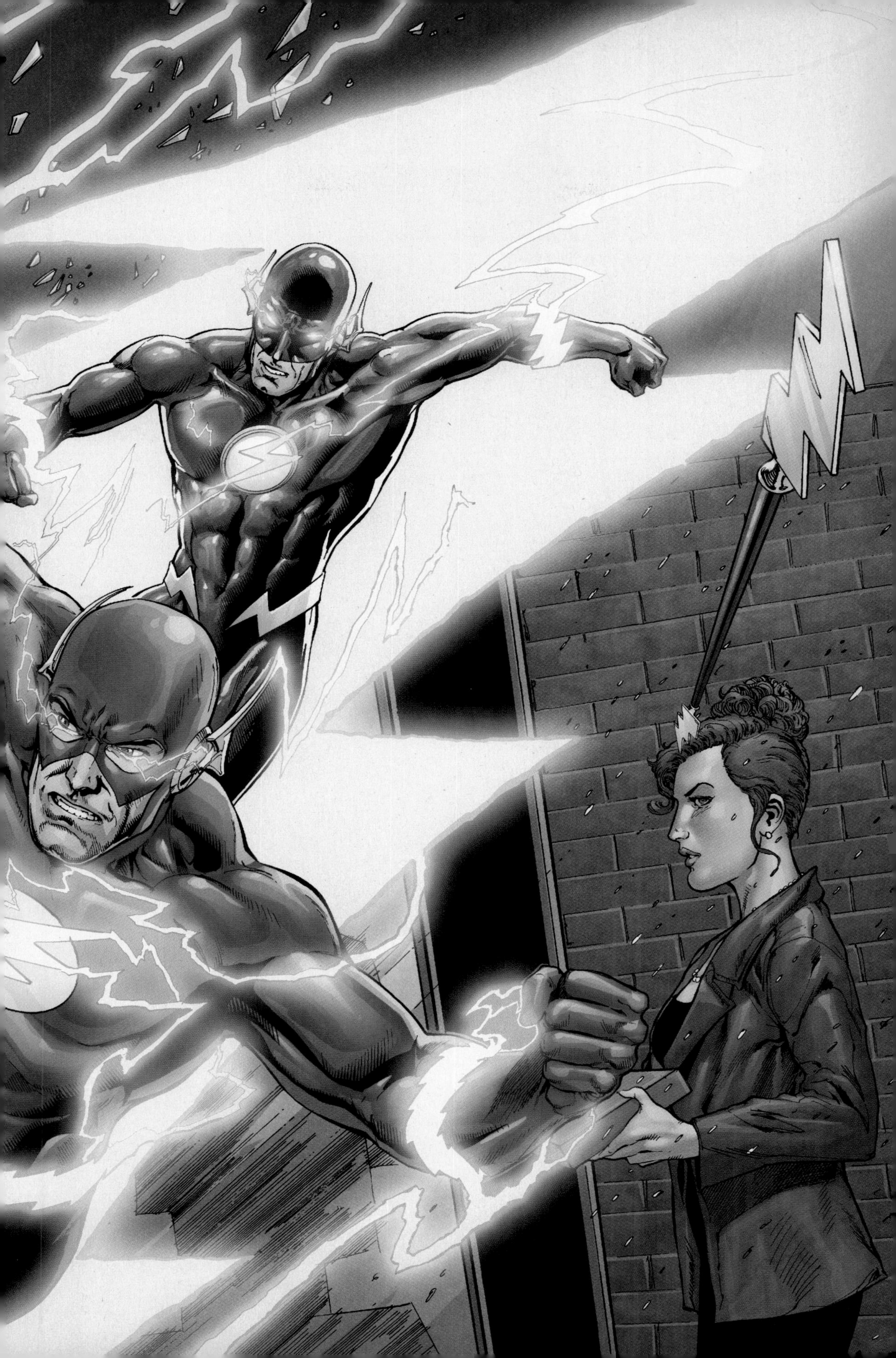

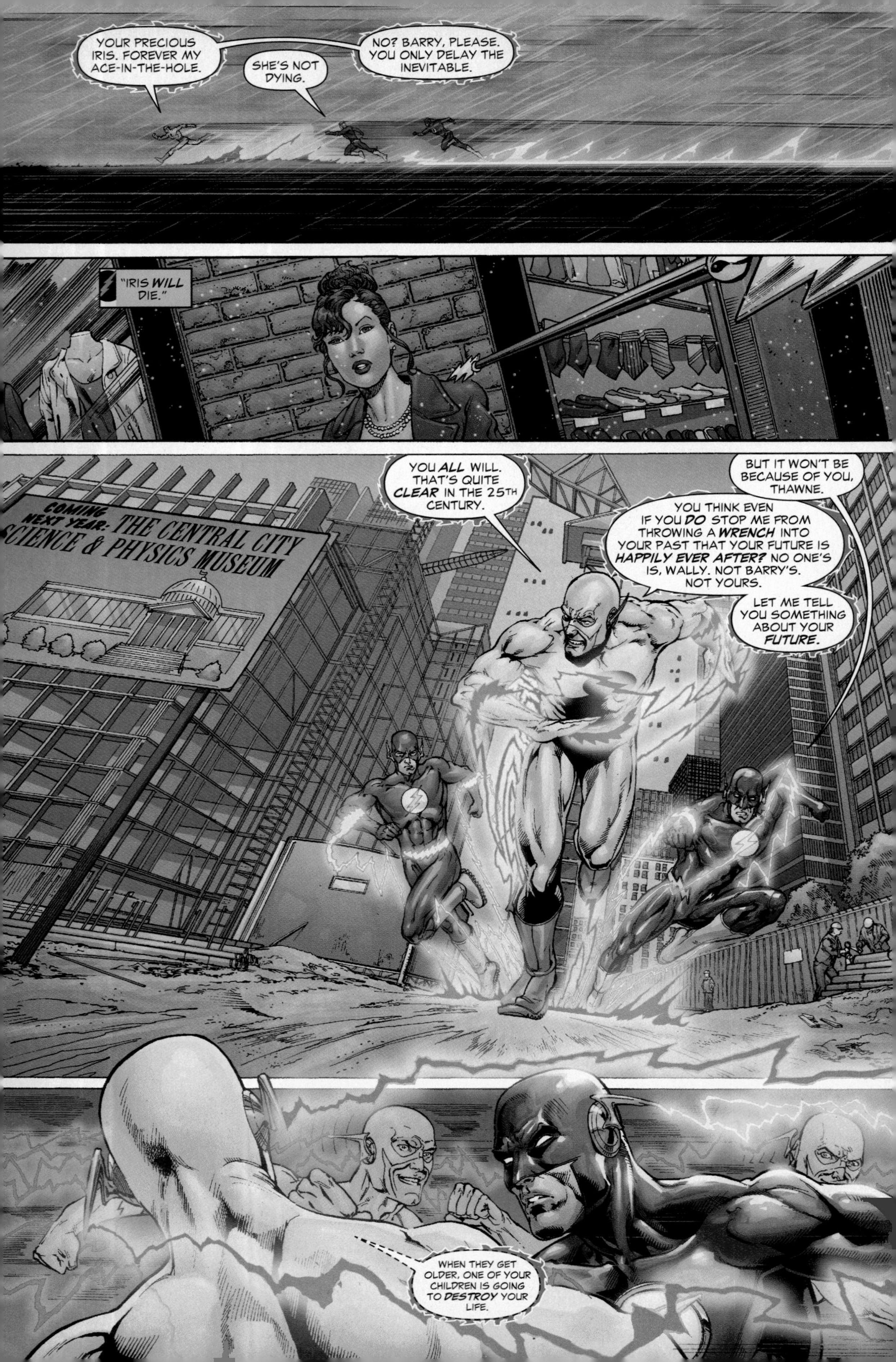

YOUR PRECIOUS IRIS. FOREVER MY ACE-IN-THE-HOLE.
SHE'S NOT DYING.
NO? BARRY, PLEASE. YOU ONLY DELAY THE INEVITABLE.
"IRIS WILL DIE."
COMING NEXT YEAR: THE CENTRAL CITY SCIENCE & PHYSICS MUSEUM
YOU ALL WILL. THAT'S QUITE CLEAR IN THE 25TH CENTURY.
BUT IT WON'T BE BECAUSE OF YOU, THAWNE.
YOU THINK EVEN IF YOU DO STOP ME FROM THROWING A WRENCH INTO YOUR PAST THAT YOUR FUTURE IS HAPPILY EVER AFTER? NO ONE'S IS, WALLY. NOT BARRY'S. NOT YOURS.
LET ME TELL YOU SOMETHING ABOUT YOUR FUTURE.
WHEN THEY GET OLDER, ONE OF YOUR CHILDREN IS GOING TO DESTROY YOUR LIFE.

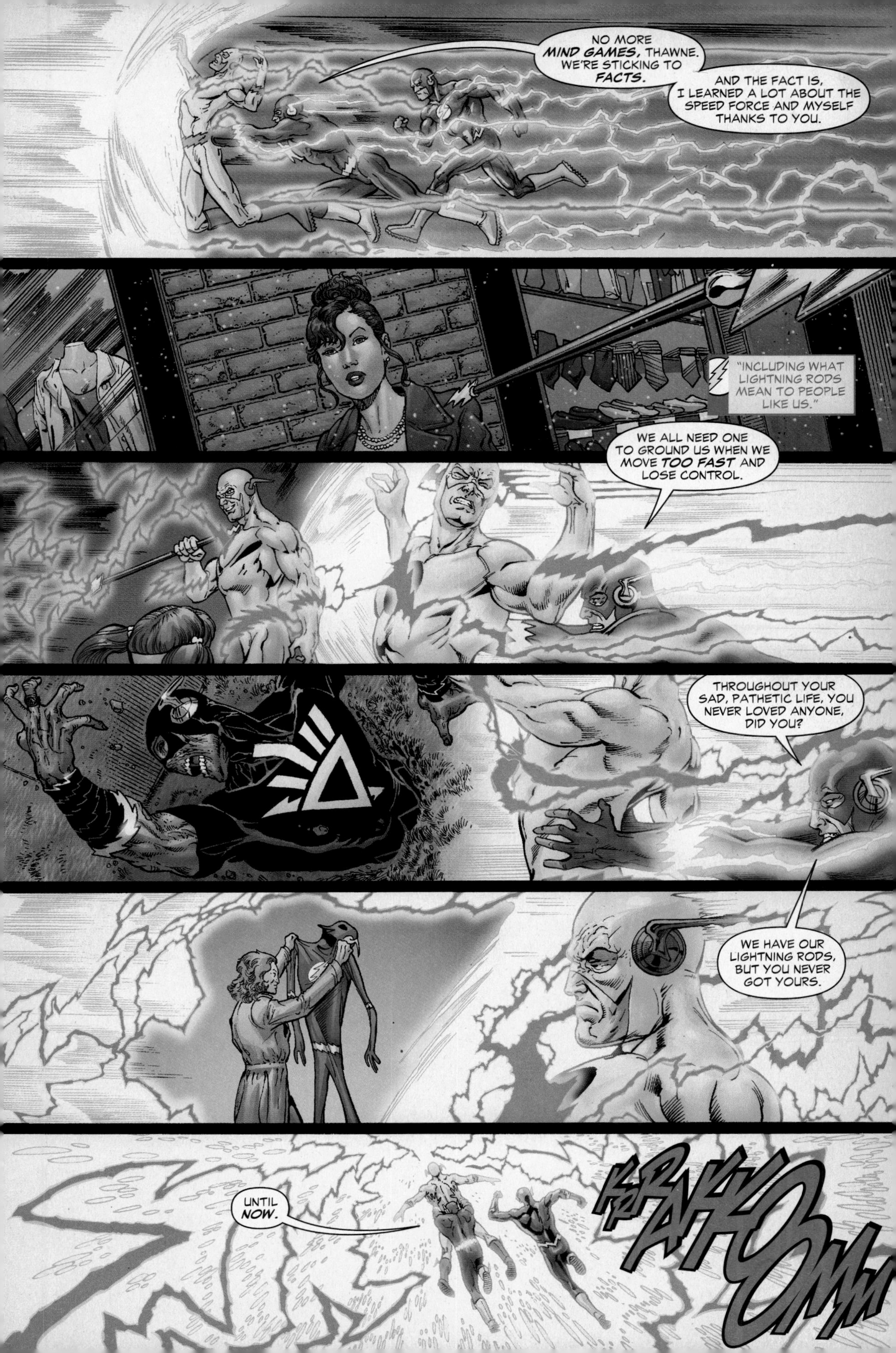

NO MORE MIND GAMES, THAWNE. WE'RE STICKING TO FACTS.
AND THE FACT IS, I LEARNED A LOT ABOUT THE SPEED FORCE AND MYSELF THANKS TO YOU.
"INCLUDING WHAT LIGHTNING RODS MEAN TO PEOPLE LIKE US."
WE ALL NEED ONE TO GROUND US WHEN WE MOVE TOO FAST AND LOSE CONTROL.
THROUGHOUT YOUR SAD, PATHETIC LIFE, YOU NEVER LOVED ANYONE, DID YOU?
WE HAVE OUR LIGHTNING RODS, BUT YOU NEVER GOT YOURS.
UNTIL NOW.

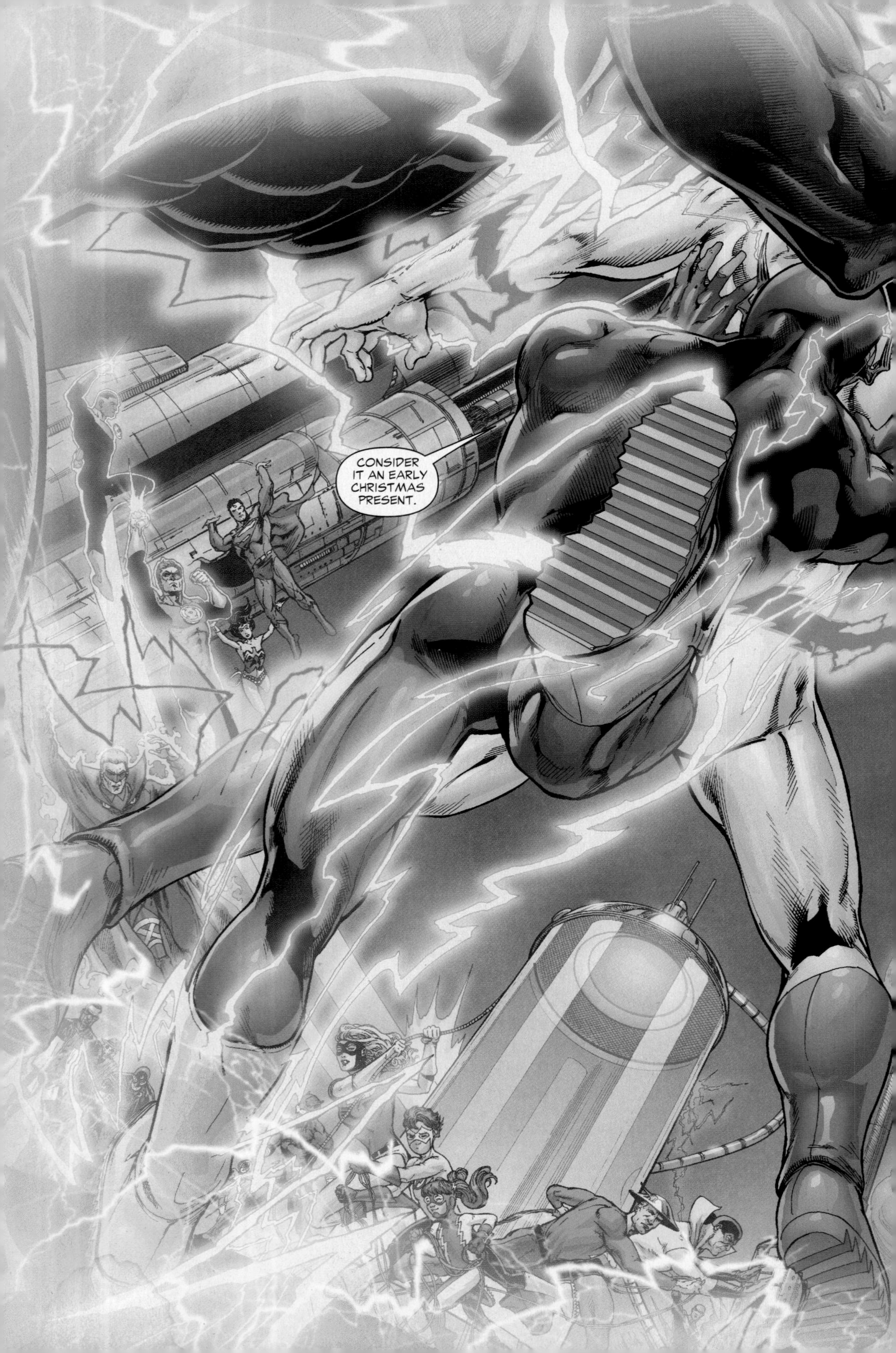
CONSIDER IT AN EARLY CHRISTMAS PRESENT.

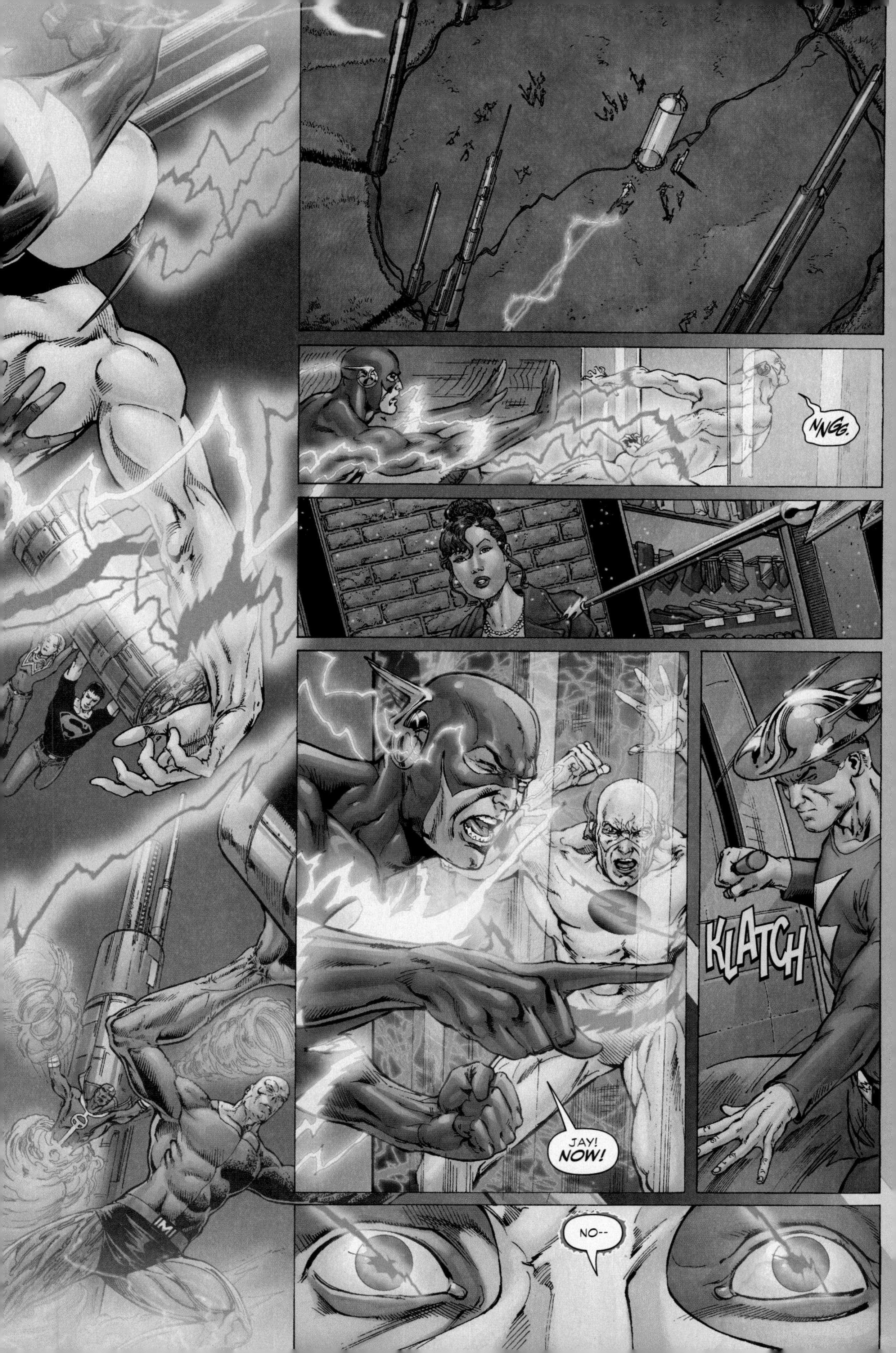
NNGG.
KLATCH
JAY! NOW!
NO--

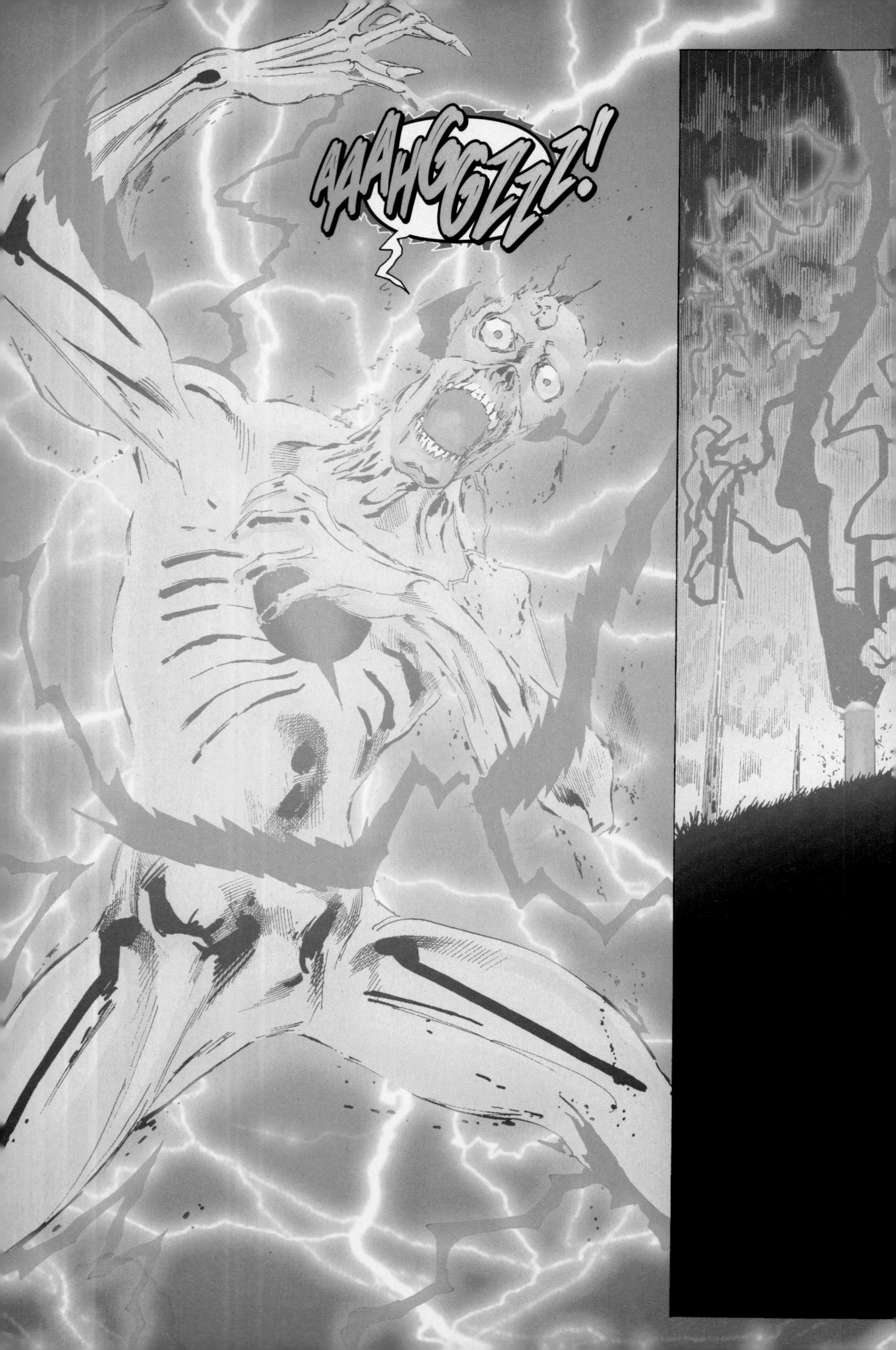
AAAHGGZZZZ!

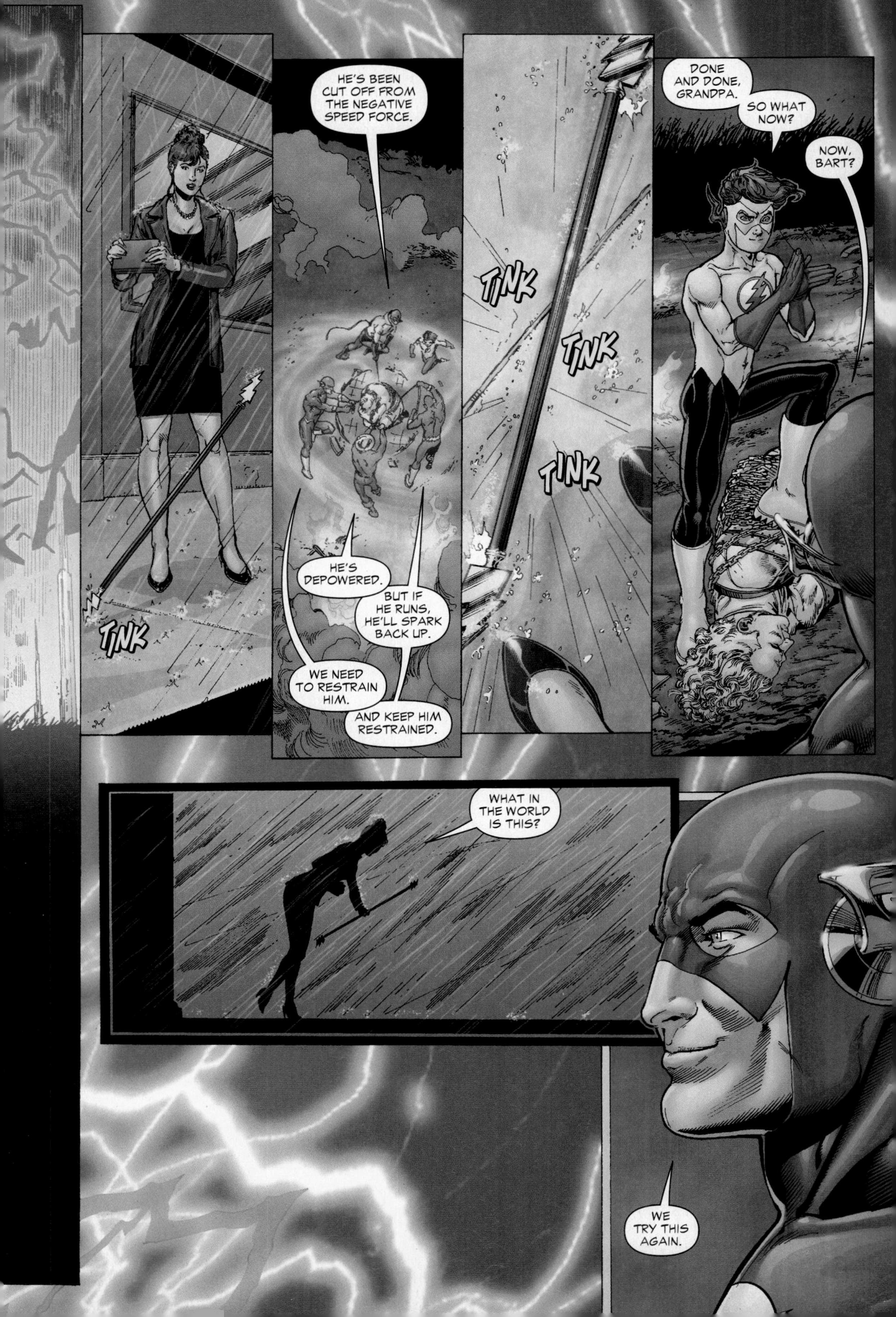
TINK
HE'S BEEN CUT OFF FROM THE NEGATIVE SPEED FORCE.
HE'S DEPOWERED.
BUT IF HE RUNS, HE'LL SPARK BACK UP.
WE NEED TO RESTRAIN HIM.
AND KEEP HIM RESTRAINED.
TINK
TINK
TINK
DONE AND DONE, GRANDPA.
SO WHAT NOW?
NOW, BART?
WHAT IN THE WORLD IS THIS?
WE TRY THIS AGAIN.

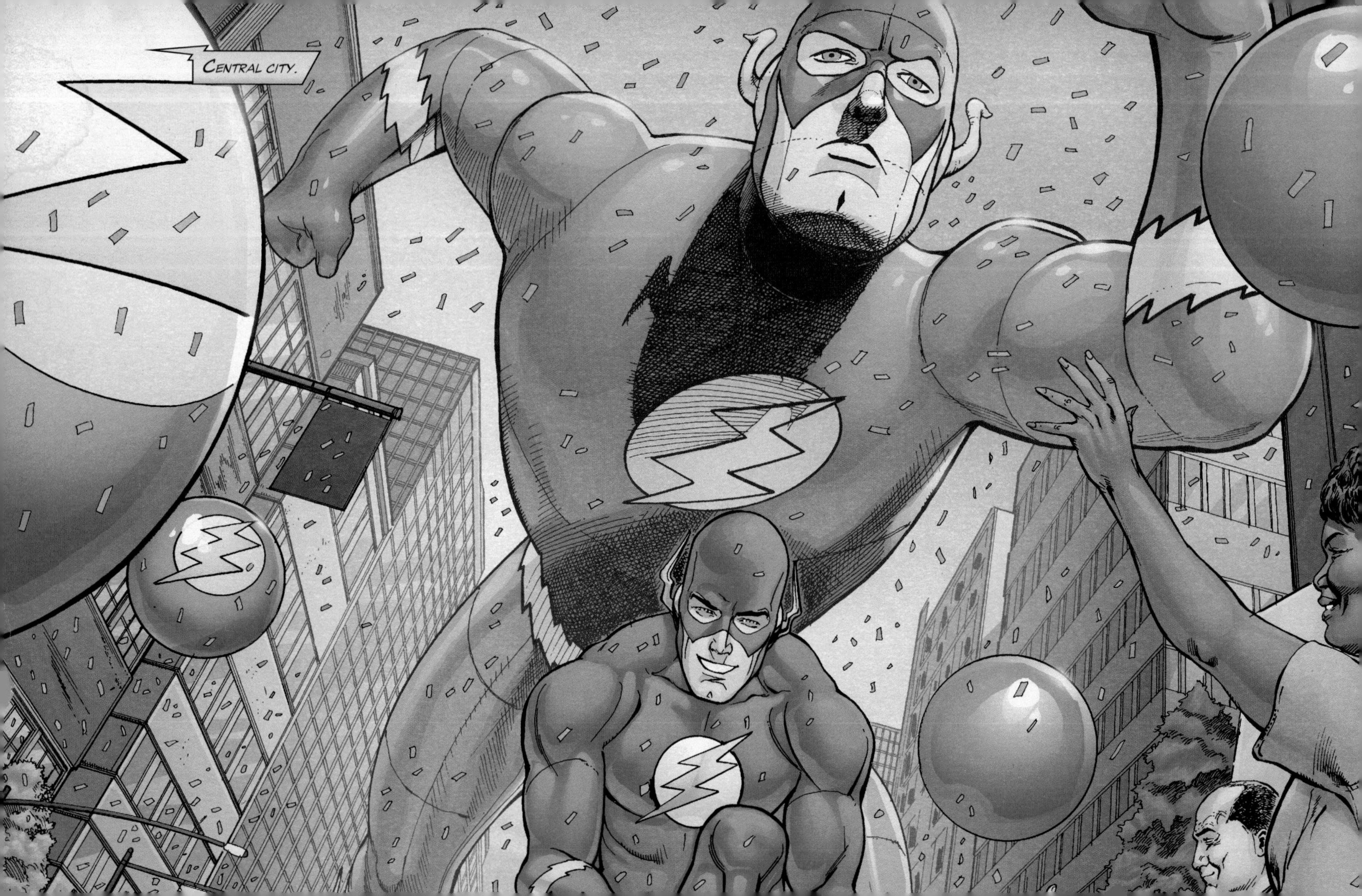
Central city.

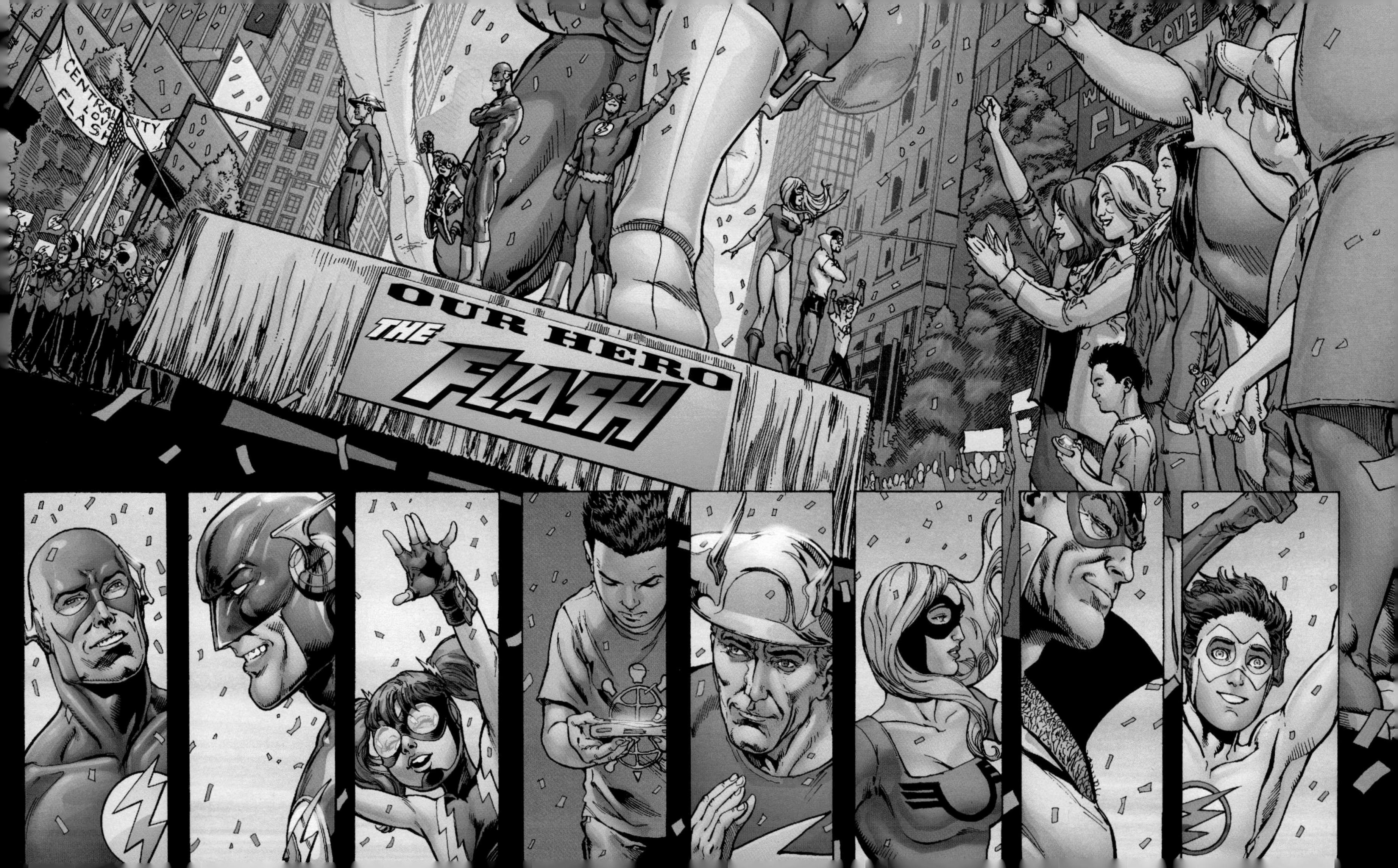
CENTRAL CITY LOVES FLASH
OUR HERO
THE FLASH

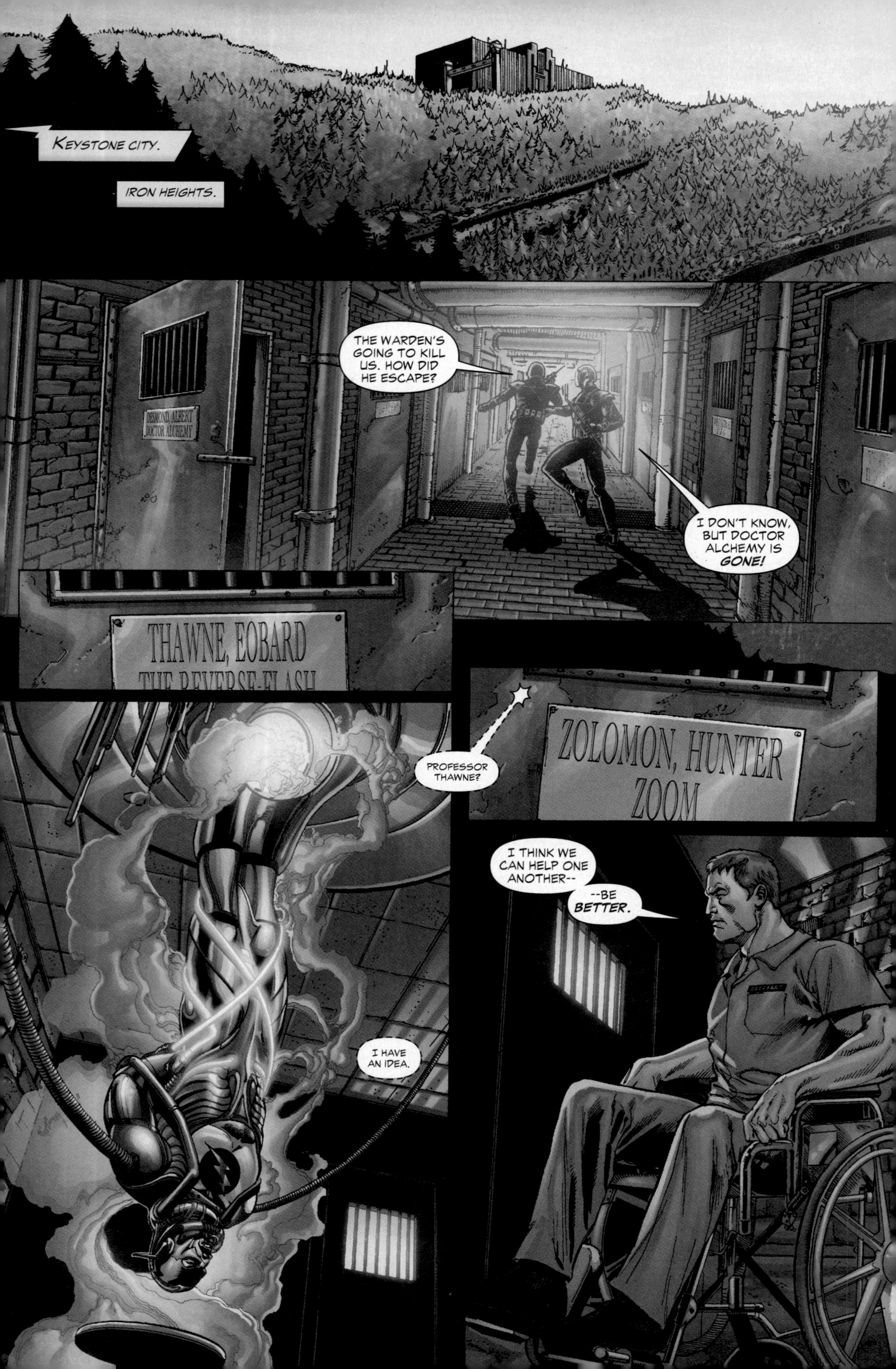

KEYSTONE CITY.
IRON HEIGHTS.
THE WARDEN'S GOING TO KILL US. HOW DID HE ESCAPE?
DESMOND, ALBERT DOCTOR ALCHEMY
I DON'T KNOW, BUT DOCTOR ALCHEMY IS GONE!
THAWNE, EOBARD
PROFESSOR THAWNE?
ZOLOMON, HUNTER ZOOM
I THINK WE CAN HELP ONE ANOTHER--
--BE BETTER.
I HAVE AN IDEA.

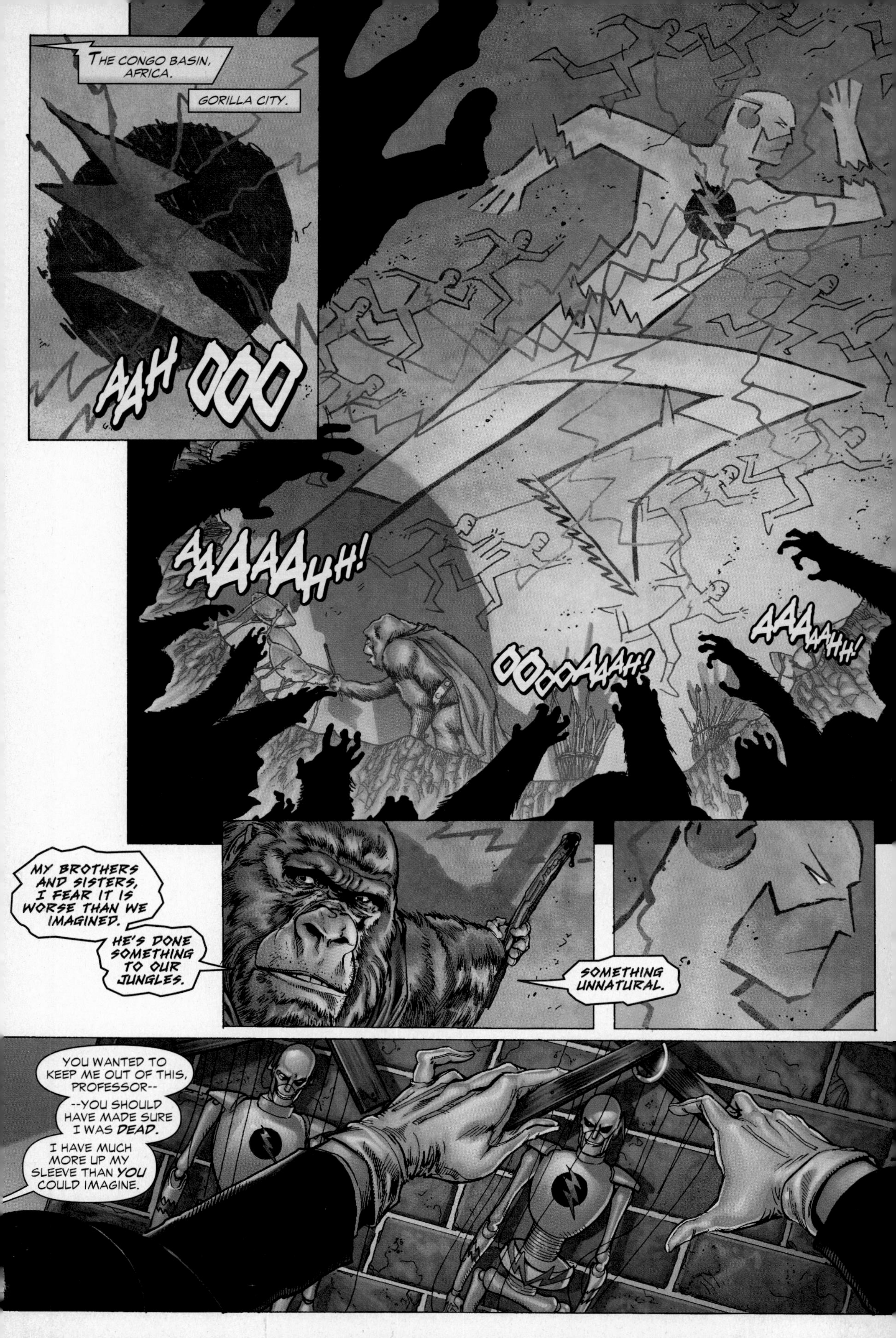
THE CONGO BASIN, AFRICA.
GORILLA CITY.
AAH OOO
AAAAAHH!
OOooAAAH!
AAAAAHH!
MY BROTHERS AND SISTERS, I FEAR IT IS WORSE THAN WE IMAGINED.
HE'S DONE SOMETHING TO OUR JUNGLES.
SOMETHING UNNATURAL.
YOU WANTED TO KEEP ME OUT OF THIS, PROFESSOR--
--YOU SHOULD HAVE MADE SURE I WAS DEAD.
I HAVE MUCH MORE UP MY SLEEVE THAN YOU COULD IMAGINE.

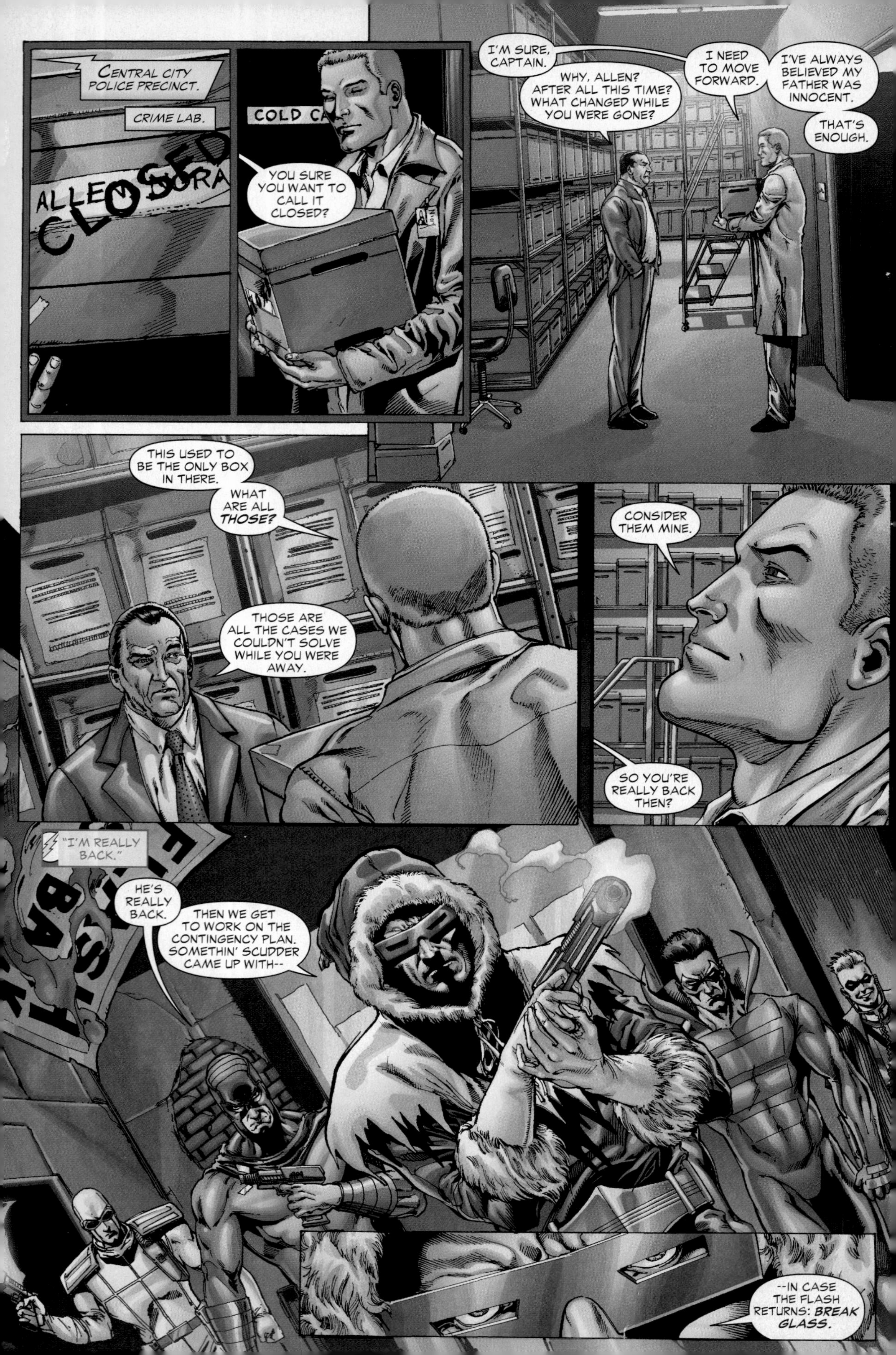
CENTRAL CITY POLICE PRECINCT.
CRIME LAB.
ALLEN DORA
CLOSED
COLD CA
YOU SURE YOU WANT TO CALL IT CLOSED?
I'M SURE, CAPTAIN.
WHY, ALLEN? AFTER ALL THIS TIME? WHAT CHANGED WHILE YOU WERE GONE?
I NEED TO MOVE FORWARD.
I'VE ALWAYS BELIEVED MY FATHER WAS INNOCENT.
THAT'S ENOUGH.
THIS USED TO BE THE ONLY BOX IN THERE.
WHAT ARE ALL THOSE?
THOSE ARE ALL THE CASES WE COULDN'T SOLVE WHILE YOU WERE AWAY.
CONSIDER THEM MINE.
SO YOU'RE REALLY BACK THEN?
"I'M REALLY BACK."
HE'S REALLY BACK.
THEN WE GET TO WORK ON THE CONTINGENCY PLAN. SOMETHIN' SCUDDER CAME UP WITH--
--IN CASE THE FLASH RETURNS: BREAK GLASS.

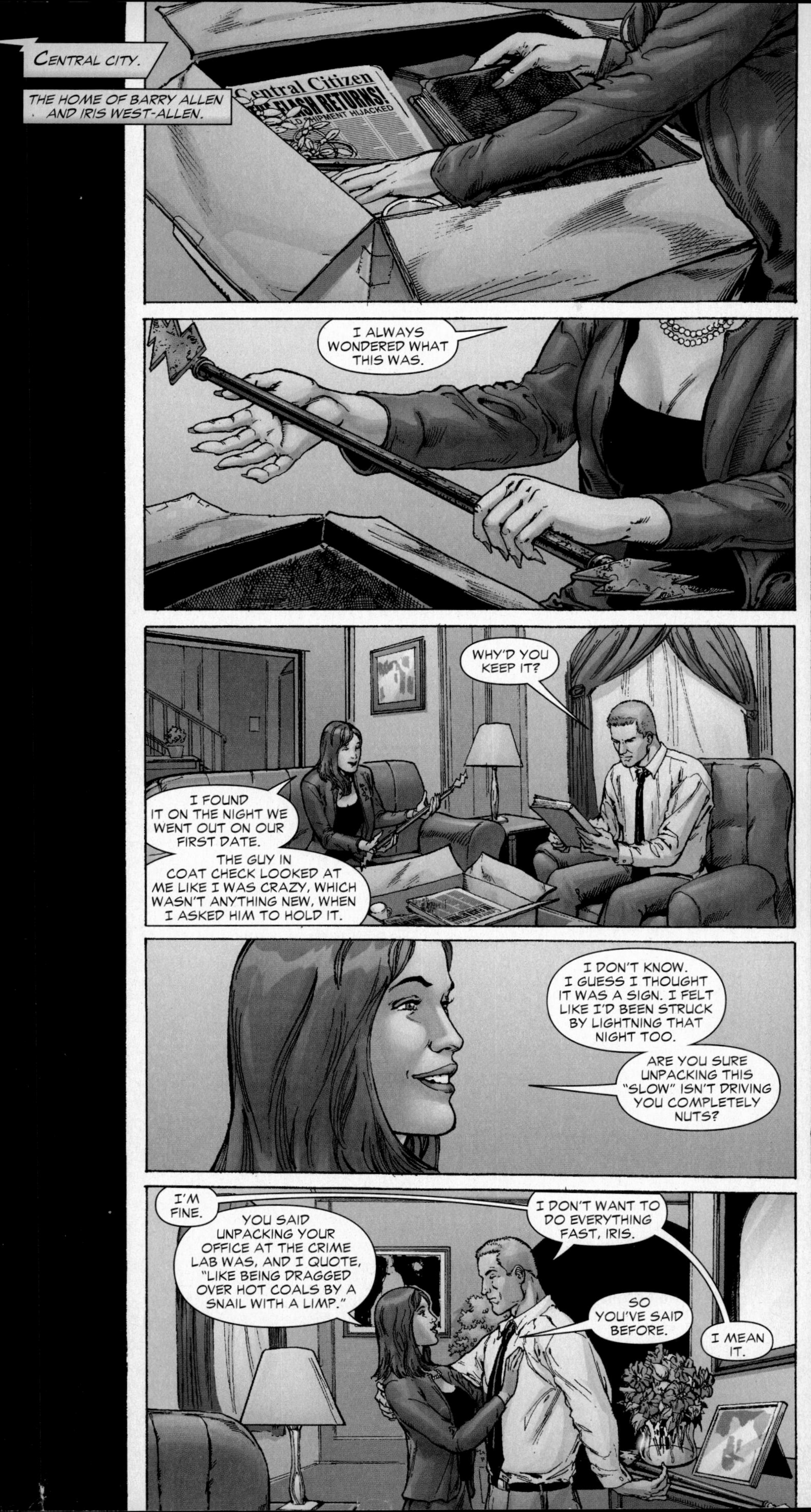

CENTRAL CITY.
THE HOME OF BARRY ALLEN AND IRIS WEST-ALLEN.
Central Citizen
FLASH RETURNS!
I ALWAYS WONDERED WHAT THIS WAS.
WHY'D YOU KEEP IT?
I FOUND IT ON THE NIGHT WE WENT OUT ON OUR FIRST DATE.
THE GUY IN COAT CHECK LOOKED AT ME LIKE I WAS CRAZY, WHICH WASN'T ANYTHING NEW, WHEN I ASKED HIM TO HOLD IT.
I DON'T KNOW. I GUESS I THOUGHT IT WAS A SIGN. I FELT LIKE I'D BEEN STRUCK BY LIGHTNING THAT NIGHT TOO.
ARE YOU SURE UNPACKING THIS "SLOW" ISN'T DRIVING YOU COMPLETELY NUTS?
I'M FINE.
YOU SAID UNPACKING YOUR OFFICE AT THE CRIME LAB WAS, AND I QUOTE, "LIKE BEING DRAGGED OVER HOT COALS BY A SNAIL WITH A LIMP."
I DON'T WANT TO DO EVERYTHING FAST, IRIS.
SO YOU'VE SAID BEFORE.
I MEAN IT.

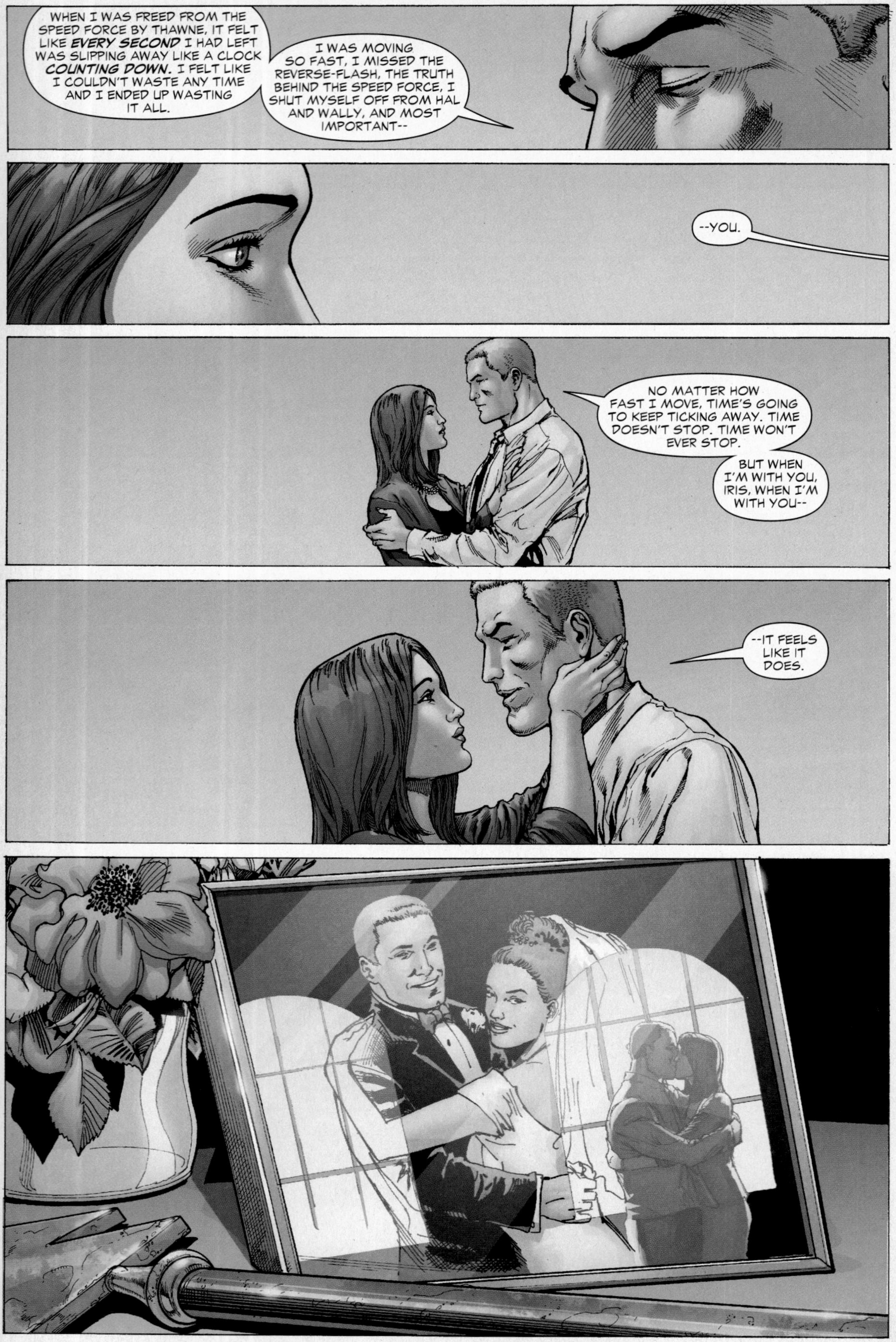
WHEN I WAS FREED FROM THE SPEED FORCE BY THAWNE, IT FELT LIKE EVERY SECOND I HAD LEFT WAS SLIPPING AWAY LIKE A CLOCK COUNTING DOWN. I FELT LIKE I COULDN'T WASTE ANY TIME AND I ENDED UP WASTING IT ALL.
I WAS MOVING SO FAST, I MISSED THE REVERSE-FLASH, THE TRUTH BEHIND THE SPEED FORCE, I SHUT MYSELF OFF FROM HAL AND WALLY, AND MOST IMPORTANT--
--YOU.
NO MATTER HOW FAST I MOVE, TIME'S GOING TO KEEP TICKING AWAY. TIME DOESN'T STOP. TIME WON'T EVER STOP.
BUT WHEN I'M WITH YOU, IRIS, WHEN I'M WITH YOU--
--IT FEELS LIKE IT DOES.

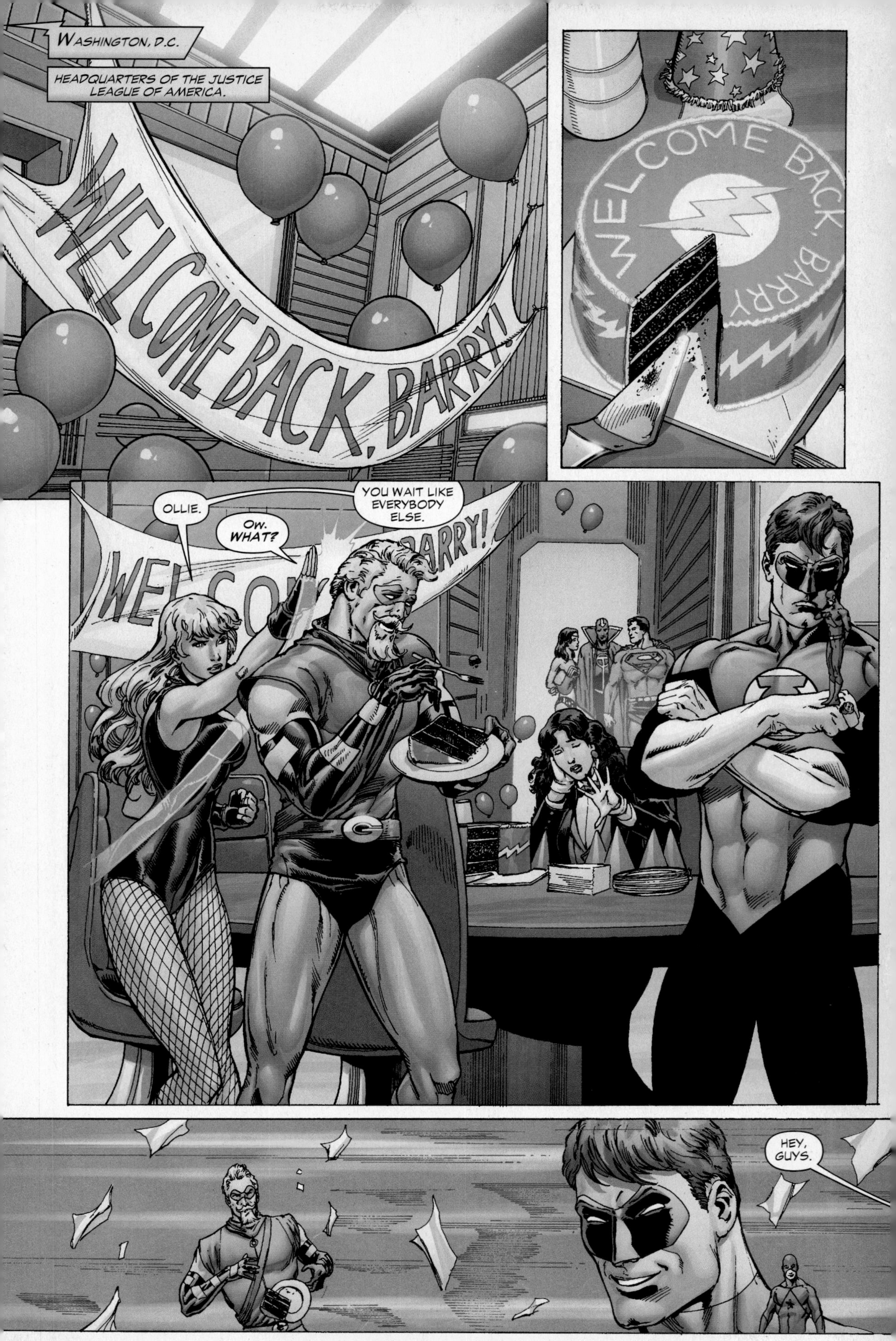

WASHINGTON, D.C.
HEADQUARTERS OF THE JUSTICE LEAGUE OF AMERICA.
WELCOME BACK, BARRY!
WELCOME BACK, BARRY
OLLIE.
OW. WHAT?
YOU WAIT LIKE EVERYBODY ELSE.
HEY, GUYS.

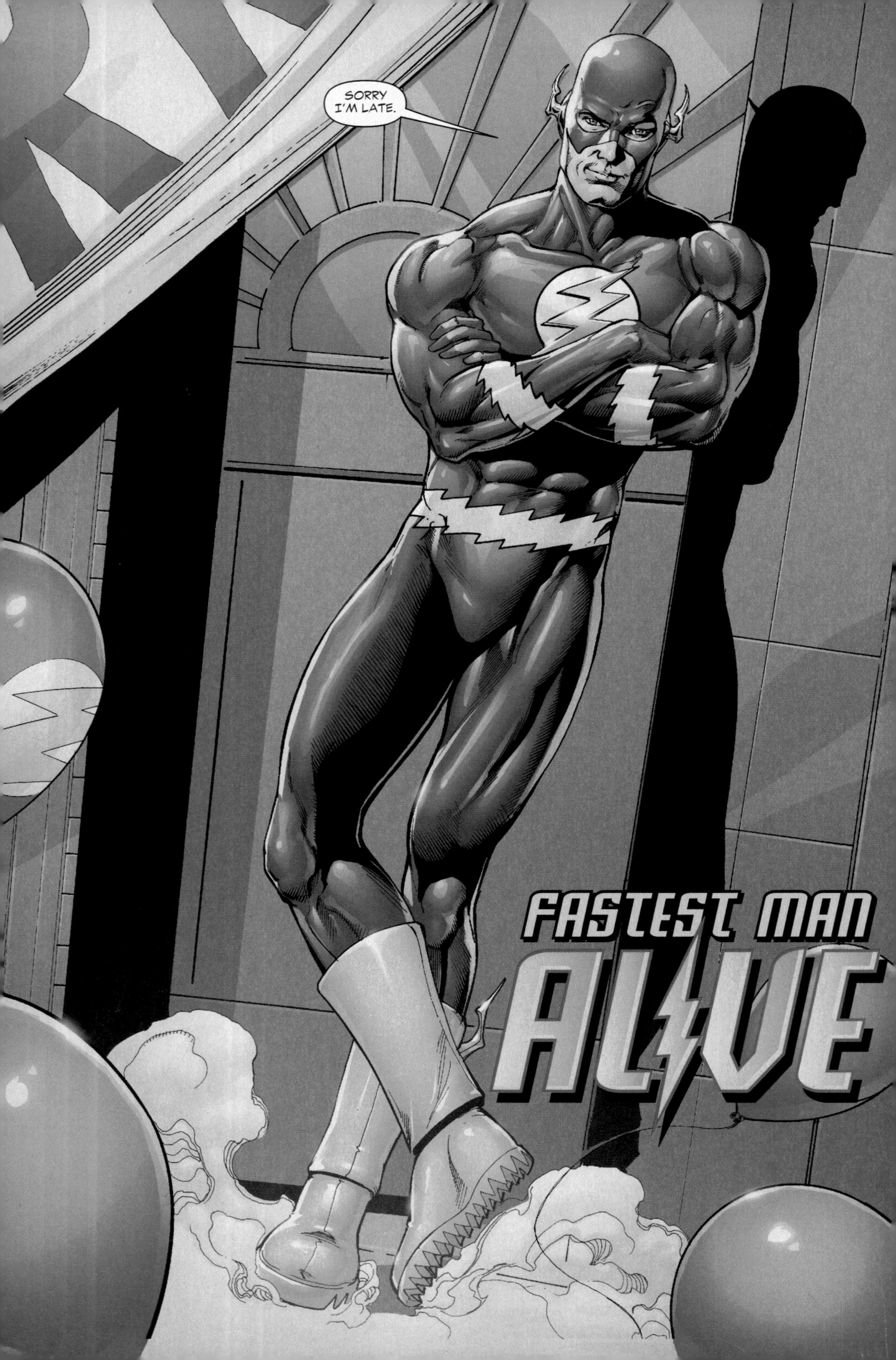
SORRY I'M LATE.
FASTEST MAN ALIVE

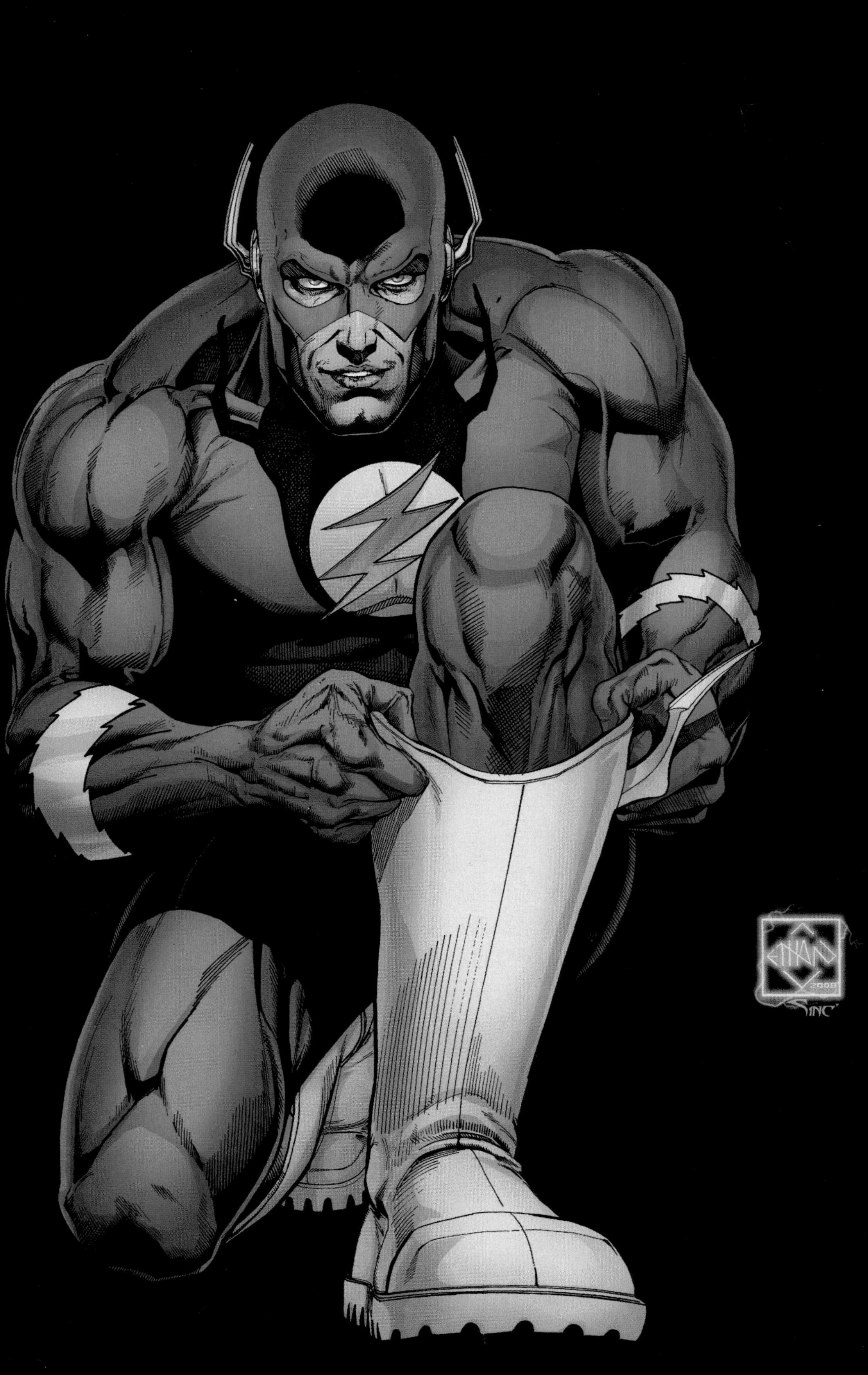
ETHAN
2008

THE FLASH: REBIRTH #1 2ND PRINTING COVER BY **ETHAN VAN SCIVER** WITH **ALEX SINCLAIR**

REBIRTH A 6-ISSUE MINISERIES GEOFF JOHNS REVISED 1/2/08

Barry Allen's first appearance in SHOWCASE #4 was the original "rebirth" of the DC Universe. Barry Allen ushered in the Silver Age. His success arguably saved super-heroes.

Springing out of FINAL CRISIS in early 2009, I'd love nothing more than to get a chance to attempt to rebuild Barry Allen and the Flash Universe the same way we've managed to rebuild Hal Jordan and the Green Lantern Universe.

Like the proposal for GREEN LANTERN: REBIRTH, I'm going to outline the basics behind the re-exploration of the Flash mythology. This is about using the best elements and characters from the Flash universe, as we did with Green Lantern, and moving it all forward with Barry Allen front and center.

WHO ARE THE MAIN PLAYERS?

Barry Allen explodes out of the Speed Force during FINAL CRISIS. I hope this proposal illustrates why he should stick around.

The other main characters in this mini-series will include Wally West, Bart Allen (who returns as KID FLASH in 2009), Jay Garrick, Wally's twins, "Iris" West-Allen and Barry's closest friends from the Justice League.

In addition, Max Mercury, the guru of the Speed Force, will return.

WHAT IS THE SECRET OF THE SPEED FORCE?

The Speed Force is a fantastic modern addition to the Flash mythos. But the true origin of the Speed Force has never been revealed. One of the major revelations in THE FLASH: REBIRTH is to reveal that origin:

The night Barry Allen was doused in chemicals and struck by lightning wasn't the night he simply "tapped" into the Speed Force. It was the night Barry Allen created the Speed Force.

The analogy of electricity and positive and negative charges will be a major part of this series. Barry is literally a human electrical generator. His muscles create the electrical energy that adds to the Speed Force. The Speed Force has been tapped and used by Wally, Jay, Bart and a host of other DCU speedsters. Since Barry's "death," the Speed Force hasn't grown.

When Barry returns, that all changes.

WHAT IS BARRY ALLEN'S TRUE LEGACY?

Without Barry Allen the Speed Force would not exist. Without Barry Allen the Flash would not exist.

With the new secret of the Speed Force revealed, Barry Allen's legacy extends well beyond Wally West and Bart Allen. He is the father of thousands of heroes.

The Speed Force that Barry created exists in all of space and time. Meaning, no matter what time period you're in, the Speed Force is there. This explains why, even in the '40s, Jay Garrick was able to tap into the Speed Force.

Again, when Barry Allen first appeared in SHOWCASE #4 in 1956 he ushered in a Silver Age of heroes that was literally a "rebirth" for the DC Universe. Taking what he means within the text of comic book history and applying that to his character you can think of his legacy another way...

When Barry Allen runs he generates more Speed Force. The Speed Force grows. It exists in all of space and time. So as Barry runs and the Speed Force grows, someone else — somewhere and somewhen — is able to tap into the Speed Force and become a great hero.

Although we won't see it, the idea is that Barry Allen is literally expanding his heroic legacy with every step he runs.

WHY SHOULD BARRY ALLEN RETURN AS DC'S MAIN FLASH?

Like Hal Jordan, Barry Allen is an icon. His origin is simple and straightforward. His secret identity as a "police scientist" is as thrilling as his masked identity as the scarlet speedster (and more relevant today than ever). And his personality and relationships within the DC Universe have never been explored in this modern age of comics.

Barry will be the Flash that created the Speed Force.

I believe Barry is as important to the DC Universe as Hal Jordan.

Also, readers can be skeptical about the "big events" in the DC Universe. It's natural and I'm right there with them. But Barry Allen's return truly makes FINAL CRISIS feel like it deserves the title "FINAL." It's the final Crisis for Barry and it's truly CRISIS ON INFINITE EARTHS coming full circle. Although his actual return is already in FINAL CRISIS, it will be explored in THE FLASH: REBIRTH.

WHO IS BARRY ALLEN?

We all had heroes we looked up to when we were children. Sometimes, when we grow up,

we have a chance to meet those heroes. And one of the most crushing things in life is meeting a hero who doesn't live up to your expectations of who you think they really are.

When you meet Barry Allen he surpasses those expectations.

Barry Allen is a valued member of the Central City C.S.I. team, but he's not the leader. Barry loves talking shop. In fact, he'd rather talk shop than anything else.

Barry was known to chat about forensics and technique with Batman for hours after a Justice League meeting ended. Batman never talked to anyone else that long.

Although Barry is much more introverted than Hal, the two are both cops. They have a similar set of morals when it comes to enforcing the law. Despite Barry keeping his feet on the ground and Hal flying off into space, they can relate to the ups and downs of organized law enforcement. No one made Barry laugh quite like Hal, and Hal was one of the few who got Barry's straight-faced humor.

Barry never really liked Green Arrow. He over-heard Ollie talk about the "growing problems of police brutality" one too many times. Barry saw Ollie as the guy who would get his best friend in the League, Hal, in trouble. He made Hal doubt himself on occasion. Barry and Ollie would never be comfortable hanging out together outside the League.

When Hal wanted to go to the bar, Ollie was always his wingmen with the women. Hal would invite Barry along, but Barry would decline. Barry was never good with women.

He married young when he met his soul mate, Iris. And when Iris died, he stumbled through a few relationships.

Barry loves being a cop. He loves piecing together evidence that not only solves the crime, but puts the criminal away. His moral code is unshakable.

Barry's intense when it comes to work, but he also has a dry wit about him. Barry is courageous. He's incorruptible (though he'll find out some of the Central City police are not).

Despite his altered perception, Barry never gets bored. He has incredible patience. Despite his quirks, and there are many, Barry's one of the purest and greatest heroes in the DC Universe.

And, of course, no matter how fast he is, Barry is always, always late.

IF BARRY'S BACK, WHAT HAPPENS TO WALLY WEST?
Like GREEN LANTERN: REBIRTH we aren't here to throw anything away or limit who is on stage, we're here to build it up into a sub-universe like Batman's and Superman's, and now Green Lantern's. Wally is still Wally, yet a Wally West with a second chance at fatherhood. He will do what he has done since day one of FLASH #1: lead and expand the legacy of the Flash with both his children and Flashes from across time, including the return of John Fox.

Wally West's kids have been growing unnaturally thanks to the Speed Force and it could kill them, as established in the current FLASH title. They have not had normal childhoods. When all is said and done, Wally's kids are "cured" and safe, though his daughter is now the new Impulse while his son loses his powers and earns the nickname "the Turtle."

Wally West will work as an auto mechanic for the police department as he has before, therefore allowing him to interact with Barry.

WHAT IS THE NEGATIVE SPEED FORCE?
The opening scene of THE FLASH: REBIRTH would be a silhouetted figure breaking and entering into the Central City Police Lab in the middle of the night. The silhouetted figure puts several deliberately chosen chemicals on a rack by a window.

He waits.

Then lightning hits in a twisted version of Barry Allen's origin!

At this moment, just like Barry created the Speed Force, this silhouetted figure has created the "Negative" Speed Force. Yin and yang — the more this figure runs, the greater the "Negative" Speed Force grows. The greater the "Negative" Speed Force grows, the more it eats away at the Speed Force.

The more this mysterious figure runs, the more he damages the speedsters tapping into the Speed Force. If he runs enough, this villain will destroy the Speed Force, and kill everyone tapping into it.

This mysterious figure will be revealed to be a time-traveling Eobard Thawne — a.k.a. Professor Zoom — a.k.a. Reverse-Flash.

Thawne has discovered the true origin of the Speed Force and has purposely set out to make its opposite charge.

Thawne knows one day Barry will kill him, but he plans to destroy the Flash legacy in revenge for it and put the guilt on Barry himself.

WHAT HAPPENS TO THE OTHER SPEEDSTERS IN THE FLASH: REBIRTH?

After the creation of the "Negative" Speed Force, unbeknownst to Barry it begins to affect the Speed Force.

At first, Jay and Bart and Wally have bursts of super-speed. All over the DC Universe, speedsters' powers are growing and increasing.

Then they do the opposite. Speedsters start to get ill. Some lose their powers.

All but Barry.

Everyone (and the reader) will be led to believe that by the end of this Barry may not only be the last speedster running, but the others will.

That's exactly what Reverse-Flash wants.

As Barry struggles with it (even transforming into the Black Flash) and the Speed Force is eaten away, the other speedsters held in it – Max Mercury, Johnny Quick and Savitar – are expelled. Max Mercury is the one that witnessed the creation and invasion of the "Negative" Speed Force.

But the physical problems Barry has to solve and overcome aren't the only things challenging him…he's also emotionaly distant. Pulled away from everyone.

But he doesn't know why…

WHAT HAS THE REVERSE-FLASH DONE?

One power the Reverse-Flash has that the Flashes have never been able to conquer is traveling through time and actually changing it. Thawne needs Barry to become the Flash and run in order to keep Thawne's pursuit of power intact, but Thawne wants Barry to be miserable.

Although we won't learn it for a while, we discover Thawne has killed Barry's mother.

This all leads to the new series and ████████ ███████████████████████████████ ███████████████████████████████ ███████████████████████████████ ███████████████████████████████

And that all leads to FLASHPOINT – the DC Universe 2011 event.

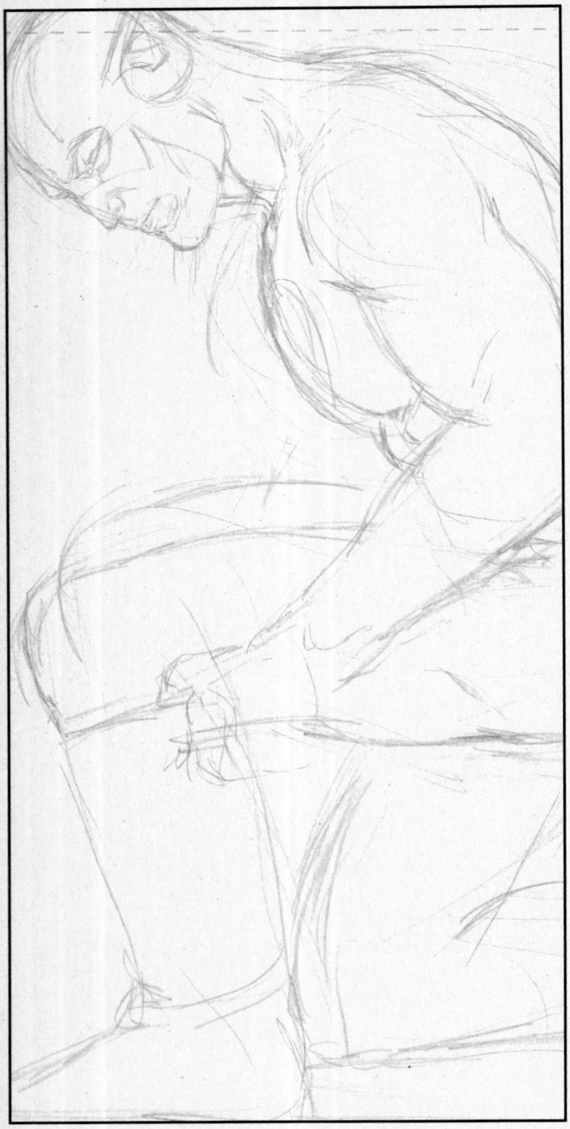

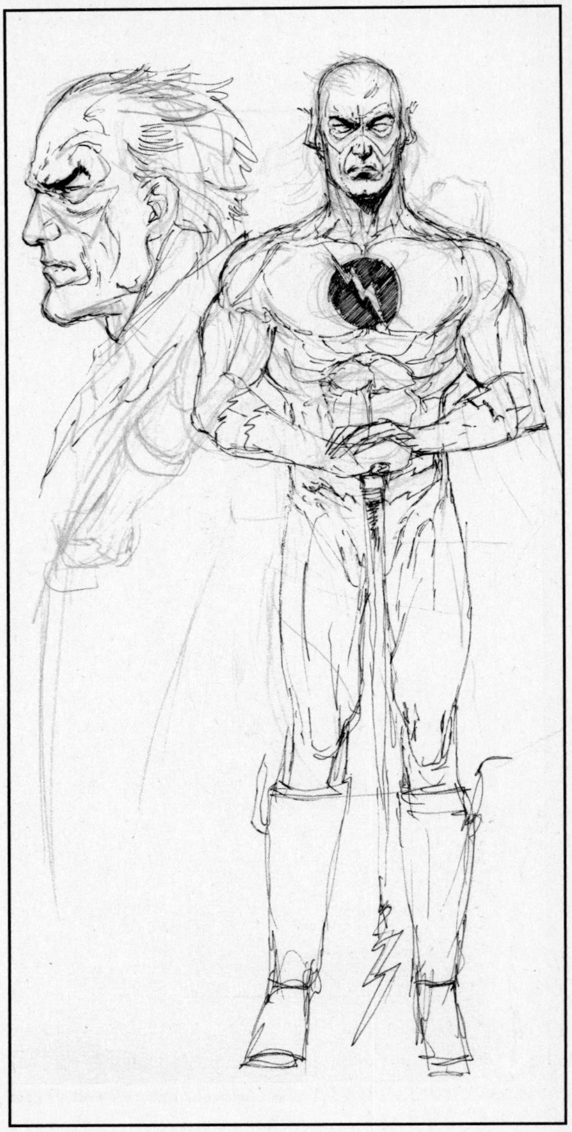

Here's an outtake for the cover of FLASH: REBIRTH #1! Done in blue line pencil, I posed for it myself, just to get the general idea down. From here, I was able to exaggerate the pose to make it more exciting and heroic, and to position the figure to fill almost the entire rectangular frame in a dramatic way.

I do so many designs and sketches in airports, when I'm bored. They're never meant to be seen, you see. I do them as a way of thinking. Before we were even sure that Professor Zoom would make his return in FLASH: REBIRTH, I started getting some ideas. Wanting to emphasize the "Professor" part of his name, to make him more scholarly, an academician, I thought he should have some sort of pointing stick, or cane. It became a lightning rod, eventually.

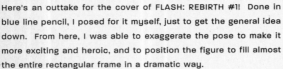

And here it is: I had this drawing of Barry Allen removing his mask done around the same time as the cover to FLASH: REBIRTH #1. I thought I'd turn it into a cover eventually, and decided to take a big chance by DESIGNING WALLY'S COSTUME RIGHT ON THE COVER! Ha ha! That was a daring, and stupid thing to do. But I got very motivated one night, and designed what I thought would be a Guy Gardner- style Flash costume. Big boots, a vest, etc, etc. Nope! I faxed this result to Joey Cavalieri, who asked me if I was out of my mind!

The color version of the Barry image. Used for solicitation of issue #6 only.

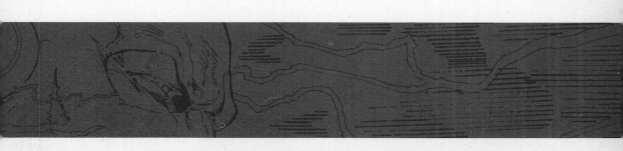

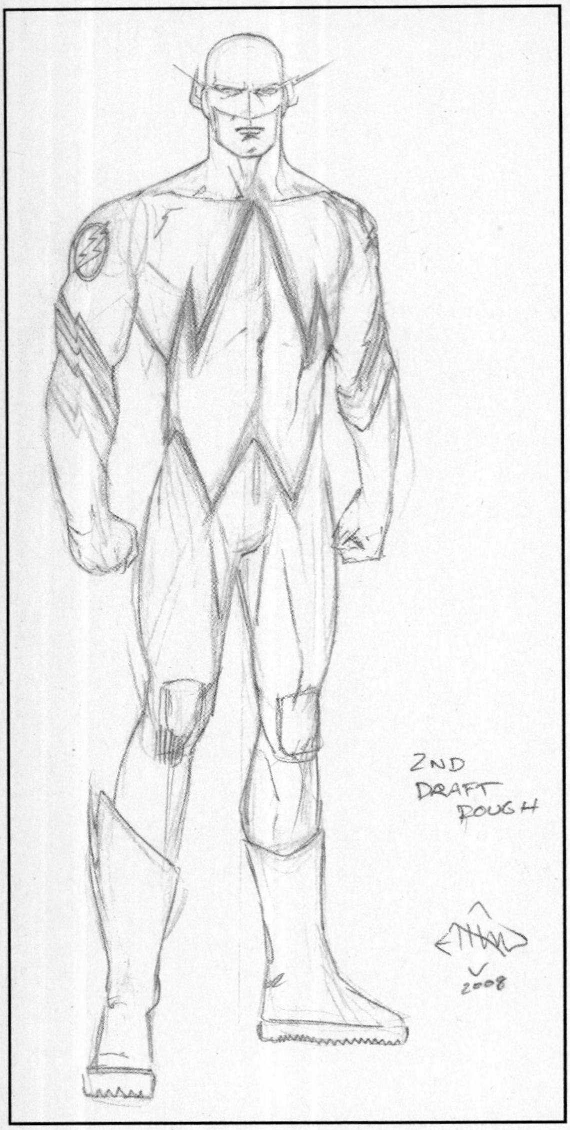
2ND DRAFT ROUGH
2008

All right, this is part of trying to find our new Wally West Flash costume design. This is actually the second stab at it. The first one looked like a gingerbread man, a vague shape with doodles on it, which is a fine way to design a costume. I felt as though the Flash logo should be taken from his chest and moved to his shoulders. And then, some lightning shapes on his chest to indicate two W's...? But it worked better in my head than it did on paper. Frustrated, I decided to try something much more drastic...

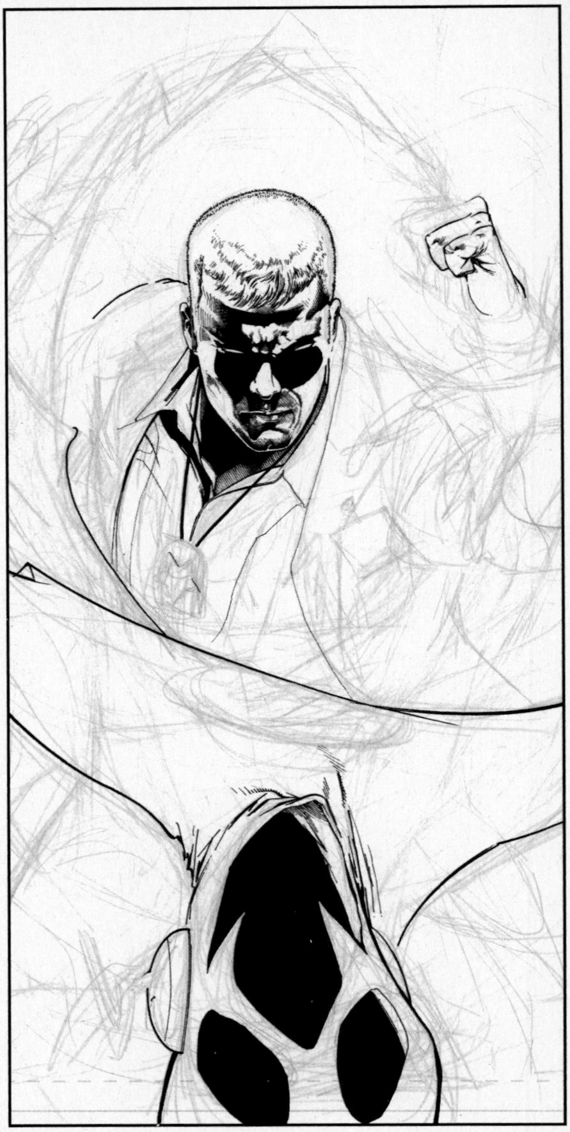

This is obviously an outtake for the FLASH: REBIRTH #2 variant cover. I quit this a few hours into it, because I was becoming aware of how dark and grim I was making our Barry. So I lightboxed it and started over.

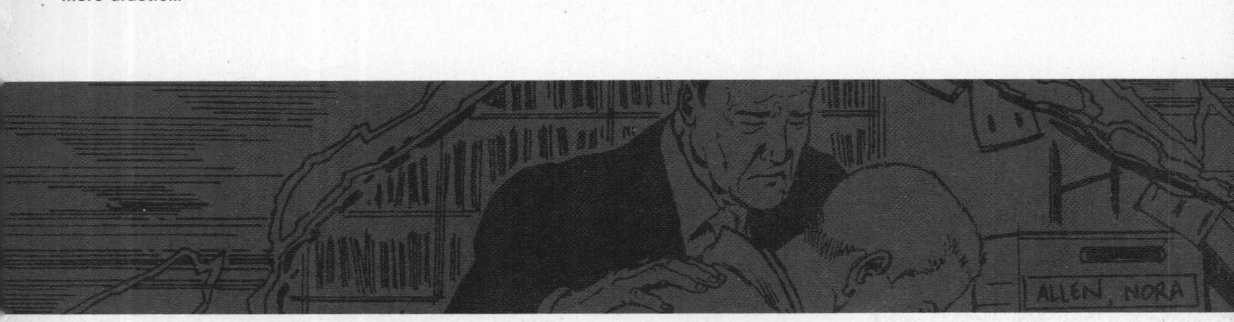
ALLEN, NORA

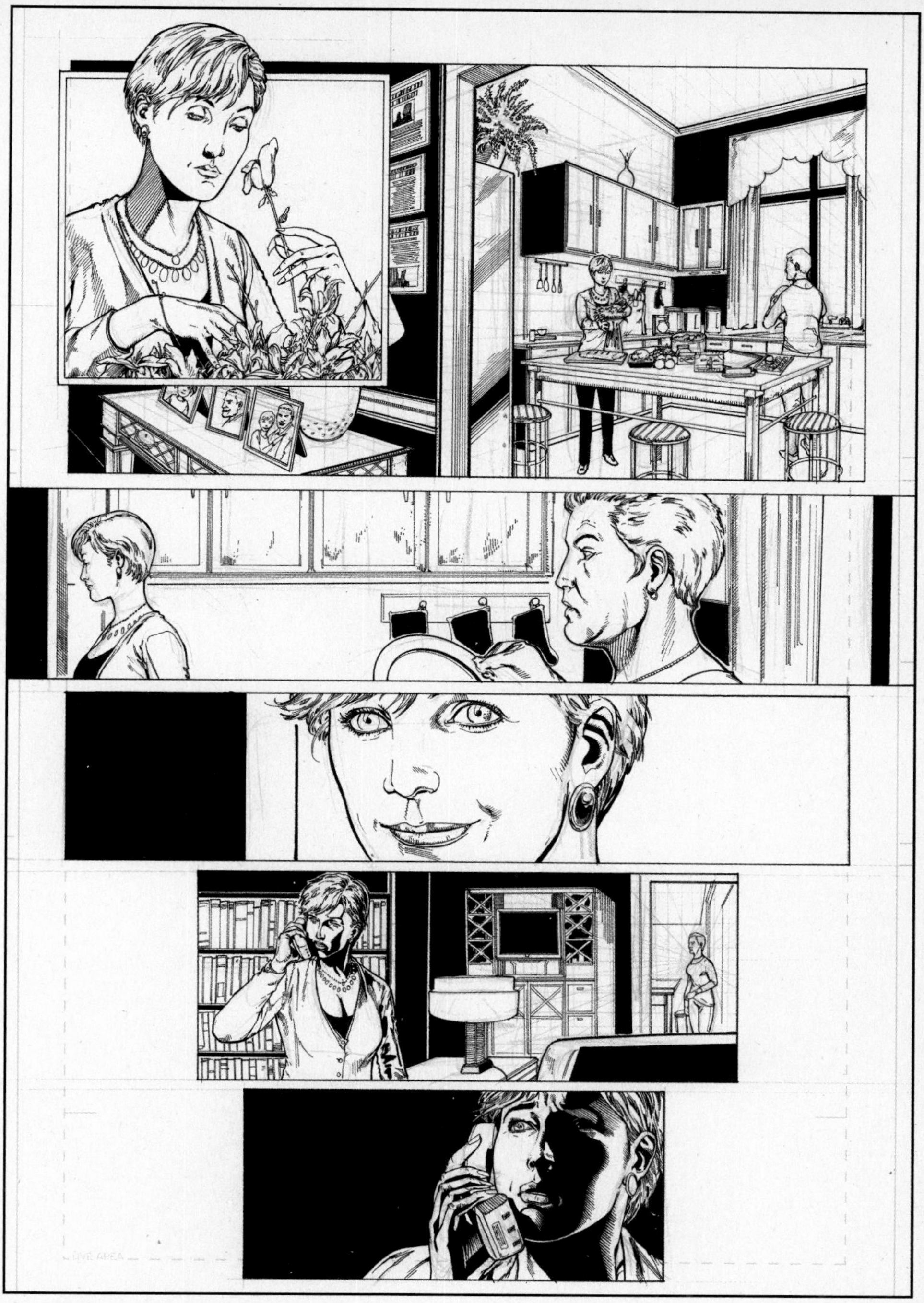

Okay, here's a deleted page from FLASH: REBIRTH #1. And it was deleted and redrawn for good reason. We were never really happy with the quality of the work on the page. This is an older Iris, which I kind of took from what I saw in FINAL CRISIS. Geoff and I knew that one thing that would be revealed about the Speedforce in this miniseries is that it "youthens" the people who come in contact with it. Iris and Barry, as well as Wally, the kids, Bart, Jay would all enjoy a rejuvenation through this story. So I redrew this page with a younger Iris and this page ended up in the circular file.

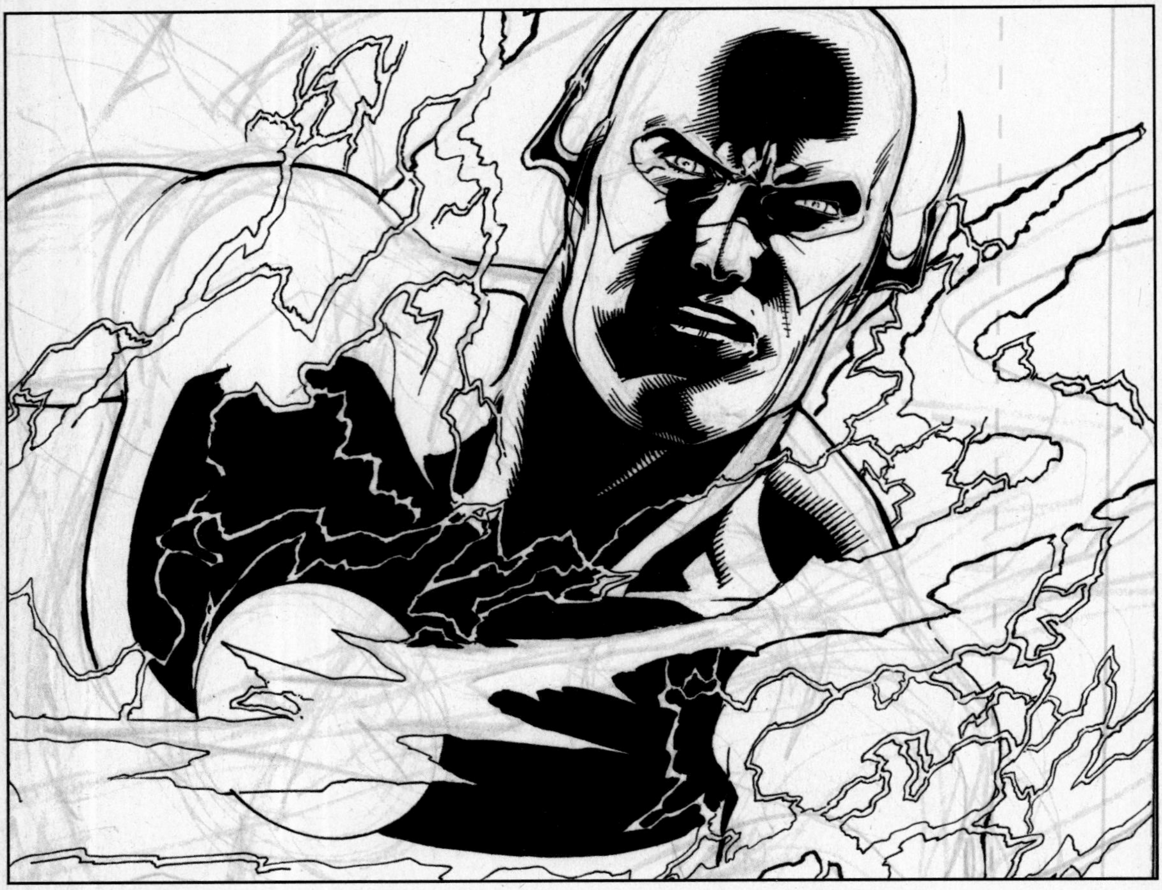

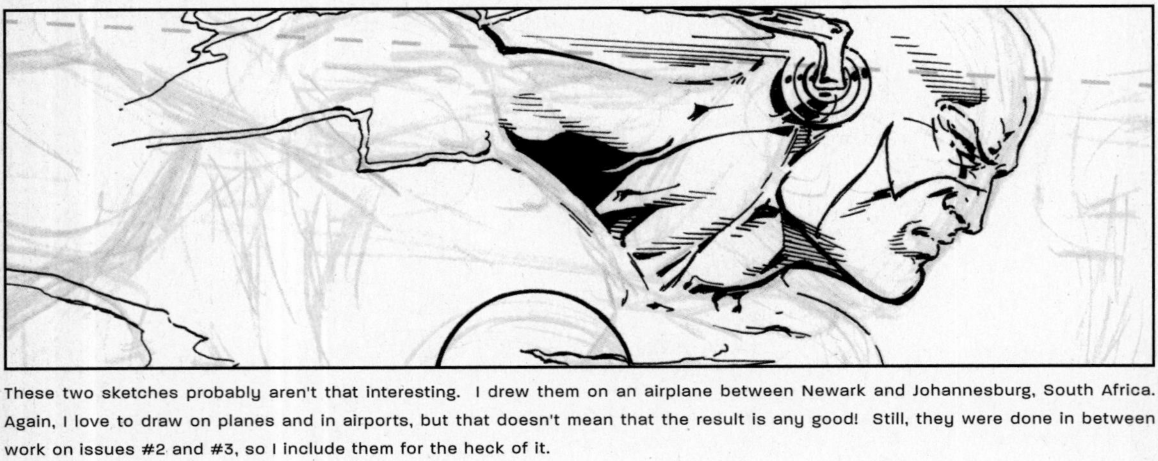

These two sketches probably aren't that interesting. I drew them on an airplane between Newark and Johannesburg, South Africa. Again, I love to draw on planes and in airports, but that doesn't mean that the result is any good! Still, they were done in between work on issues #2 and #3, so I include them for the heck of it.

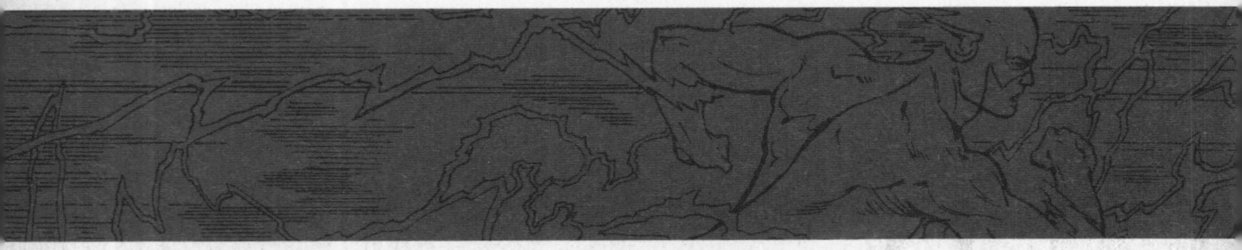